ARCHANGEL STUDIOS PRESENTS

CHRISTIAN GOSSETT'S

THE RED STAR

NOKGORKA

TABLE OF CONTENTS

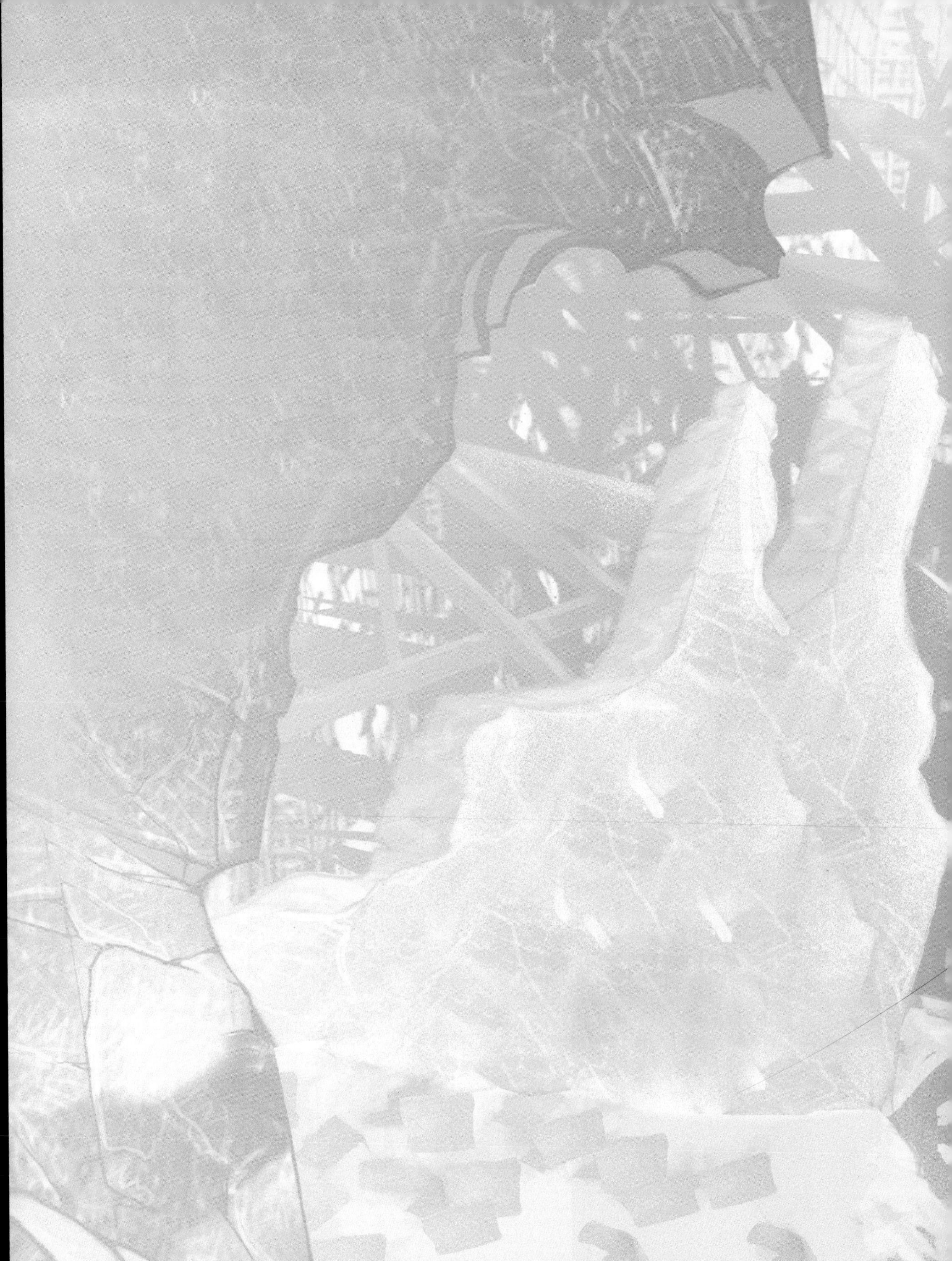

WWW.THEREDSTAR.COM

PRINTED IN CANADA

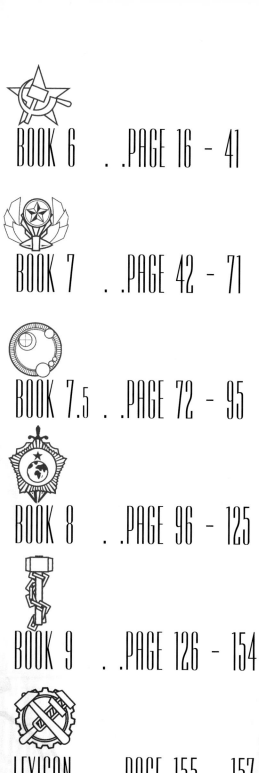

ARCHANGEL
STUDIOS

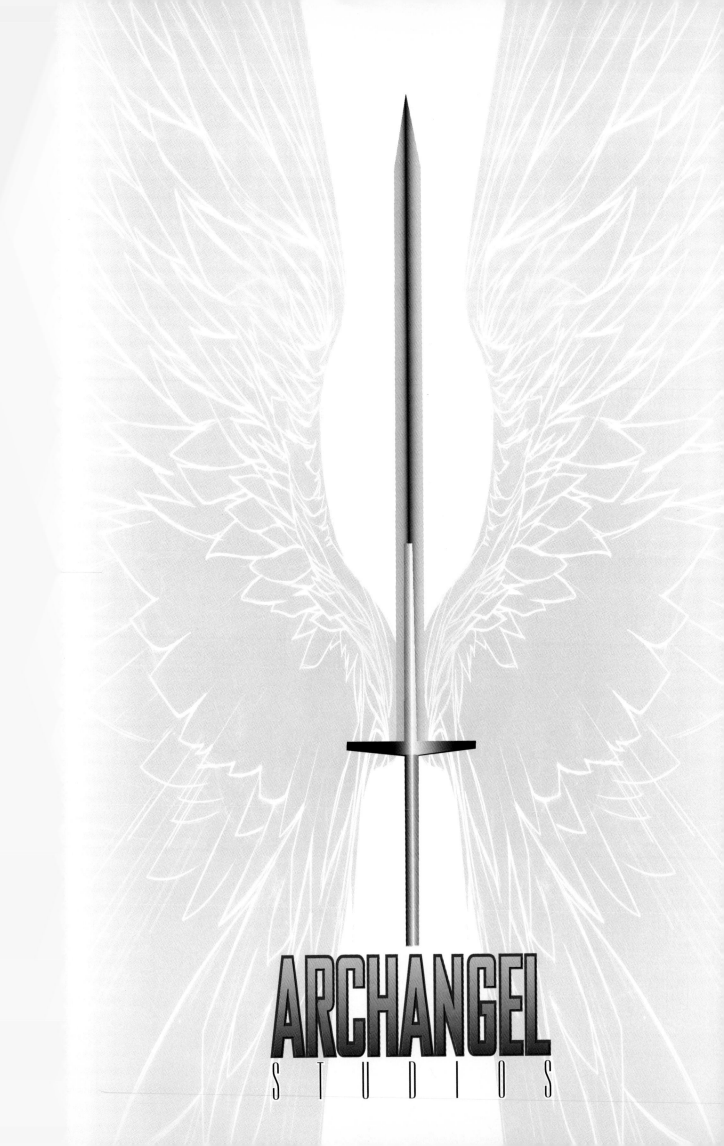

TEAM RED STAR

Christian Gossett:
Creator - Penciller - Writer
Bradley Kayl: Writer

Snakebite: Colorist - Composites

3D Teams:
Jon Moberly
K.G.B.
Paul Schrier

Johanna Olson, MD: Publisher

Nathaniel Downes: Ministry of Finance

Richard Starkings: Letterer

JG Roshell: Font Designer

Saida Temofonte: Letterer

Oscar Gongora: Issue Production

Creative Visions: TPB Design

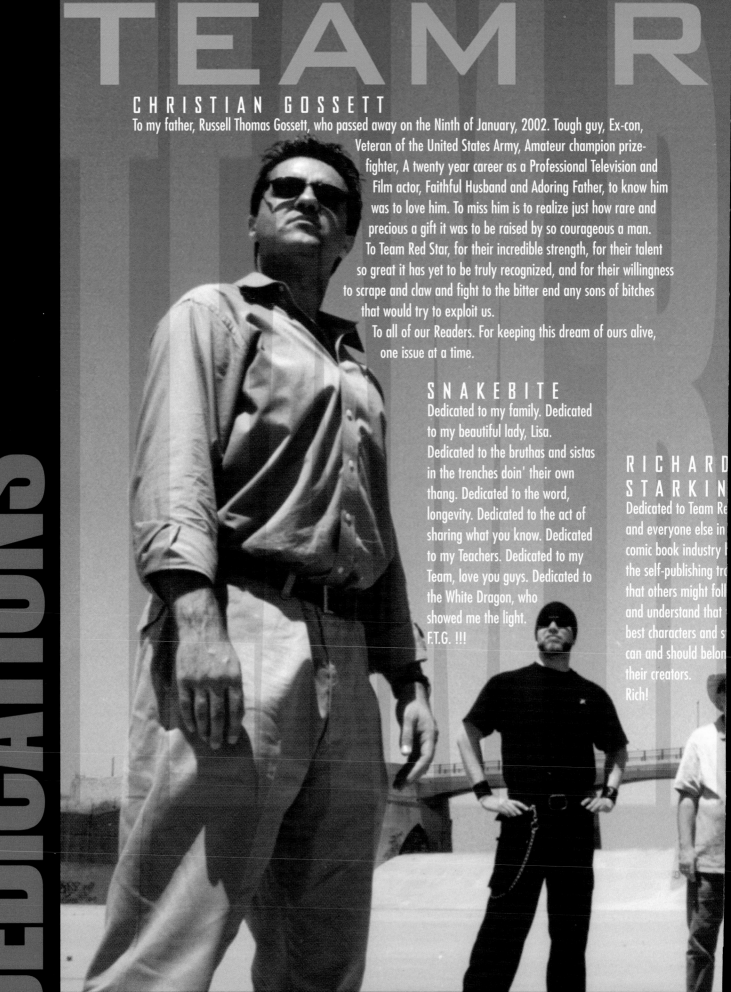

DEDICATIONS

CHRISTIAN GOSSETT

To my father, Russell Thomas Gossett, who passed away on the Ninth of January, 2002. Tough guy, Ex-con, Veteran of the United States Army, Amateur champion prize-fighter, A twenty year career as a Professional Television and Film actor, Faithful Husband and Adoring Father, to know him was to love him. To miss him is to realize just how rare and precious a gift it was to be raised by so courageous a man. To Team Red Star, for their incredible strength, for their talent so great it has yet to be truly recognized, and for their willingness to scrape and claw and fight to the bitter end any sons of bitches that would try to exploit us.

To all of our Readers. For keeping this dream of ours alive, one issue at a time.

SNAKEBITE

Dedicated to my family. Dedicated to my beautiful lady, Lisa. Dedicated to the bruthas and sistas in the trenches doin' their own thang. Dedicated to the word, longevity. Dedicated to the act of sharing what you know. Dedicated to my Teachers. Dedicated to my Team, love you guys. Dedicated to the White Dragon, who showed me the light. F.T.G. !!!

RICHARD STARKIN

Dedicated to Team Re
and everyone else in
comic book industry
the self-publishing tr
that others might foll
and understand that
best characters and s
can and should belon
their creators.
Rich!

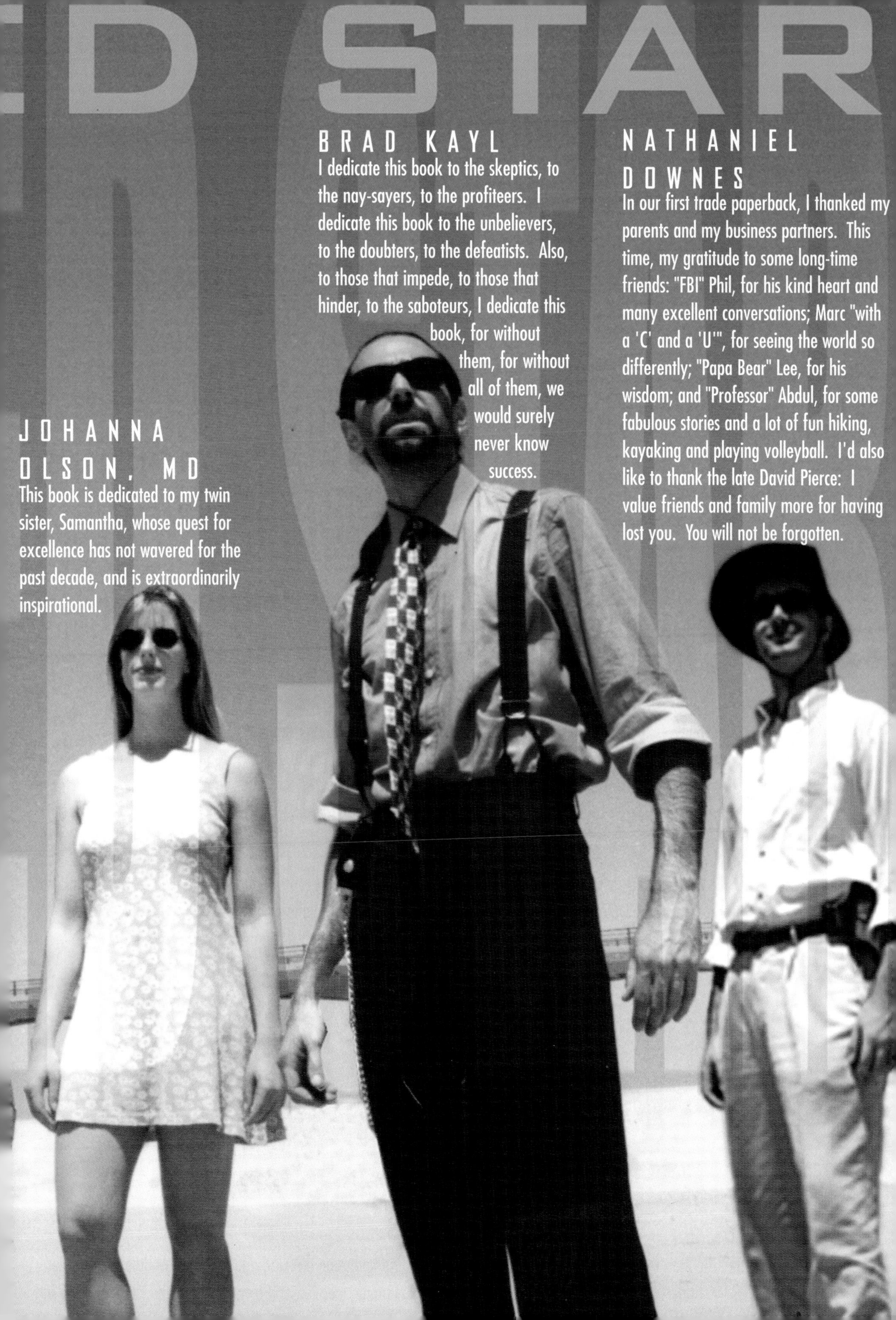
ED STAR

JOHANNA OLSON, MD

This book is dedicated to my twin sister, Samantha, whose quest for excellence has not wavered for the past decade, and is extraordinarily inspirational.

BRAD KAYL

I dedicate this book to the skeptics, to the nay-sayers, to the profiteers. I dedicate this book to the unbelievers, to the doubters, to the defeatists. Also, to those that impede, to those that hinder, to the saboteurs, I dedicate this book, for without them, for without all of them, we would surely never know success.

NATHANIEL DOWNES

In our first trade paperback, I thanked my parents and my business partners. This time, my gratitude to some long-time friends: "FBI" Phil, for his kind heart and many excellent conversations; Marc "with a 'C' and a 'U'", for seeing the world so differently; "Papa Bear" Lee, for his wisdom; and "Professor" Abdul, for some fabulous stories and a lot of fun hiking, kayaking and playing volleyball. I'd also like to thank the late David Pierce: I value friends and family more for having lost you. You will not be forgotten.

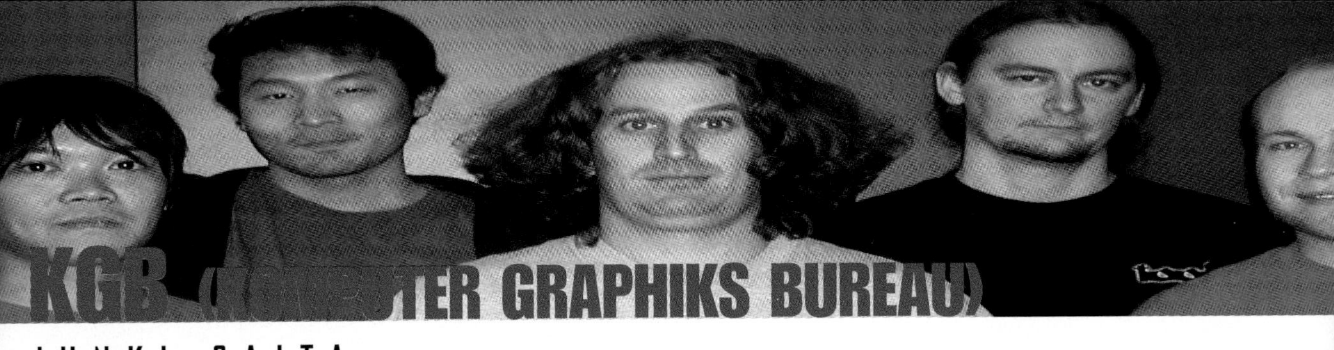

KGB (COMPUTER GRAPHIKS BUREAU)

JUNKI SAITA

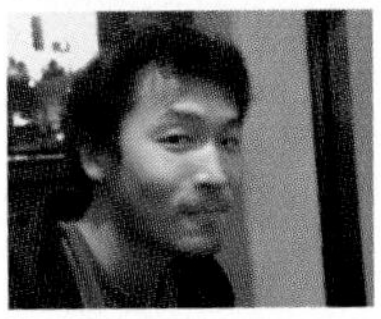

With eight published game titles under his belt Junki Saita could be considered something of a veteran in the video game industry... well sorta... kinda... ok... so he's not really sure what that would make him... besides a happy camper.

The reason for this is because rather than the projects he's worked on, he prefers to measure the progress and passing of his time in the industry by the friendships he's made ... including the one he has with Christian.

So when Christian asked for his help with a proposal for a new idea he had, something novel called The Red Star, he was more than happy to oblige him, and months later when Gossett called him for assistance on his book, Junki assembled a team of talented computer artists, named them the KGB and answered the call.

Not a big deal really, it's simply the way of things amongst friends.

EDWIN FONG

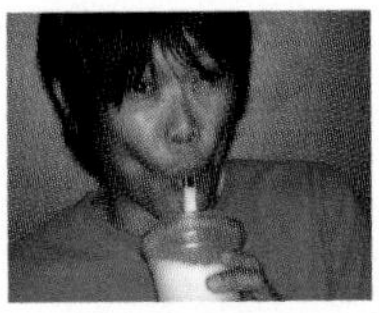

i love to draw.
i love to skateboard.
i love all your girlfriends.
i was born in Hong Kong, raised mostly in Boston. peace to Neversoft and Tony Hawk Pro Skater. it was fun while it lasted. i am working on Artafact, along with Daewon Song. i love Red Star fans.

NOLAN NELSON

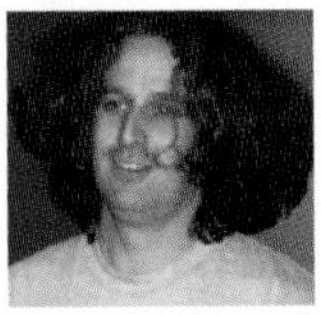

Born in Alberta, Canada, Nolan Nelson moved to the U.S. (Utah) with his family and started computer art geekin it on the Atari 800XL. Eventually he graduated and got a job at Viewpoint Datalabs where he worked for several years, then got on the videogame wagon at Kodiak Interactive. Nolan is currently working at Neversoft Entertainment in California.

CHRIS GLENN

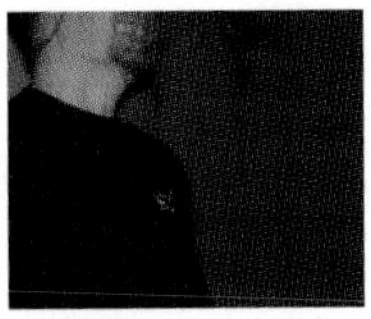

After many years in the oppressively hot wasteland known as Phoenix Arizona, Chris made his way to California for fortune and glory. After a few years at Neversoft Entertainment working as a 3d environment artist, Chris moved over to Troika Games to do concept design and creature modeling. When he's not operating for the KGB, Chris spends his free time with his wife Sarah and 1 year old daughter Alexin.

AARON SKILLMAN AKA SKILLZ

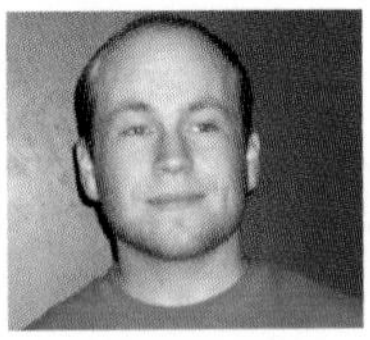

"Four years ago a crack commando was sent to prison by a military court for a crime he didn't commit. This man promptly escaped from a maximum security stockade to the Los Angeles underground. Today, still wanted by the government, he survives as soldier of fortune. If you have a problem, if no one else can help, and if you can find hi maybe you can hire the Skillzilla."

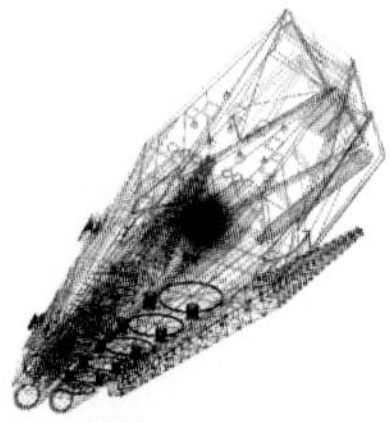

JON MOBERLY

Jon Moberly, the Iron Horse of Team Red Star's 3D onslaught. A true professional, Jon has been with the team from the very beginning of the Saga back in the spring of 2000. From the Citadel Railcar to Alex's Krawl and Makita's heavy gun (issue #9) Jon's technique has helped establish that 3D in comics is here to stay.

WHITE ARMY

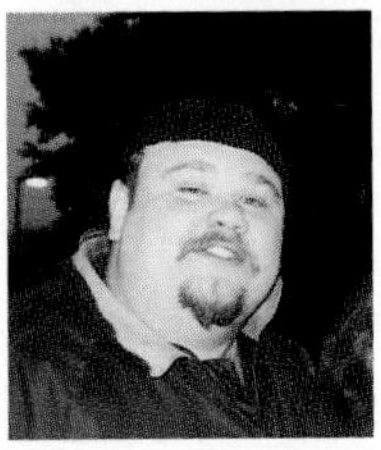

PAUL SCHRIER

The Big Man is a recovering professional actor, sometime television director, and the latest addition to The Red Fleet. Under the nom de guer "White Army", his task is model creation and scene construction. He sends the Big Love out to his wife, Carissa.

3D TEAMS

"What you are about to read is the beginning of an allegory, the prelude to a fairy tale, inspired by the history of Russia..."

With those words began the Foreword from the first Red Star Trade Paperback, "The Battle of Kar Dathra's Gate." Honestly, I couldn't think of any other words to begin the second. The story has gone from the blazing desert of Al'Istaan to the frozen ruins of Nokgorka, our unique process of production has graced another story arc with page after page of work so stunning that the entire industry has taken notice, and another character has fallen in battle, but the core source of the story has remained.

Russia. The people of Russia.

The mysterious, frozen lands that are too far East to be Europe, too far West to be Asia, too far North to be inhabited by anyone but a most particular and rare kind of human. Descendants of the Vikings and Slavs, whose cultural volatility throughout the centuries has been so unpredictable, that the great Winston Churchill could only describe Russia as:

"A Riddle inside of a Mystery, wrapped in an Enigma..."

And yet, being an American born in one of the most truly American places, New York City; The Red Star cannot help but be about my own people's perceptions of that other side of the planet. About my own people's role in the global community, and what lessons history has been trying to teach us since the Berlin Wall came down and the United States ascended into a perilous, almost unimaginable status of power and influence.

Such power has its price, and we imperials have been reminded recently of such cost. If my dear friends and I can inspire anything with the efforts that go into this work, I dearly hope that it is the study of the history of world power. That young people might be influenced to read of Britain's war in Afghanistan in the Nineteenth Century. To read of Rome's conquests. To read of the glorious days only decades ago when our people and the Russians defeated Hitler together. Read the facts. Read the fictions. Read. The world's shocks will have less peril for you if you listen to the collected voices of those who have lived before us.

Your cable commentators have no answers. Your talk show hosts do not have the answers. No advertisement or music video has the answers. Only history, only the recorded document of human success and failure is of any use when reality defies the abstract boundaries of civilization.

CHRISTIAN GOSSETT

TESTAMENT OF THE CHRONICLES

Our land is a vast treasure of riches,

But Chaos, more than Peace, has marked our ancient history.

We have known the heavy chains of servitude

And faced the horrors of the conquered.

Yet time and again, throughout the centuries,

Heroes of our native land have risen up

To wield the Red Sword of our people's liberation.

To honor their sacrifice, these Chronicles are written,

So their deeds may not ever be forgotten.

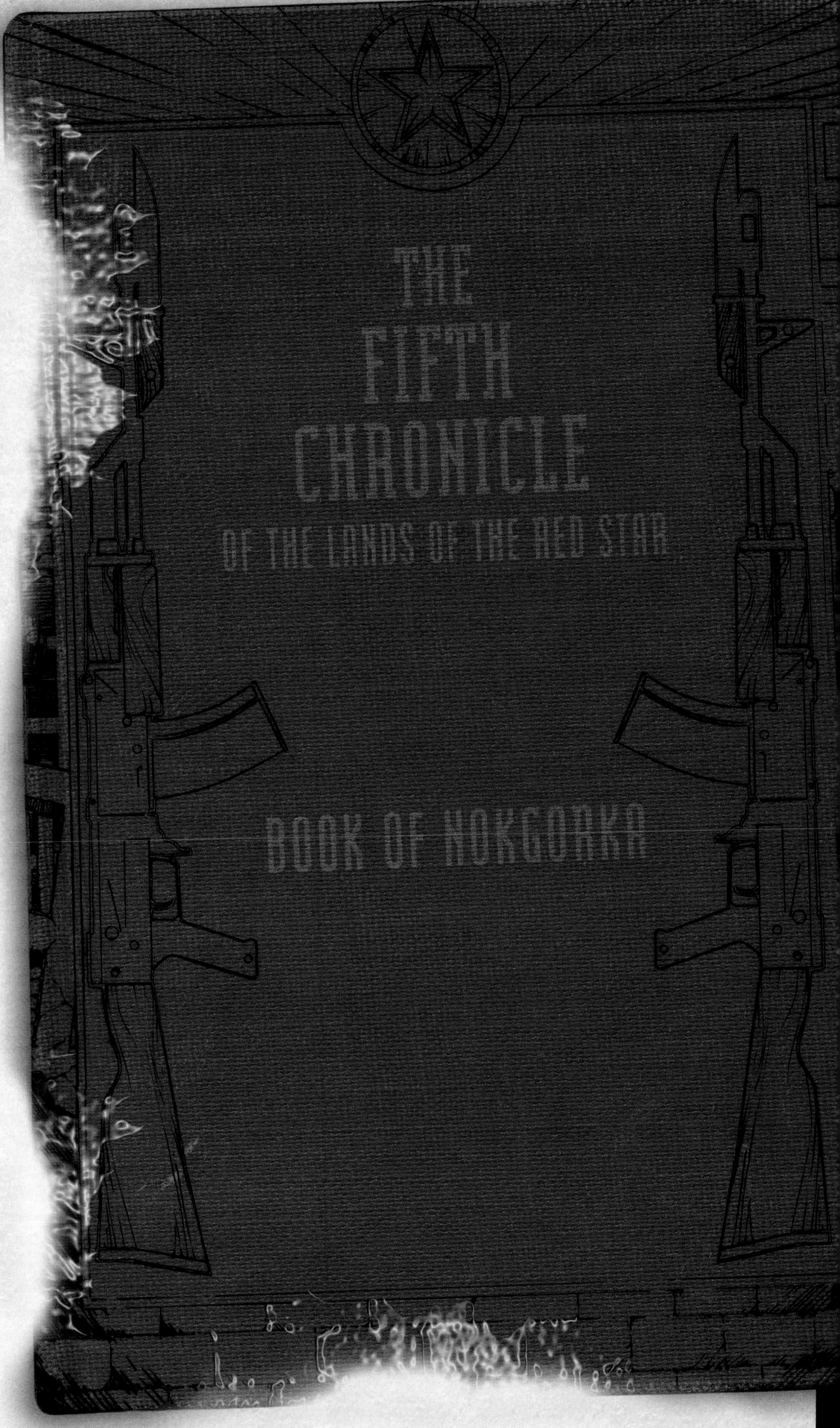
THE
FIFTH
CHRONICLE
OF THE LANDS OF THE RED STAR
BOOK OF NOKGORKA

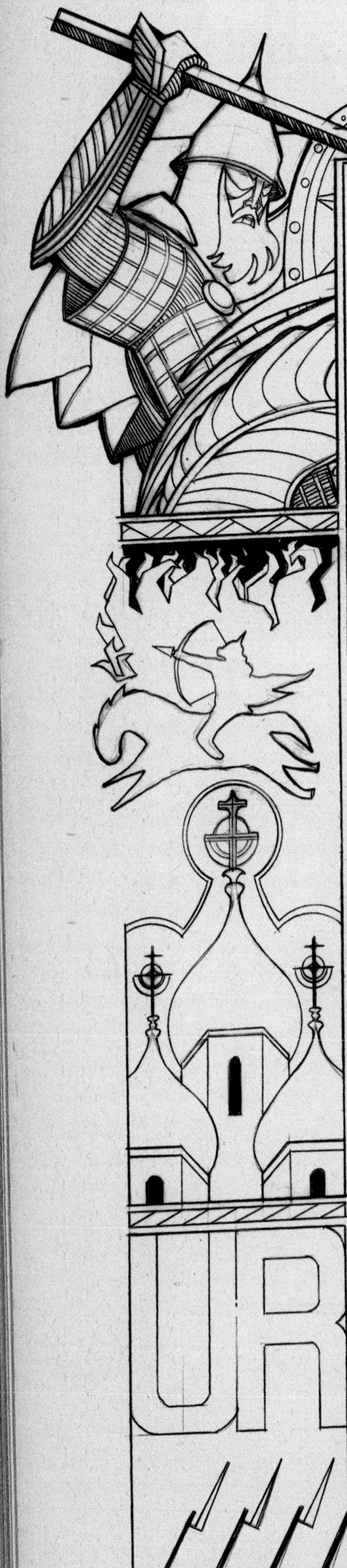

THE FIRST CHRONICLE

Wherein is told the Saga of the

mighty prince Urik I.

Who united the ancient

tribes of our land into a single nation.

FOUR CENTURIES

THE SECOND CHRONICLE

The Great Darkness.

Our lands are conquered by foreign invasion.

The Mounted Hordes of the Lands of the
Dragon hold us 'neath their yoke.

THREE CENTURIES

THE THIRD CHRONICLE

The Warrior Kings, Dmitri and Ivan III, break
the shackles of our heathen captors.

Beginning the rule of the Ancient Dynasties.

THREE CENTURIES

THE FOURTH CHRONICLE

The Revolution overthrows the Ancient Dynasties,
establishing the rule of the Red Councils.

At great cost, our nation becomes a world power,
locked in a struggle for domination
against a rival empire:

The Western Transnationalist Alliance.

ONE CENTURY

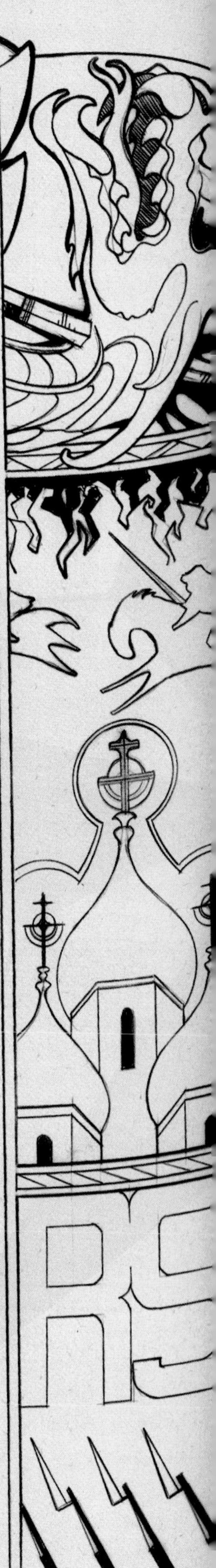

THE FIFTH CHRONICLE

BOOK 3:
NOKGORKA

These pages you are about to read continue the saga of our people.

As Book 1 documented the War of Al'Istaan, and the Battle of Kar Dathra's Gate in which the great Marcus Antares faced the demon-servants of Imbohl and was saved from damnation by the power of The Red Woman--

As Book 2 recorded the Fall of the Red Councils and the catastrophic aftermath in which the United Republics of The Red Star were shattered into a loose commonwealth of states sending our nation into a period of seemingly endless internal conflict--

This Book you hold in your hands tells of the bloodiest of the Civil Wars of this period. The War of Nokgorka.

Nokgorka, ever defiant: a mountainous, rugged nation on the Sea of Hyrkahn.

Since the time of the Ancient Dynasties they had resisted becoming subjects of the Lands of the Red Star.

After hundreds of years of conflict between our two people, only the terrible wrath of Imbohl, Supreme Overlord of the Red Councils, settled the matter.

In the violent period of forgotten conquests before the Great Patriotic War, the leading nations, fully aware that global conflict was inevitable, prepared for battle by occupying smaller countries of strategic importance.

The Western Transnationalists and their allies used their vast wealth to operate on several continents, spilling rivers of foreign blood in the process, securing vital reserves of resource and routes of supply.

It is during this period of rampant imperialism that Imbohl, never to be outdone in the game of global domination, ordered the slaughter of countless Nokgorkans. Faced with no less than the extinction of their people, they surrender and became a southern province of the U.R.R.S.

Throughout the Great War and for almost a century afterward, the Red Councils profited from the vast natural resou Nokgorka's territory.

The Nokgorkans waited, biding their time, dreaming of vengeance.

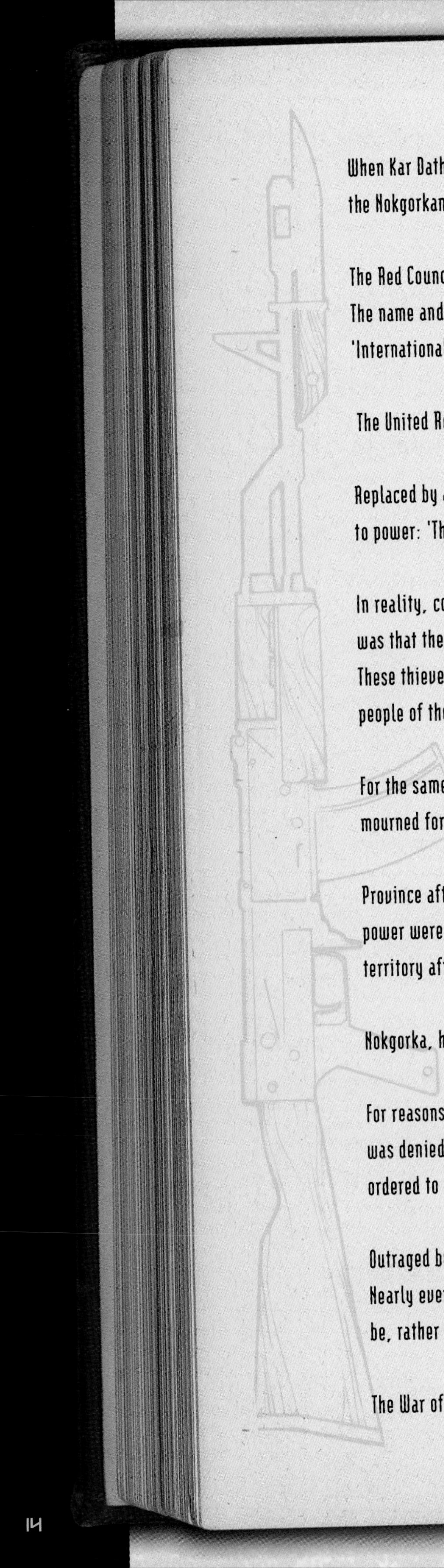

When Kar Dathra's immortal power struck down the Red Fleet, ending the War of Al'Istaan, the Nokgorkans realized their time had come.

The Red Councils were finished. Nothing could stop the collapse of the United Republics. The name and doctrines of the government changed. The economic philosophy of 'Internationalism' was abandoned in favor of the 'Transnationalism' of the Western world.

The United Republics of The Red Star had fallen into the dustbin of history.

Replaced by a government whose very name seemed to suggest that an imposter had come to power: 'The Commonwealth of Red States.'

In reality, comrades, most of the power was held in the same pairs of hands. The difference was that there was no longer any need to espouse any doctrine or direction for the country. These thieves were free to show their true colors, raping our lands of her resources and our people of their hope.

For the same decade that Maya Antares mourned at Marcus' empty grave, our motherland mourned for all of our people as our nation descended into the Abyss.

Province after province demanded independence from their former masters. The thieves in power were too busy looting our national treasury to give any thought to statecraft, and so territory after territory was granted this new freedom.

Nokgorka, however, was not.

For reasons only the Commonwealth could answer, the Nokgorkan claim for sovereignty was denied under pain of death. The Red Fleet made dark the skies over the small country, ordered to crush any resistance.

Outraged by the Commonwealth's decision, the Nokgorkan Resistance Militia was formed. Nearly every able-bodied man, woman and child joined the rebellion, ready to die if need be, rather than continue to live under Imbohl's legacy.

The War of Nokgorka had begun.

It was into this maelstrom, this collision of global circumstance, that our heroes once more enter the stage.

Skymarshall Urik Antares, commanding officer of the mighty R.S.S. Konstantinov. For him, like many of his soldiers, this was a bitter duty. In childhood he had dreamed of bringing glory to his nation, not presiding over the slaughter of innocents to preserve the fortunes of tyrants.

Sorceress Major Maya Antares, widow of Urik's younger brother Marcus, had been shrouded in mourning: not only by the loss of her husband at Al'Istaan, but also by her own profound perceptions of how wretched life had become for her people.

As brilliant as she was, as powerful a sorceress, she could not free herself of her sorrow.

She prayed, privately, for death in battle. Little could she have known that upon her descent into Bahamut, what she would find would not be her destruction, but a glorious Rebirth.

None of these veterans of Al'Istaan, not Urik, not Maya, nor her guardsman Kyuzo, could have foreseen that their fate, and the fate of their beloved Marcus, was waiting for them in the ruins of the city...

...In the form of a delicate, if dirty, pair of hands--

Belonging to a soldier of the enemy--

A child, tempered by war, aged far beyond her years.

Her destiny to bring word to a defeated nation--

That all Hope had not been lost...

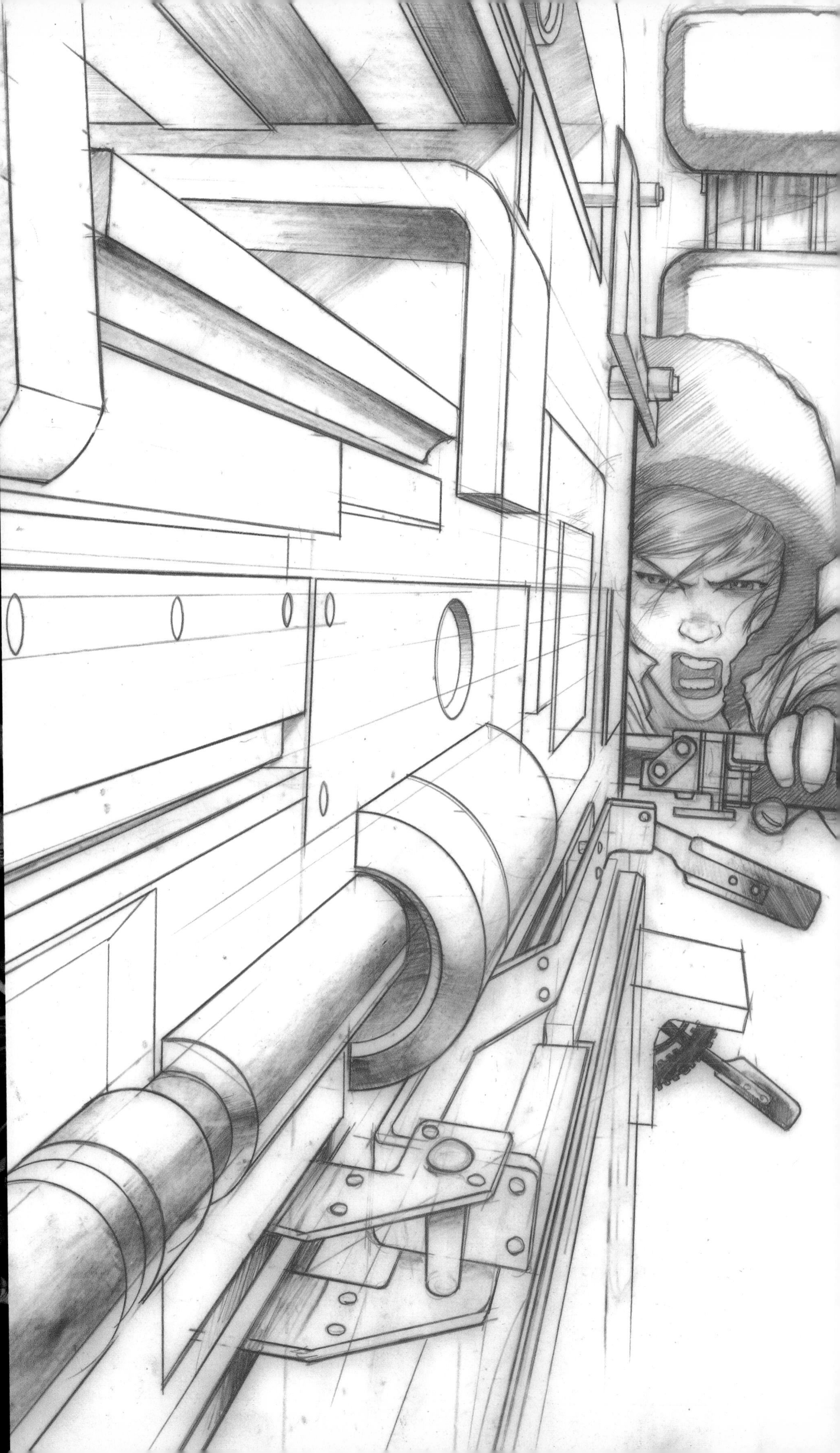

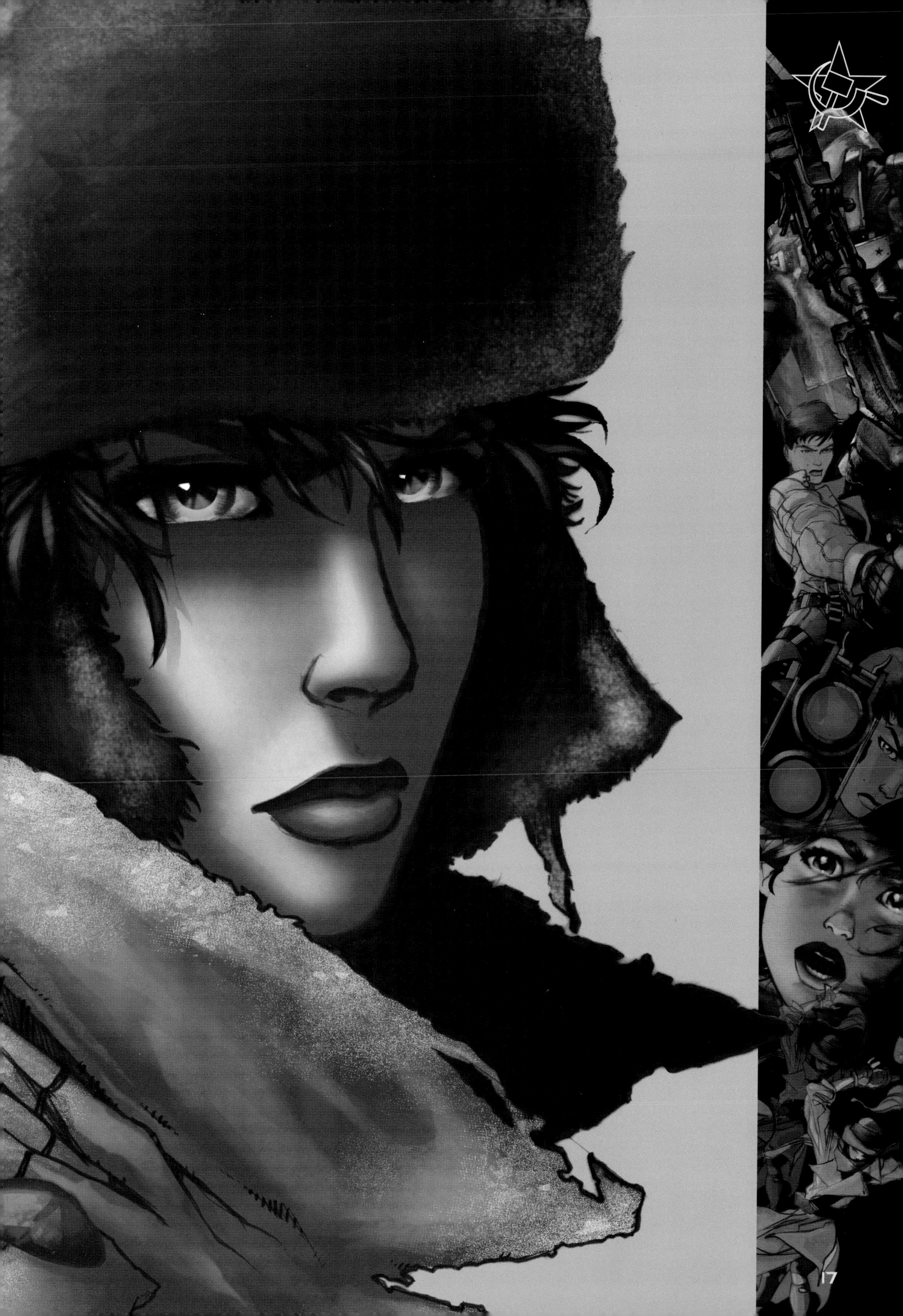

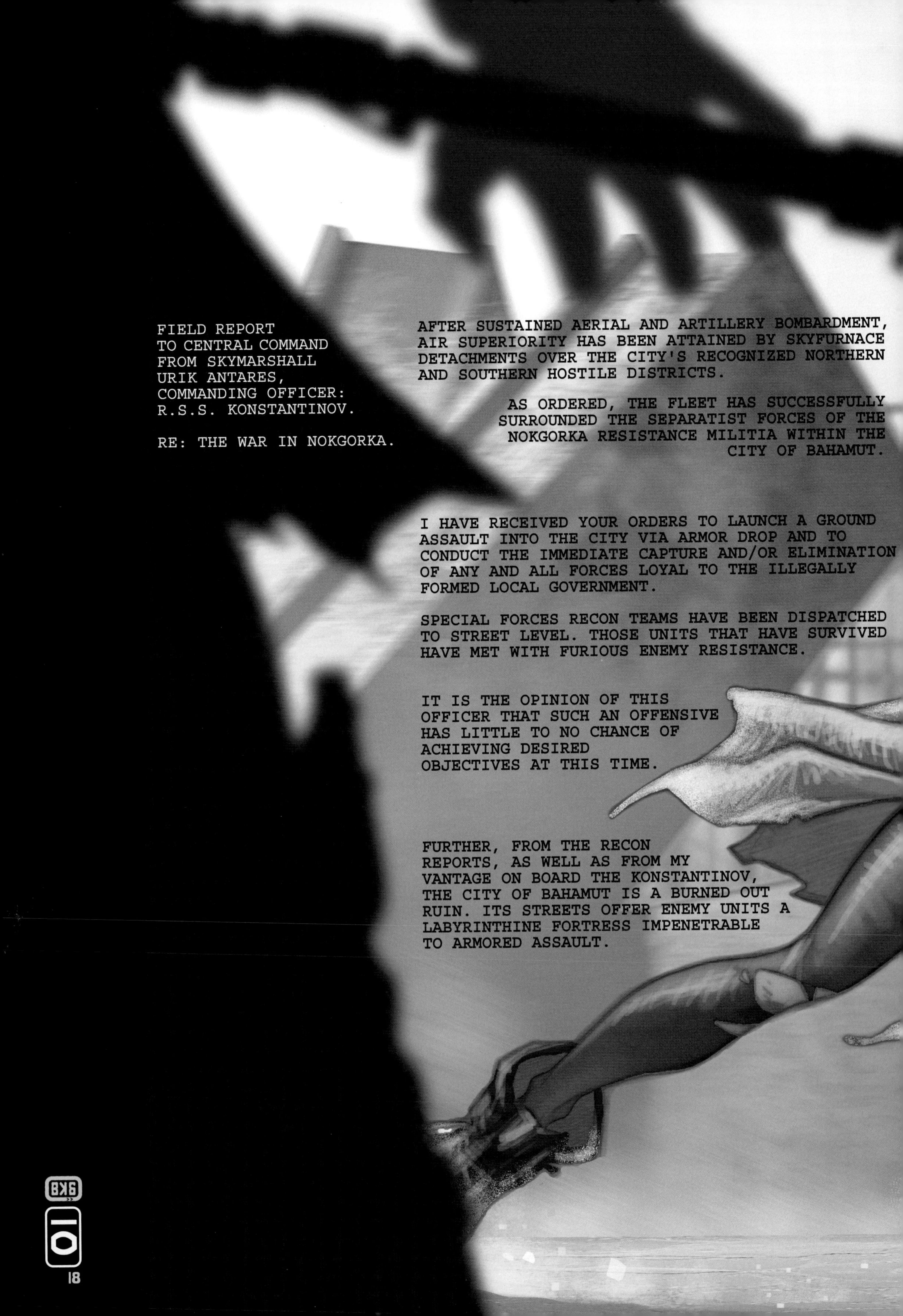

FIELD REPORT TO CENTRAL COMMAND FROM SKYMARSHALL URIK ANTARES, COMMANDING OFFICER: R.S.S. KONSTANTINOV.
RE: THE WAR IN NOKGORKA.
AFTER SUSTAINED AERIAL AND ARTILLERY BOMBARDMENT, AIR SUPERIORITY HAS BEEN ATTAINED BY SKYFURNACE DETACHMENTS OVER THE CITY'S RECOGNIZED NORTHERN AND SOUTHERN HOSTILE DISTRICTS.
AS ORDERED, THE FLEET HAS SUCCESSFULLY SURROUNDED THE SEPARATIST FORCES OF THE NOKGORKA RESISTANCE MILITIA WITHIN THE CITY OF BAHAMUT.
I HAVE RECEIVED YOUR ORDERS TO LAUNCH A GROUND ASSAULT INTO THE CITY VIA ARMOR DROP AND TO CONDUCT THE IMMEDIATE CAPTURE AND/OR ELIMINATION OF ANY AND ALL FORCES LOYAL TO THE ILLEGALLY FORMED LOCAL GOVERNMENT.
SPECIAL FORCES RECON TEAMS HAVE BEEN DISPATCHED TO STREET LEVEL. THOSE UNITS THAT HAVE SURVIVED HAVE MET WITH FURIOUS ENEMY RESISTANCE.
IT IS THE OPINION OF THIS OFFICER THAT SUCH AN OFFENSIVE HAS LITTLE TO NO CHANCE OF ACHIEVING DESIRED OBJECTIVES AT THIS TIME.
FURTHER, FROM THE RECON REPORTS, AS WELL AS FROM MY VANTAGE ON BOARD THE KONSTANTINOV, THE CITY OF BAHAMUT IS A BURNED OUT RUIN. ITS STREETS OFFER ENEMY UNITS A LABYRINTHINE FORTRESS IMPENETRABLE TO ARMORED ASSAULT.

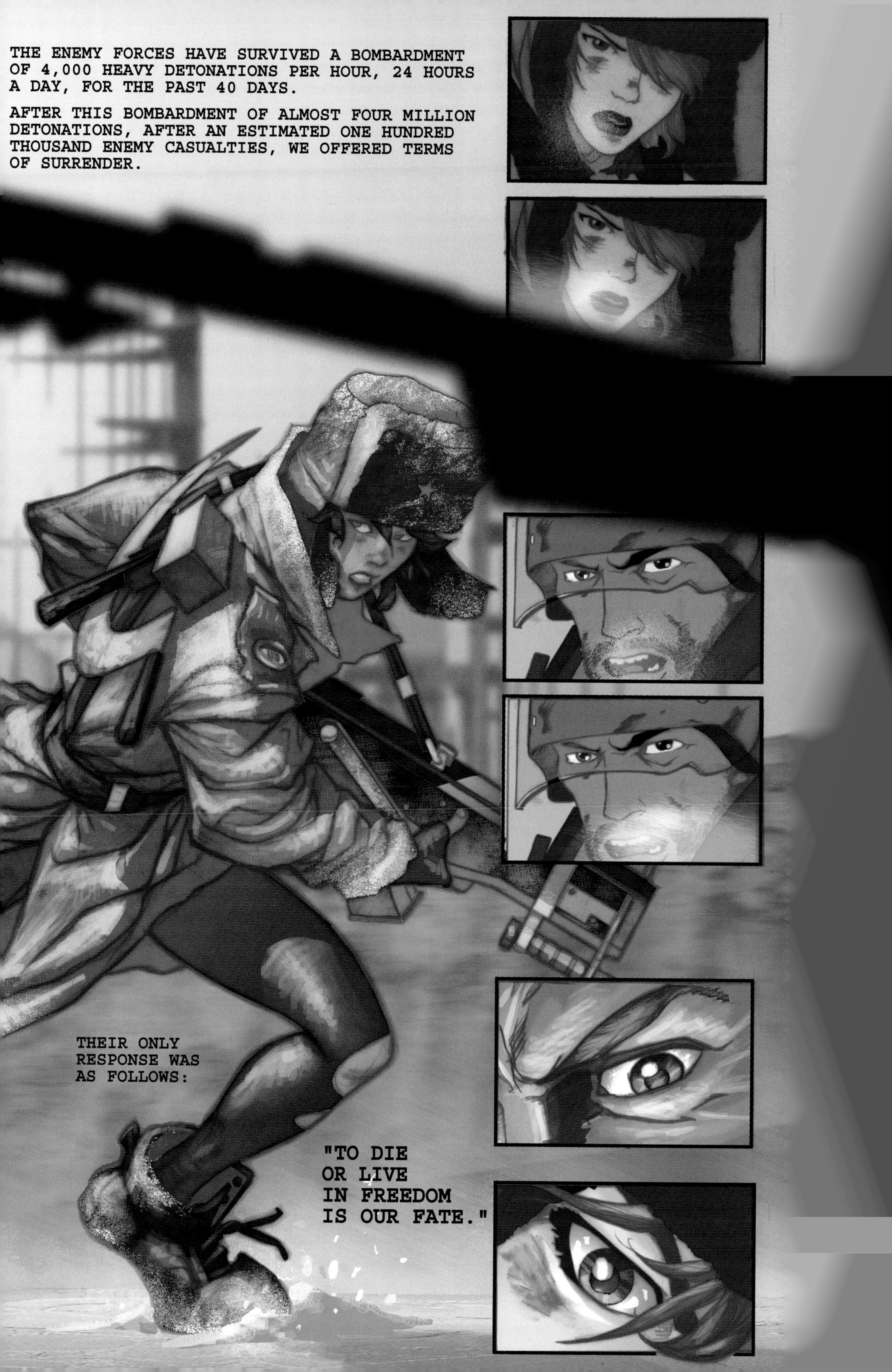
THE ENEMY FORCES HAVE SURVIVED A BOMBARDMENT OF 4,000 HEAVY DETONATIONS PER HOUR, 24 HOURS A DAY, FOR THE PAST 40 DAYS.
AFTER THIS BOMBARDMENT OF ALMOST FOUR MILLION DETONATIONS, AFTER AN ESTIMATED ONE HUNDRED THOUSAND ENEMY CASUALTIES, WE OFFERED TERMS OF SURRENDER.
THEIR ONLY RESPONSE WAS AS FOLLOWS:
"TO DIE OR LIVE IN FREEDOM IS OUR FATE."

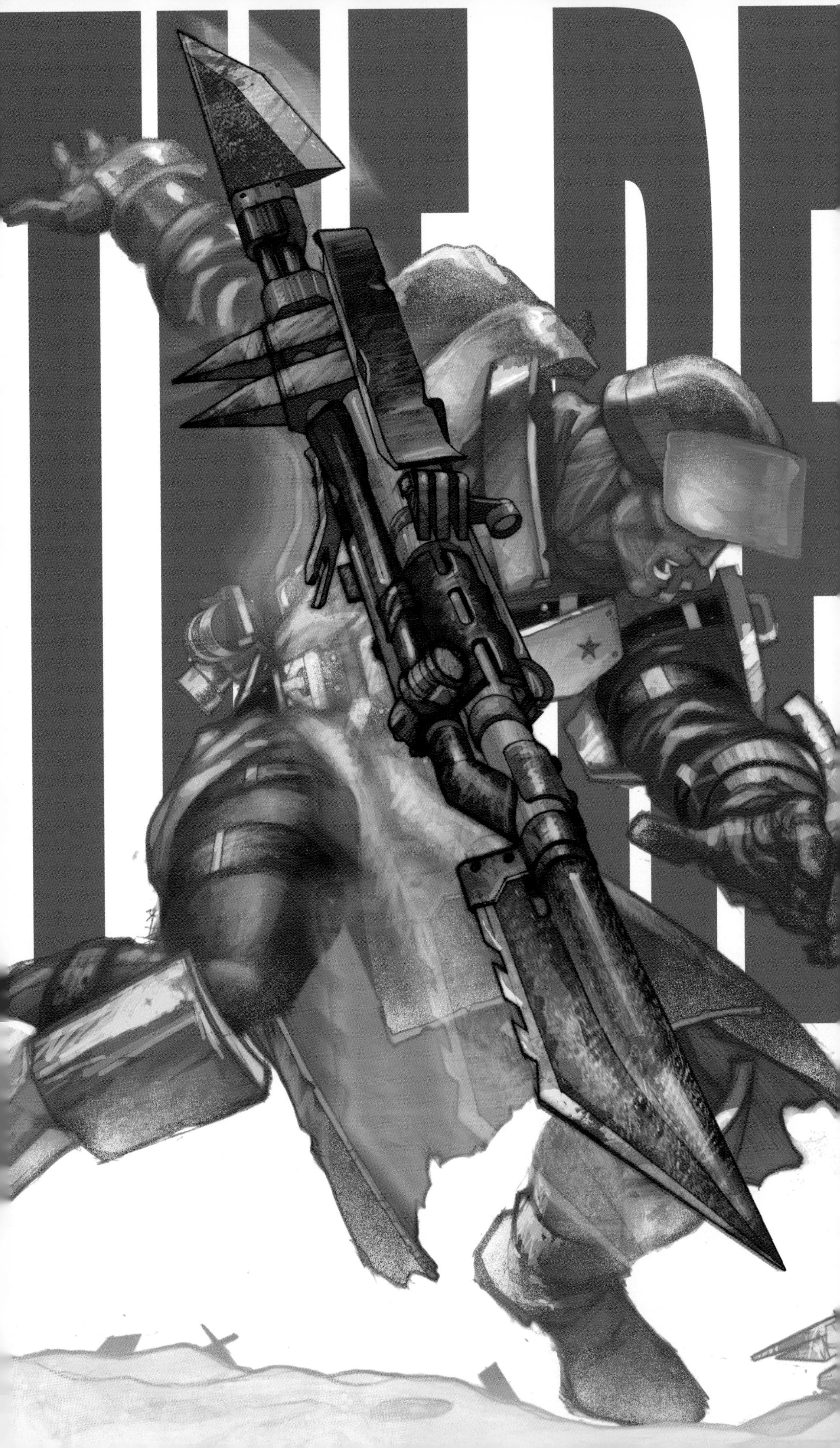

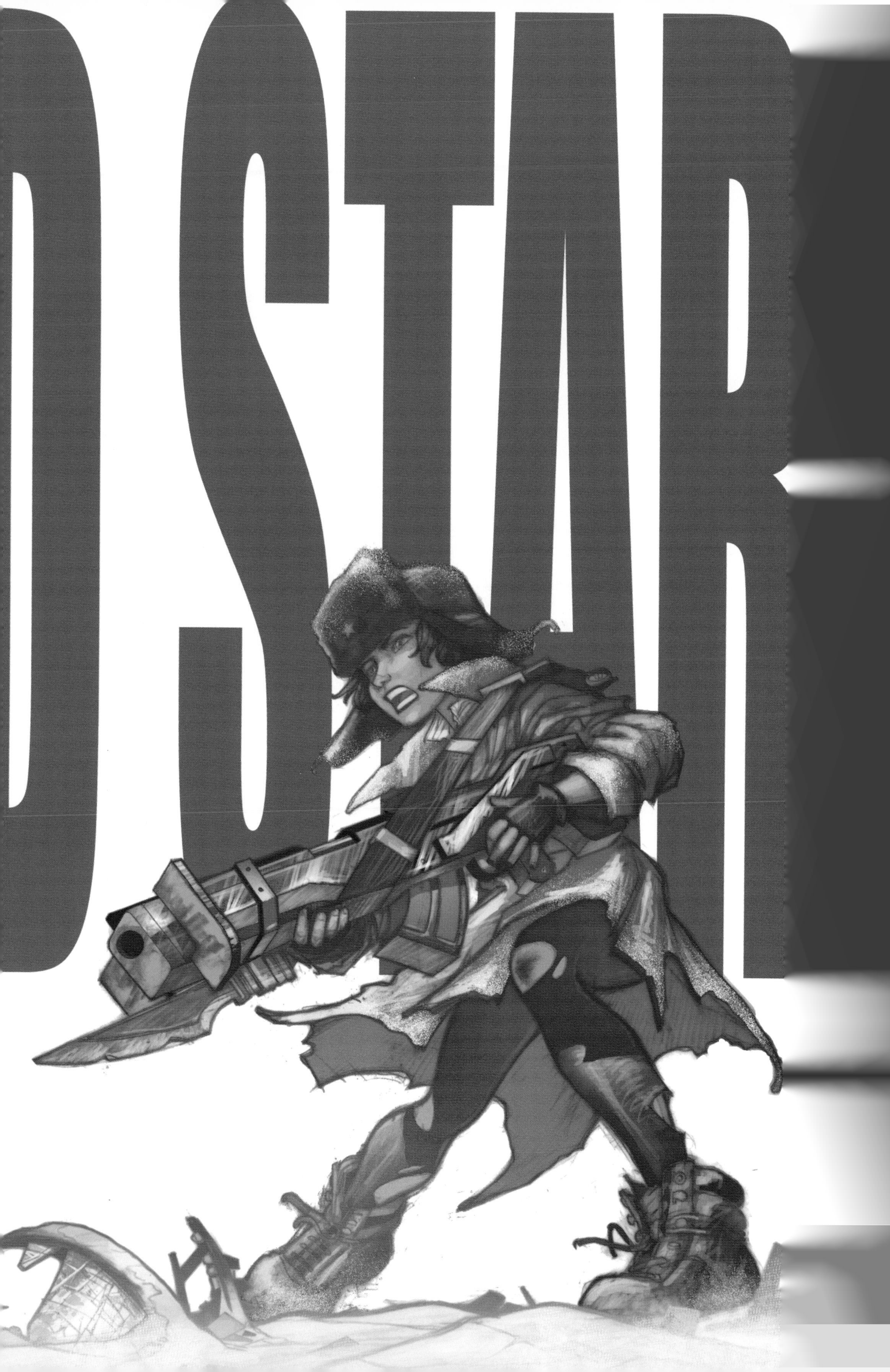
D STAR

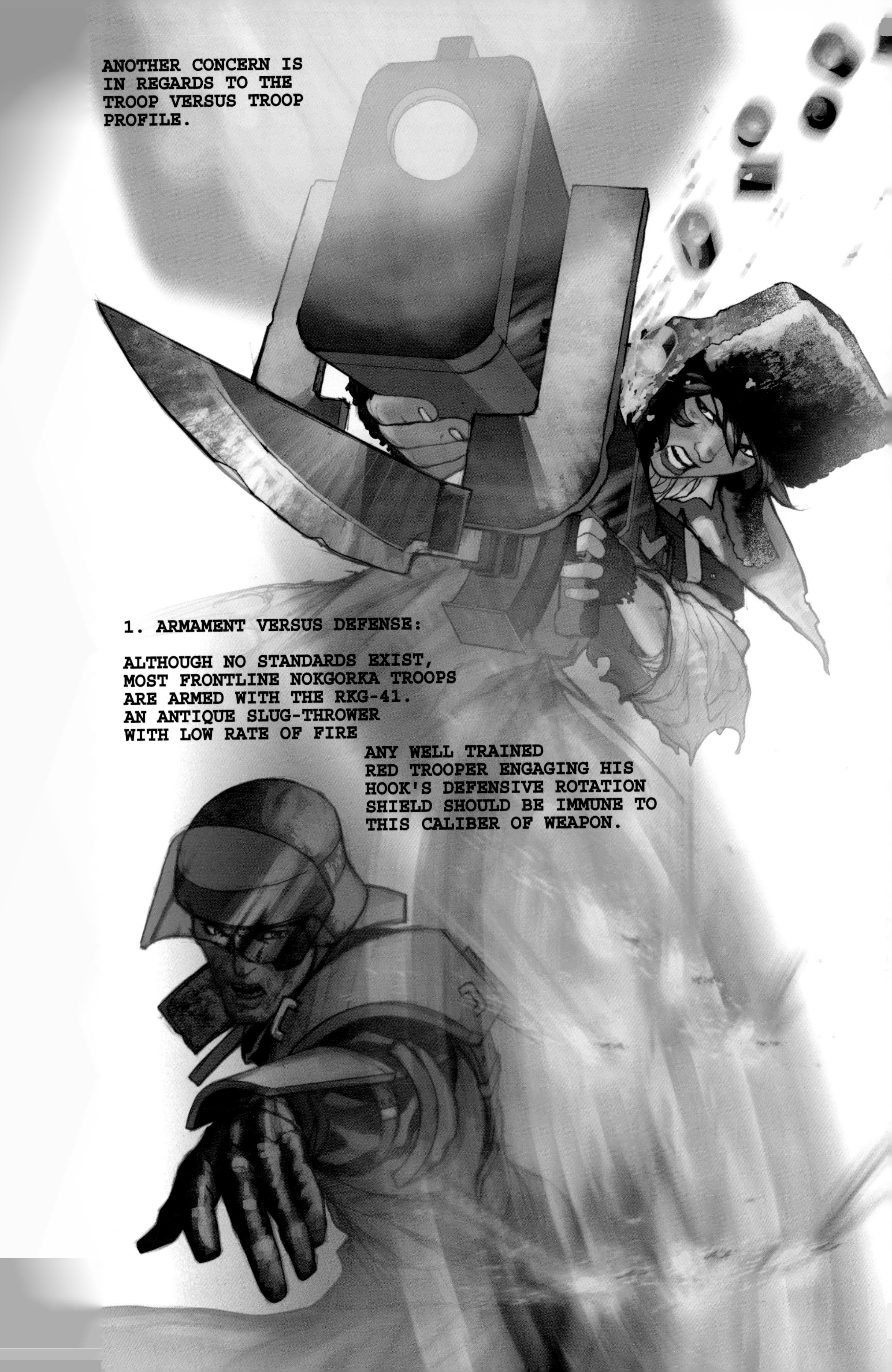
ANOTHER CONCERN IS IN REGARDS TO THE TROOP VERSUS TROOP PROFILE.
1. ARMAMENT VERSUS DEFENSE:
ALTHOUGH NO STANDARDS EXIST, MOST FRONTLINE NOKGORKA TROOPS ARE ARMED WITH THE RKG-41. AN ANTIQUE SLUG-THROWER WITH LOW RATE OF FIRE
ANY WELL TRAINED RED TROOPER ENGAGING HIS HOOK'S DEFENSIVE ROTATION SHIELD SHOULD BE IMMUNE TO THIS CALIBER OF WEAPON.

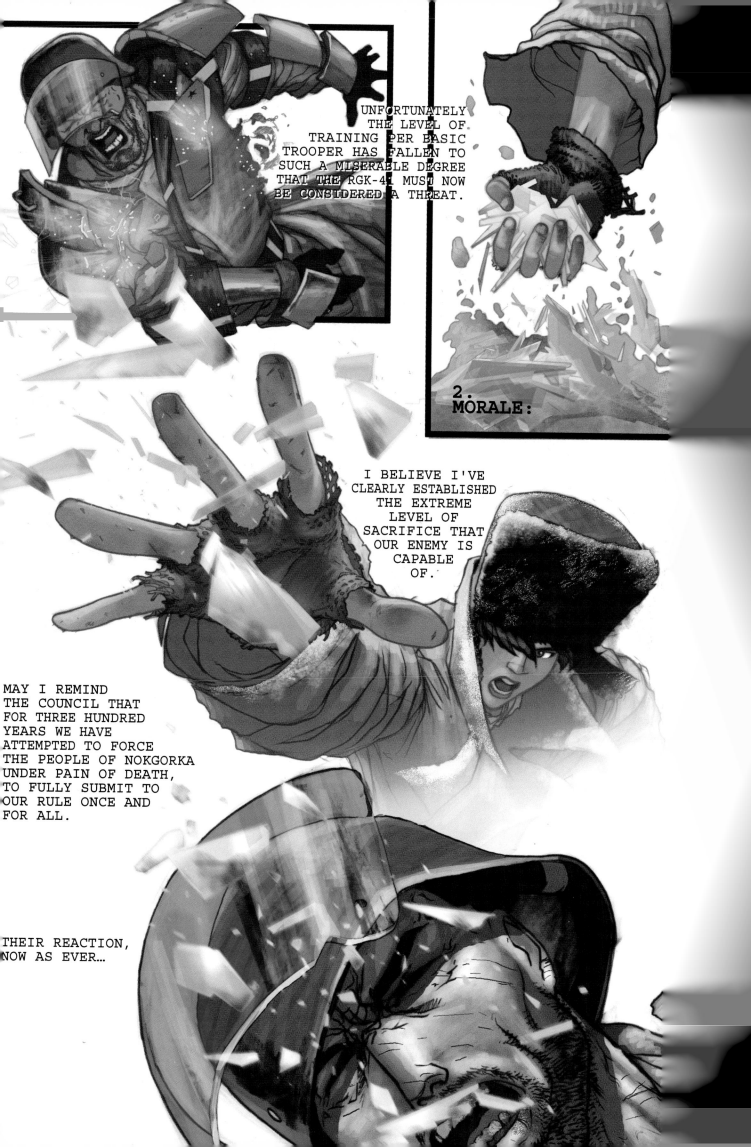

UNFORTUNATELY THE LEVEL OF TRAINING PER BASIC TROOPER HAS FALLEN TO SUCH A MISERABLE DEGREE THAT THE RGK-41 MUST NOW BE CONSIDERED A THREAT.

2. MORALE:

I BELIEVE I'VE CLEARLY ESTABLISHED THE EXTREME LEVEL OF SACRIFICE THAT OUR ENEMY IS CAPABLE OF.

MAY I REMIND THE COUNCIL THAT FOR THREE HUNDRED YEARS WE HAVE ATTEMPTED TO FORCE THE PEOPLE OF NOKGORKA UNDER PAIN OF DEATH, TO FULLY SUBMIT TO OUR RULE ONCE AND FOR ALL.

THEIR REACTION, NOW AS EVER...

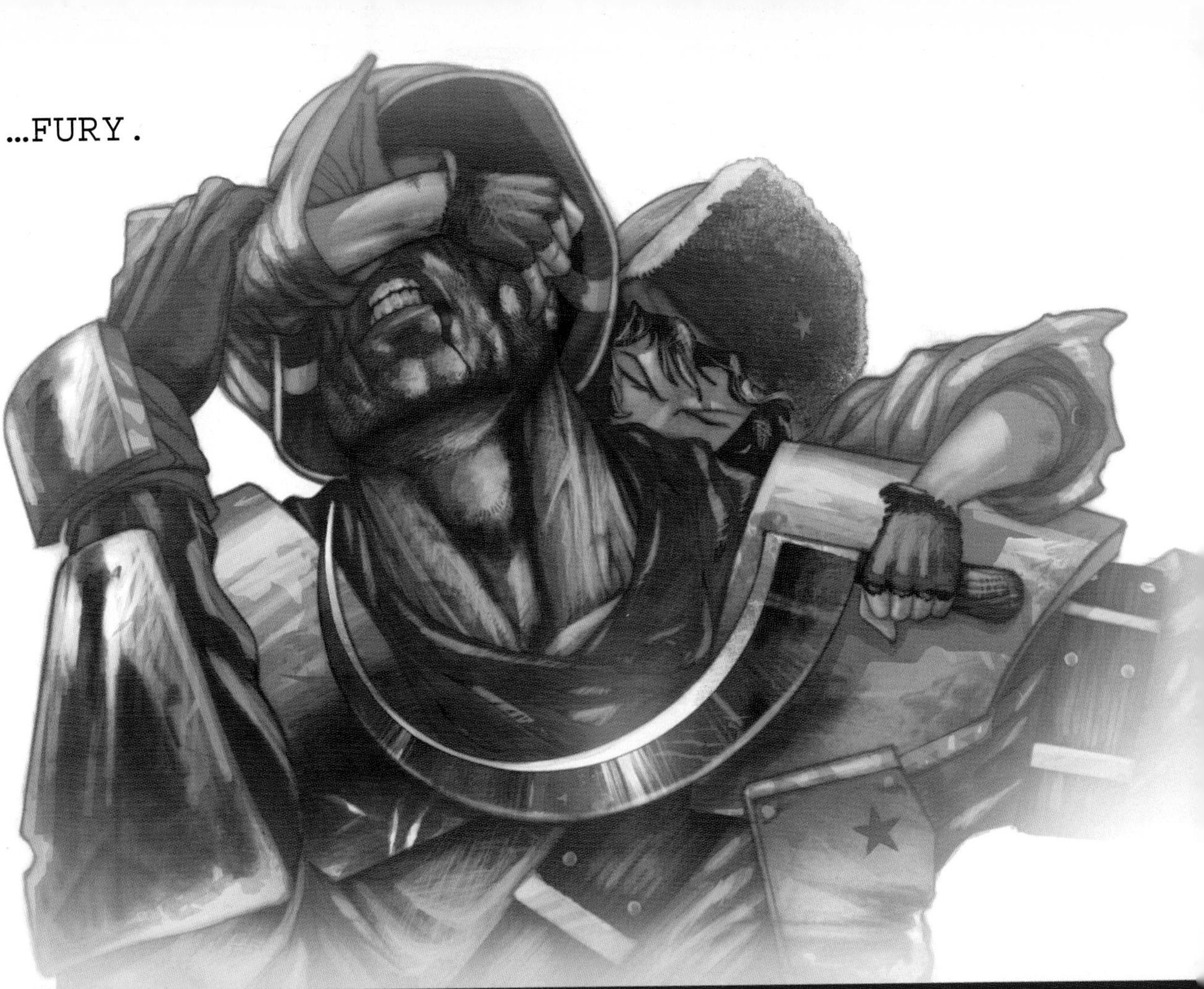
…FURY.

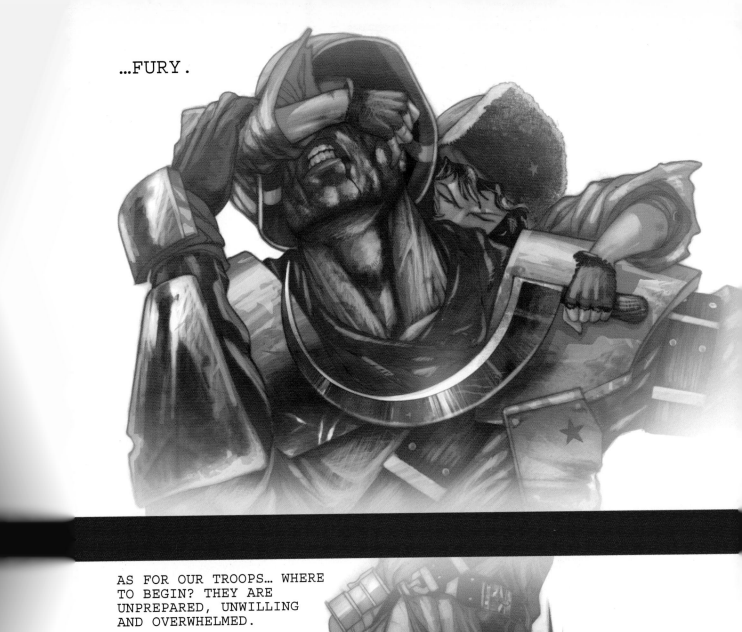

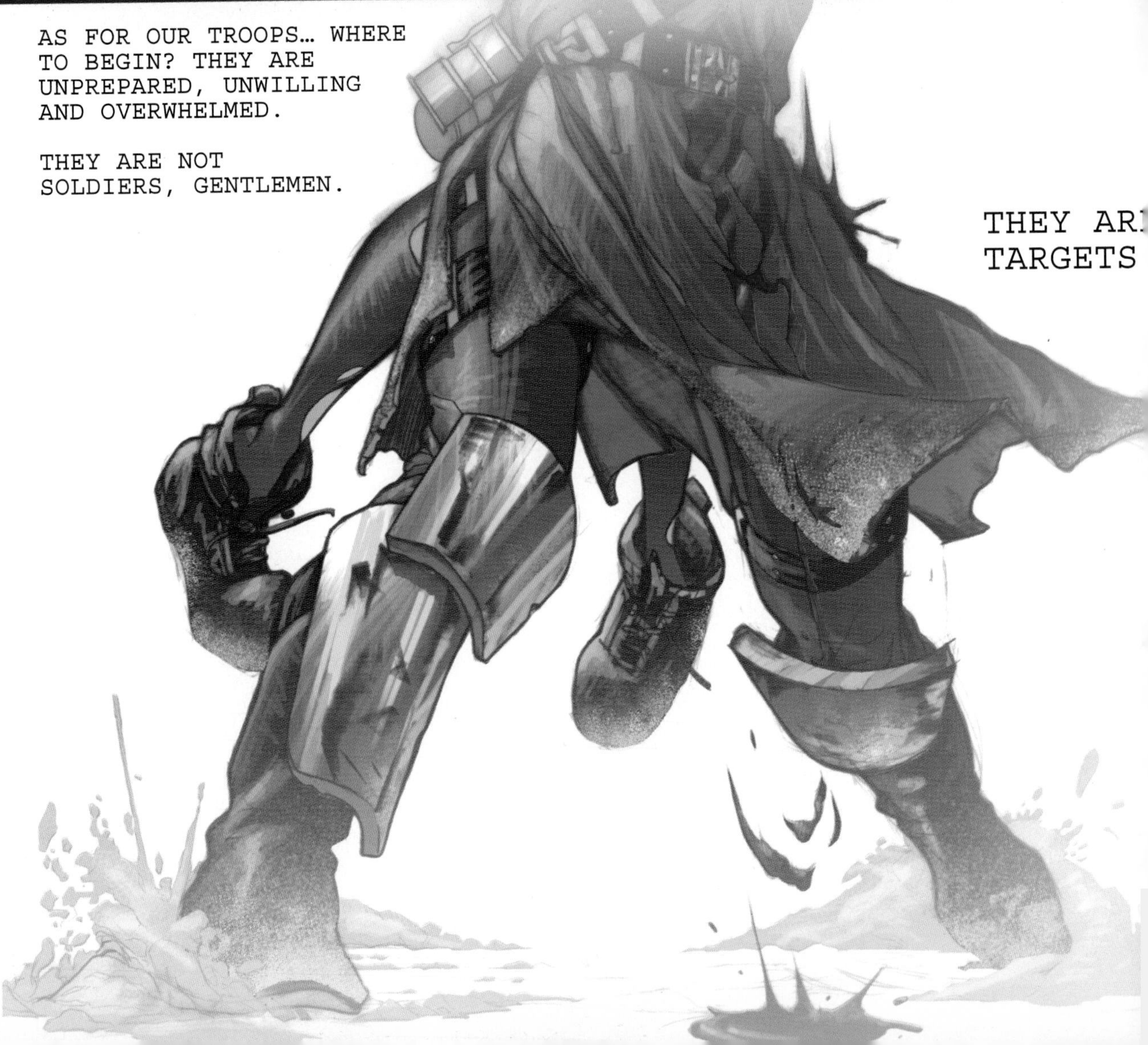
AS FOR OUR TROOPS… WHERE TO BEGIN? THEY ARE UNPREPARED, UNWILLING AND OVERWHELMED.
THEY ARE NOT SOLDIERS, GENTLEMEN.
THEY AR
TARGETS

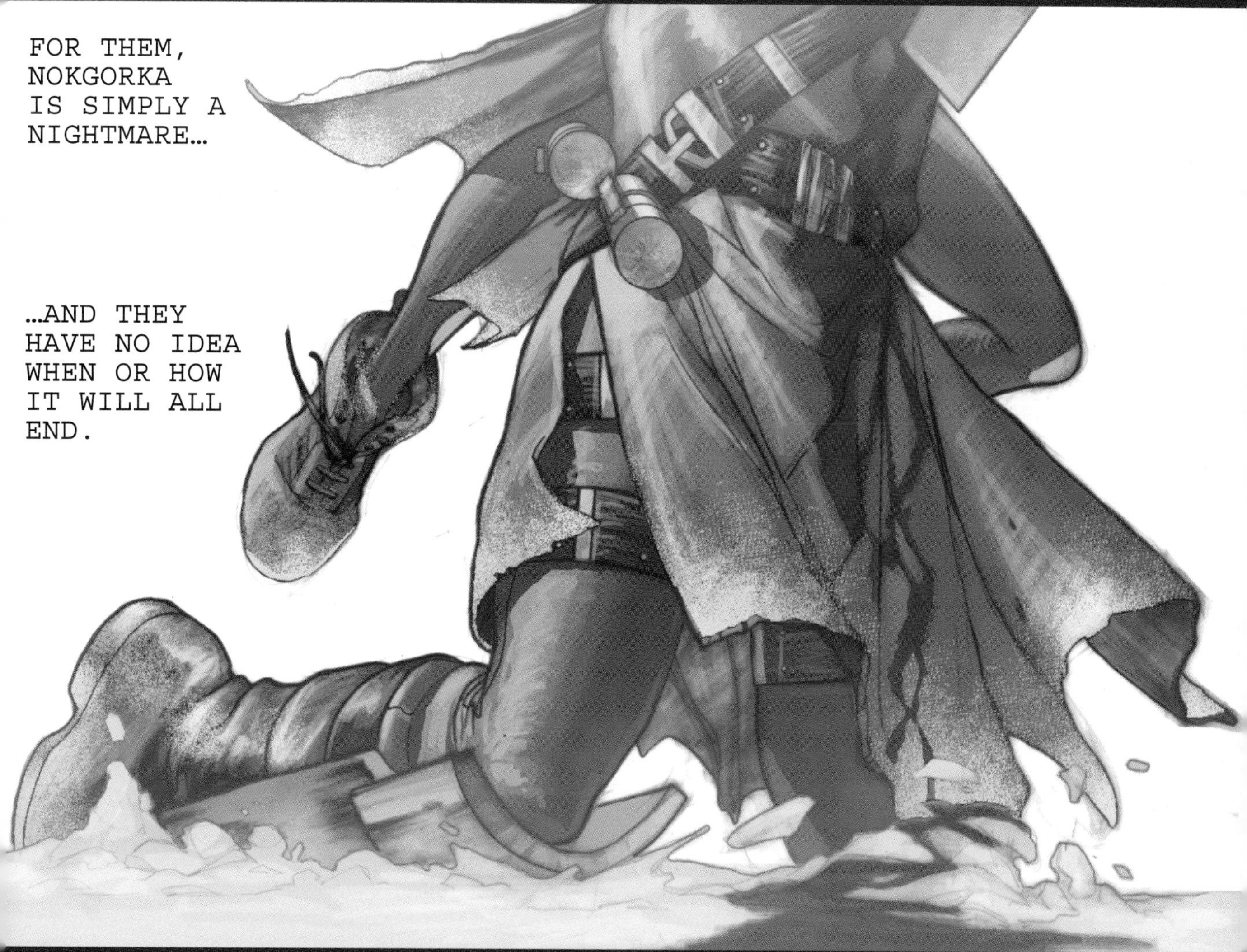
FOR THEM, NOKGORKA IS SIMPLY A NIGHTMARE…
…AND THEY HAVE NO IDEA WHEN OR HOW IT WILL ALL END.

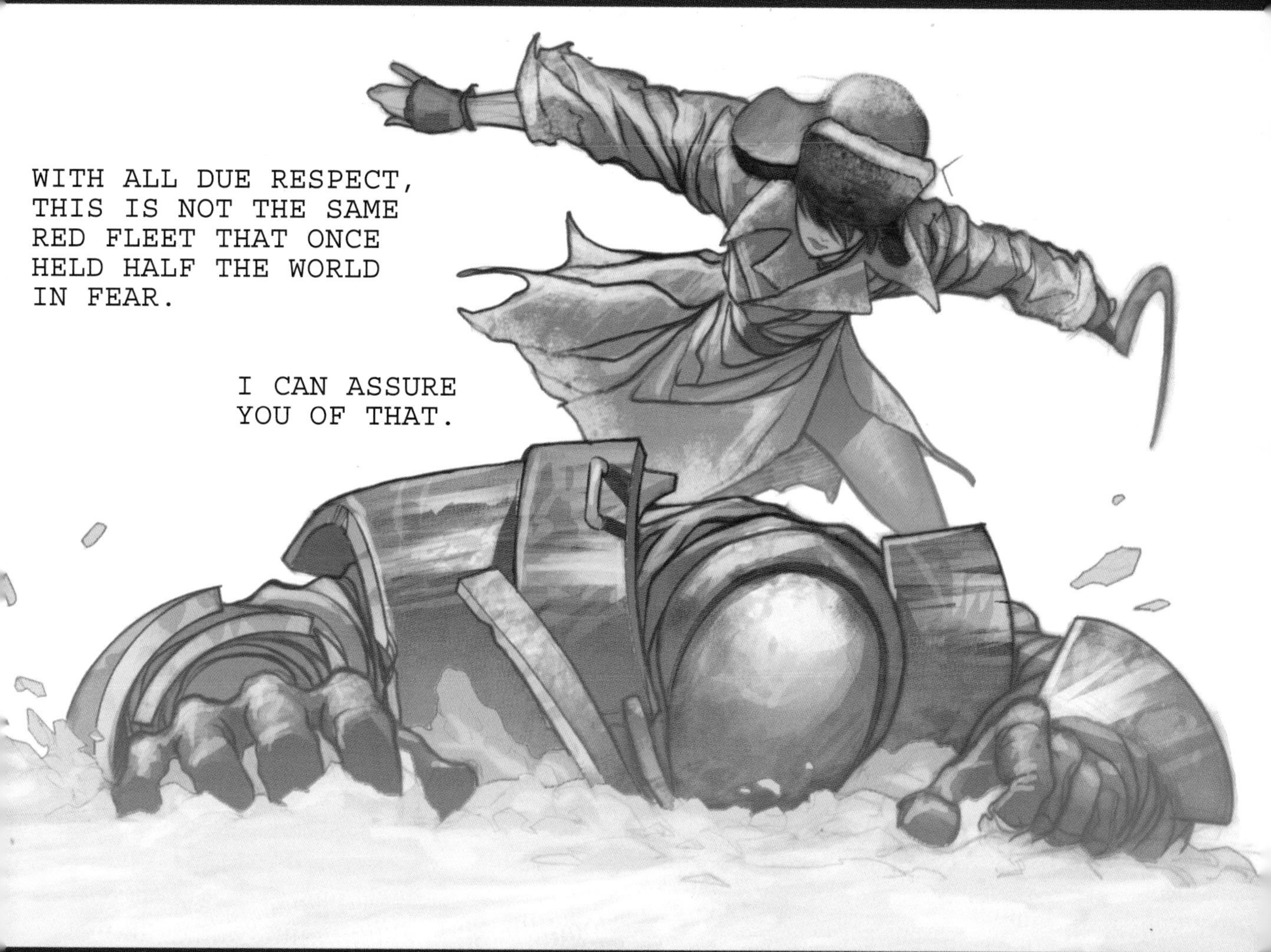
WITH ALL DUE RESPECT, THIS IS NOT THE SAME RED FLEET THAT ONCE HELD HALF THE WORLD IN FEAR.
I CAN ASSURE YOU OF THAT.

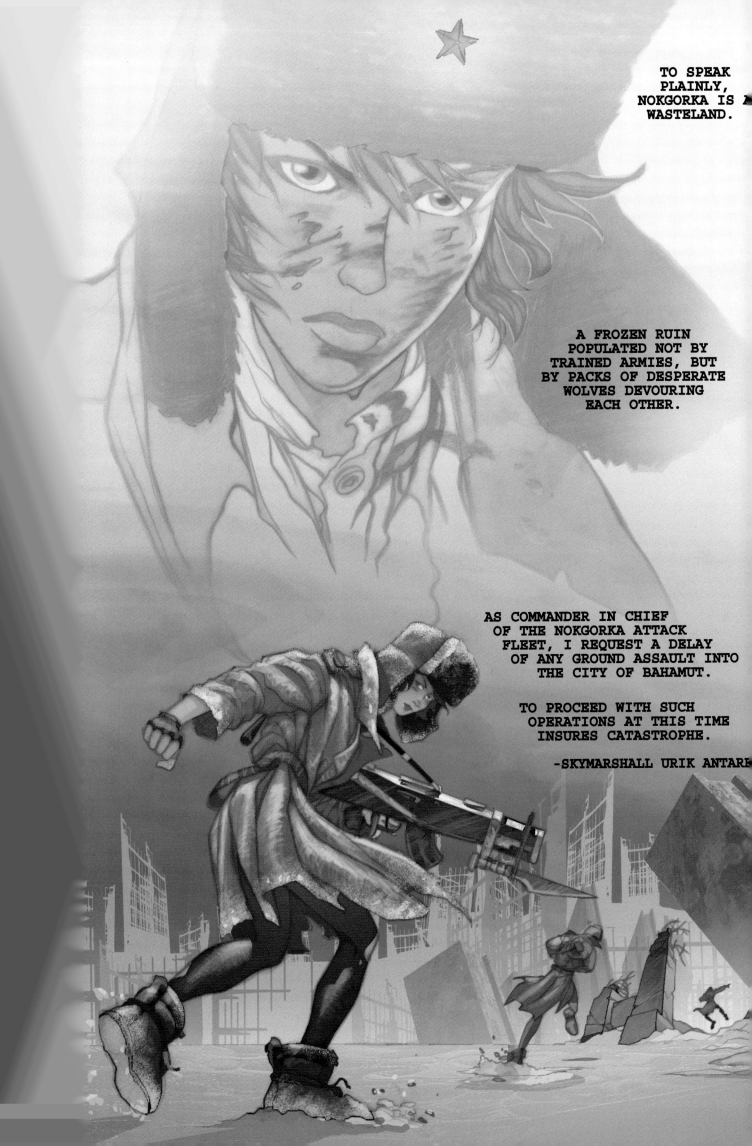

TO SPEAK PLAINLY, NOKGORKA IS A WASTELAND.

A FROZEN RUIN POPULATED NOT BY TRAINED ARMIES, BUT BY PACKS OF DESPERATE WOLVES DEVOURING EACH OTHER.

AS COMMANDER IN CHIEF OF THE NOKGORKA ATTACK FLEET, I REQUEST A DELAY OF ANY GROUND ASSAULT INTO THE CITY OF BAHAMUT.

TO PROCEED WITH SUCH OPERATIONS AT THIS TIME INSURES CATASTROPHE.

-SKYMARSHALL URIK ANTARE

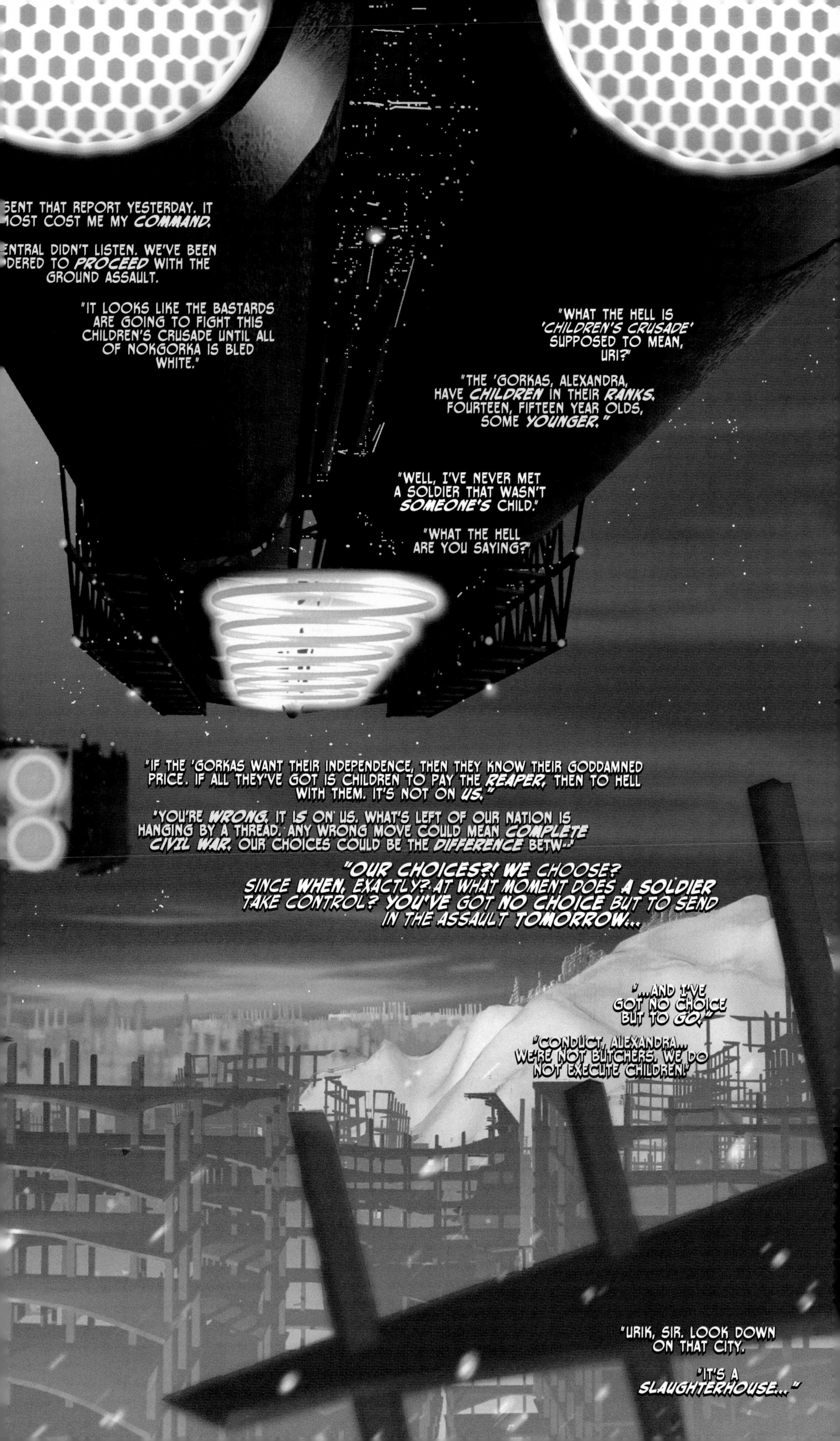

SENT THAT REPORT YESTERDAY. IT MOST COST ME MY COMMAND.
ENTRAL DIDN'T LISTEN. WE'VE BEEN DERED TO PROCEED WITH THE GROUND ASSAULT.
"IT LOOKS LIKE THE BASTARDS ARE GOING TO FIGHT THIS CHILDREN'S CRUSADE UNTIL ALL OF NOKGORKA IS BLED WHITE."
"WHAT THE HELL IS 'CHILDREN'S CRUSADE' SUPPOSED TO MEAN, URI?"
"THE 'GORKAS, ALEXANDRA, HAVE CHILDREN IN THEIR RANKS. FOURTEEN, FIFTEEN YEAR OLDS, SOME YOUNGER."
"WELL, I'VE NEVER MET A SOLDIER THAT WASN'T SOMEONE'S CHILD."
"WHAT THE HELL ARE YOU SAYING?"
"IF THE 'GORKAS WANT THEIR INDEPENDENCE, THEN THEY KNOW THEIR GODDAMNED PRICE. IF ALL THEY'VE GOT IS CHILDREN TO PAY THE REAPER, THEN TO HELL WITH THEM. IT'S NOT ON US."
"YOU'RE WRONG. IT IS ON US. WHAT'S LEFT OF OUR NATION IS HANGING BY A THREAD. ANY WRONG MOVE COULD MEAN COMPLETE CIVIL WAR. OUR CHOICES COULD BE THE DIFFERENCE BETW--"
"OUR CHOICES?! WE CHOOSE? SINCE WHEN, EXACTLY? AT WHAT MOMENT DOES A SOLDIER TAKE CONTROL? YOU'VE GOT NO CHOICE BUT TO SEND IN THE ASSAULT TOMORROW...
"...AND I'VE GOT NO CHOICE BUT TO GO."
"CONDUCT, ALEXANDRA... WE'RE NOT BUTCHERS. WE DO NOT EXECUTE CHILDREN."
"URIK, SIR. LOOK DOWN ON THAT CITY.
"IT'S A SLAUGHTERHOUSE..."

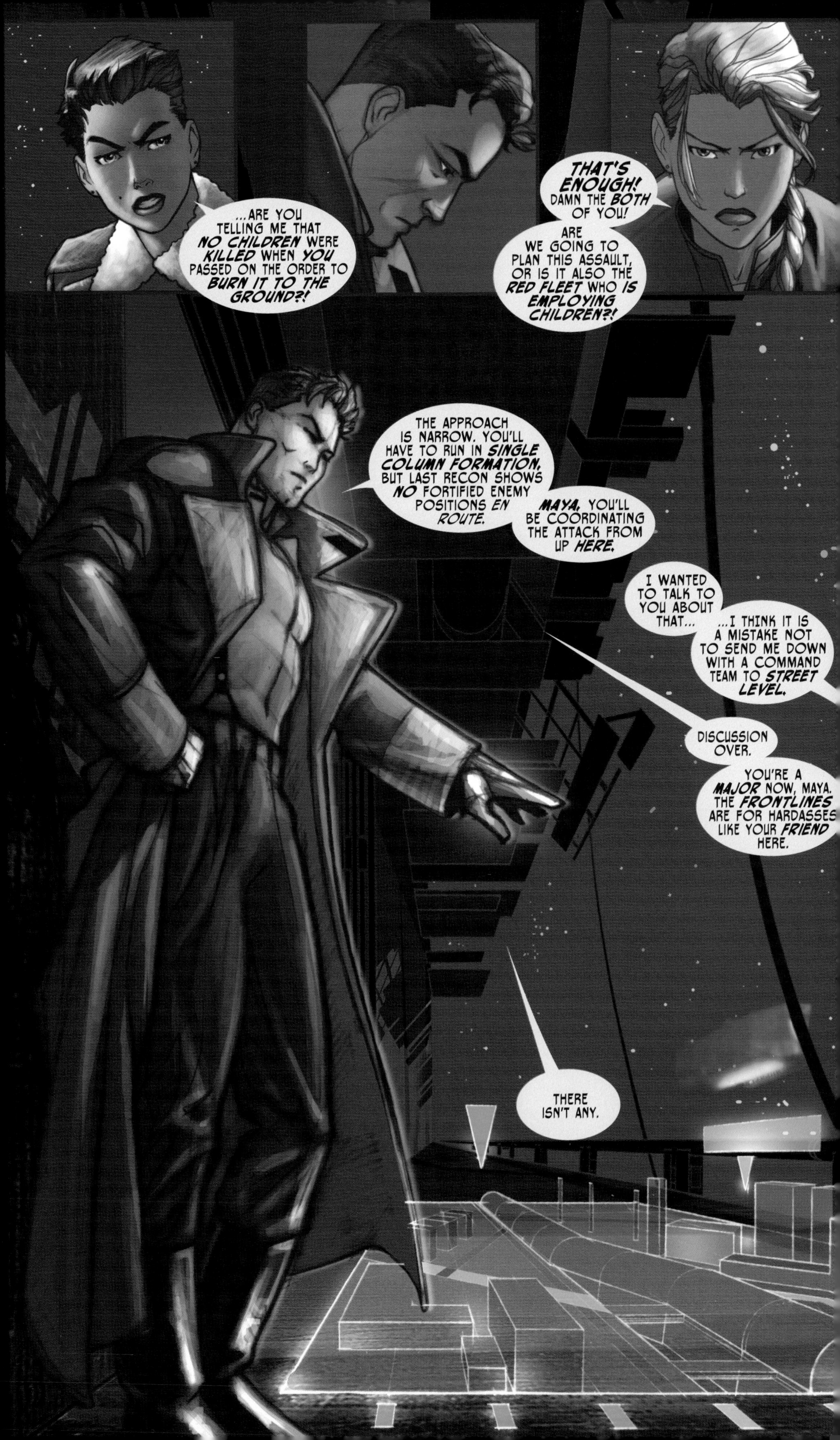

...ARE YOU TELLING ME THAT NO CHILDREN WERE KILLED WHEN YOU PASSED ON THE ORDER TO BURN IT TO THE GROUND?!
THAT'S ENOUGH! DAMN THE BOTH OF YOU!
ARE WE GOING TO PLAN THIS ASSAULT, OR IS IT ALSO THE RED FLEET WHO IS EMPLOYING CHILDREN?!
THE APPROACH IS NARROW. YOU'LL HAVE TO RUN IN SINGLE COLUMN FORMATION, BUT LAST RECON SHOWS NO FORTIFIED ENEMY POSITIONS EN ROUTE.
MAYA, YOU'LL BE COORDINATING THE ATTACK FROM UP HERE.
I WANTED TO TALK TO YOU ABOUT THAT...
...I THINK IT IS A MISTAKE NOT TO SEND ME DOWN WITH A COMMAND TEAM TO STREET LEVEL.
DISCUSSION OVER.
YOU'RE A MAJOR NOW, MAYA. THE FRONTLINES ARE FOR HARDASSES LIKE YOUR FRIEND HERE.
THERE ISN'T ANY.

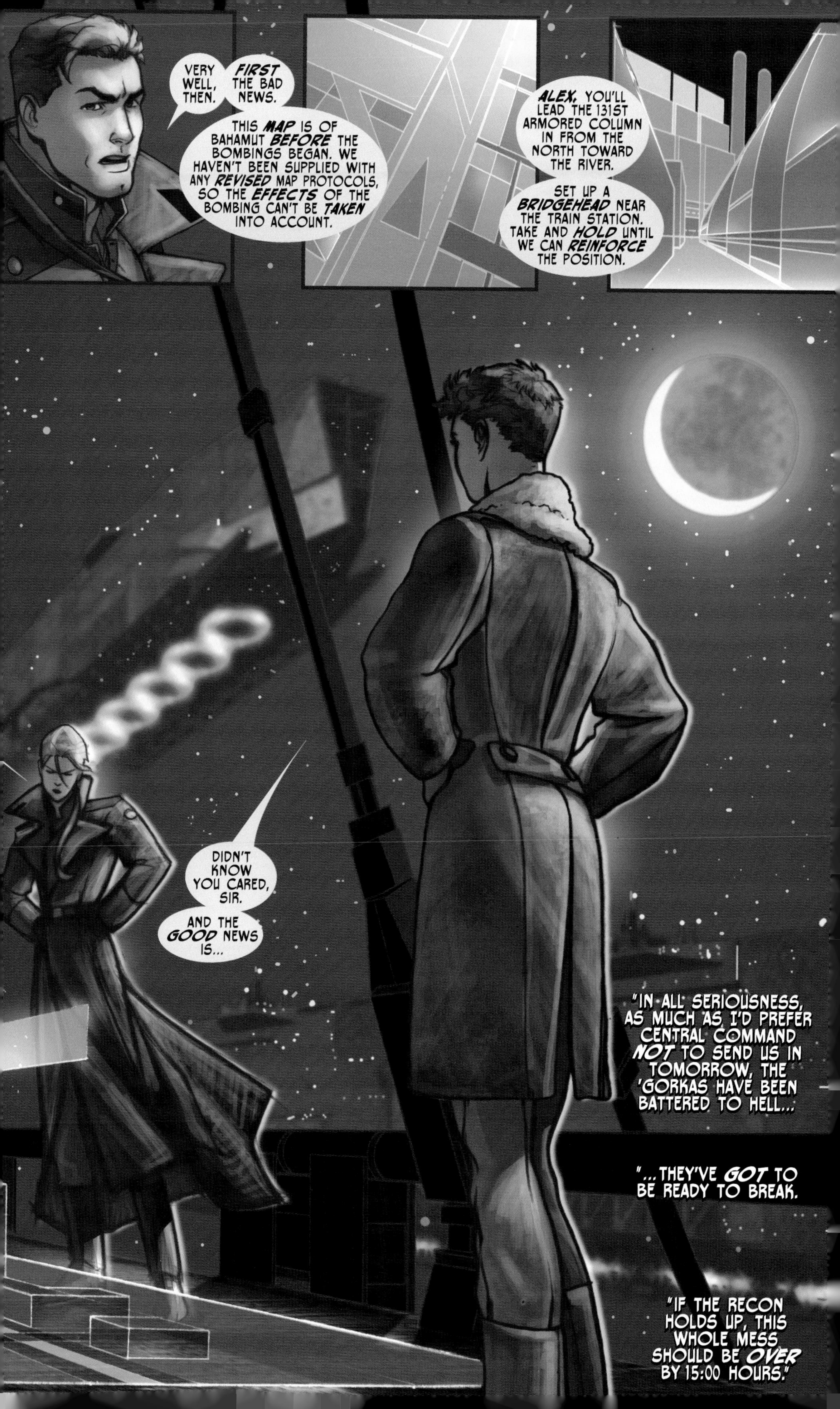
VERY WELL, THEN.
FIRST THE BAD NEWS.
THIS MAP IS OF BAHAMUT BEFORE THE BOMBINGS BEGAN. WE HAVEN'T BEEN SUPPLIED WITH ANY REVISED MAP PROTOCOLS, SO THE EFFECTS OF THE BOMBING CAN'T BE TAKEN INTO ACCOUNT.
ALEX, YOU'LL LEAD THE 131ST ARMORED COLUMN IN FROM THE NORTH TOWARD THE RIVER.
SET UP A BRIDGEHEAD NEAR THE TRAIN STATION. TAKE AND HOLD UNTIL WE CAN REINFORCE THE POSITION.
DIDN'T KNOW YOU CARED, SIR.
AND THE GOOD NEWS IS...
"IN ALL SERIOUSNESS, AS MUCH AS I'D PREFER CENTRAL COMMAND NOT TO SEND US IN TOMORROW, THE 'GORKAS HAVE BEEN BATTERED TO HELL...
"...THEY'VE GOT TO BE READY TO BREAK.
"IF THE RECON HOLDS UP, THIS WHOLE MESS SHOULD BE OVER BY 15:00 HOURS."

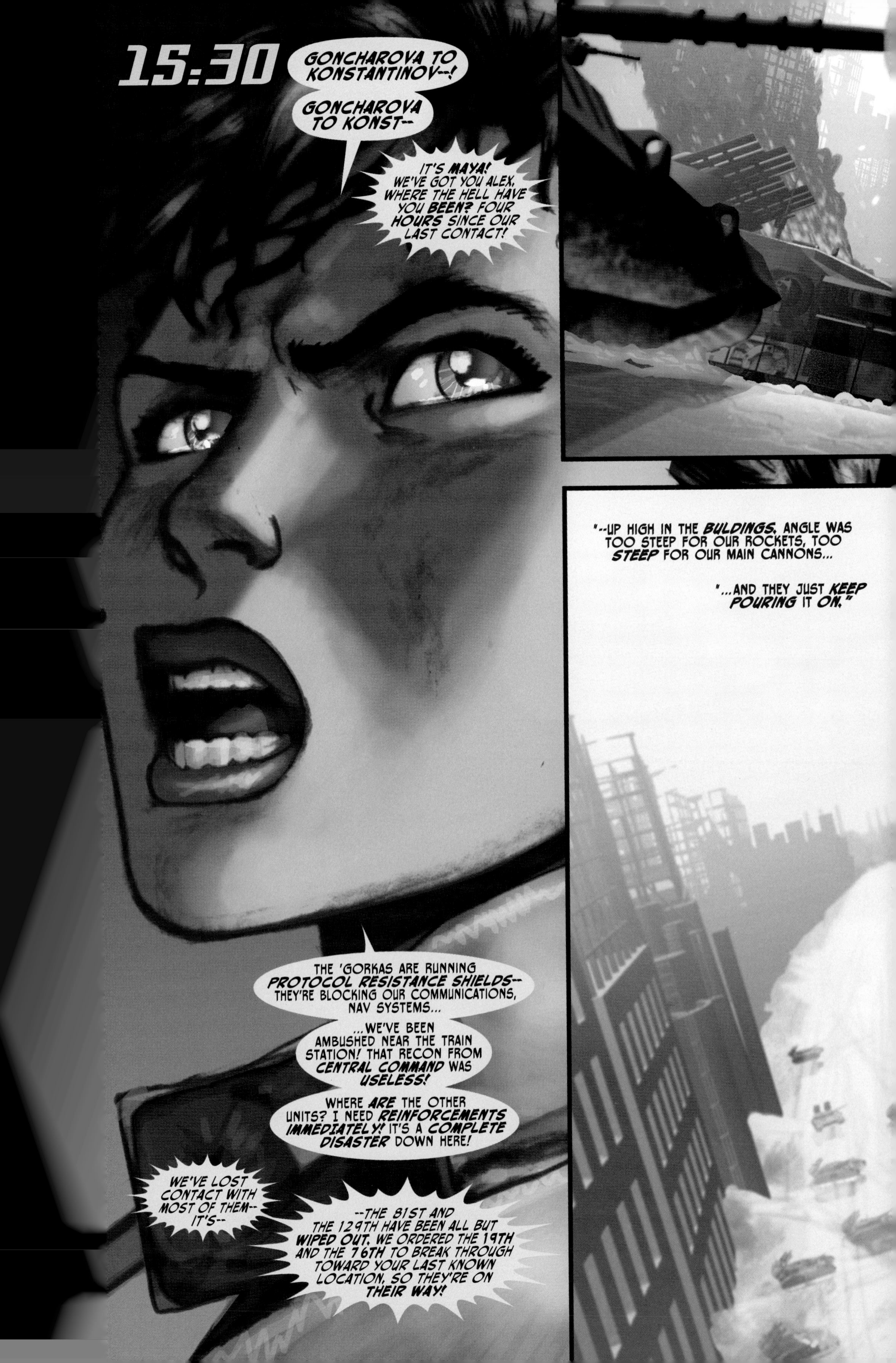
15:30
GONCHAROVA TO KONSTANTINOV--!
GONCHAROVA TO KONST--
IT'S MAYA! WE'VE GOT YOU ALEX. WHERE THE HELL HAVE YOU BEEN? FOUR HOURS SINCE OUR LAST CONTACT!
THE 'GORKAS ARE RUNNING PROTOCOL RESISTANCE SHIELDS-- THEY'RE BLOCKING OUR COMMUNICATIONS, NAV SYSTEMS...
...WE'VE BEEN AMBUSHED NEAR THE TRAIN STATION! THAT RECON FROM CENTRAL COMMAND WAS USELESS!
WHERE ARE THE OTHER UNITS? I NEED REINFORCEMENTS IMMEDIATELY! IT'S A COMPLETE DISASTER DOWN HERE!
WE'VE LOST CONTACT WITH MOST OF THEM-- IT'S--
--THE 81ST AND THE 129TH HAVE BEEN ALL BUT WIPED OUT. WE ORDERED THE 19TH AND THE 76TH TO BREAK THROUGH TOWARD YOUR LAST KNOWN LOCATION, SO THEY'RE ON THEIR WAY!
"--UP HIGH IN THE BULDINGS. ANGLE WAS TOO STEEP FOR OUR ROCKETS, TOO STEEP FOR OUR MAIN CANNONS...
"...AND THEY JUST KEEP POURING IT ON."

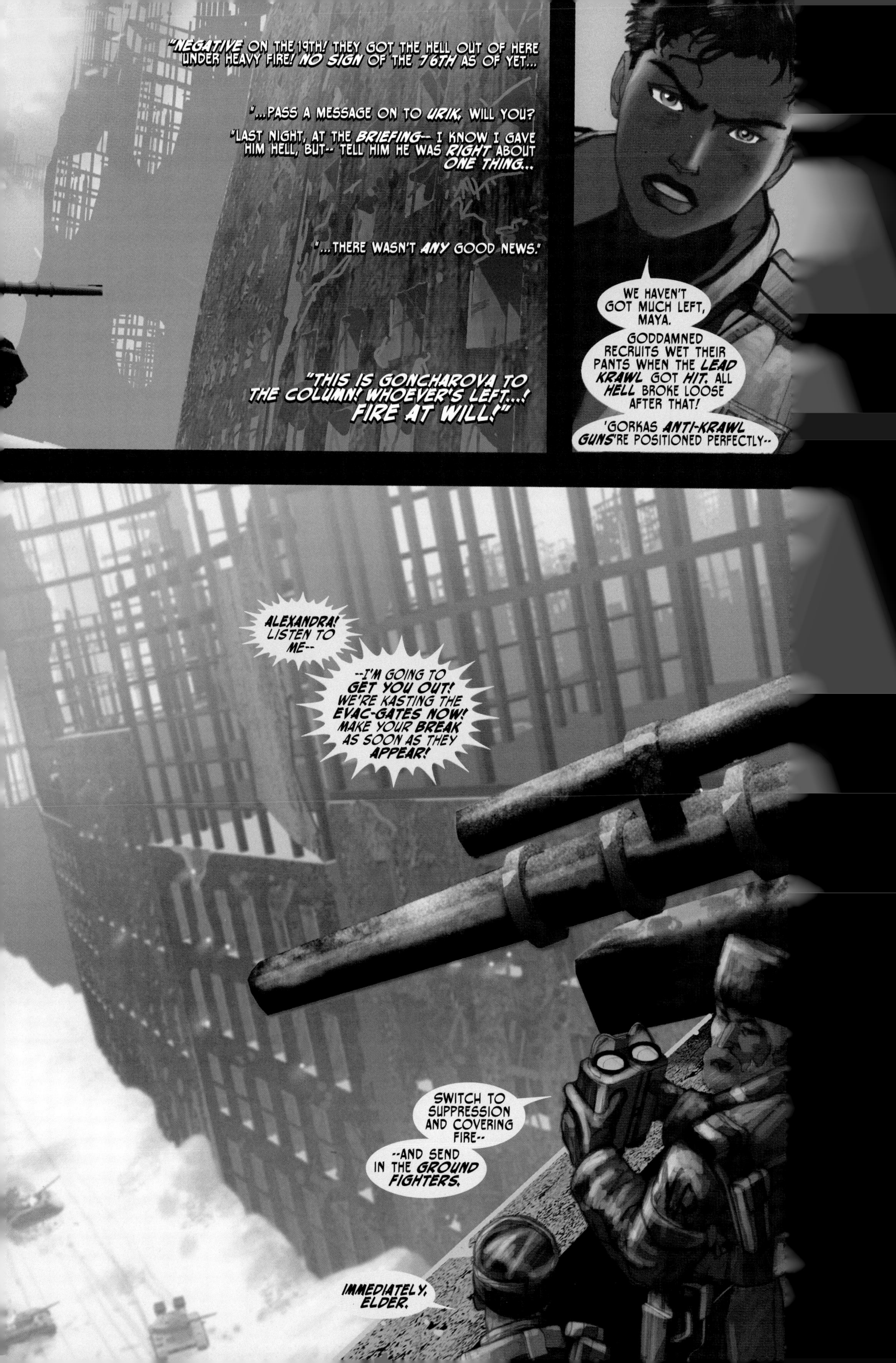
"NEGATIVE ON THE 19TH! THEY GOT THE HELL OUT OF HERE UNDER HEAVY FIRE! NO SIGN OF THE 76TH AS OF YET...
"...PASS A MESSAGE ON TO URIK, WILL YOU?
"LAST NIGHT, AT THE BRIEFING-- I KNOW I GAVE HIM HELL, BUT-- TELL HIM HE WAS RIGHT ABOUT ONE THING...
"...THERE WASN'T ANY GOOD NEWS."
"THIS IS GONCHAROVA TO THE COLUMN! WHOEVER'S LEFT...! FIRE AT WILL!"
WE HAVEN'T GOT MUCH LEFT, MAYA.
GODDAMNED RECRUITS WET THEIR PANTS WHEN THE LEAD KRAWL GOT HIT. ALL HELL BROKE LOOSE AFTER THAT!
'GORKAS ANTI-KRAWL GUNS'RE POSITIONED PERFECTLY--
ALEXANDRA! LISTEN TO ME--
--I'M GOING TO GET YOU OUT! WE'RE KASTING THE EVAC-GATES NOW! MAKE YOUR BREAK AS SOON AS THEY APPEAR!
SWITCH TO SUPPRESSION AND COVERING FIRE--
--AND SEND IN THE GROUND FIGHTERS.
IMMEDIATELY, ELDER.

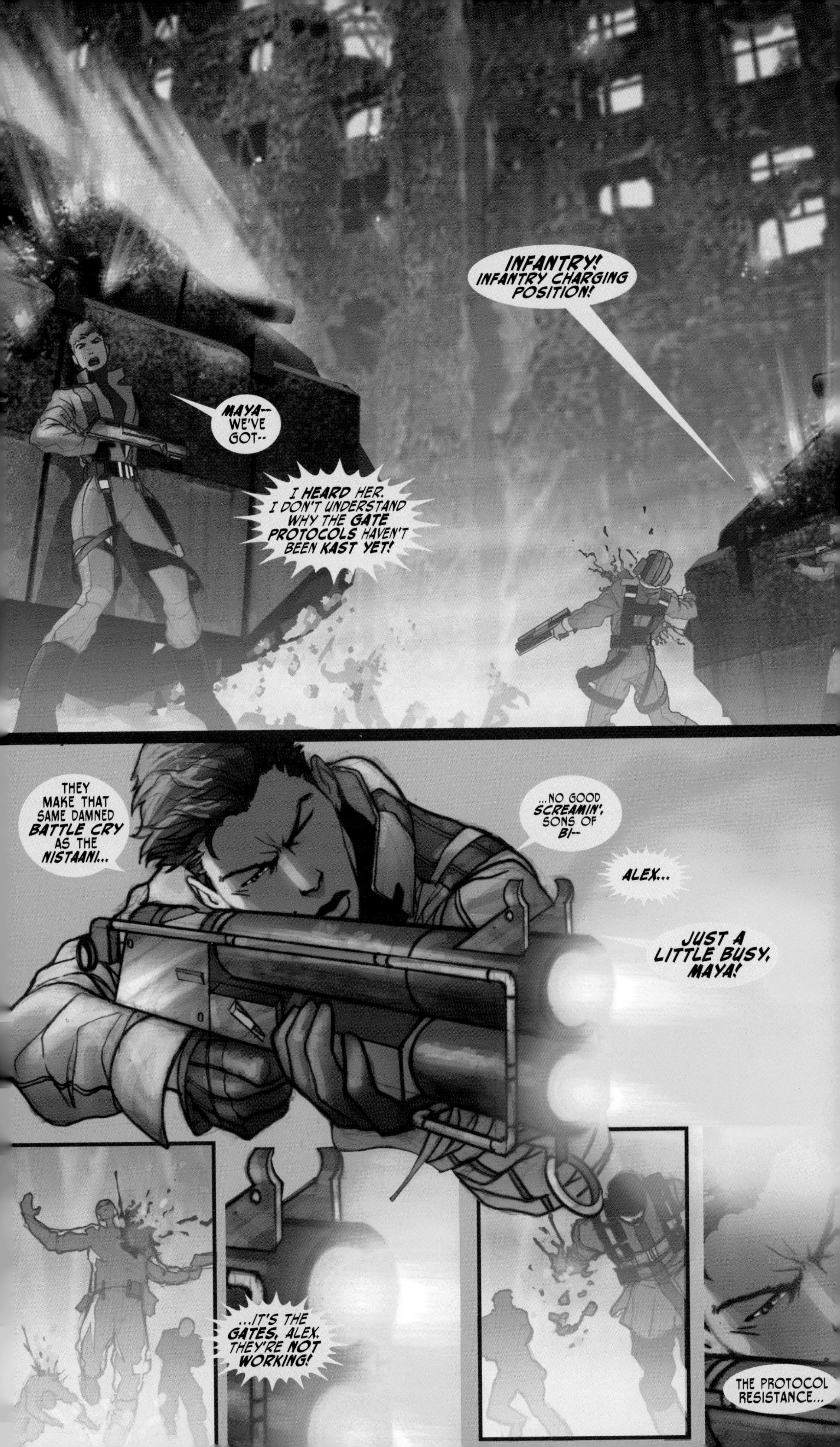
INFANTRY! INFANTRY CHARGING POSITION!
MAYA-- WE'VE GOT--
I HEARD HER. I DON'T UNDERSTAND WHY THE GATE PROTOCOLS HAVEN'T BEEN KAST YET!
THEY MAKE THAT SAME DAMNED BATTLE CRY AS THE NISTAANI...
...NO GOOD SCREAMIN', SONS OF BI--
ALEX...
JUST A LITTLE BUSY, MAYA!
...IT'S THE GATES, ALEX. THEY'RE NOT WORKING!
THE PROTOCOL RESISTANCE...

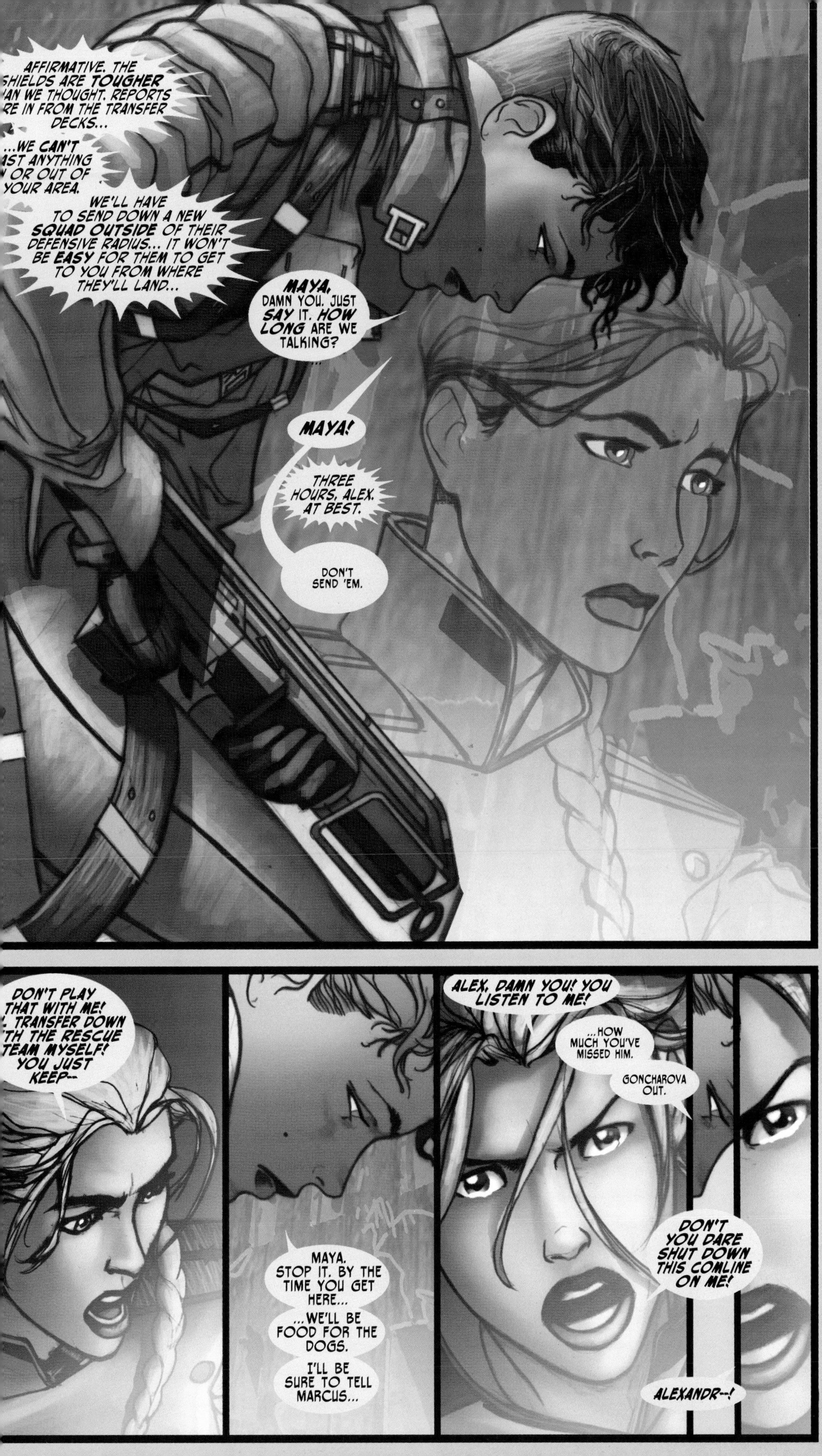
AFFIRMATIVE. THE SHIELDS ARE TOUGHER AN WE THOUGHT. REPORTS RE IN FROM THE TRANSFER DECKS...
...WE CAN'T AST ANYTHING N OR OUT OF YOUR AREA.
WE'LL HAVE TO SEND DOWN A NEW SQUAD OUTSIDE OF THEIR DEFENSIVE RADIUS... IT WON'T BE EASY FOR THEM TO GET TO YOU FROM WHERE THEY'LL LAND...
MAYA, DAMN YOU. JUST SAY IT. HOW LONG ARE WE TALKING?
...
MAYA!
THREE HOURS, ALEX. AT BEST.
DON'T SEND 'EM.
DON'T PLAY THAT WITH ME! TRANSFER DOWN TH THE RESCUE TEAM MYSELF! YOU JUST KEEP--
MAYA. STOP IT. BY THE TIME YOU GET HERE...
...WE'LL BE FOOD FOR THE DOGS.
I'LL BE SURE TO TELL MARCUS...
ALEX, DAMN YOU! YOU LISTEN TO ME!
...HOW MUCH YOU'VE MISSED HIM.
GONCHAROVA OUT.
DON'T YOU DARE SHUT DOWN THIS COMLINE ON ME!
ALEXANDR--!

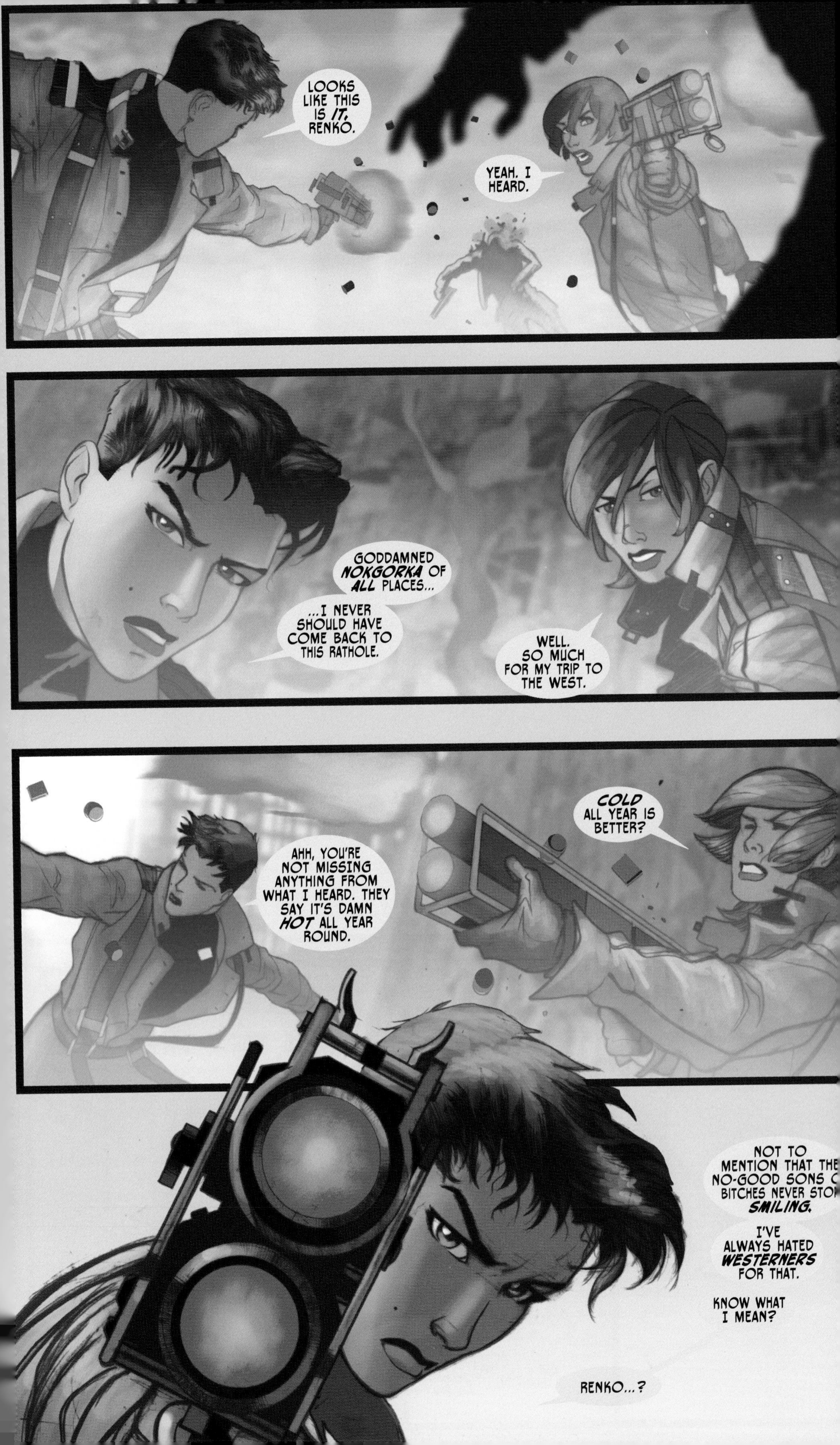
LOOKS LIKE THIS IS IT, RENKO.
YEAH. I HEARD.
GODDAMNED NOKGORKA OF ALL PLACES...
...I NEVER SHOULD HAVE COME BACK TO THIS RATHOLE.
WELL. SO MUCH FOR MY TRIP TO THE WEST.
AHH, YOU'RE NOT MISSING ANYTHING FROM WHAT I HEARD. THEY SAY IT'S DAMN HOT ALL YEAR ROUND.
COLD ALL YEAR IS BETTER?
I'VE ALWAYS HATED WESTERNERS FOR THAT.
KNOW WHAT I MEAN?
RENKO...?

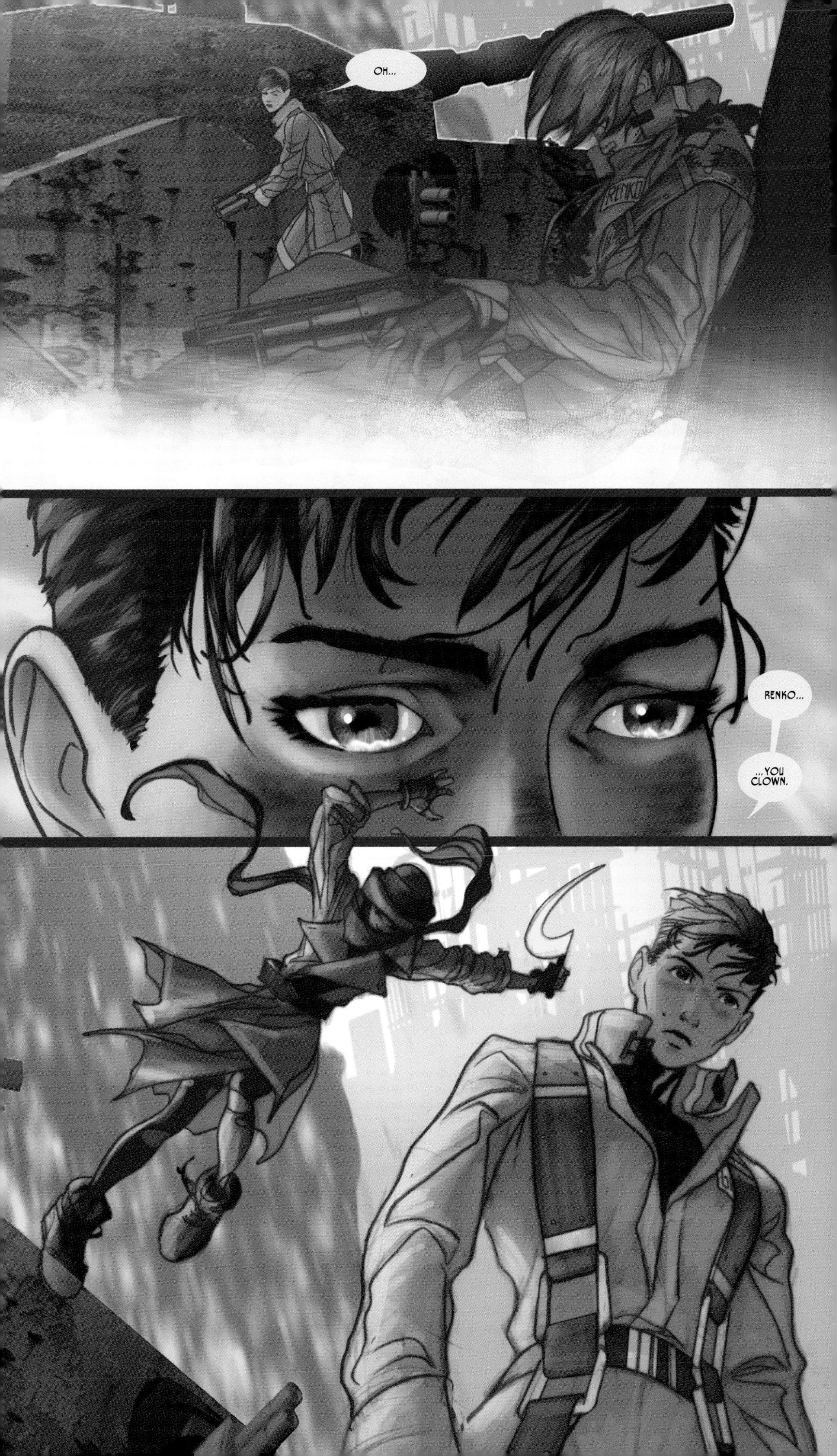
OH...
RENKO
RENKO...
...YOU CLOWN.

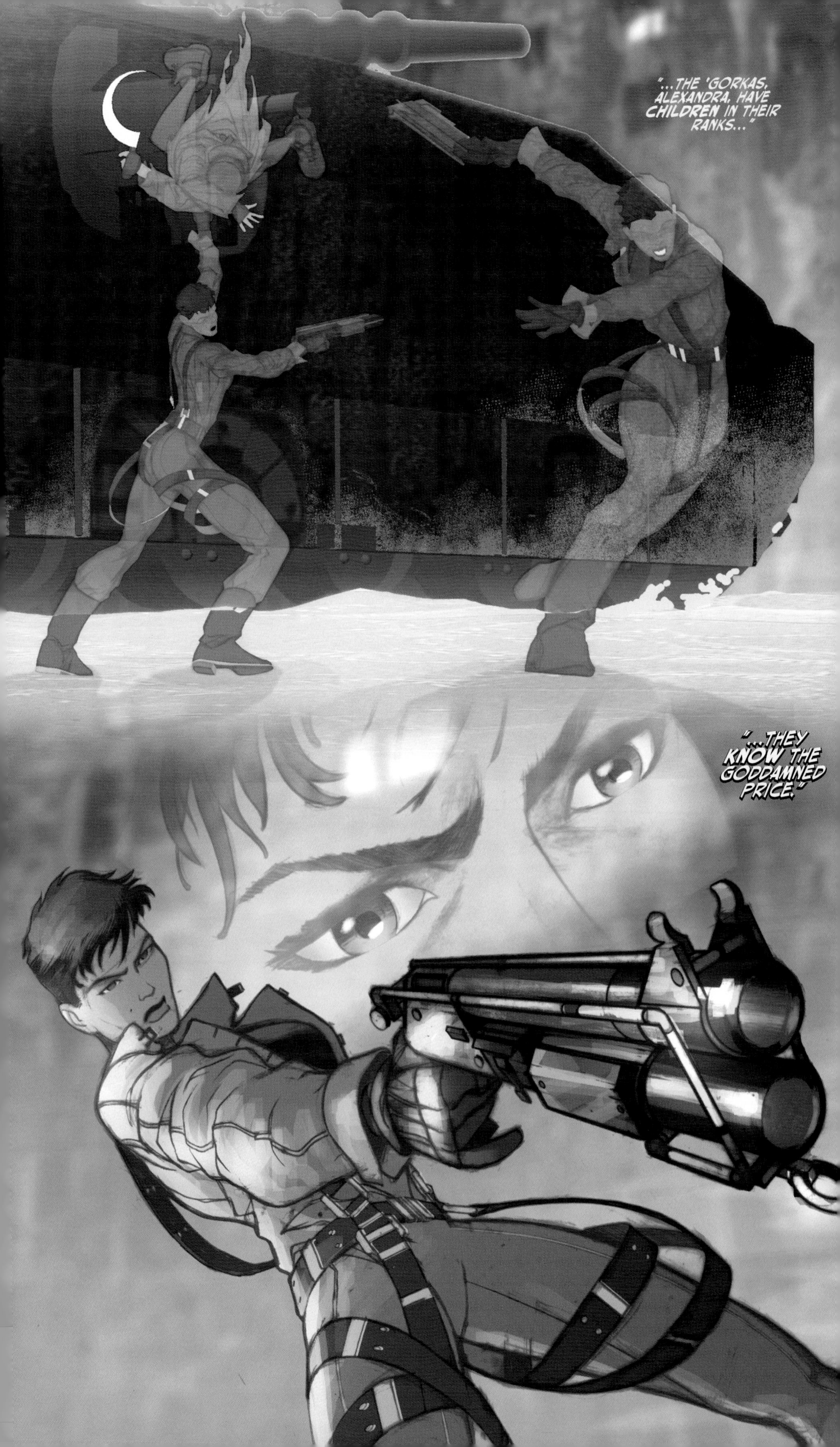
"...THE 'GORKAS, ALEXANDRA, HAVE CHILDREN IN THEIR RANKS..."
"...THEY KNOW THE GODDAMNED PRICE."

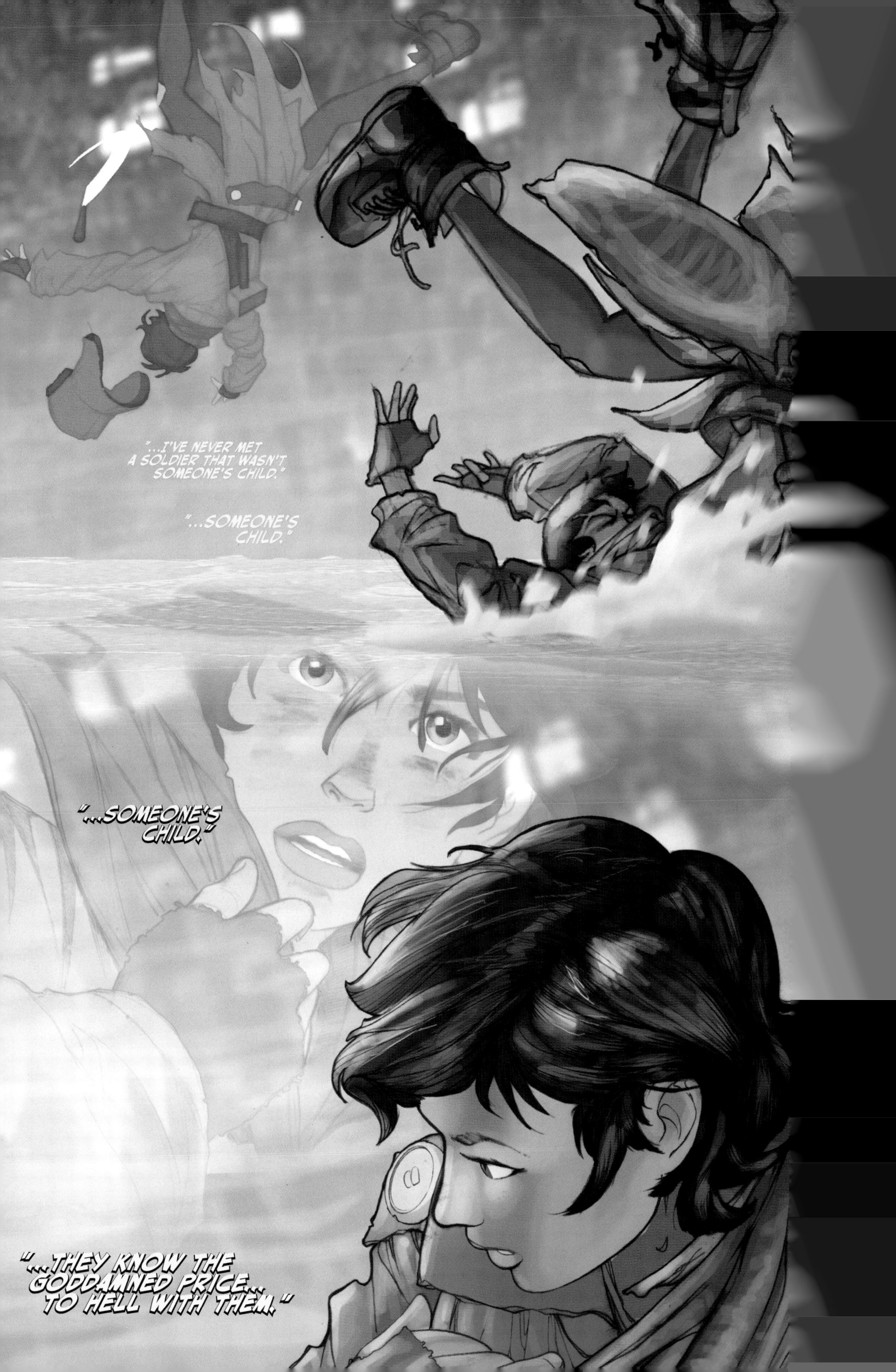
"...I'VE NEVER MET A SOLDIER THAT WASN'T SOMEONE'S CHILD."
"...SOMEONE'S CHILD."
"...SOMEONE'S CHILD."
"...THEY KNOW THE GODDAMNED PRICE... TO HELL WITH THEM."

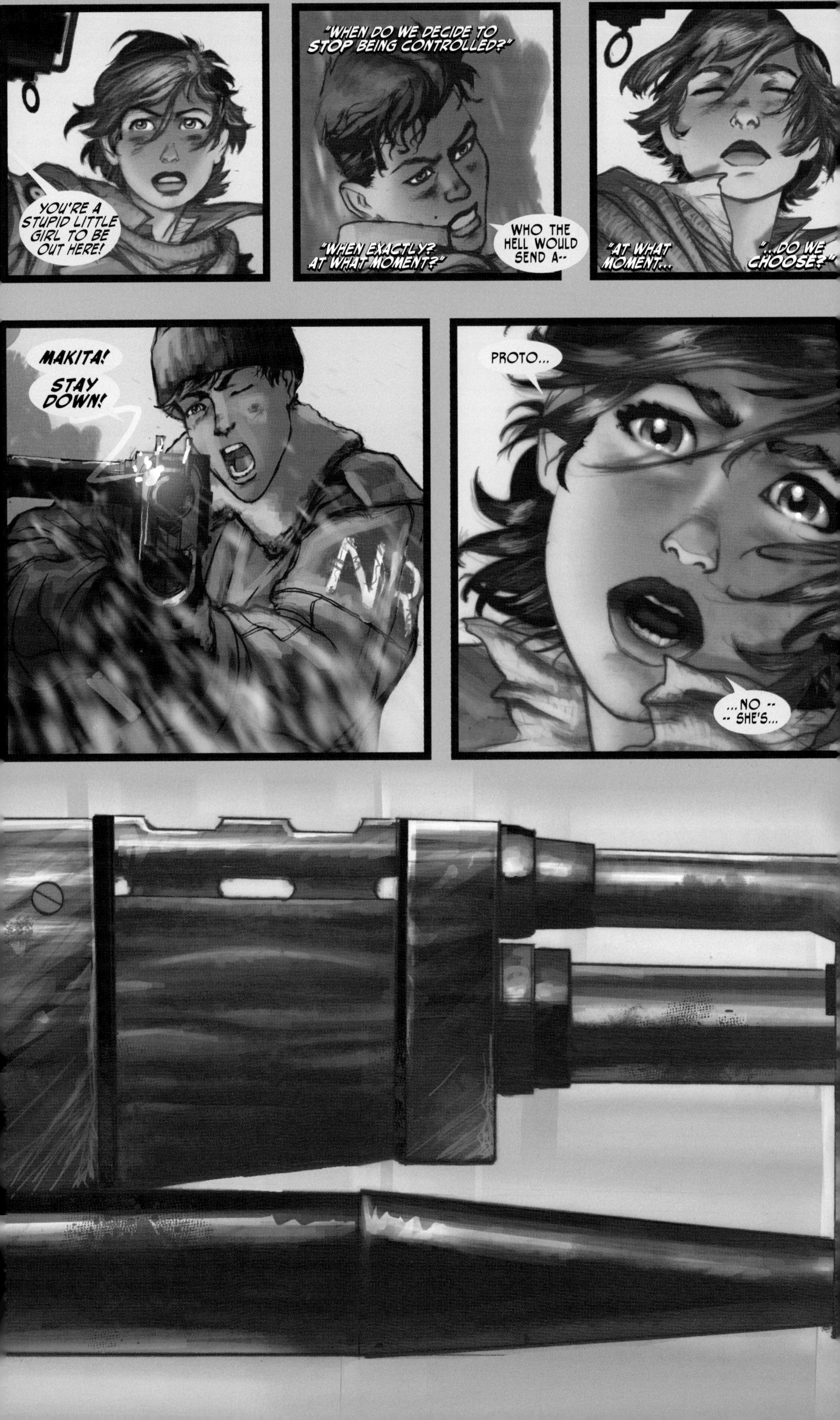
YOU'RE A STUPID LITTLE GIRL TO BE OUT HERE!
"WHEN DO WE DECIDE TO STOP BEING CONTROLLED?"
"WHEN EXACTLY? AT WHAT MOMENT?"
WHO THE HELL WOULD SEND A--
"AT WHAT MOMENT...
"...DO WE CHOOSE?"
MAKITA!
STAY DOWN!
PROTO...
...NO --
-- SHE'S...

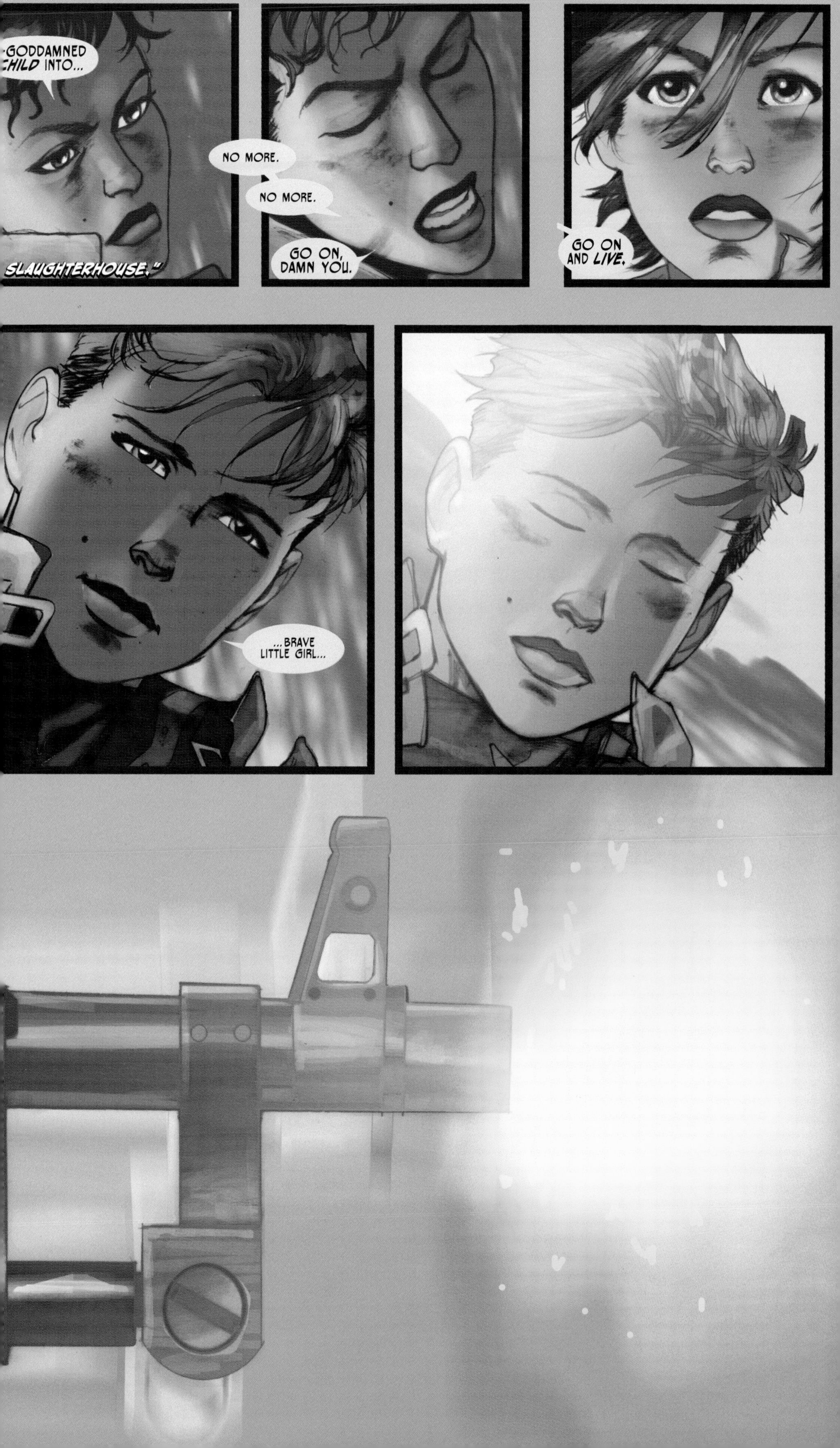
—GODDAMNED CHILD INTO...
SLAUGHTERHOUSE."
NO MORE.
NO MORE.
GO ON, DAMN YOU.
GO ON AND LIVE.
...BRAVE LITTLE GIRL...

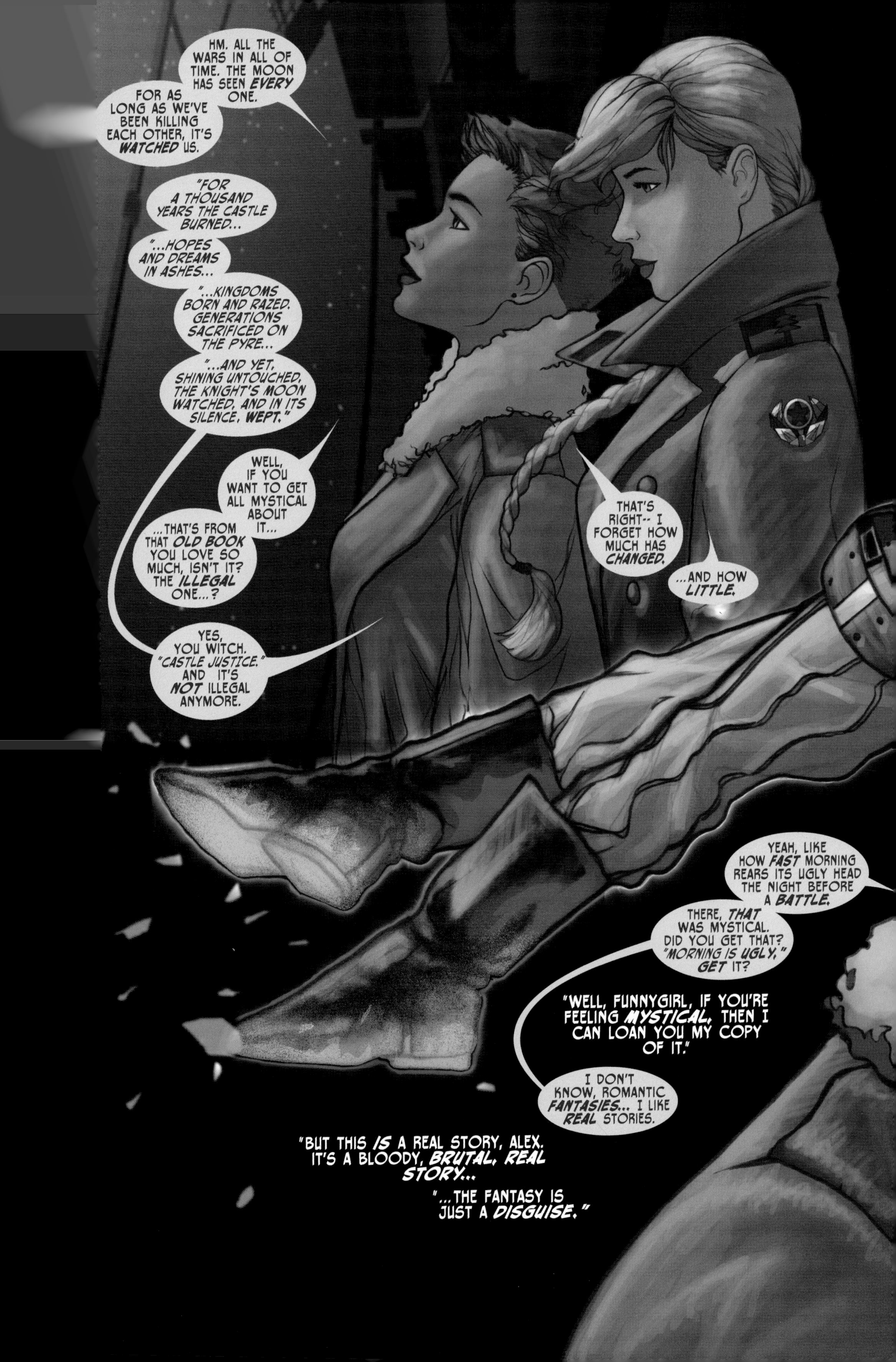
HM. ALL THE WARS IN ALL OF TIME. THE MOON HAS SEEN EVERY ONE.
FOR AS LONG AS WE'VE BEEN KILLING EACH OTHER, IT'S WATCHED US.
"FOR A THOUSAND YEARS THE CASTLE BURNED...
"...HOPES AND DREAMS IN ASHES...
"...KINGDOMS BORN AND RAZED. GENERATIONS SACRIFICED ON THE PYRE...
"...AND YET, SHINING UNTOUCHED, THE KNIGHT'S MOON WATCHED, AND IN ITS SILENCE, WEPT."
WELL, IF YOU WANT TO GET ALL MYSTICAL ABOUT IT...
...THAT'S FROM THAT OLD BOOK YOU LOVE SO MUCH, ISN'T IT? THE ILLEGAL ONE...?
YES, YOU WITCH. "CASTLE JUSTICE." AND IT'S NOT ILLEGAL ANYMORE.
THAT'S RIGHT-- I FORGET HOW MUCH HAS CHANGED.
...AND HOW LITTLE.
YEAH, LIKE HOW FAST MORNING REARS ITS UGLY HEAD THE NIGHT BEFORE A BATTLE.
THERE, THAT WAS MYSTICAL. DID YOU GET THAT? "MORNING IS UGLY," GET IT?
"WELL, FUNNYGIRL, IF YOU'RE FEELING MYSTICAL, THEN I CAN LOAN YOU MY COPY OF IT."
I DON'T KNOW, ROMANTIC FANTASIES... I LIKE REAL STORIES.
"BUT THIS IS A REAL STORY, ALEX. IT'S A BLOODY, BRUTAL, REAL STORY...
"...THE FANTASY IS JUST A DISGUISE."

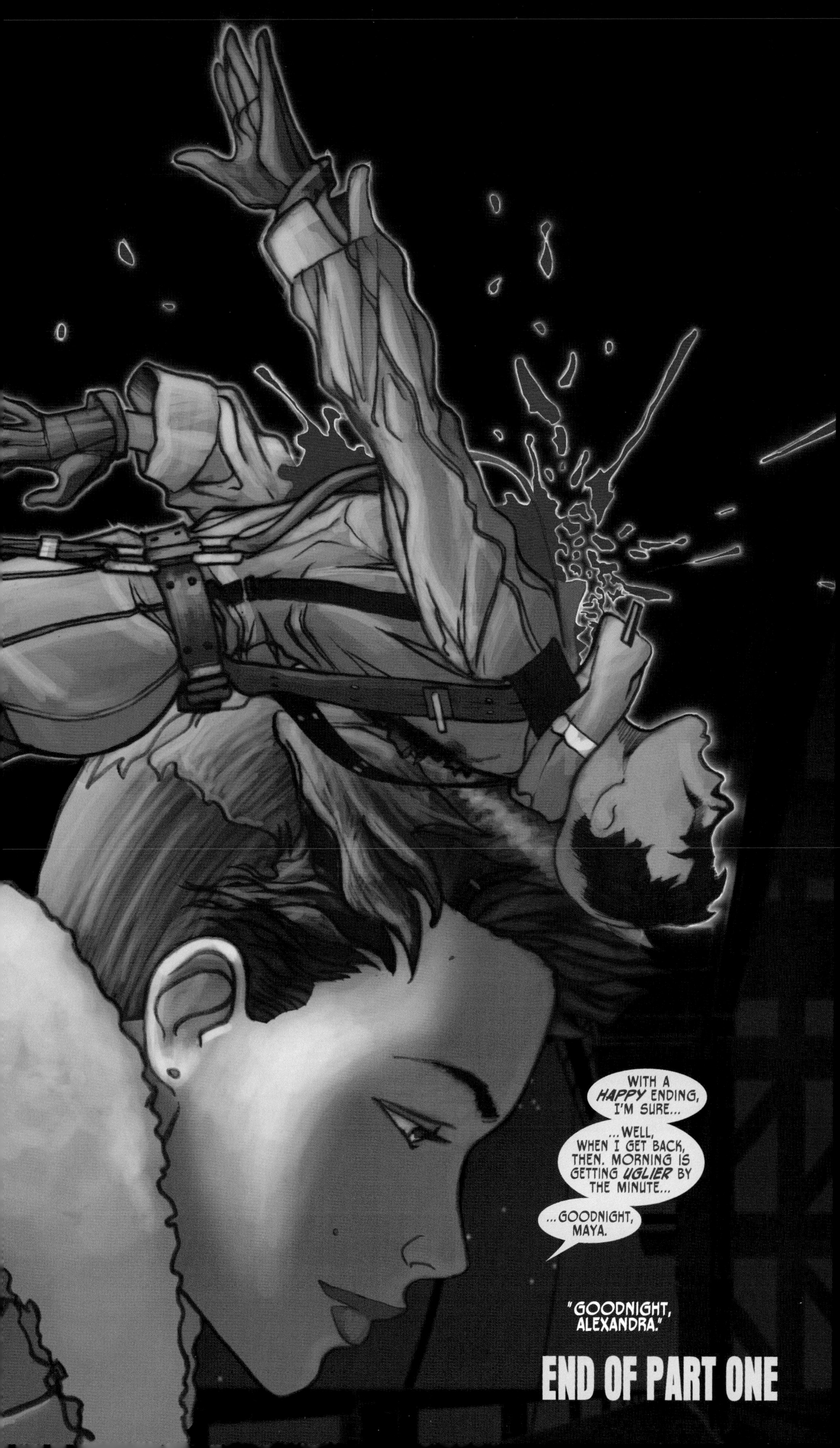
WITH A *HAPPY* ENDING, I'M SURE...
...WELL, WHEN I GET BACK, THEN. MORNING IS GETTING *UGLIER* BY THE MINUTE...
...GOODNIGHT, MAYA.
"GOODNIGHT, ALEXANDRA."
END OF PART ONE

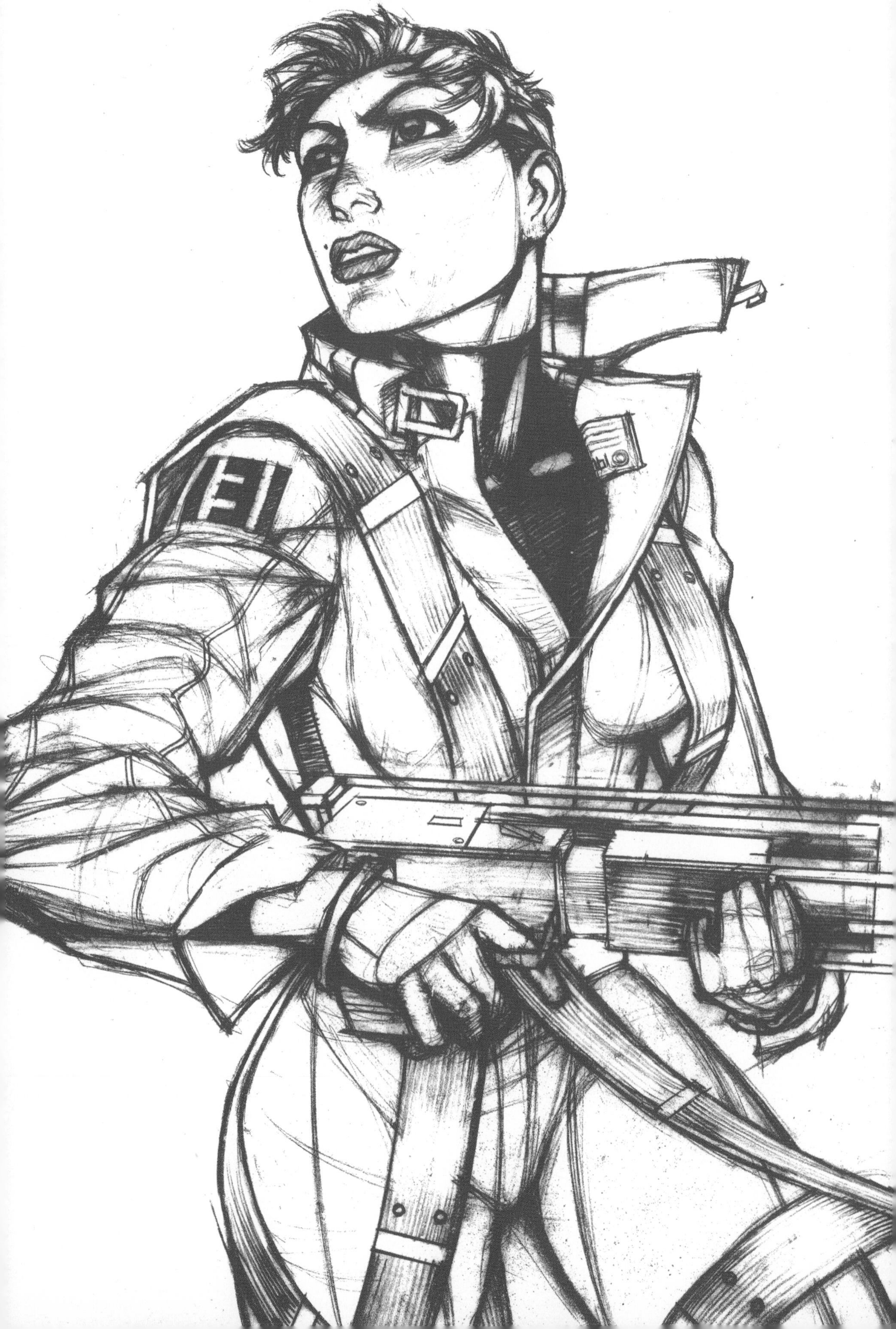

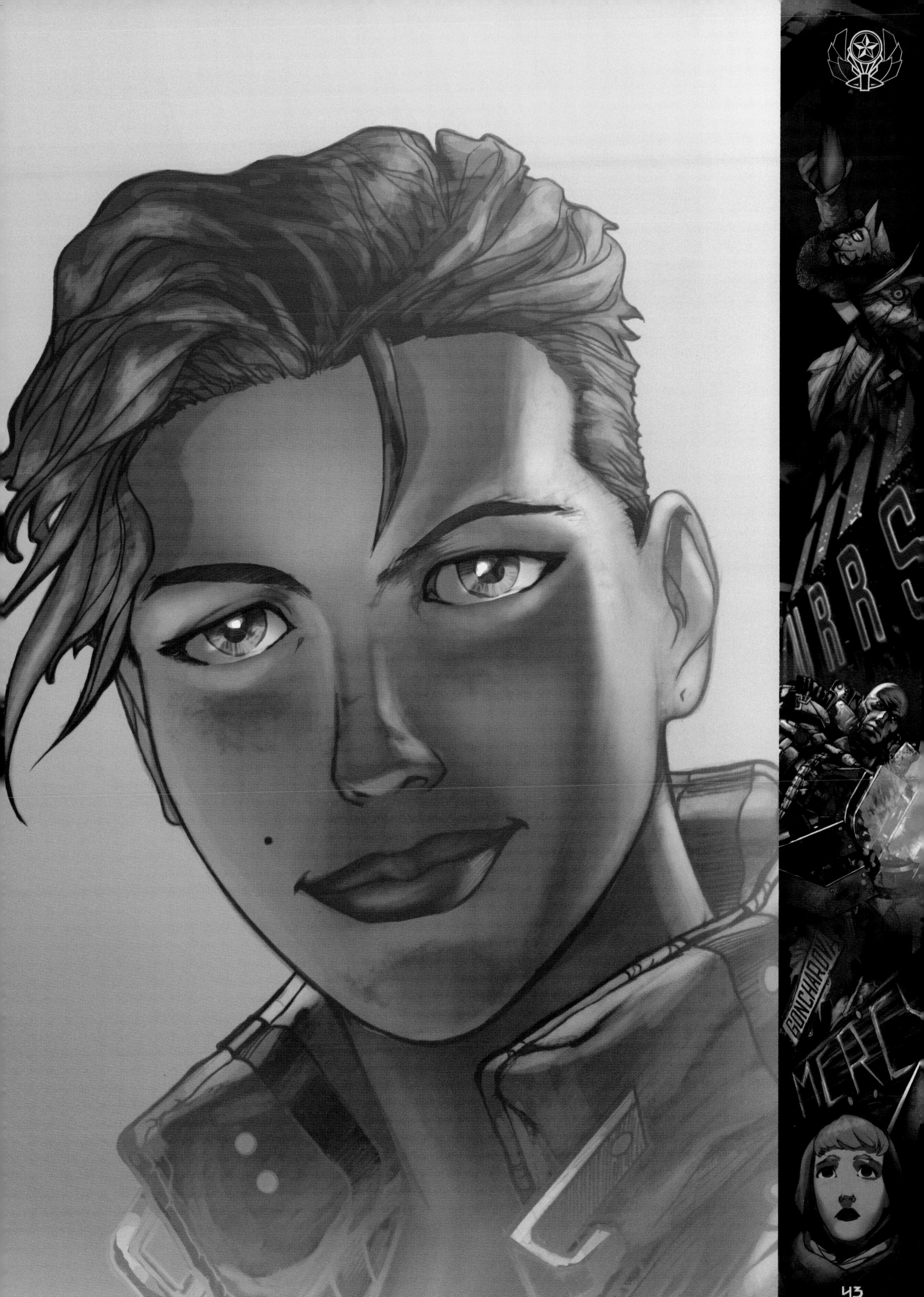

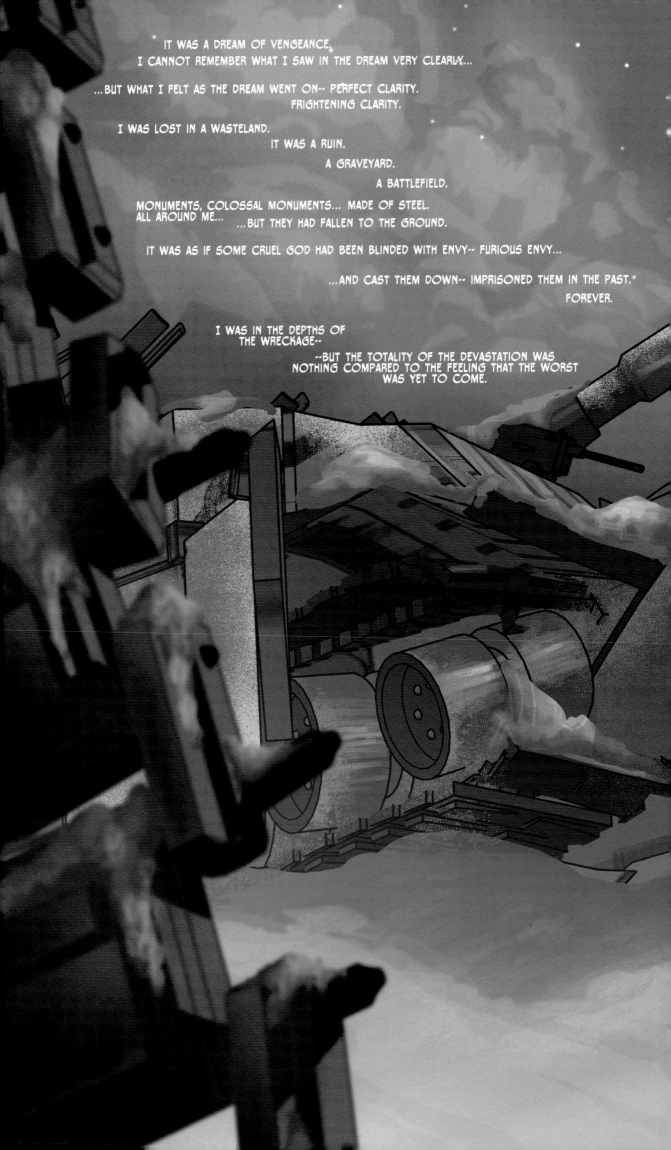

IT WAS A DREAM OF VENGEANCE.
I CANNOT REMEMBER WHAT I SAW IN THE DREAM VERY CLEARLY...

...BUT WHAT I FELT AS THE DREAM WENT ON-- PERFECT CLARITY.
FRIGHTENING CLARITY.

I WAS LOST IN A WASTELAND.
IT WAS A RUIN.
A GRAVEYARD.
A BATTLEFIELD.

MONUMENTS, COLOSSAL MONUMENTS... MADE OF STEEL.
ALL AROUND ME...   ...BUT THEY HAD FALLEN TO THE GROUND.

IT WAS AS IF SOME CRUEL GOD HAD BEEN BLINDED WITH ENVY-- FURIOUS ENVY...

...AND CAST THEM DOWN-- IMPRISONED THEM IN THE PAST.
FOREVER.

I WAS IN THE DEPTHS OF
THE WRECKAGE--
--BUT THE TOTALITY OF THE DEVASTATION WAS
NOTHING COMPARED TO THE FEELING THAT THE WORST
WAS YET TO COME.

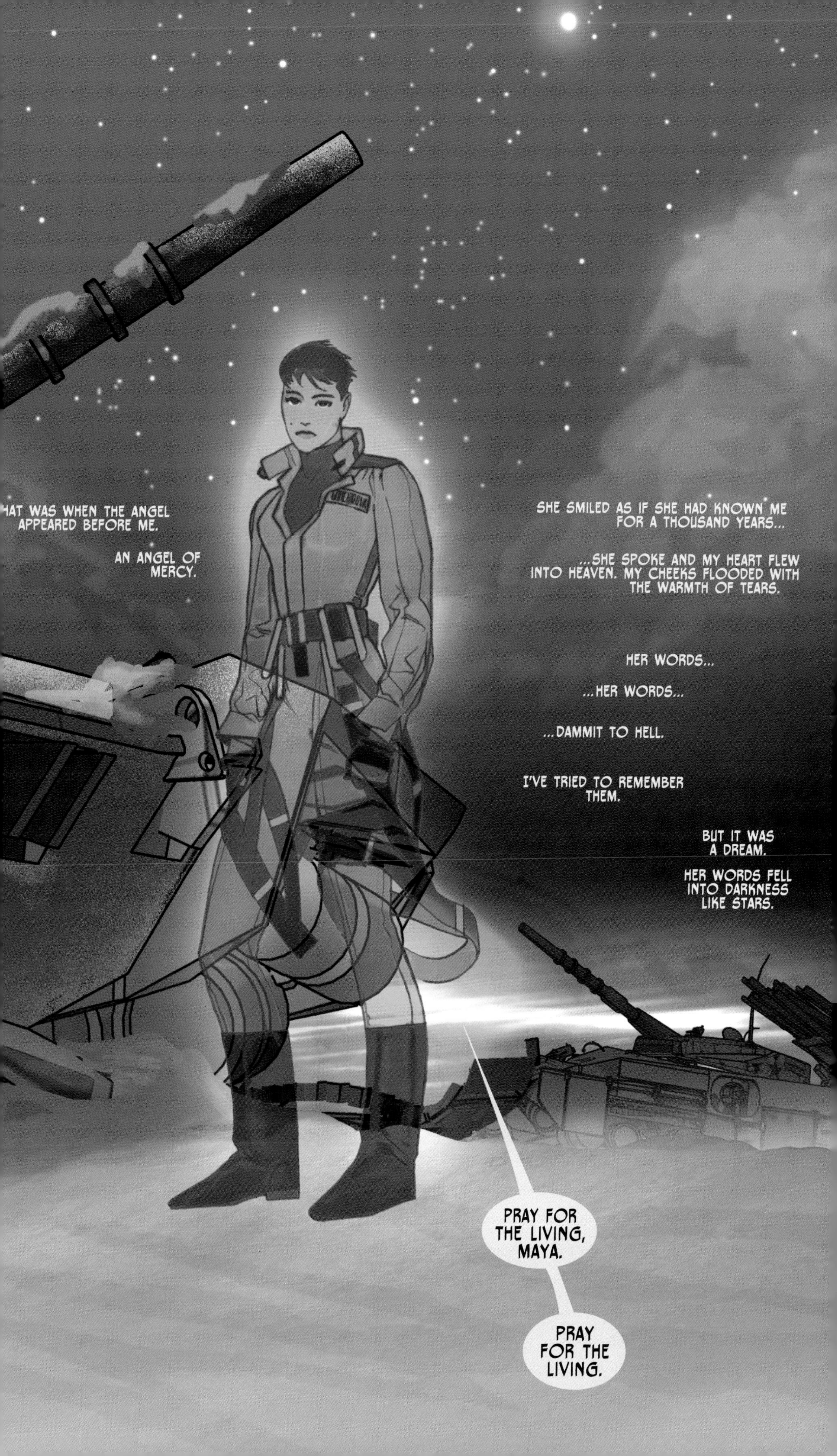
HAT WAS WHEN THE ANGEL APPEARED BEFORE ME.
AN ANGEL OF MERCY.
SHE SMILED AS IF SHE HAD KNOWN ME FOR A THOUSAND YEARS...
...SHE SPOKE AND MY HEART FLEW INTO HEAVEN. MY CHEEKS FLOODED WITH THE WARMTH OF TEARS.
HER WORDS...
...HER WORDS...
...DAMMIT TO HELL.
I'VE TRIED TO REMEMBER THEM.
BUT IT WAS A DREAM.
HER WORDS FELL INTO DARKNESS LIKE STARS.
PRAY FOR THE LIVING, MAYA.
PRAY FOR THE LIVING.

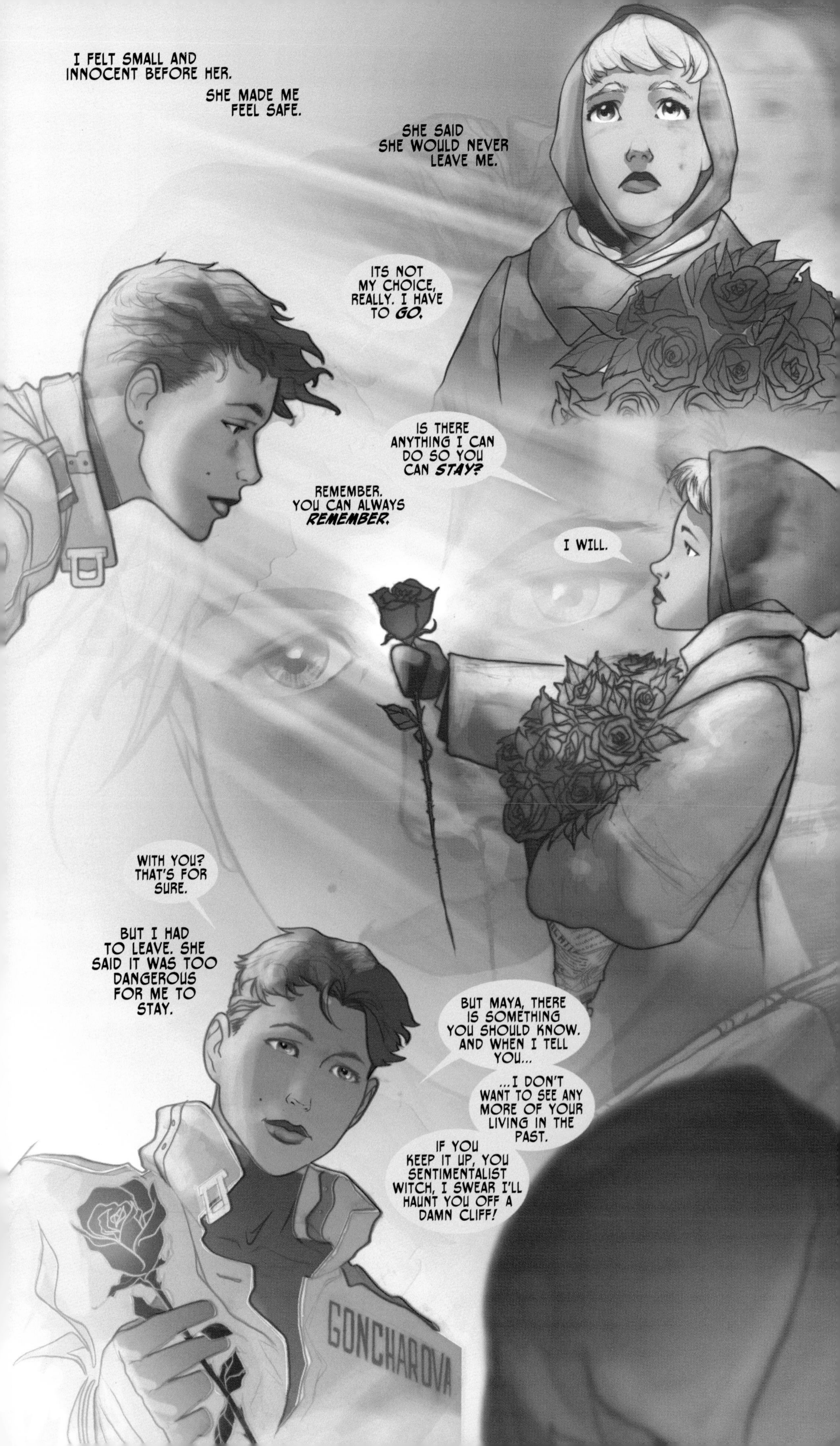
I FELT SMALL AND INNOCENT BEFORE HER.
SHE MADE ME FEEL SAFE.
SHE SAID SHE WOULD NEVER LEAVE ME.
ITS NOT MY CHOICE, REALLY. I HAVE TO *GO*.
IS THERE ANYTHING I CAN DO SO YOU CAN *STAY?*
REMEMBER. YOU CAN ALWAYS *REMEMBER.*
I WILL.
WITH YOU? THAT'S FOR SURE.
BUT I HAD TO LEAVE. SHE SAID IT WAS TOO DANGEROUS FOR ME TO STAY.
BUT MAYA, THERE IS SOMETHING YOU SHOULD KNOW. AND WHEN I TELL YOU...
...I DON'T WANT TO SEE ANY MORE OF YOUR LIVING IN THE PAST.
IF YOU KEEP IT UP, YOU SENTIMENTALIST WITCH, I SWEAR I'LL HAUNT YOU OFF A DAMN CLIFF!
GONCHAROVA

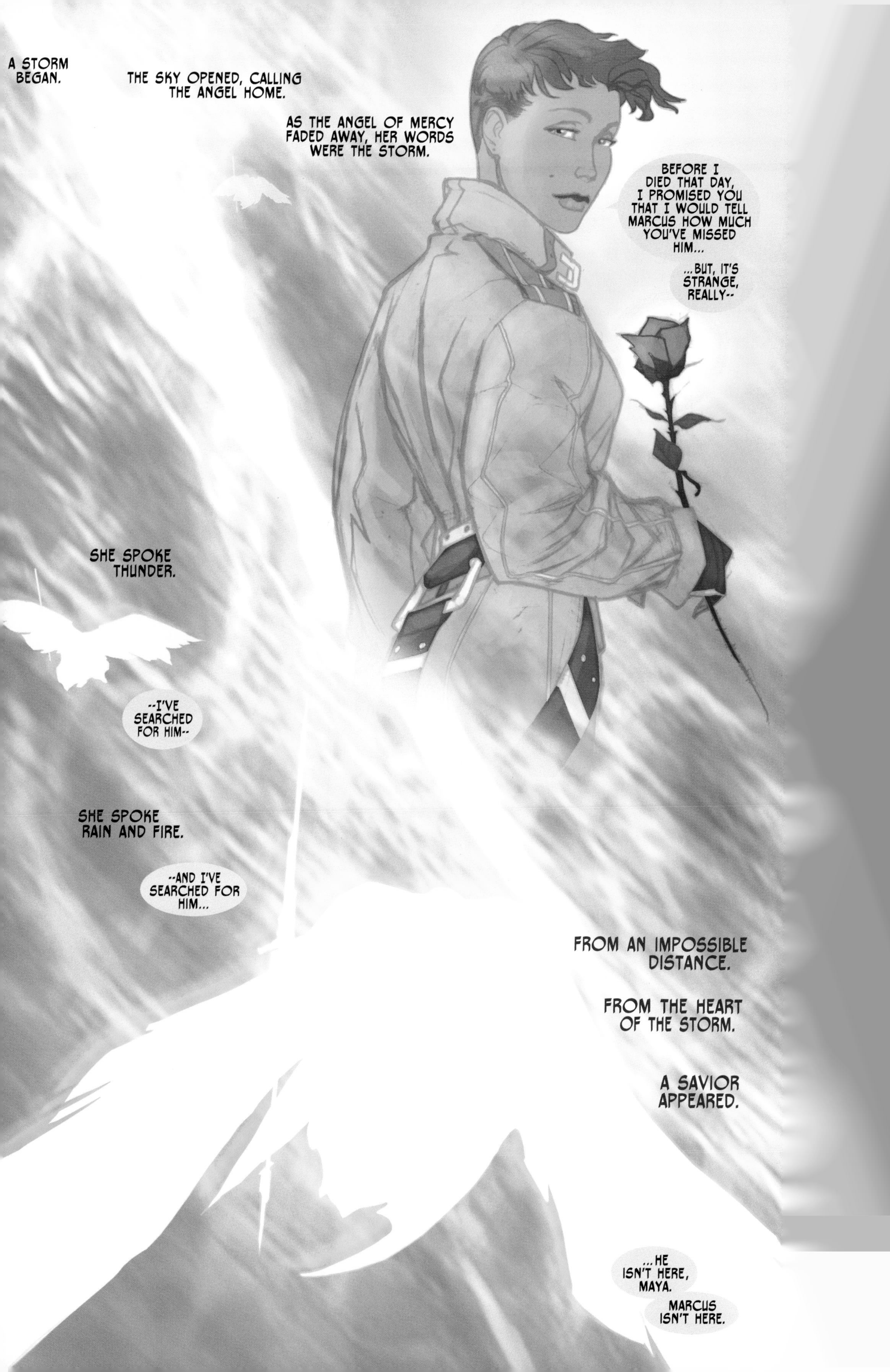
A STORM BEGAN.
THE SKY OPENED, CALLING THE ANGEL HOME.
AS THE ANGEL OF MERCY FADED AWAY, HER WORDS WERE THE STORM.
BEFORE I DIED THAT DAY, I PROMISED YOU THAT I WOULD TELL MARCUS HOW MUCH YOU'VE MISSED HIM...
...BUT, IT'S STRANGE, REALLY--
SHE SPOKE THUNDER.
--I'VE SEARCHED FOR HIM--
SHE SPOKE RAIN AND FIRE.
--AND I'VE SEARCHED FOR HIM...
FROM AN IMPOSSIBLE DISTANCE.
FROM THE HEART OF THE STORM.
A SAVIOR APPEARED.
...HE ISN'T HERE, MAYA.
MARCUS ISN'T HERE.

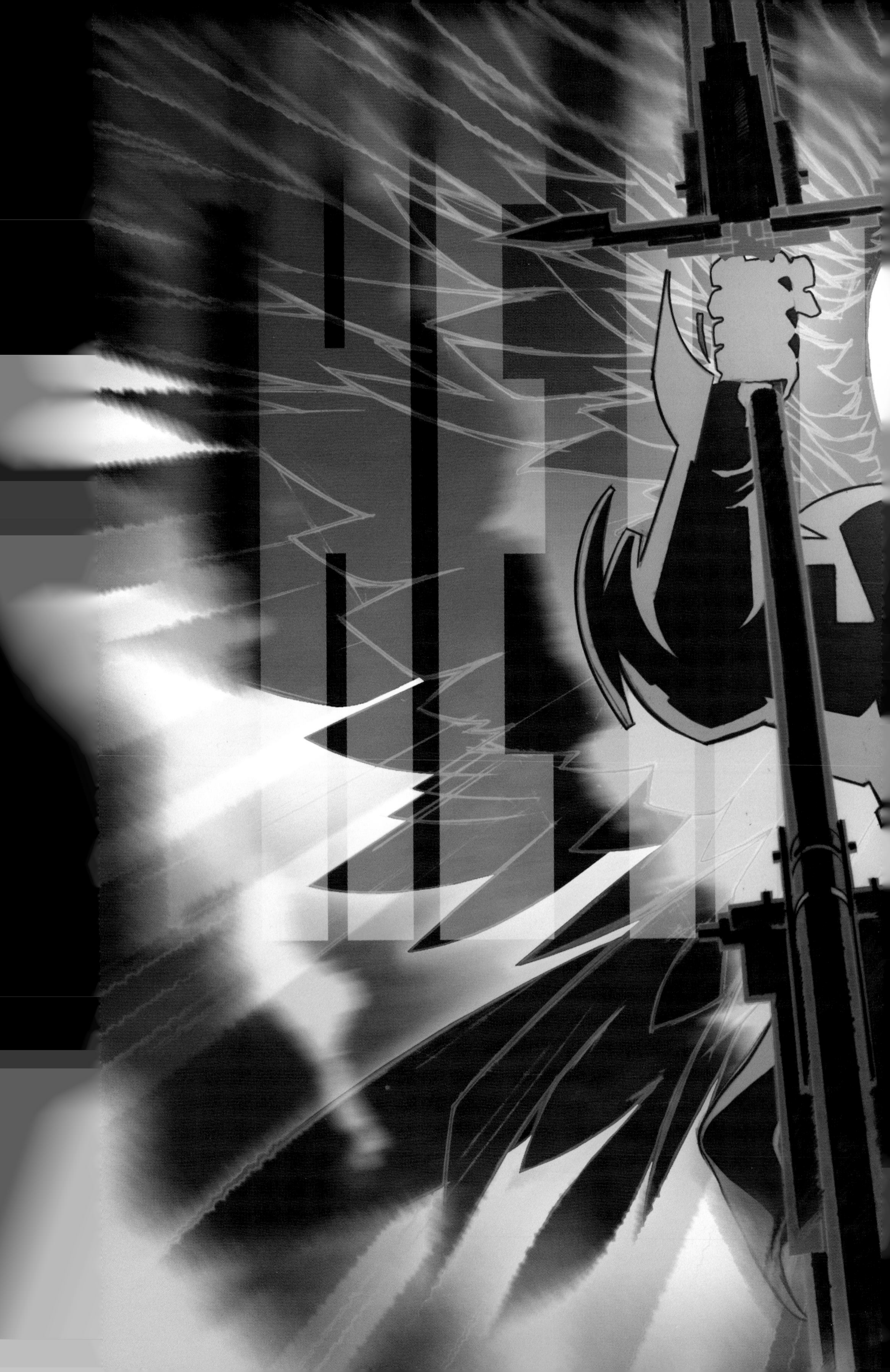

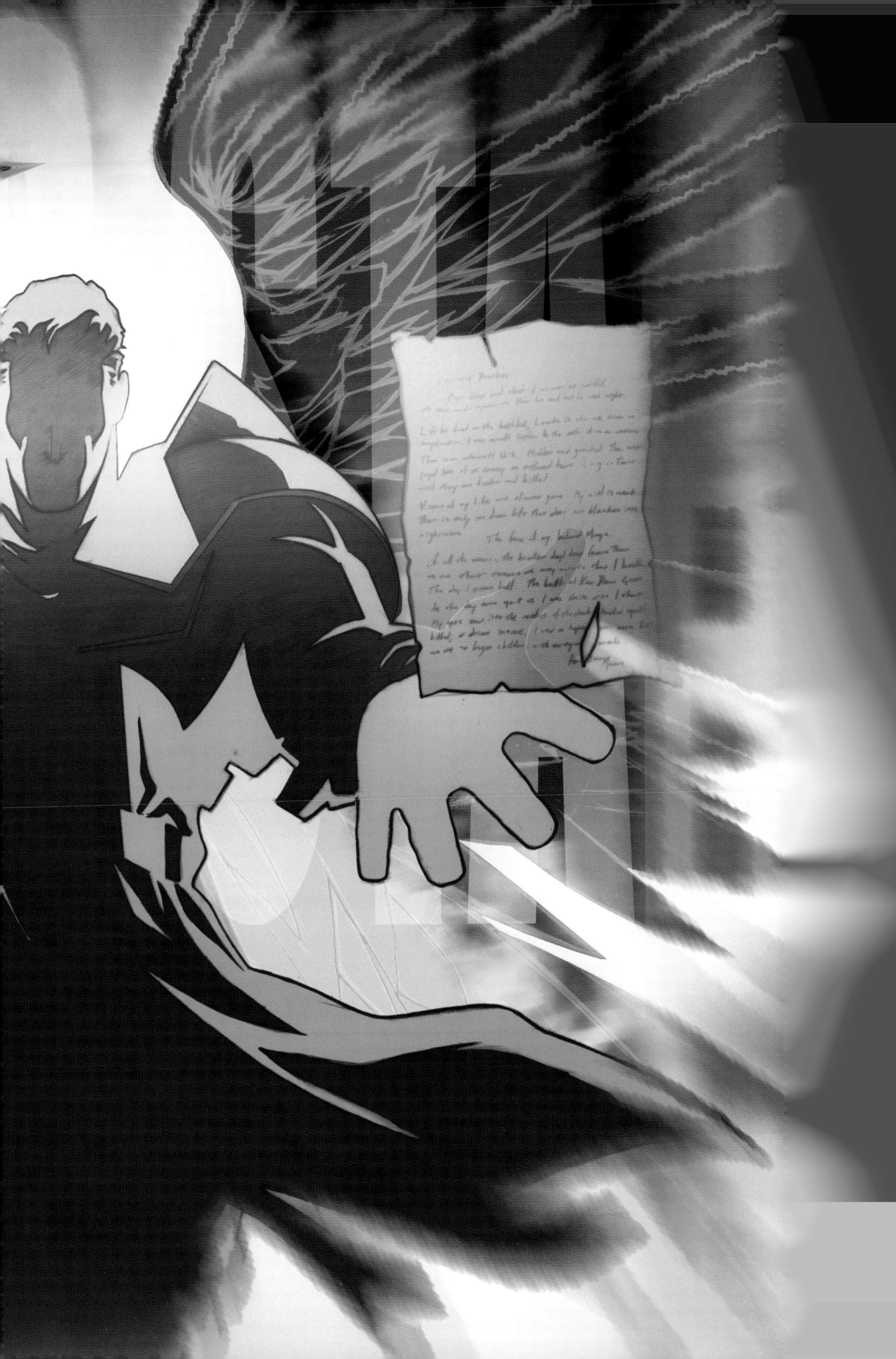
The face of my beloved Maya.

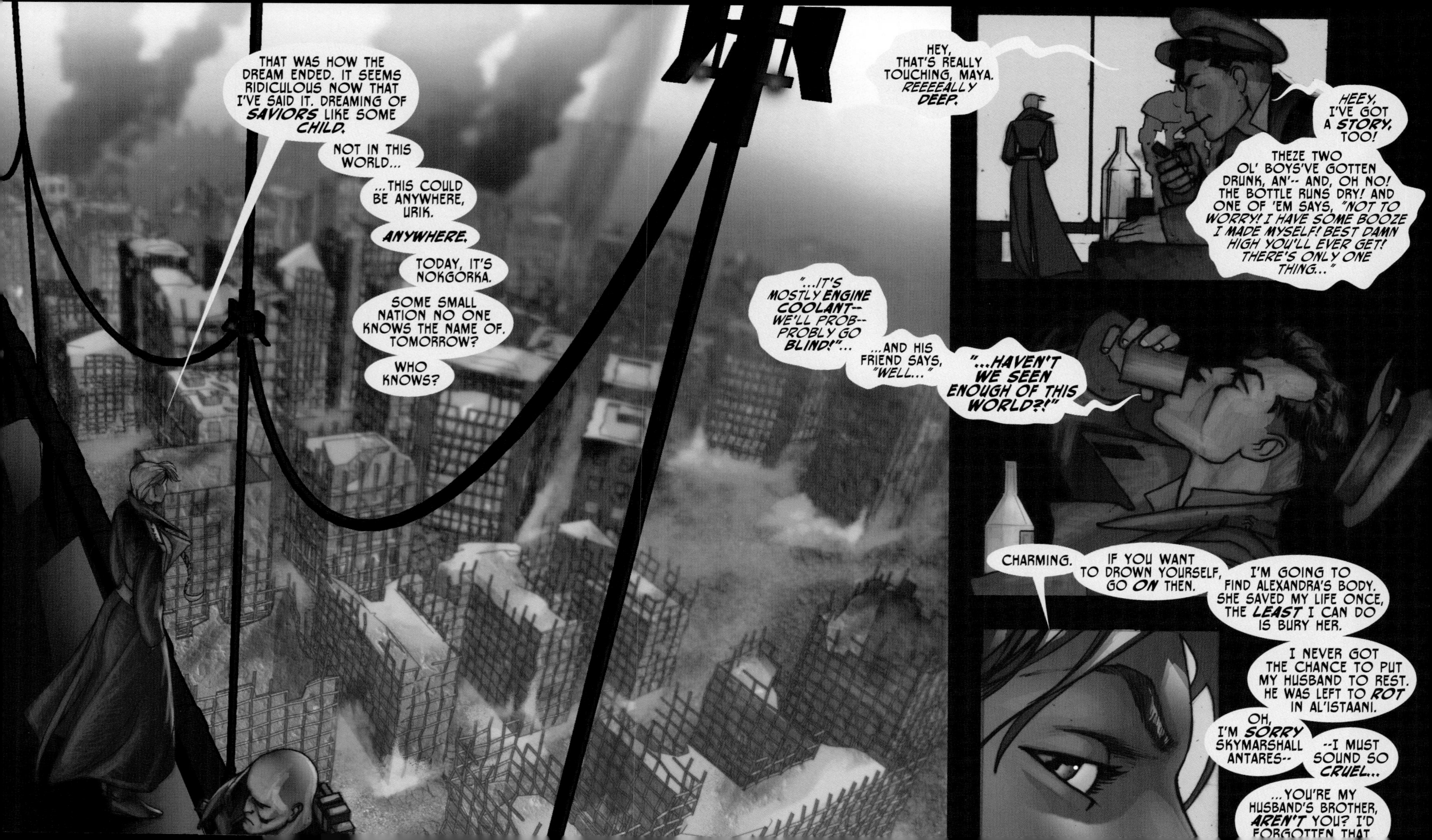
THAT WAS HOW THE DREAM ENDED. IT SEEMS RIDICULOUS NOW THAT I'VE SAID IT. DREAMING OF SAVIORS LIKE SOME CHILD.
NOT IN THIS WORLD...
...THIS COULD BE ANYWHERE, URIK.
ANYWHERE.
TODAY, IT'S NOKGORKA.
SOME SMALL NATION NO ONE KNOWS THE NAME OF. TOMORROW?
WHO KNOWS?
HEY, THAT'S REALLY TOUCHING, MAYA. REEEEALLY DEEP.
HEEY, I'VE GOT A STORY, TOO!
THEZE TWO OL' BOYS'VE GOTTEN DRUNK, AN'-- AND, OH NO! THE BOTTLE RUNS DRY! AND ONE OF 'EM SAYS, "NOT TO WORRY! I HAVE SOME BOOZE I MADE MYSELF! BEST DAMN HIGH YOU'LL EVER GET! THERE'S ONLY ONE THING..."
"...IT'S MOSTLY ENGINE COOLANT-- WE'LL PROB-- PROBLY GO BLIND!"...
...AND HIS FRIEND SAYS, "WELL..."
"...HAVEN'T WE SEEN ENOUGH OF THIS WORLD?!"
CHARMING.
IF YOU WANT TO DROWN YOURSELF, GO ON THEN.
I'M GOING TO FIND ALEXANDRA'S BODY. SHE SAVED MY LIFE ONCE, THE LEAST I CAN DO IS BURY HER.
I NEVER GOT THE CHANCE TO PUT MY HUSBAND TO REST. HE WAS LEFT TO ROT IN AL'ISTAANI.
OH, I'M SORRY SKYMARSHALL ANTARES--
--I MUST SOUND SO CRUEL...
...YOU'RE MY HUSBAND'S BROTHER, AREN'T YOU? I'D FORGOTTEN THAT

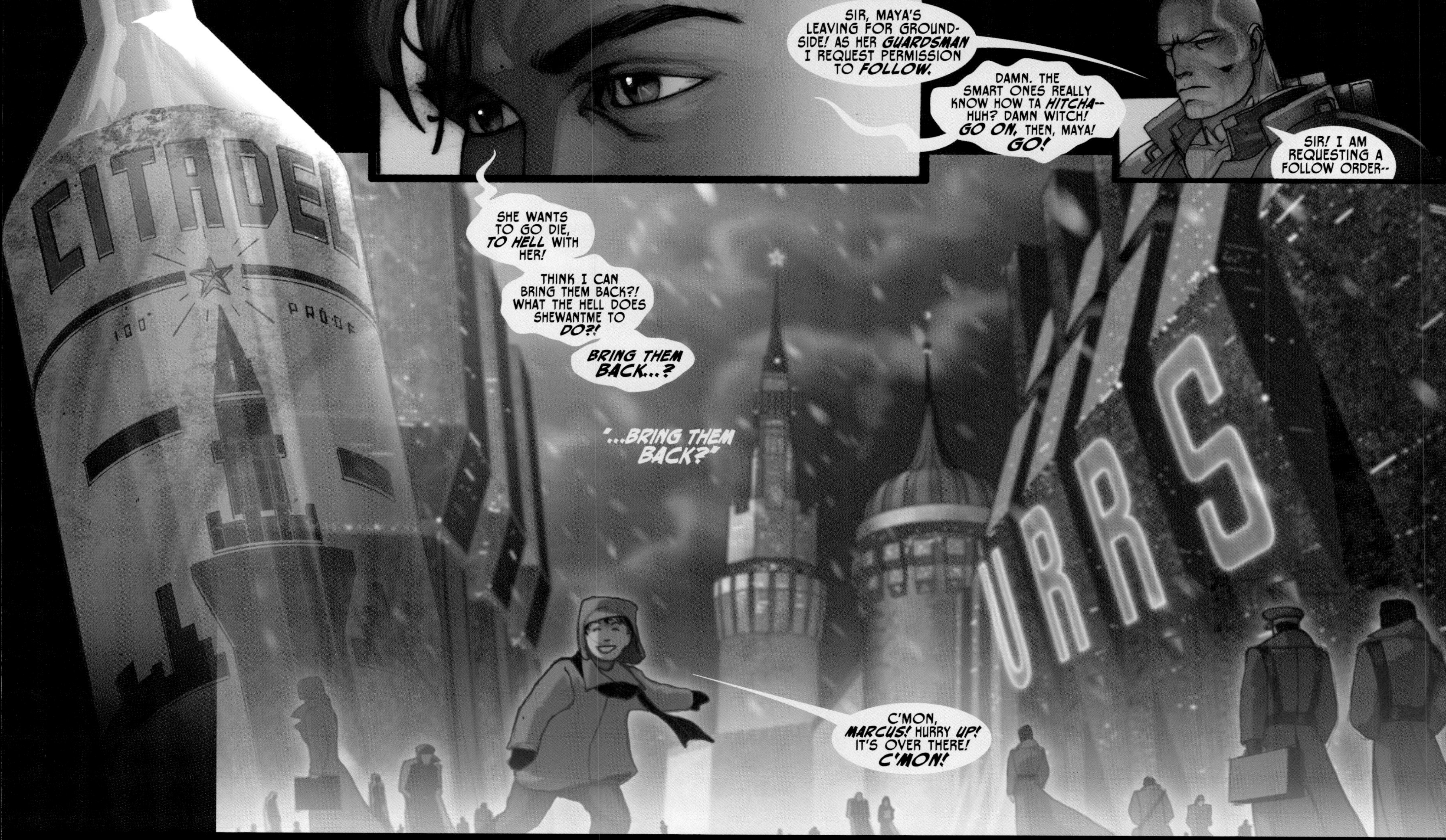
SIR, MAYA'S LEAVING FOR GROUND-SIDE! AS HER GUARDSMAN I REQUEST PERMISSION TO FOLLOW.
DAMN. THE SMART ONES REALLY KNOW HOW TA HITCHA-- HUH? DAMN WITCH! GO ON, THEN, MAYA! GO!
SIR! I AM REQUESTING A FOLLOW ORDER--
SHE WANTS TO GO DIE, TO HELL WITH HER!
THINK I CAN BRING THEM BACK?! WHAT THE HELL DOES SHEWANTME TO DO?!
BRING THEM BACK...?
"...BRING THEM BACK?"
C'MON, MARCUS! HURRY UP! IT'S OVER THERE! C'MON!
CITADEL
100 PROOF
URRS

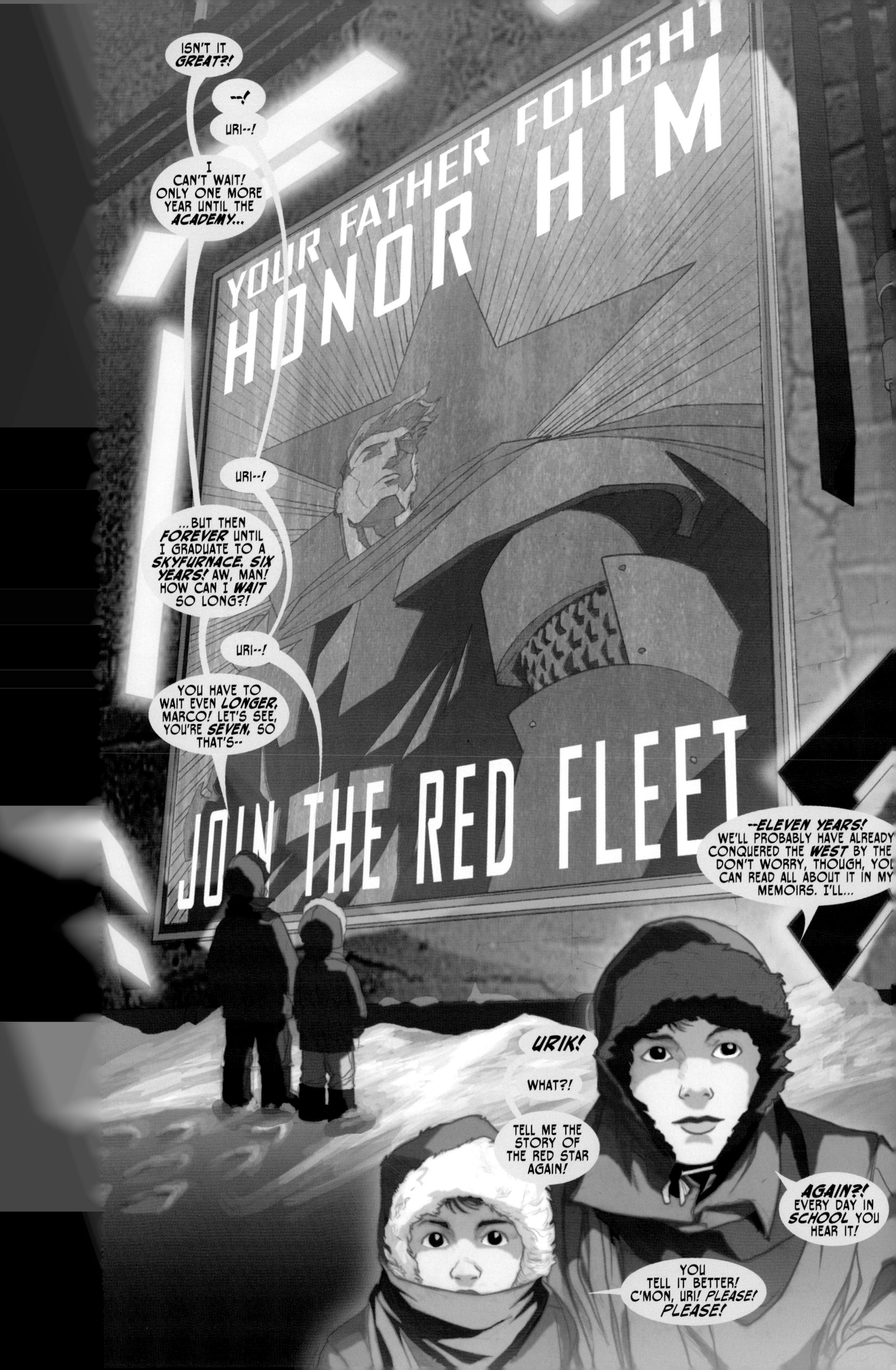
YOUR FATHER FOUGHT
HONOR HIM
ISN'T IT GREAT?!
--!
URI--!
I CAN'T WAIT! ONLY ONE MORE YEAR UNTIL THE ACADEMY...
URI--!
...BUT THEN FOREVER UNTIL I GRADUATE TO A SKYFURNACE. SIX YEARS! AW, MAN! HOW CAN I WAIT SO LONG?!
URI--!
YOU HAVE TO WAIT EVEN LONGER, MARCO! LET'S SEE, YOU'RE SEVEN, SO THAT'S--
JOIN THE RED FLEET
--ELEVEN YEARS! WE'LL PROBABLY HAVE ALREADY CONQUERED THE WEST BY THE DON'T WORRY, THOUGH, YO CAN READ ALL ABOUT IT IN MY MEMOIRS. I'LL...
URIK!
WHAT?!
TELL ME THE STORY OF THE RED STAR AGAIN!
AGAIN?! EVERY DAY IN SCHOOL YOU HEAR IT!
YOU TELL IT BETTER! C'MON, URI! PLEASE! PLEASE!

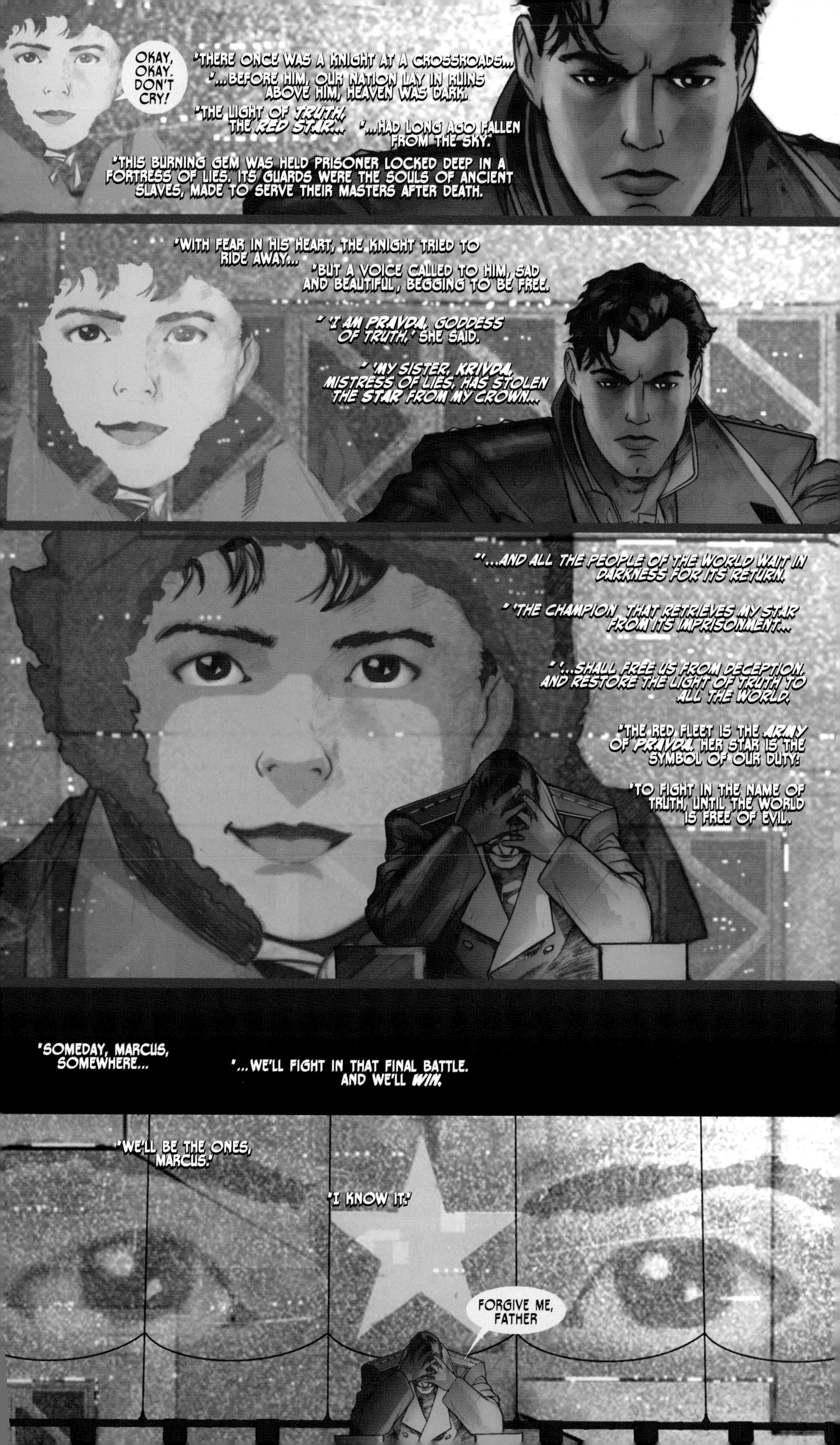

OKAY, OKAY. DON'T CRY!
"THERE ONCE WAS A KNIGHT AT A CROSSROADS...
"...BEFORE HIM, OUR NATION LAY IN RUINS ABOVE HIM, HEAVEN WAS DARK.
"THE LIGHT OF TRUTH, THE RED STAR...
"...HAD LONG AGO FALLEN FROM THE SKY.
"THIS BURNING GEM WAS HELD PRISONER LOCKED DEEP IN A FORTRESS OF LIES. ITS GUARDS WERE THE SOULS OF ANCIENT SLAVES, MADE TO SERVE THEIR MASTERS AFTER DEATH.
"WITH FEAR IN HIS HEART, THE KNIGHT TRIED TO RIDE AWAY...
"BUT A VOICE CALLED TO HIM, SAD AND BEAUTIFUL, BEGGING TO BE FREE.
" 'I AM PRAVDA, GODDESS OF TRUTH,' SHE SAID.
" 'MY SISTER, KRIVDA, MISTRESS OF LIES, HAS STOLEN THE STAR FROM MY CROWN...
" '...AND ALL THE PEOPLE OF THE WORLD WAIT IN DARKNESS FOR ITS RETURN.
" 'THE CHAMPION THAT RETRIEVES MY STAR FROM ITS IMPRISONMENT...
" '...SHALL FREE US FROM DECEPTION, AND RESTORE THE LIGHT OF TRUTH TO ALL THE WORLD.
"THE RED FLEET IS THE ARMY OF PRAVDA. HER STAR IS THE SYMBOL OF OUR DUTY!
"TO FIGHT IN THE NAME OF TRUTH, UNTIL THE WORLD IS FREE OF EVIL.
"SOMEDAY, MARCUS, SOMEWHERE...
"...WE'LL FIGHT IN THAT FINAL BATTLE. AND WE'LL WIN.
"WE'LL BE THE ONES, MARCUS."
"I KNOW IT."
FORGIVE ME, FATHER

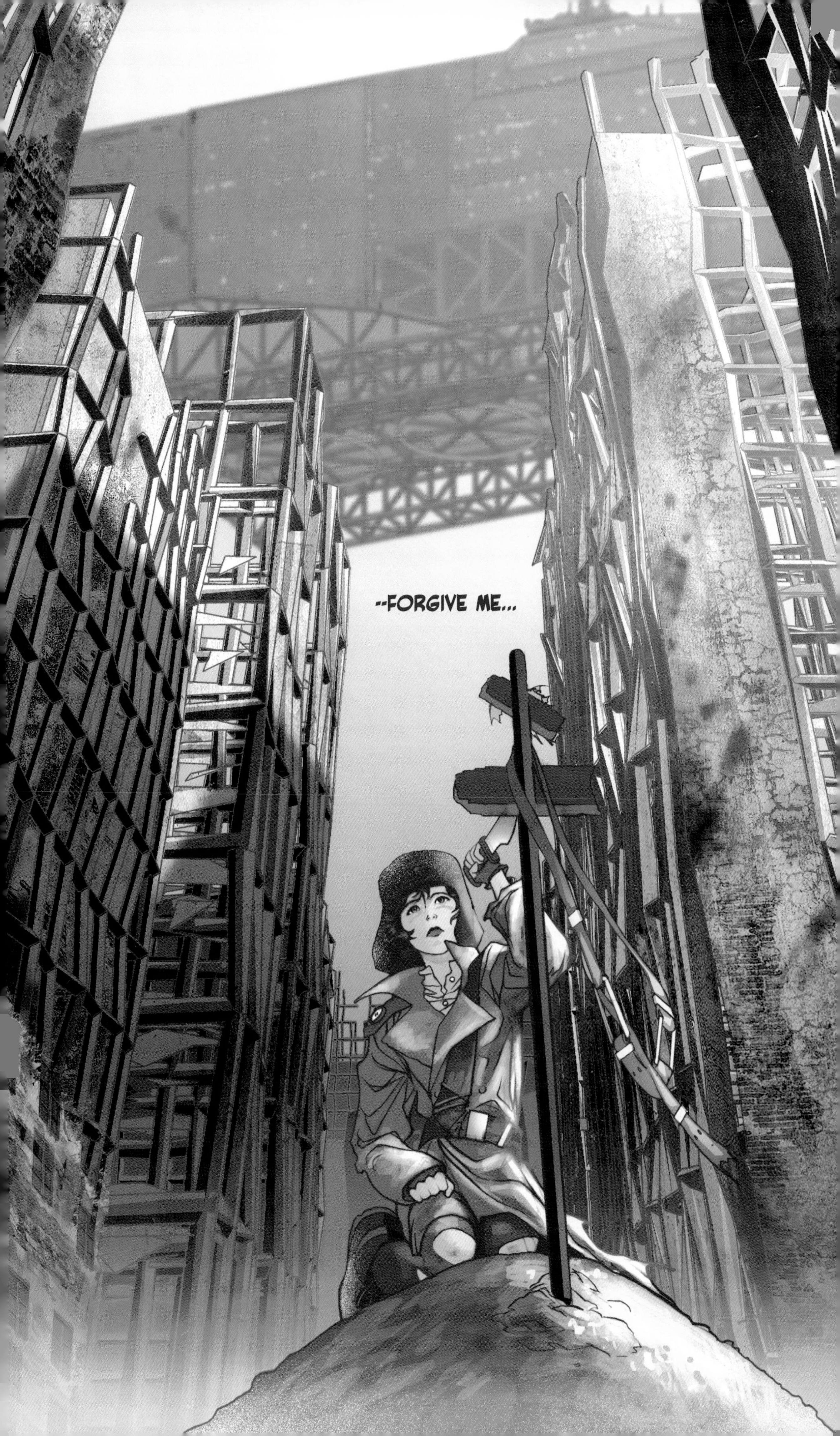
--FORGIVE ME...

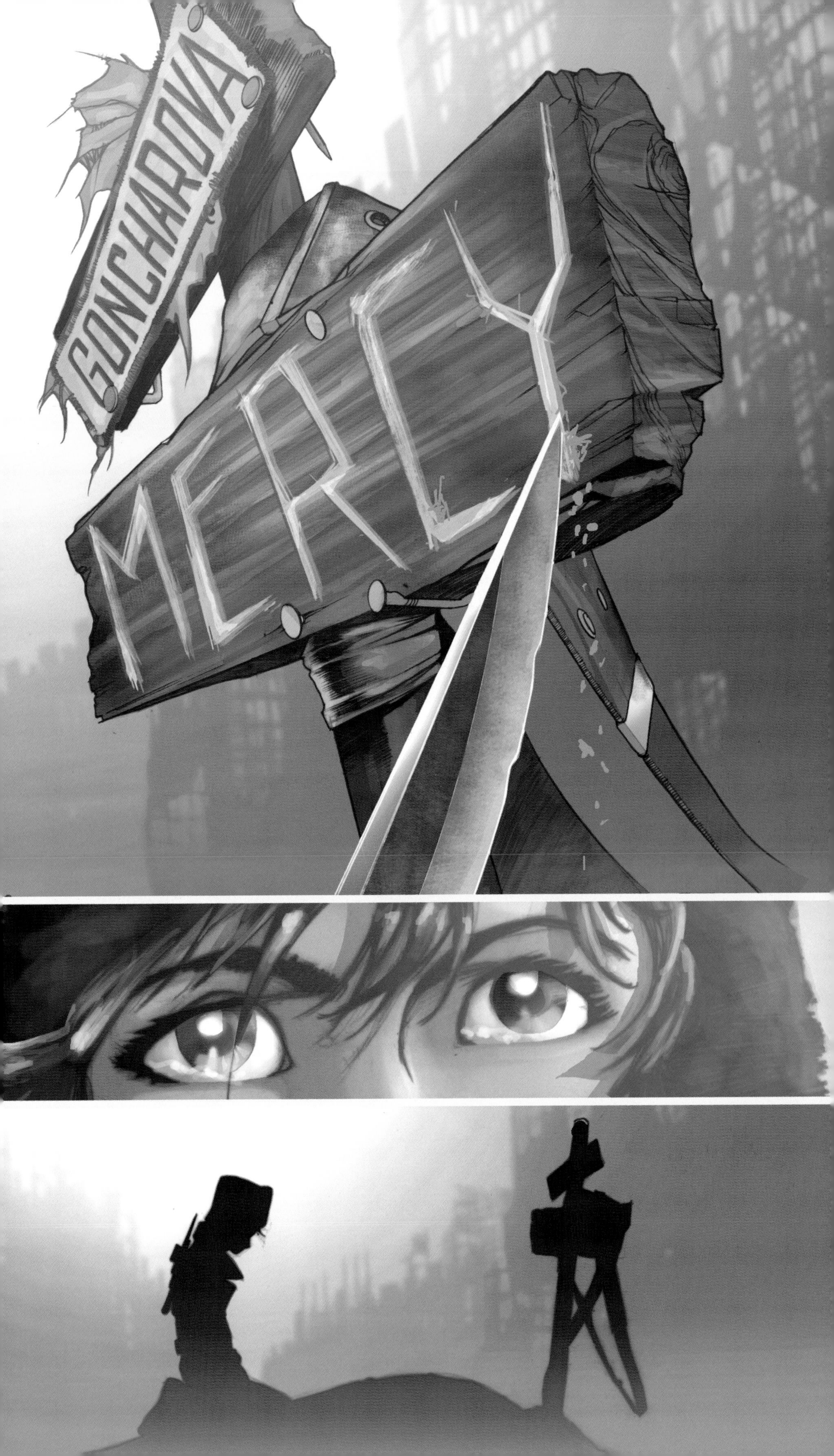
GONCHAROVA
MERCY

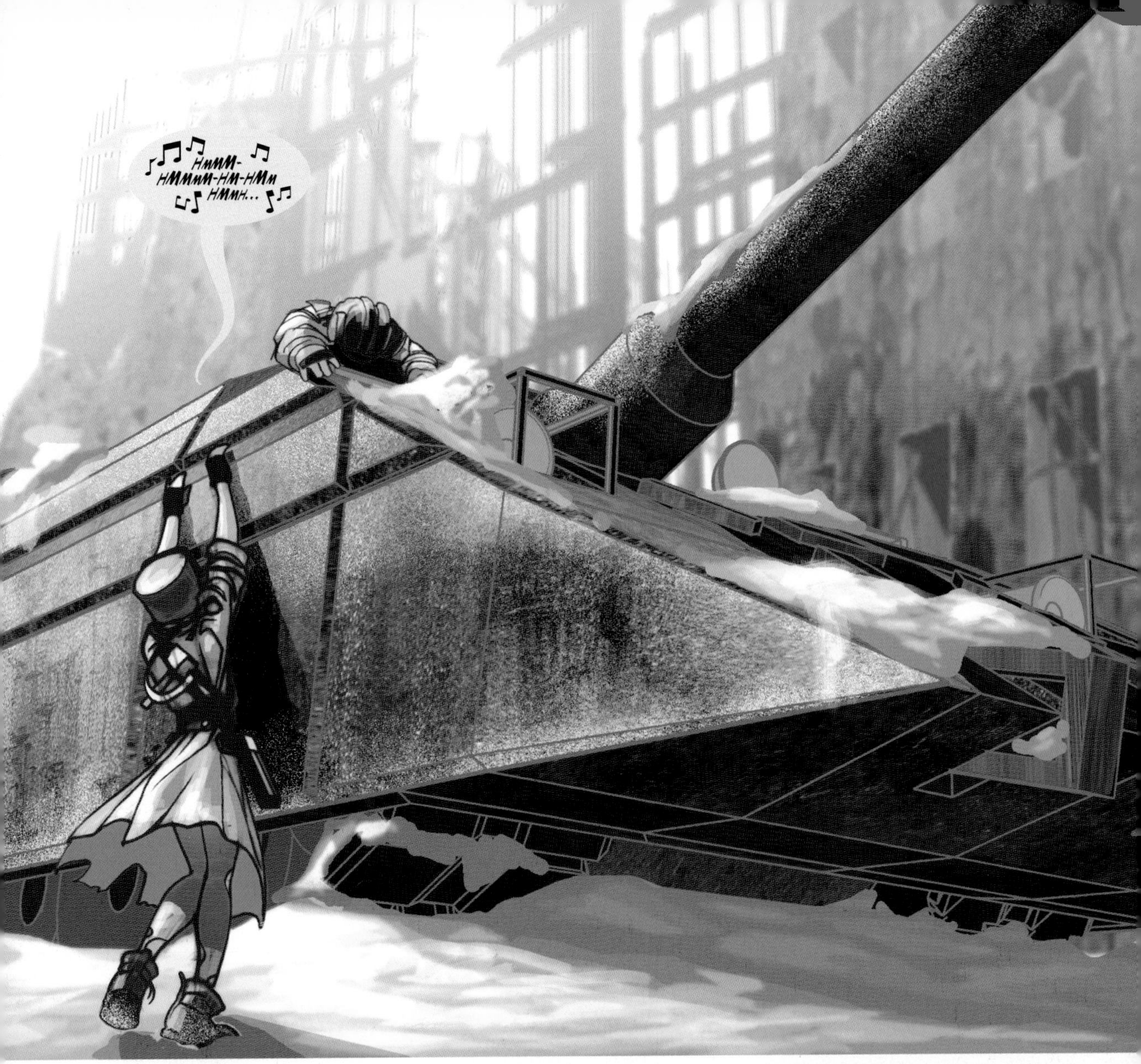
HMMM- HMMMM-HM-HMM HMMH...

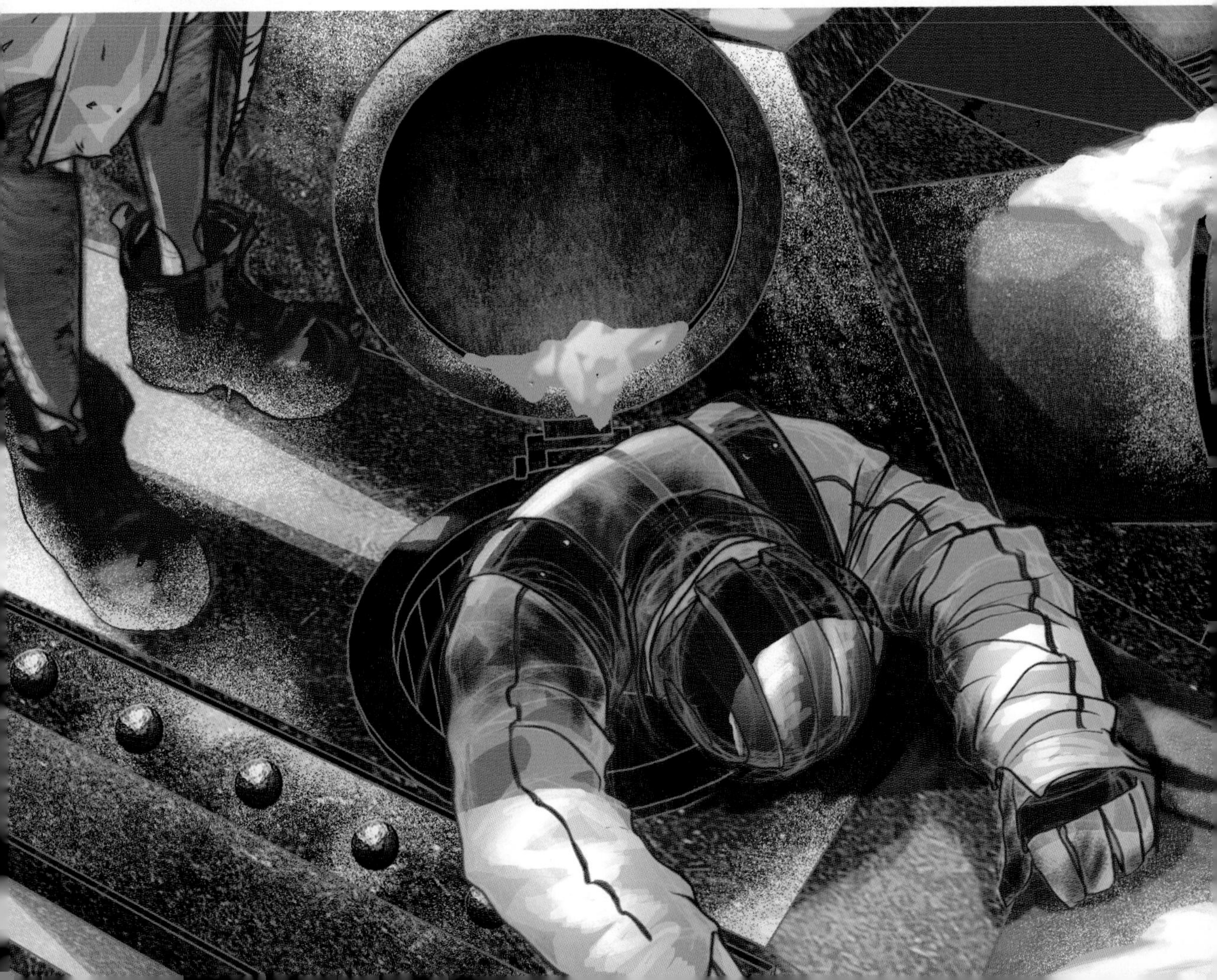

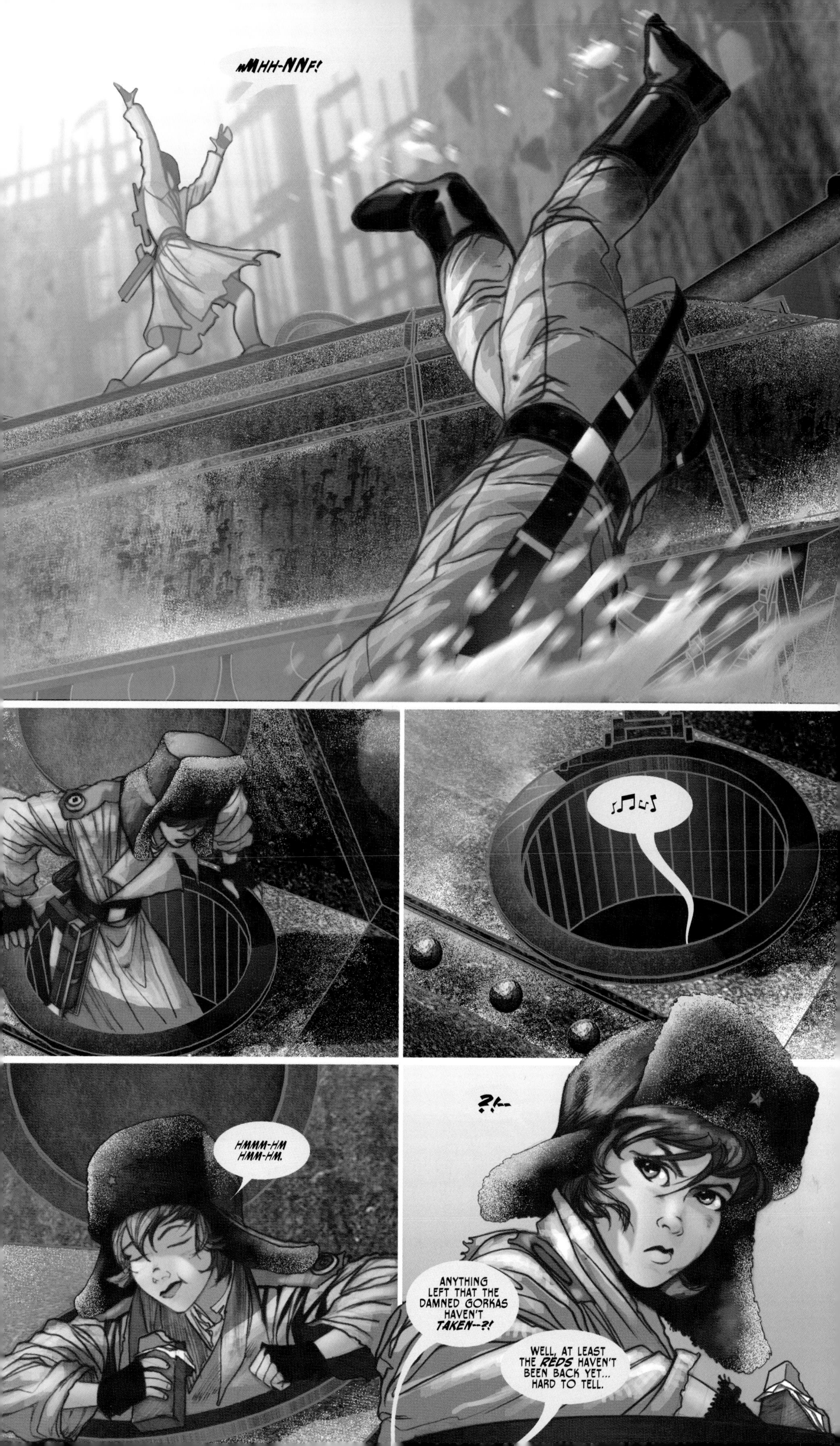
mMHH-NNF!
HMMM-HM HMM-HM.
?!--
ANYTHING LEFT THAT THE DAMNED GORKAS HAVEN'T *TAKEN*--?!
WELL, AT LEAST THE *REDS* HAVEN'T BEEN BACK YET... HARD TO TELL.

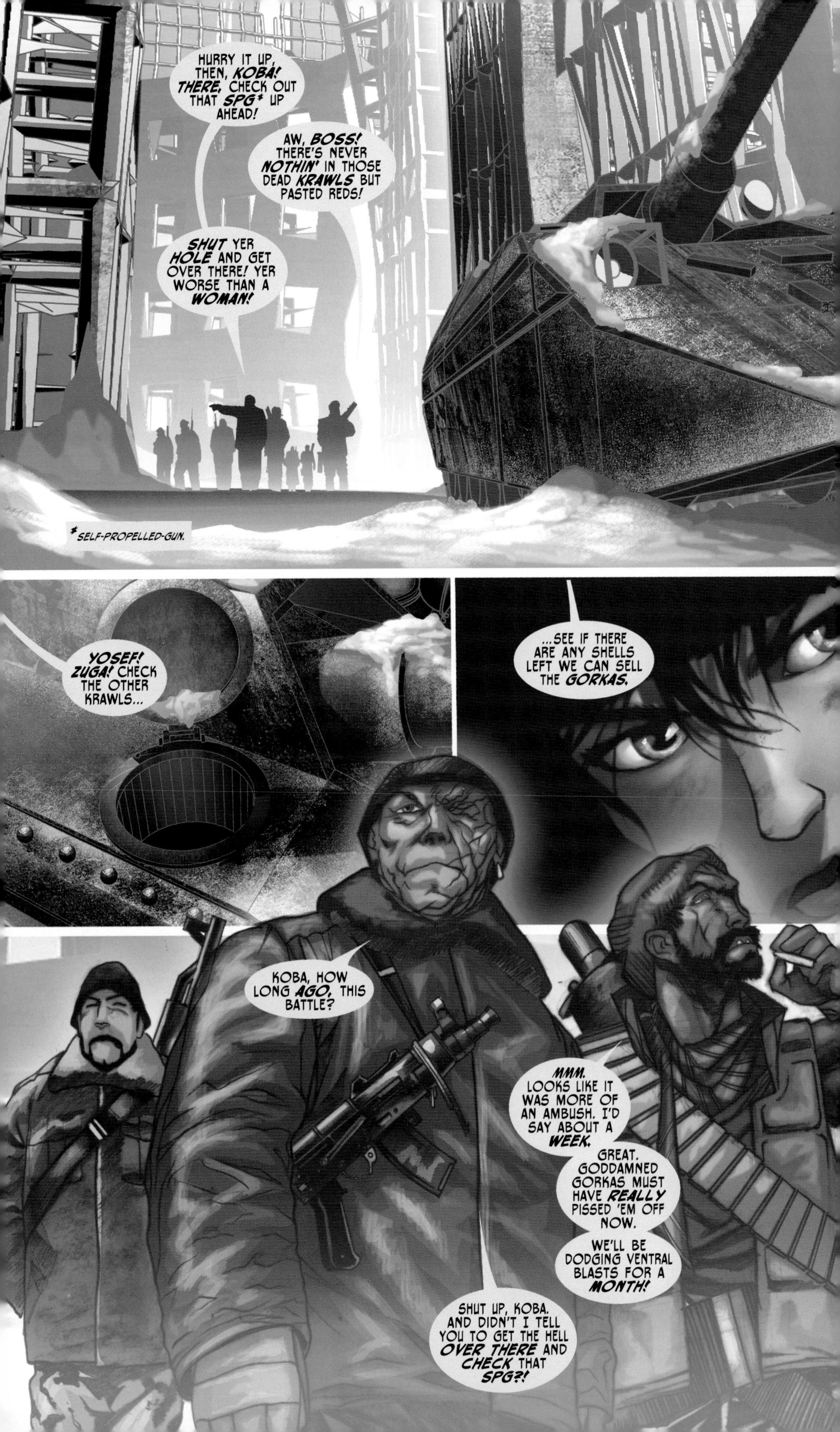

HURRY IT UP, THEN, KOBA! THERE, CHECK OUT THAT SPG* UP AHEAD!
AW, BOSS! THERE'S NEVER NOTHIN' IN THOSE DEAD KRAWLS BUT PASTED REDS!
SHUT YER HOLE AND GET OVER THERE! YER WORSE THAN A WOMAN!
*SELF-PROPELLED-GUN.
YOSEF! ZUGA! CHECK THE OTHER KRAWLS...
...SEE IF THERE ARE ANY SHELLS LEFT WE CAN SELL THE GORKAS.
KOBA, HOW LONG AGO, THIS BATTLE?
MMM. LOOKS LIKE IT WAS MORE OF AN AMBUSH. I'D SAY ABOUT A WEEK.
GREAT. GODDAMNED GORKAS MUST HAVE REALLY PISSED 'EM OFF NOW.
WE'LL BE DODGING VENTRAL BLASTS FOR A MONTH!
SHUT UP, KOBA. AND DIDN'T I TELL YOU TO GET THE HELL OVER THERE AND CHECK THAT SPG?!

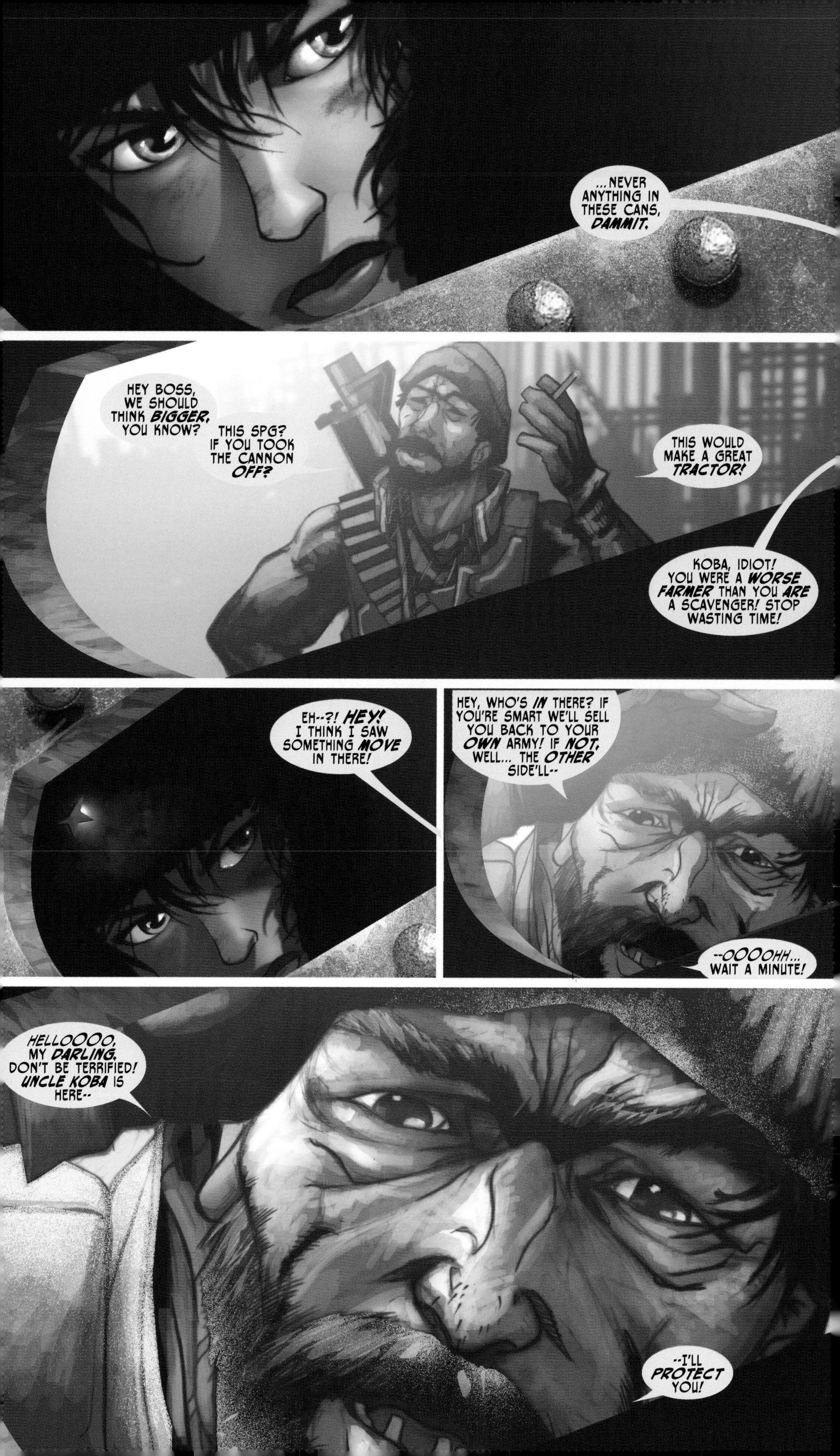
...NEVER ANYTHING IN THESE CANS, DAMMIT.
HEY BOSS, WE SHOULD THINK BIGGER, YOU KNOW?
THIS SPG? IF YOU TOOK THE CANNON OFF?
THIS WOULD MAKE A GREAT TRACTOR!
KOBA, IDIOT! YOU WERE A WORSE FARMER THAN YOU ARE A SCAVENGER! STOP WASTING TIME!
EH--?! HEY! I THINK I SAW SOMETHING MOVE IN THERE!
HEY, WHO'S IN THERE? IF YOU'RE SMART WE'LL SELL YOU BACK TO YOUR OWN ARMY! IF NOT, WELL... THE OTHER SIDE'LL--
--OOOOHH... WAIT A MINUTE!
HELLOOOO, MY DARLING. DON'T BE TERRIFIED! UNCLE KOBA IS HERE--
--I'LL PROTECT YOU!

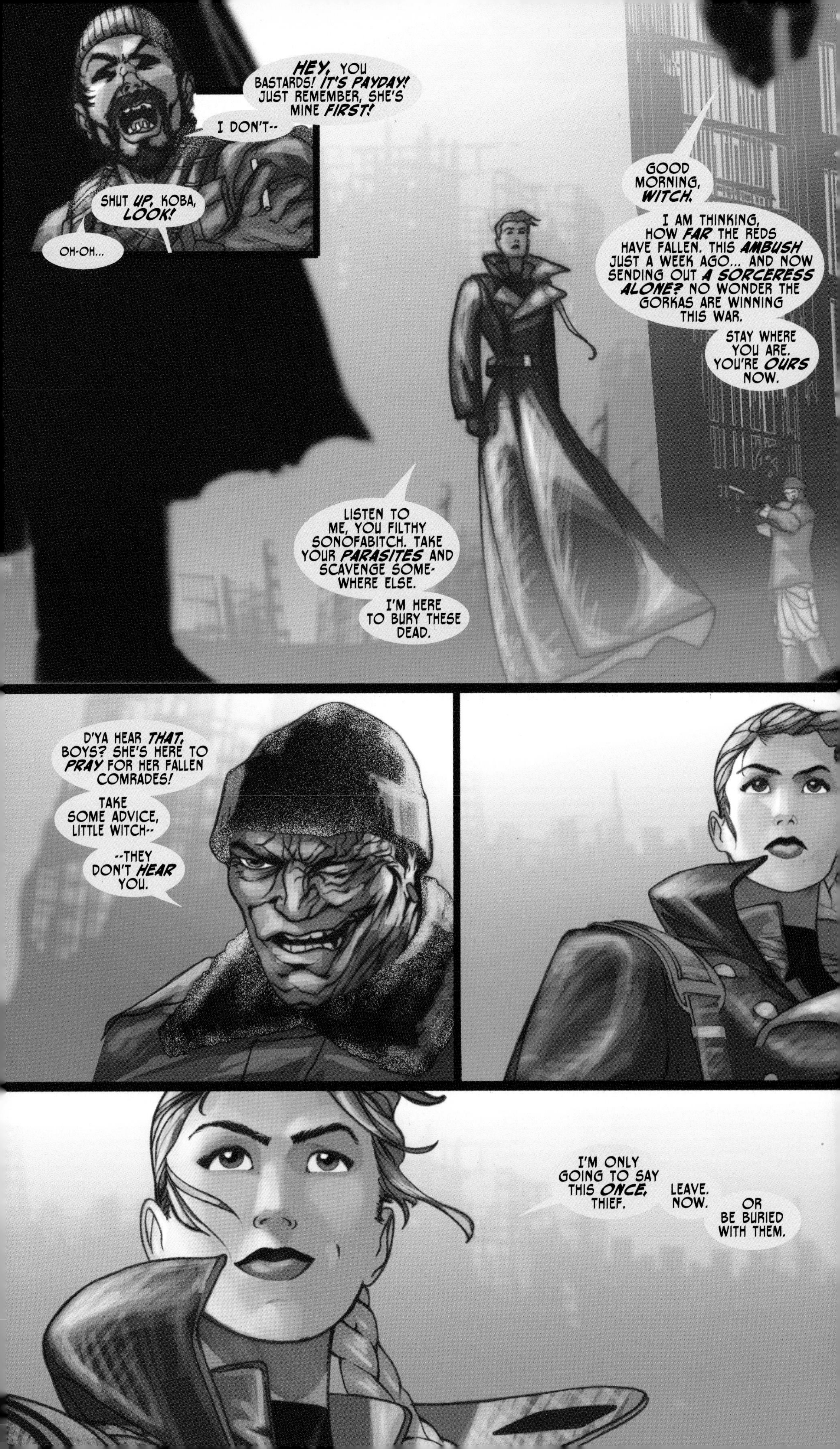
HEY, YOU BASTARDS! IT'S PAYDAY! JUST REMEMBER, SHE'S MINE FIRST!
I DON'T--
SHUT UP, KOBA, LOOK!
OH-OH...
GOOD MORNING, WITCH.
I AM THINKING, HOW FAR THE REDS HAVE FALLEN. THIS AMBUSH JUST A WEEK AGO... AND NOW SENDING OUT A SORCERESS ALONE? NO WONDER THE GORKAS ARE WINNING THIS WAR.
STAY WHERE YOU ARE. YOU'RE OURS NOW.
LISTEN TO ME, YOU FILTHY SONOFABITCH. TAKE YOUR PARASITES AND SCAVENGE SOMEWHERE ELSE.
I'M HERE TO BURY THESE DEAD.
D'YA HEAR THAT, BOYS? SHE'S HERE TO PRAY FOR HER FALLEN COMRADES!
TAKE SOME ADVICE, LITTLE WITCH--
--THEY DON'T HEAR YOU.
I'M ONLY GOING TO SAY THIS ONCE, THIEF.
LEAVE. NOW.
OR BE BURIED WITH THEM.

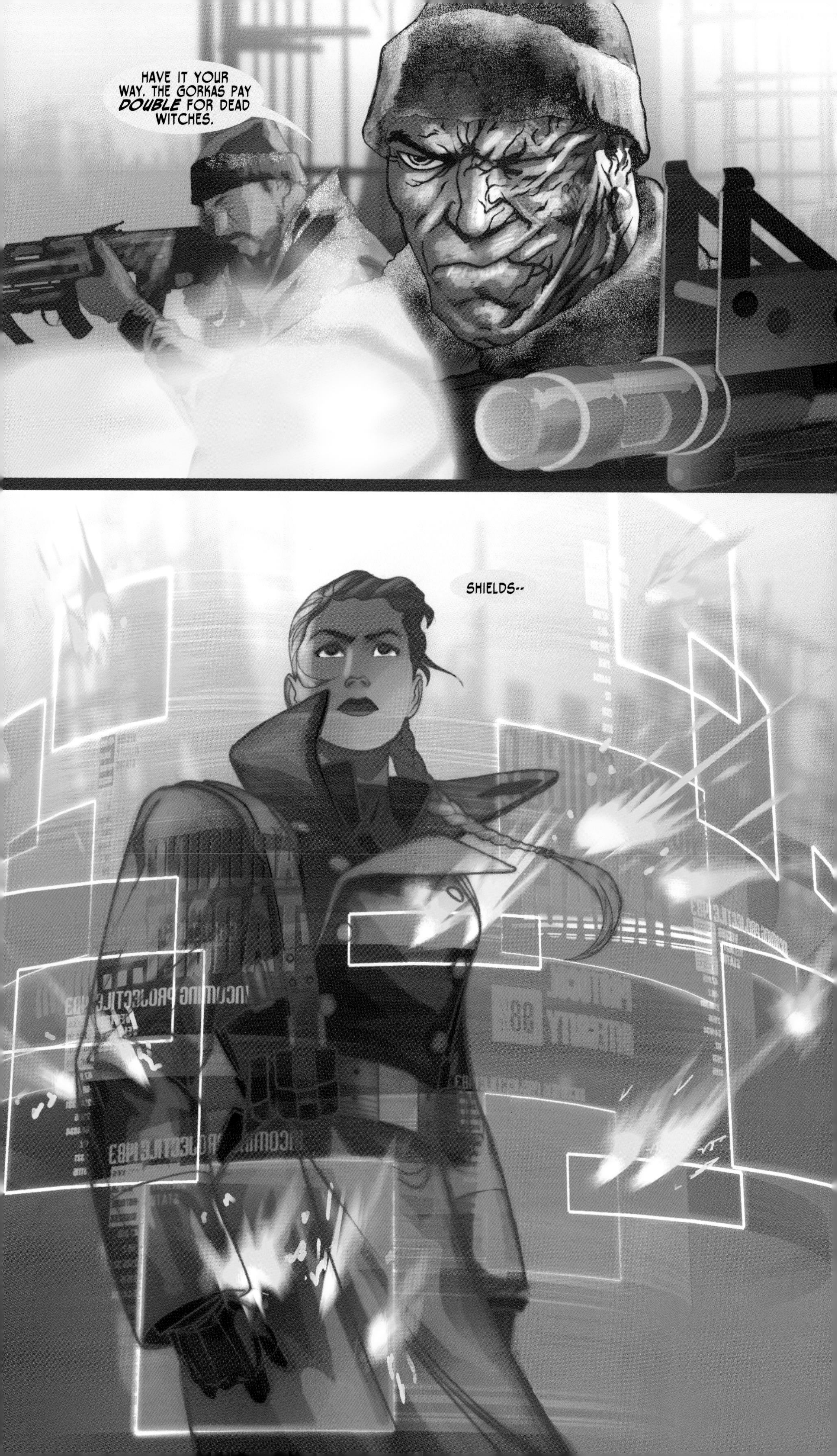
HAVE IT YOUR WAY. THE GORKAS PAY DOUBLE FOR DEAD WITCHES.
SHIELDS--

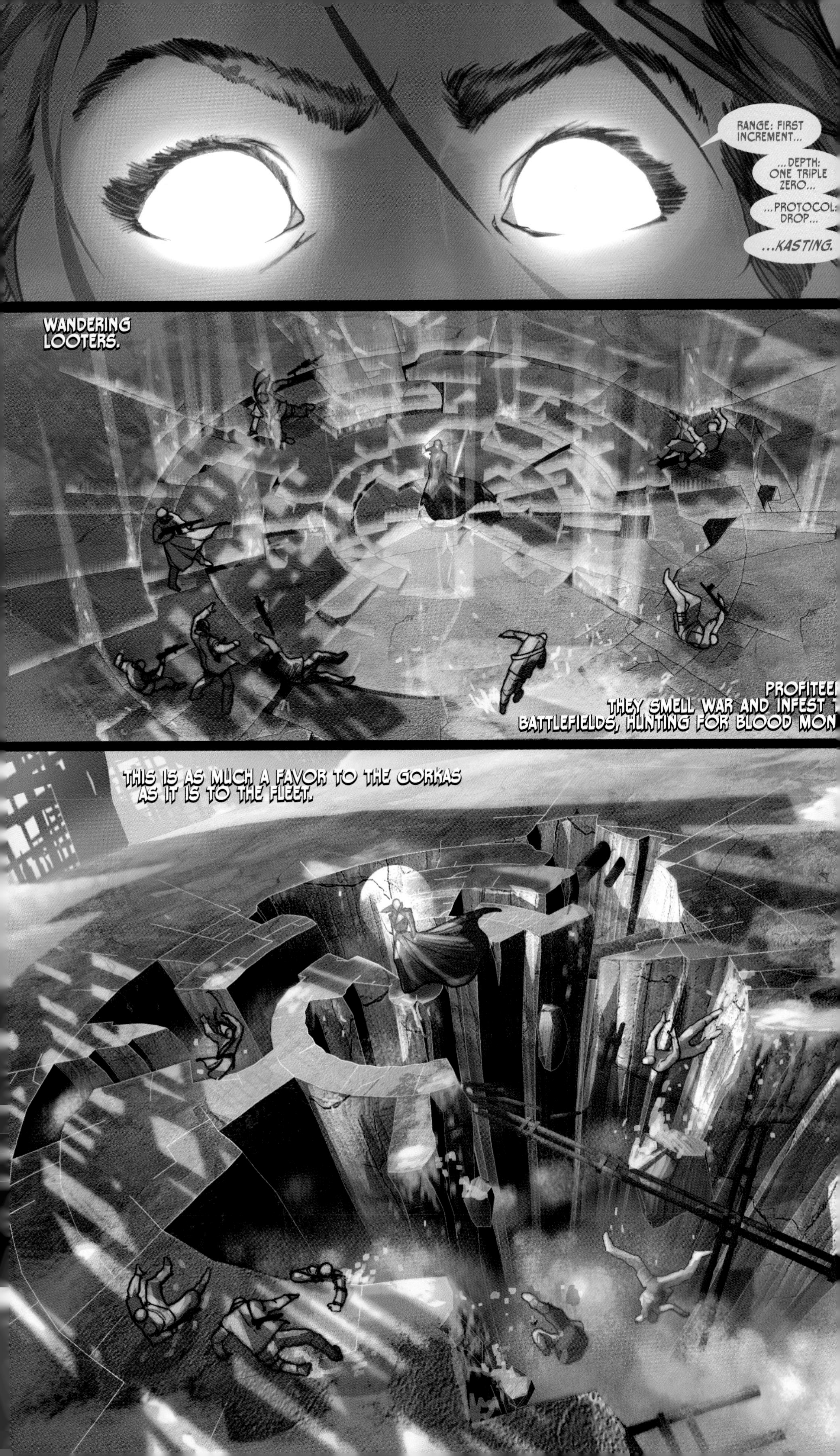
RANGE: FIRST INCREMENT...
...DEPTH: ONE TRIPLE ZERO...
...PROTOCOL: DROP...
...KASTING.
WANDERING LOOTERS.
PROFITEE
THEY SMELL WAR AND INFEST T
BATTLEFIELDS, HUNTING FOR BLOOD MON
THIS IS AS MUCH A FAVOR TO THE GORKAS AS IT IS TO THE FLEET.

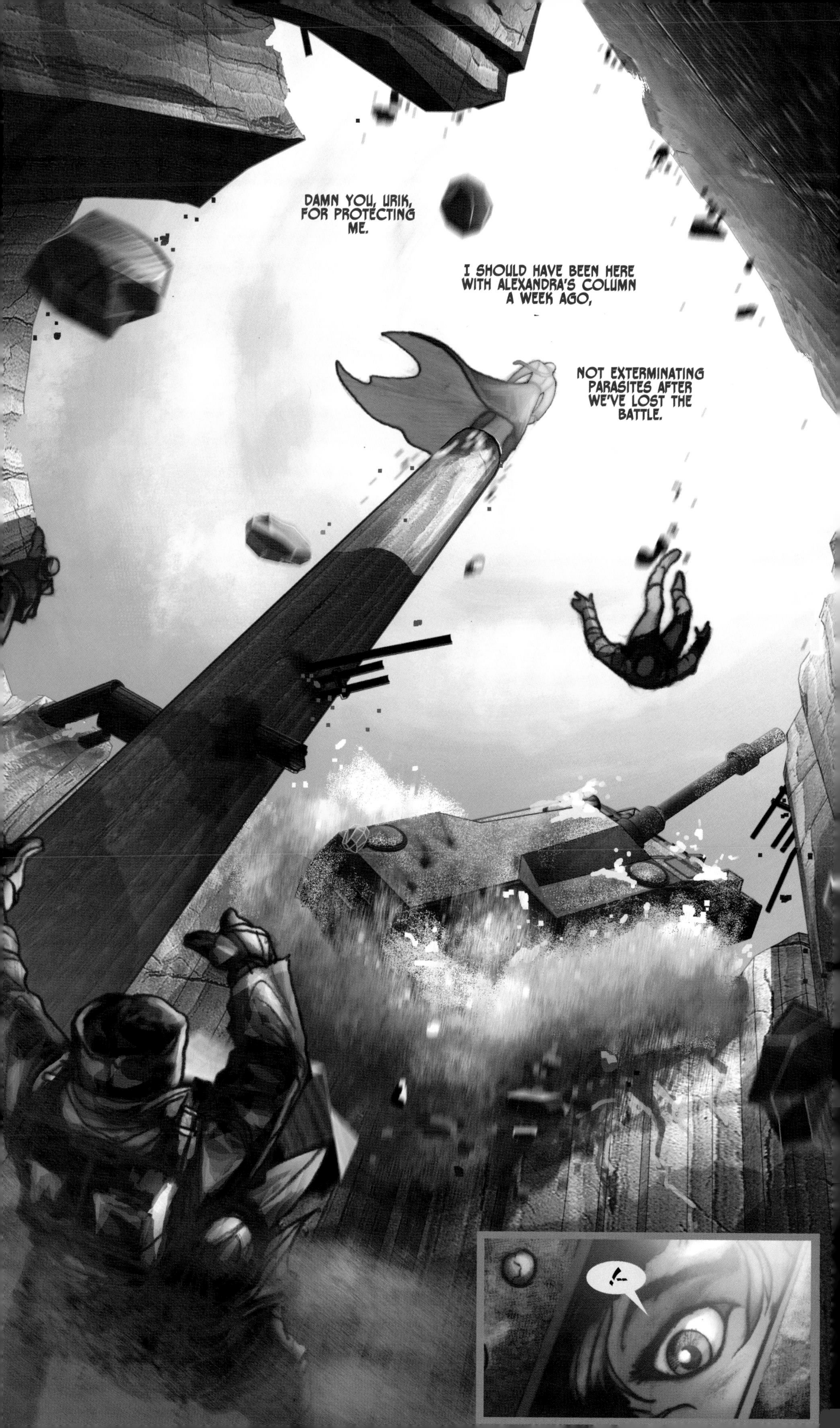
DAMN YOU, URIK, FOR PROTECTING ME.
I SHOULD HAVE BEEN HERE WITH ALEXANDRA'S COLUMN A WEEK AGO,
NOT EXTERMINATING PARASITES AFTER WE'VE LOST THE BATTLE.
!--

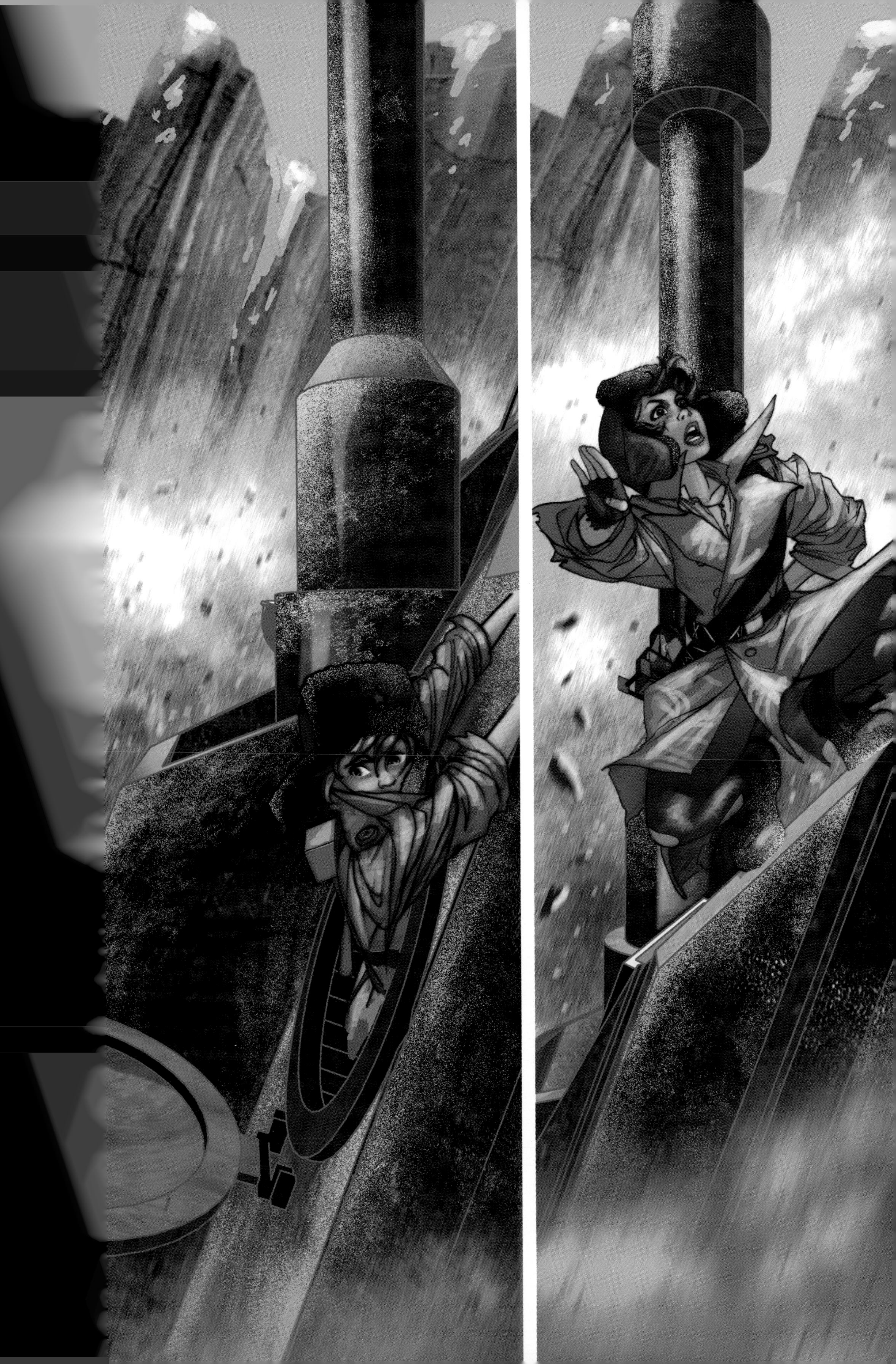

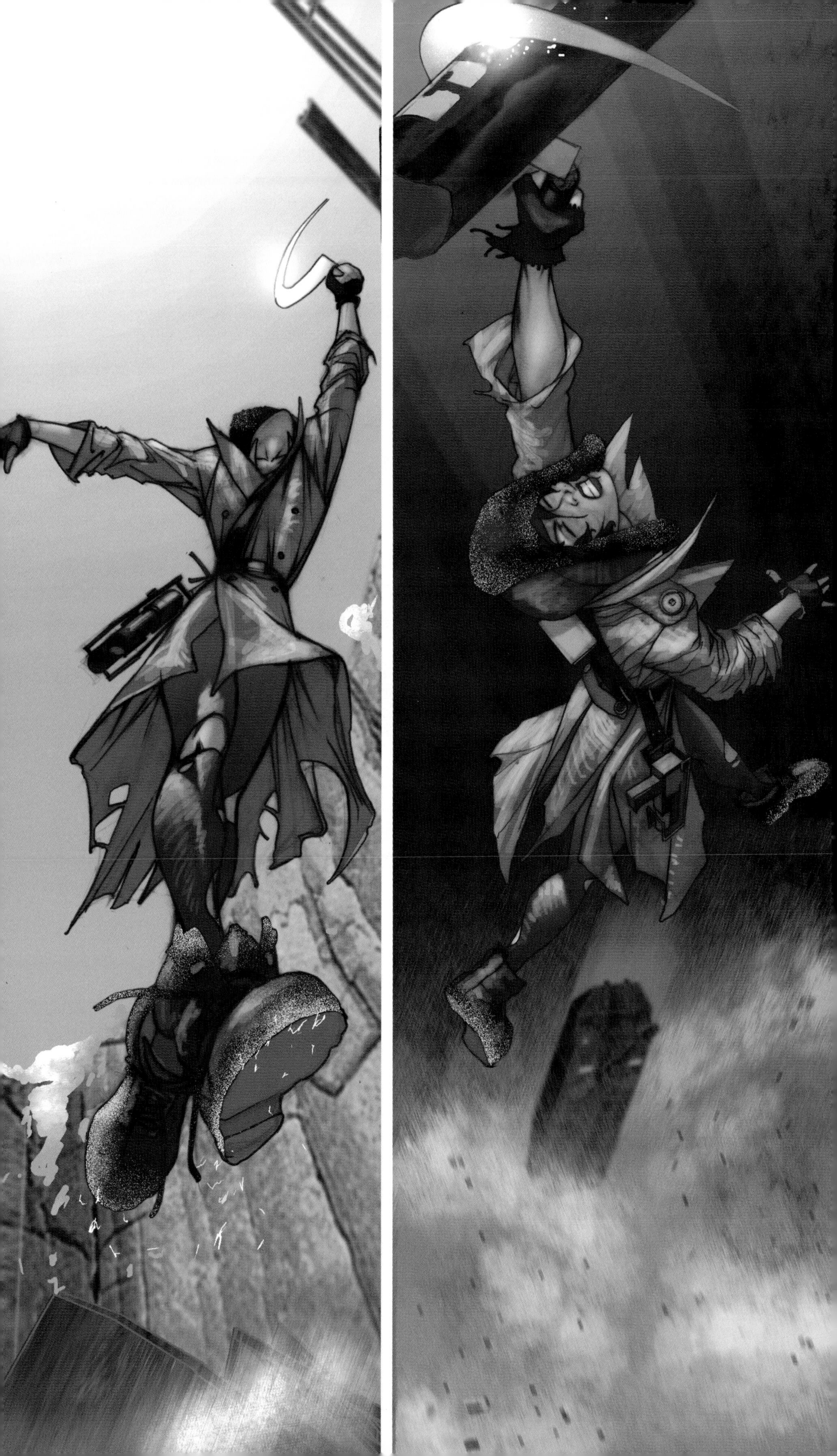

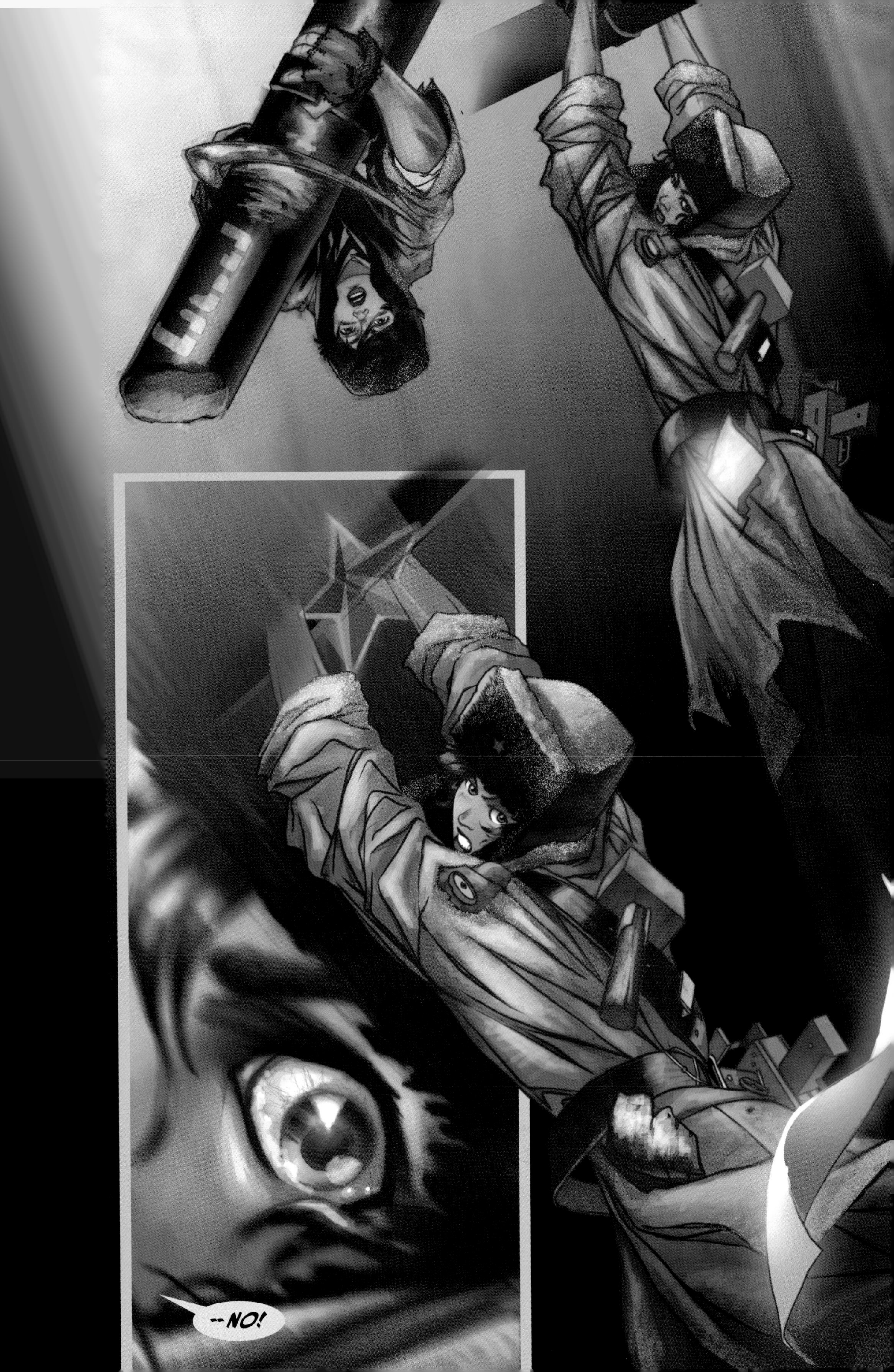
--NO!

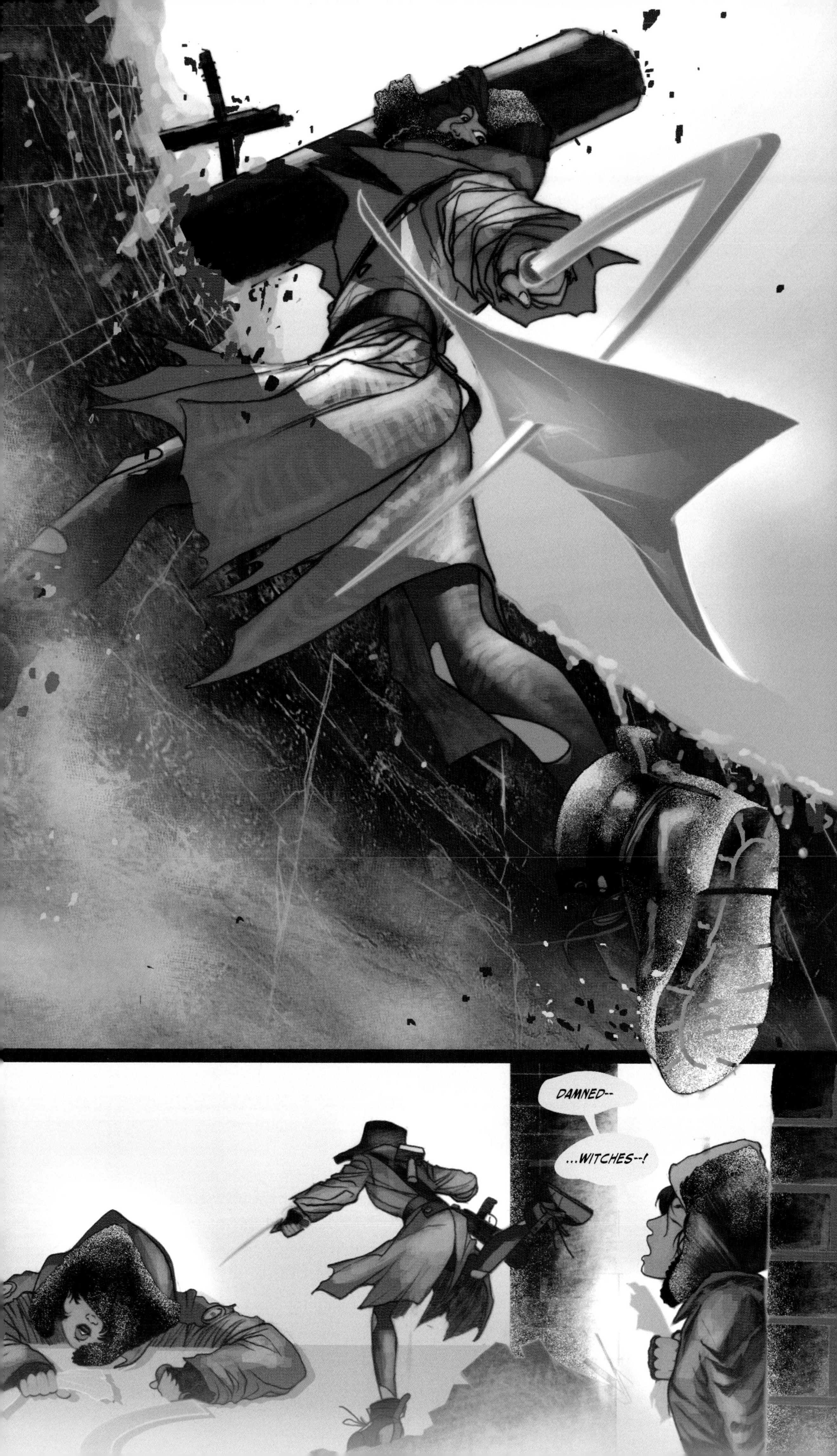
DAMNED--
...WITCHES--!

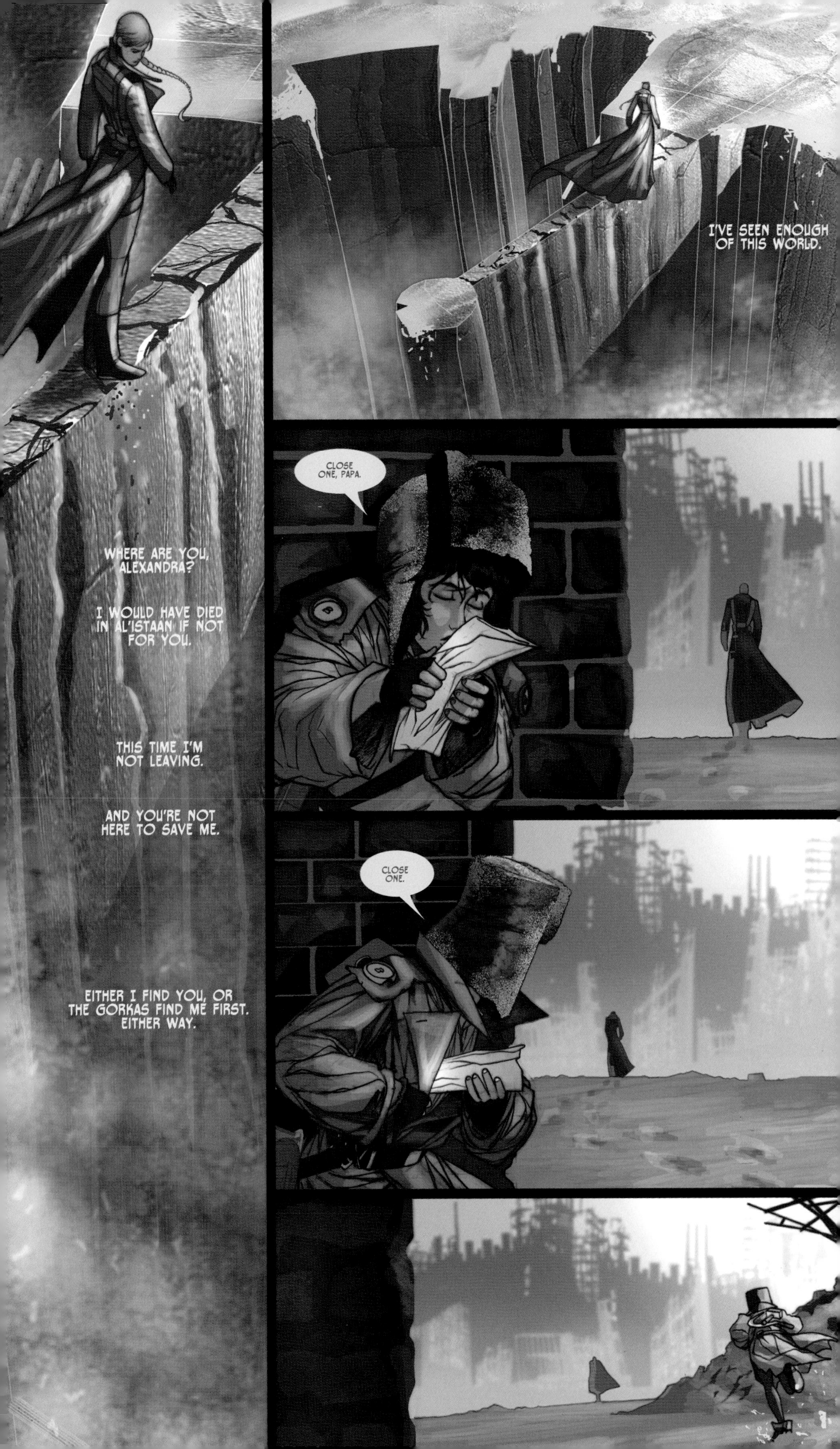
WHERE ARE YOU, ALEXANDRA?
I WOULD HAVE DIED IN AL'ISTAAN IF NOT FOR YOU.
THIS TIME I'M NOT LEAVING.
AND YOU'RE NOT HERE TO SAVE ME.
EITHER I FIND YOU, OR THE GORKAS FIND ME FIRST. EITHER WAY.
I'VE SEEN ENOUGH OF THIS WORLD.
CLOSE ONE, PAPA.
CLOSE ONE.

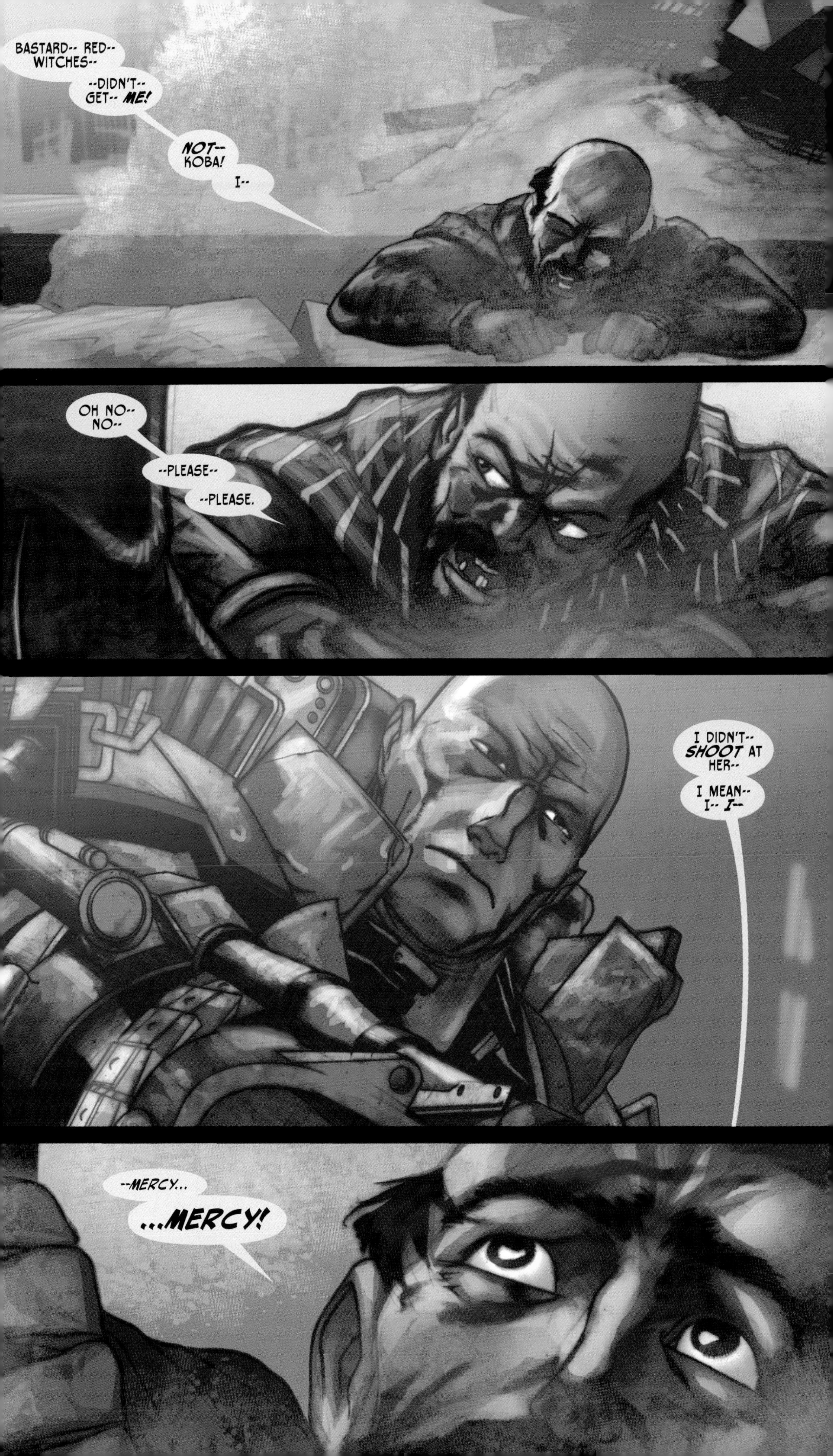
BASTARD-- RED-- WITCHES--
--DIDN'T-- GET-- ME!
NOT-- KOBA!
I--
OH NO-- NO--
--PLEASE--
--PLEASE.
I DIDN'T-- SHOOT AT HER--
I MEAN-- I-- I--
--MERCY...
...MERCY!

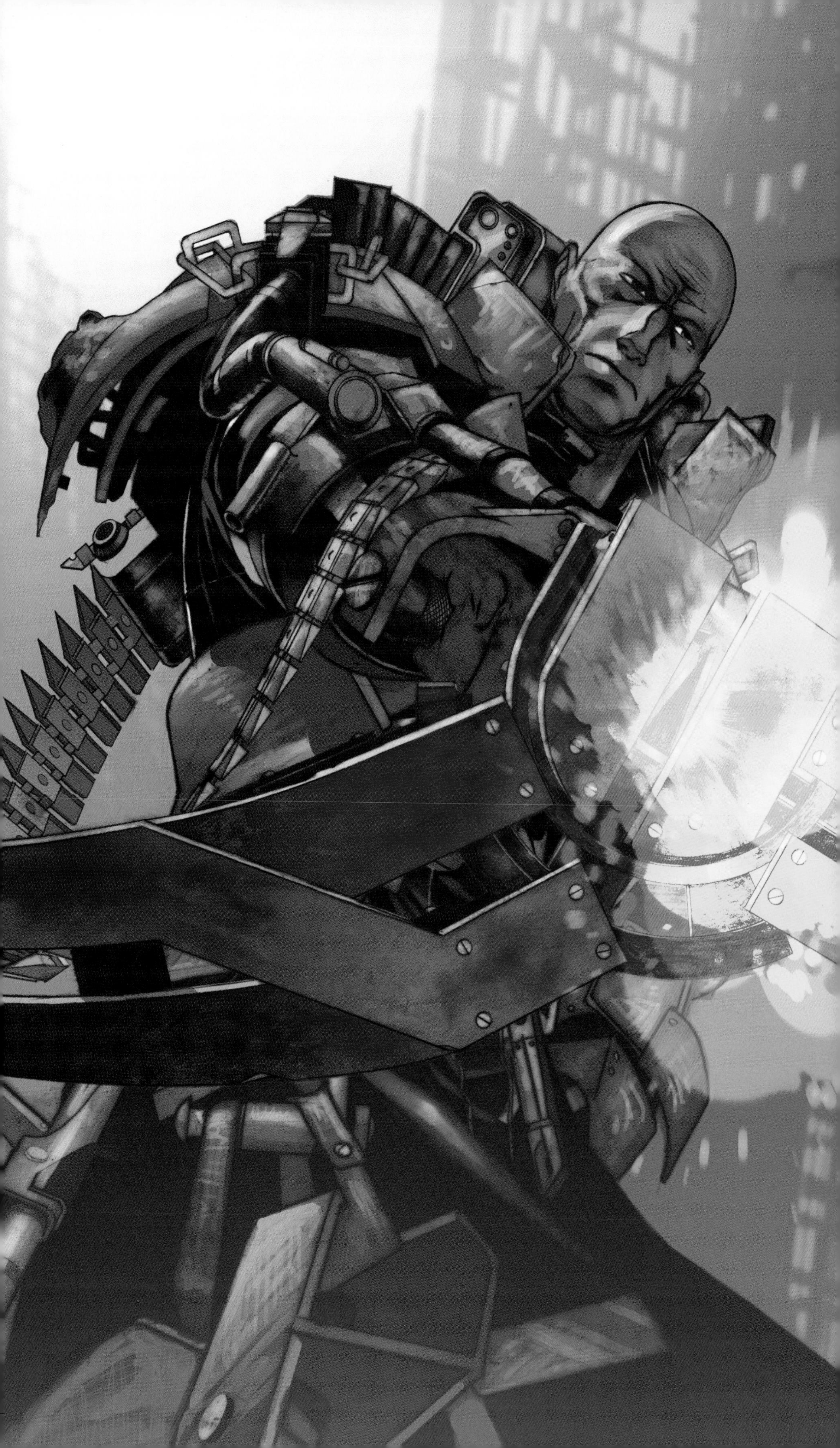

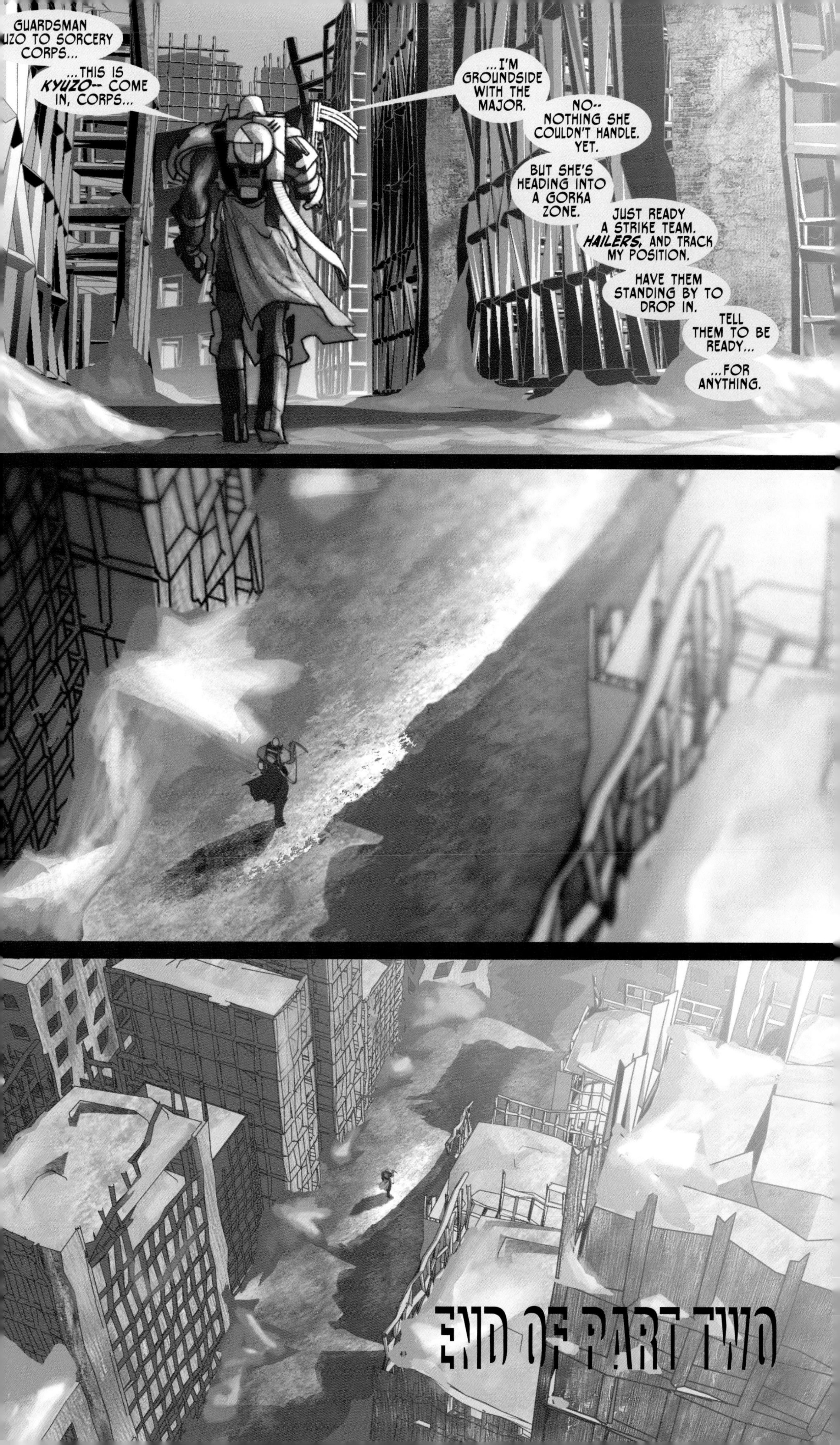

GUARDSMAN UZO TO SORCERY CORPS...
...THIS IS *KYUZO*-- COME IN, CORPS...
...I'M GROUNDSIDE WITH THE MAJOR.
NO-- NOTHING SHE COULDN'T HANDLE. YET.
BUT SHE'S HEADING INTO A GORKA ZONE.
JUST READY A STRIKE TEAM. *HAILERS,* AND TRACK MY POSITION.
HAVE THEM STANDING BY TO DROP IN.
TELL THEM TO BE READY...
...FOR ANYTHING.
END OF PART TWO

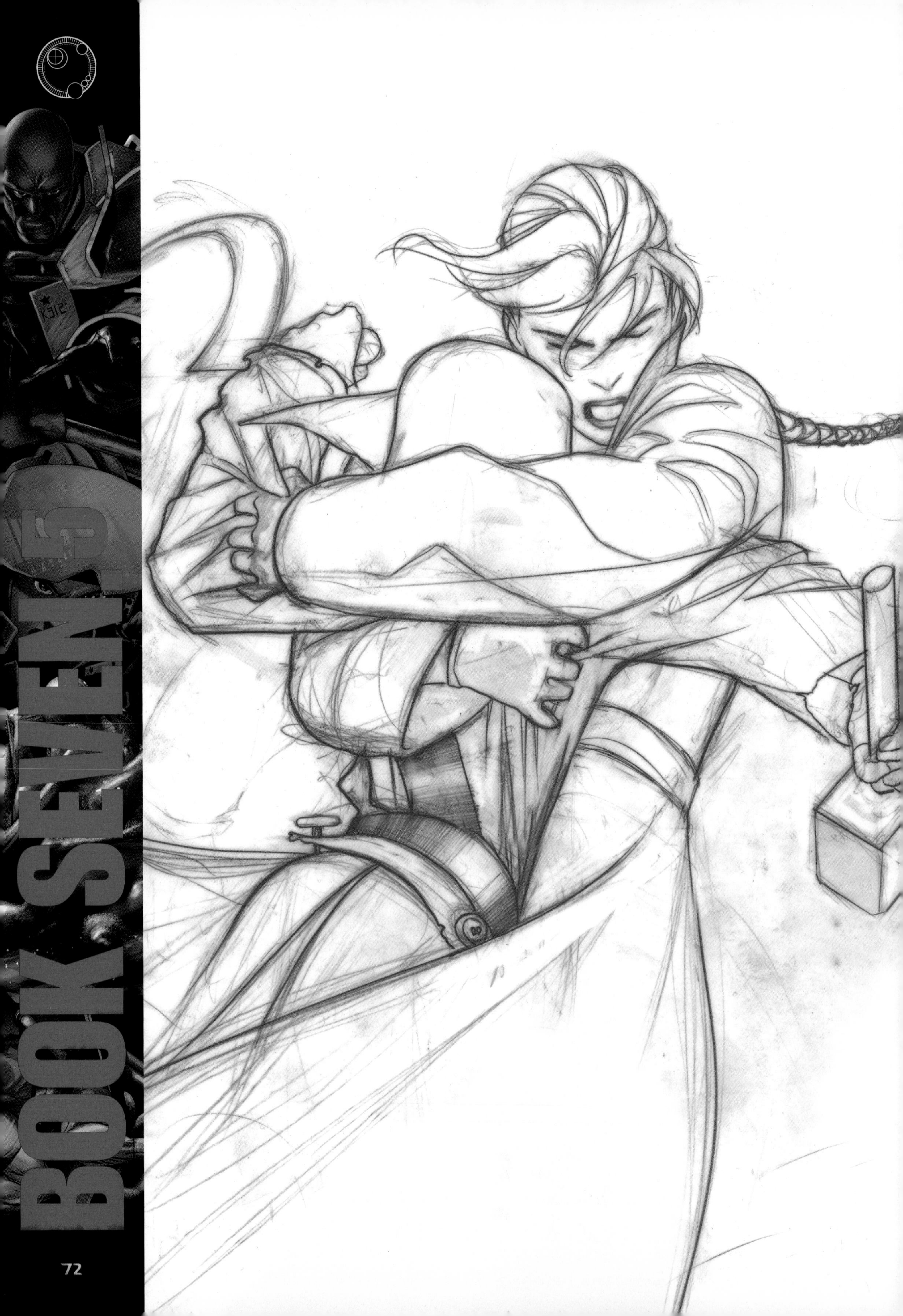

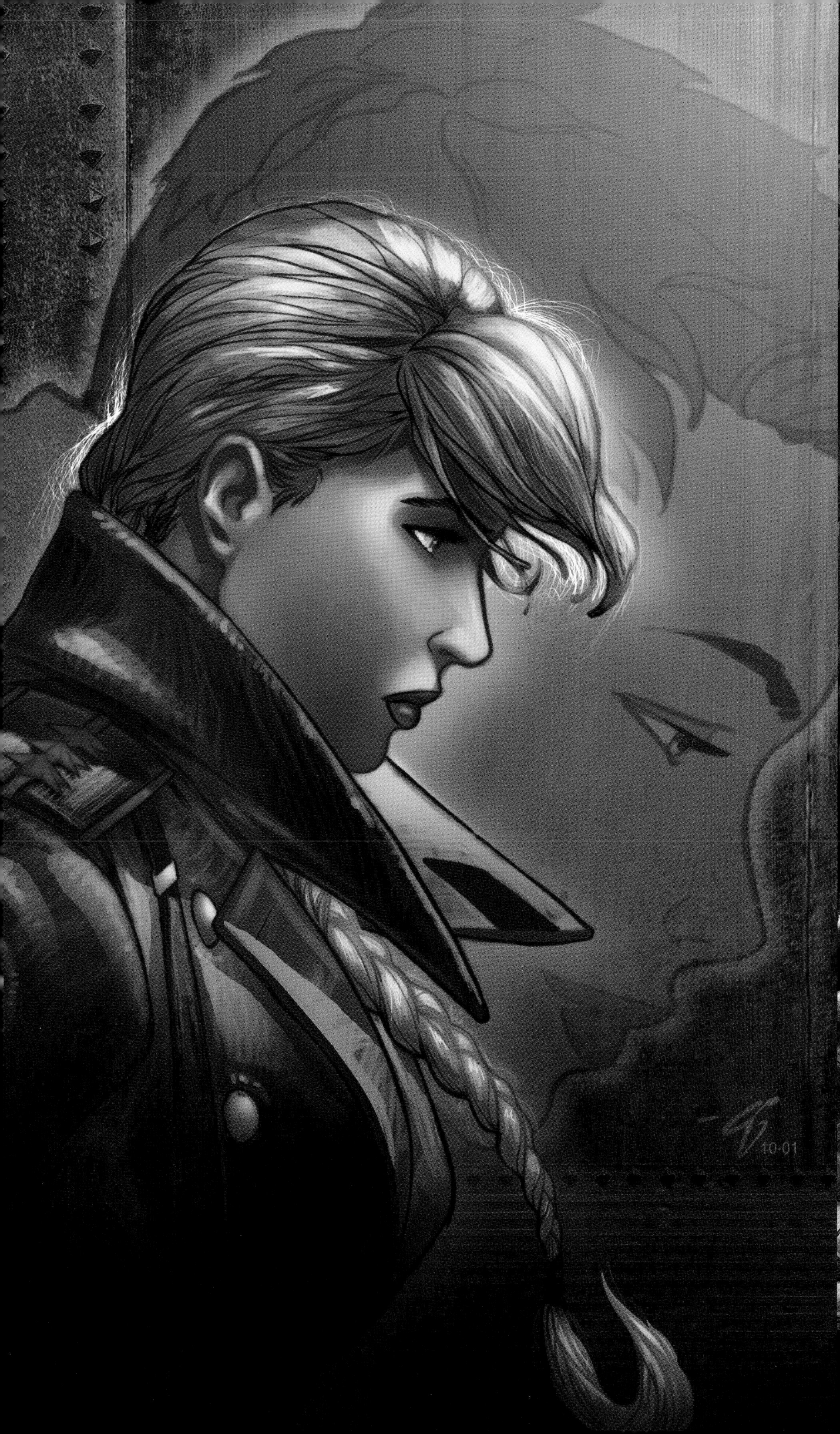
10-01
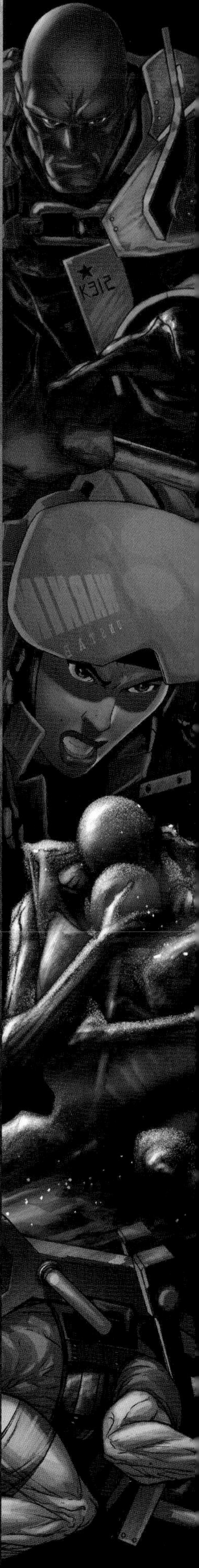

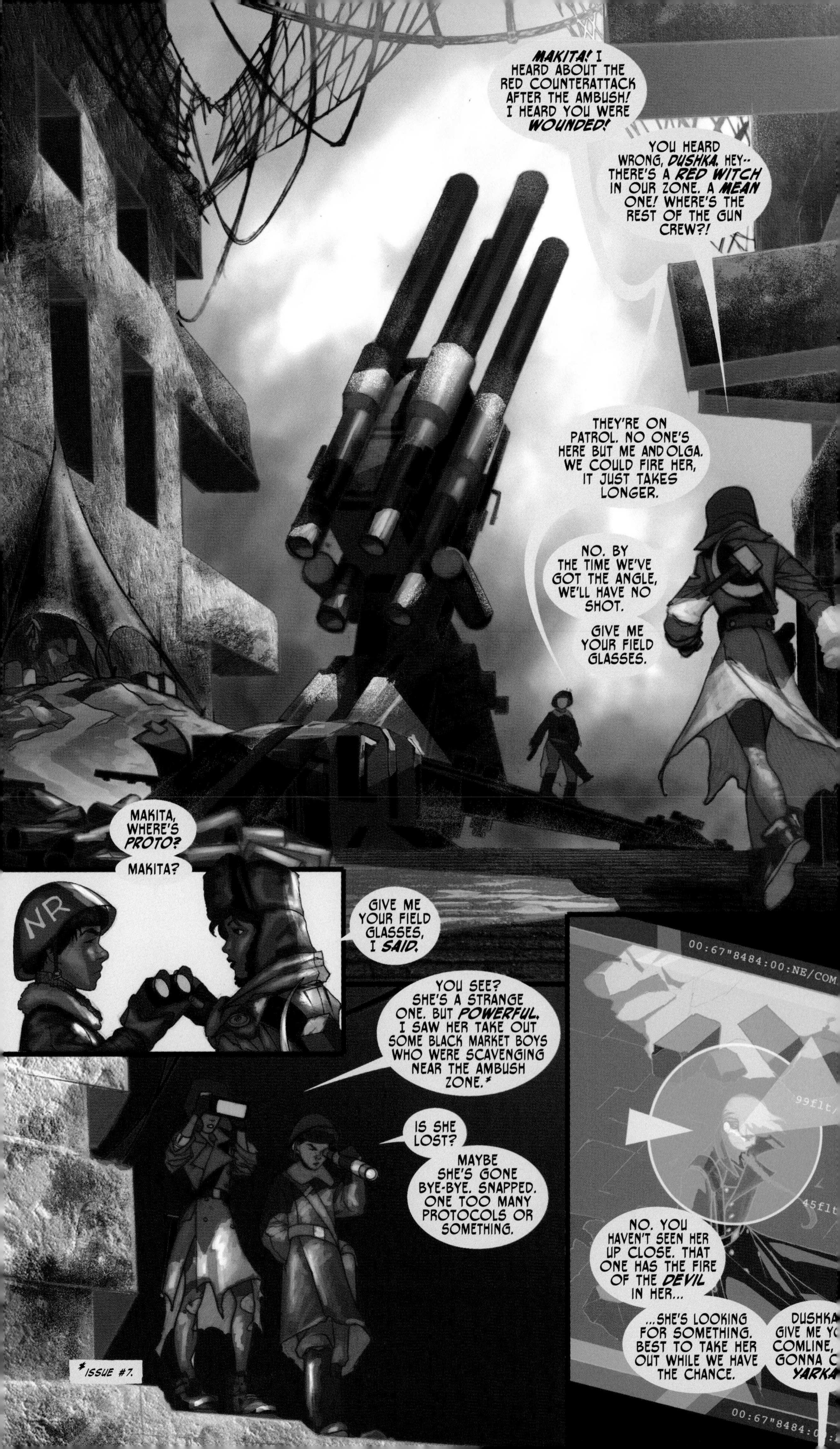
MAKITA! I HEARD ABOUT THE RED COUNTERATTACK AFTER THE AMBUSH! I HEARD YOU WERE WOUNDED!
YOU HEARD WRONG, DUSHKA. HEY-- THERE'S A RED WITCH IN OUR ZONE. A MEAN ONE! WHERE'S THE REST OF THE GUN CREW?!
THEY'RE ON PATROL. NO ONE'S HERE BUT ME AND OLGA. WE COULD FIRE HER, IT JUST TAKES LONGER.
NO. BY THE TIME WE'VE GOT THE ANGLE, WE'LL HAVE NO SHOT.
GIVE ME YOUR FIELD GLASSES.
MAKITA, WHERE'S PROTO?
MAKITA?
NR
GIVE ME YOUR FIELD GLASSES, I SAID.
YOU SEE? SHE'S A STRANGE ONE. BUT POWERFUL. I SAW HER TAKE OUT SOME BLACK MARKET BOYS WHO WERE SCAVENGING NEAR THE AMBUSH ZONE.*
IS SHE LOST?
MAYBE SHE'S GONE BYE-BYE. SNAPPED. ONE TOO MANY PROTOCOLS OR SOMETHING.
*ISSUE #7.
00:67"8484:00:NE/COM
99flt
45flt
NO. YOU HAVEN'T SEEN HER UP CLOSE. THAT ONE HAS THE FIRE OF THE DEVIL IN HER...
...SHE'S LOOKING FOR SOMETHING. BEST TO TAKE HER OUT WHILE WE HAVE THE CHANCE.
DUSHKA GIVE ME YO COMLINE, GONNA C YARKA
00:67"8484:0

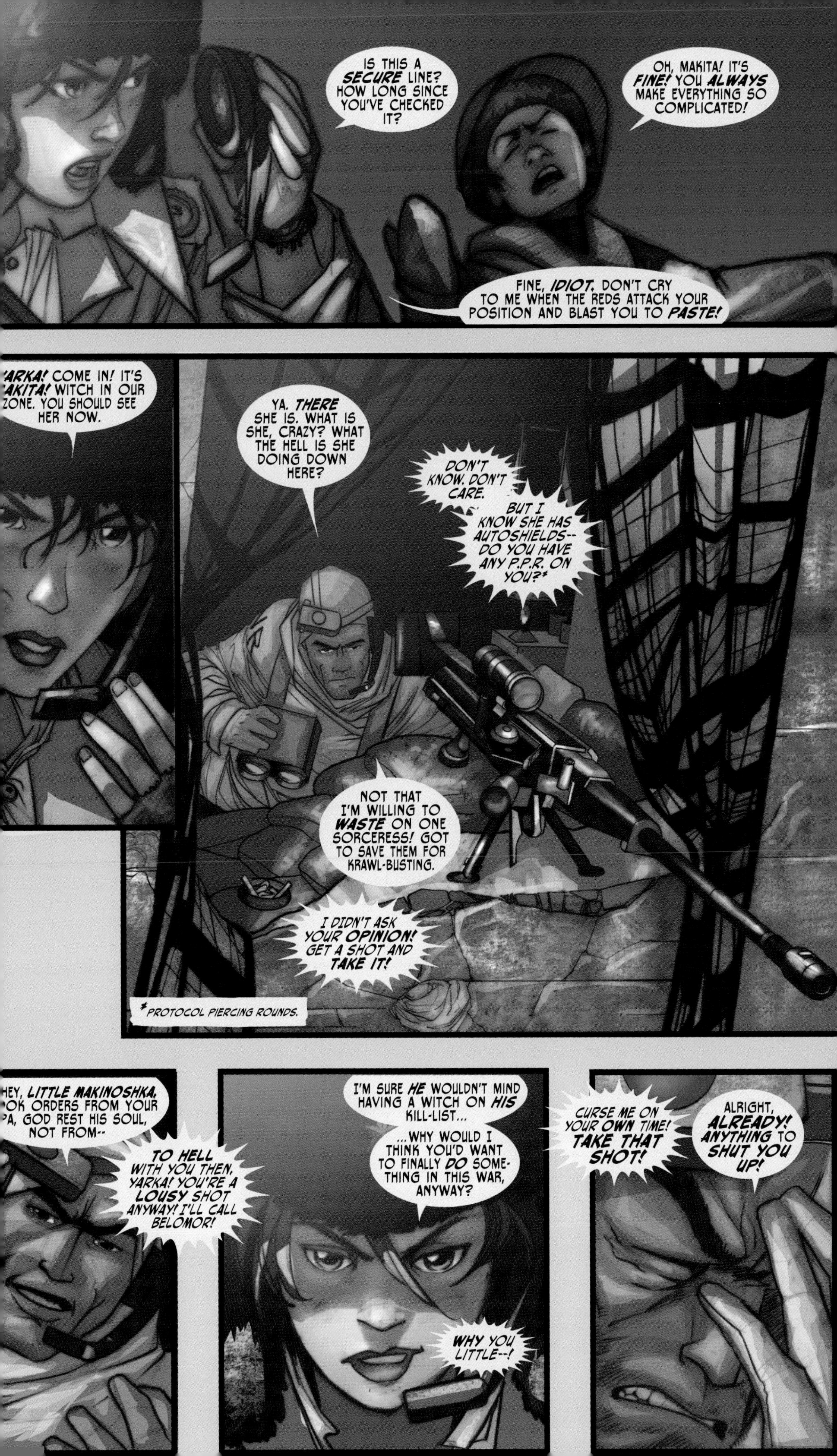
IS THIS A SECURE LINE? HOW LONG SINCE YOU'VE CHECKED IT?
OH, MAKITA! IT'S FINE! YOU ALWAYS MAKE EVERYTHING SO COMPLICATED!
FINE, IDIOT. DON'T CRY TO ME WHEN THE REDS ATTACK YOUR POSITION AND BLAST YOU TO PASTE!
YARKA! COME IN! IT'S MAKITA! WITCH IN OUR ZONE. YOU SHOULD SEE HER NOW.
YA. THERE SHE IS. WHAT IS SHE, CRAZY? WHAT THE HELL IS SHE DOING DOWN HERE?
DON'T KNOW. DON'T CARE.
BUT I KNOW SHE HAS AUTOSHIELDS-- DO YOU HAVE ANY P.P.R. ON YOU?*
NOT THAT I'M WILLING TO WASTE ON ONE SORCERESS! GOT TO SAVE THEM FOR KRAWL-BUSTING.
I DIDN'T ASK YOUR OPINION! GET A SHOT AND TAKE IT!
*PROTOCOL PIERCING ROUNDS.
HEY, LITTLE MAKINOSHKA, I TOOK ORDERS FROM YOUR PA, GOD REST HIS SOUL, NOT FROM--
TO HELL WITH YOU THEN, YARKA! YOU'RE A LOUSY SHOT ANYWAY! I'LL CALL BELOMOR!
I'M SURE HE WOULDN'T MIND HAVING A WITCH ON HIS KILL-LIST...
...WHY WOULD I THINK YOU'D WANT TO FINALLY DO SOMETHING IN THIS WAR, ANYWAY?
WHY YOU LITTLE--!
CURSE ME ON YOUR OWN TIME! TAKE THAT SHOT!
ALRIGHT, ALREADY! ANYTHING TO SHUT YOU UP!

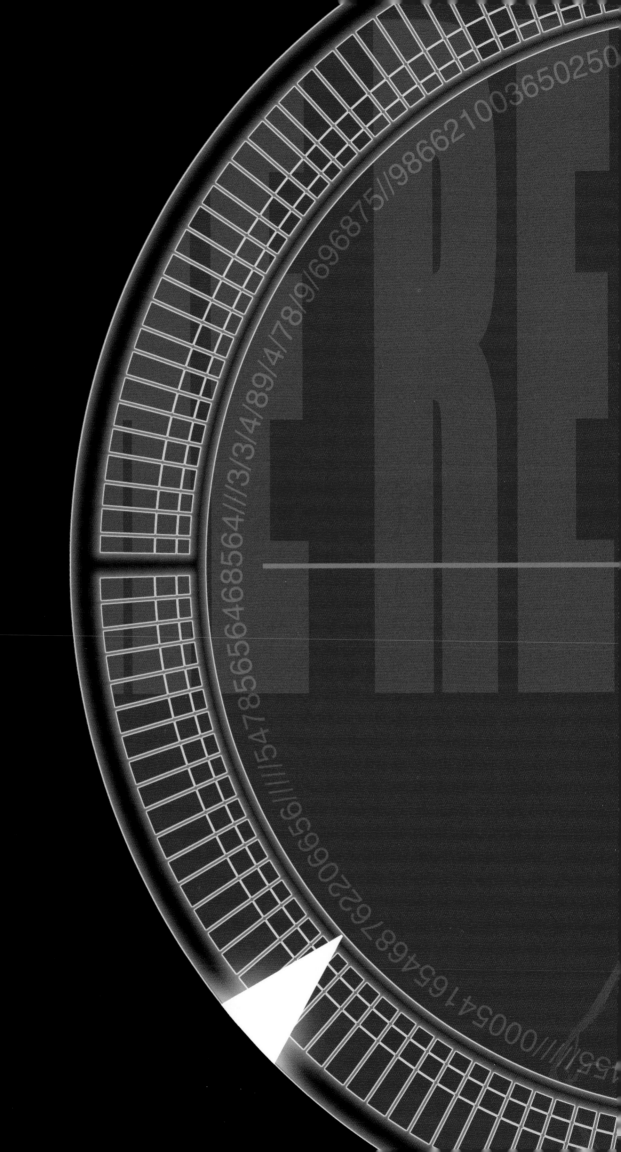

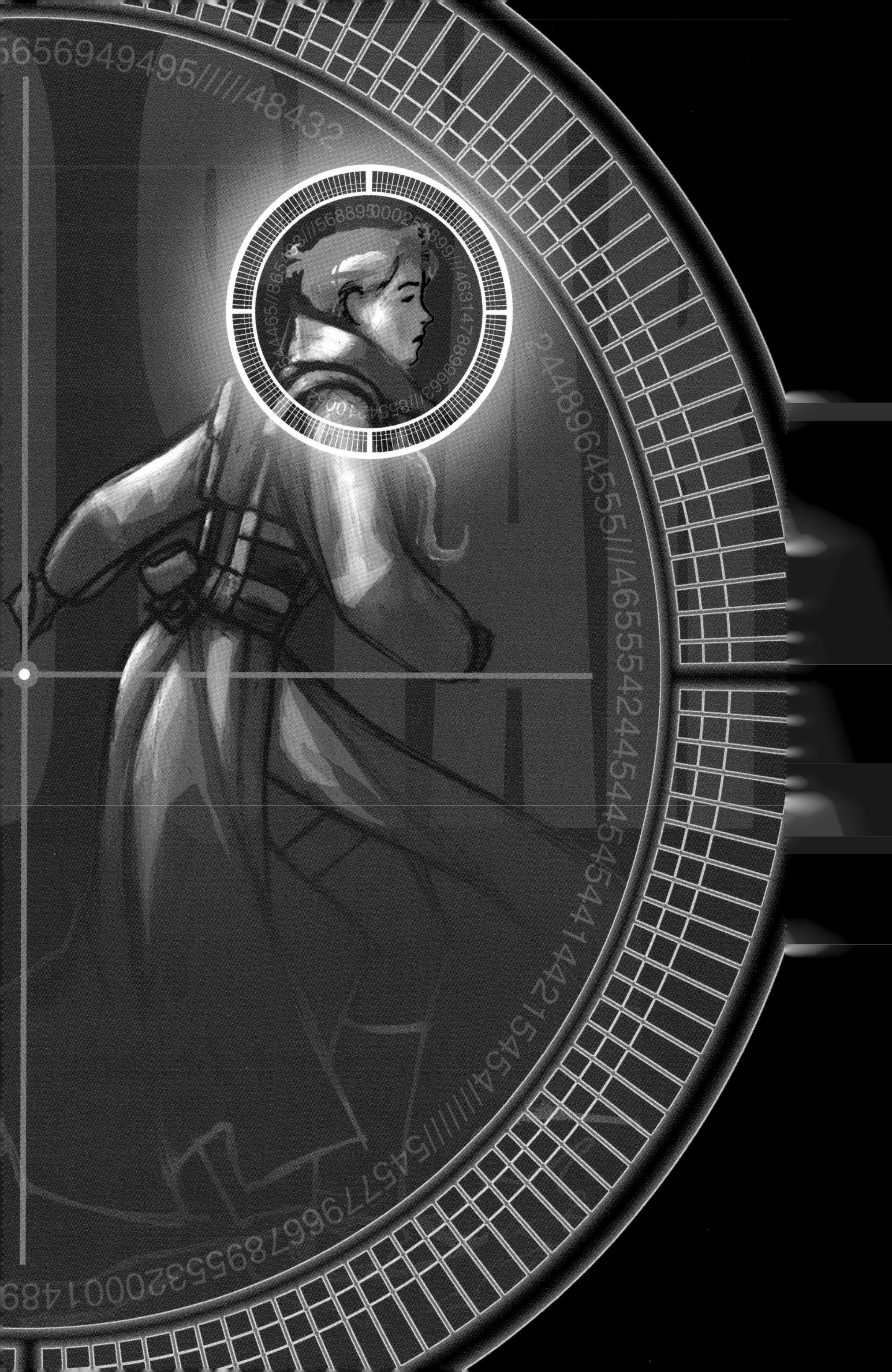
5656949495//////48432

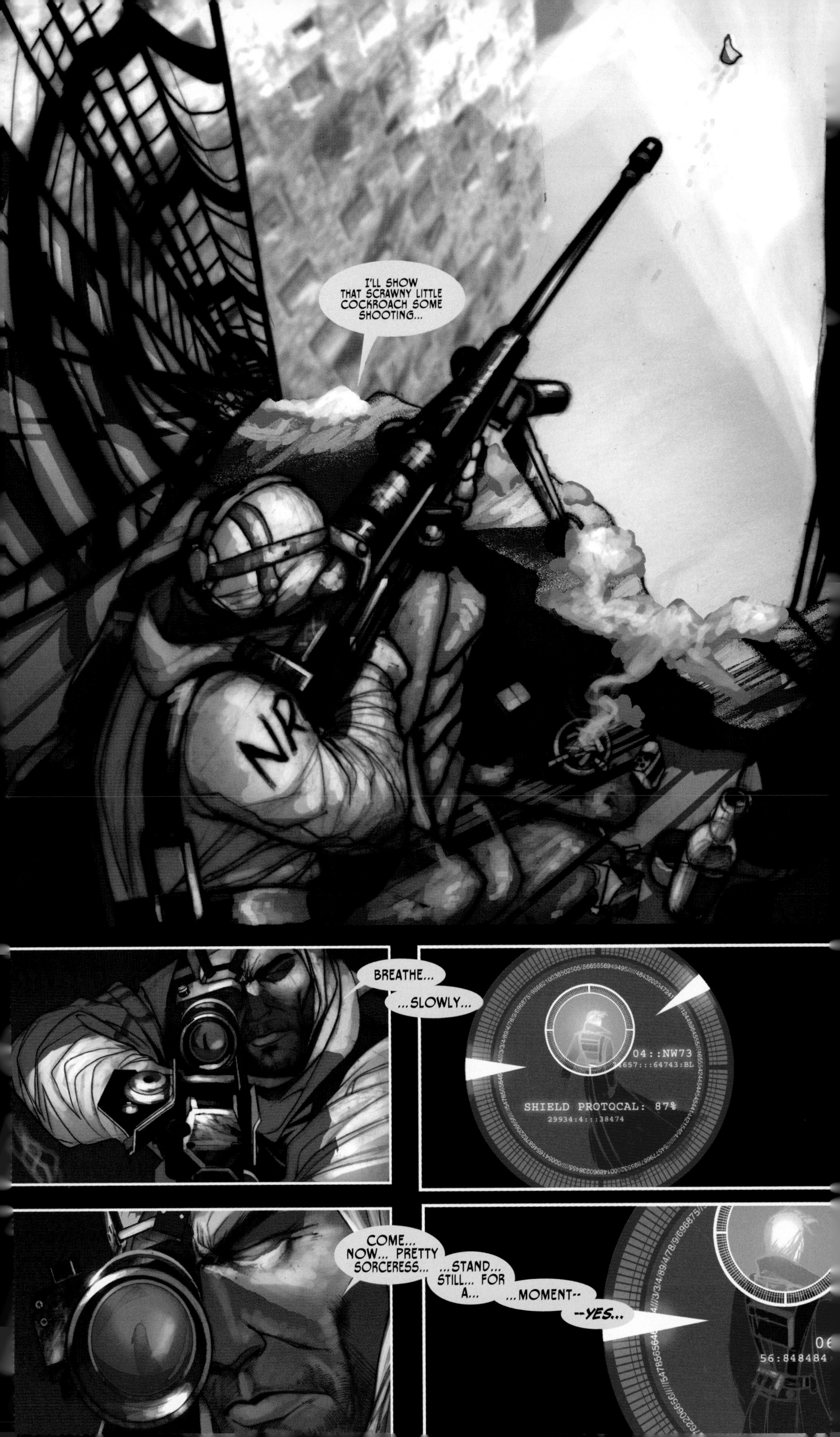
I'LL SHOW THAT SCRAWNY LITTLE COCKROACH SOME SHOOTING...
BREATHE...
...SLOWLY...
04::NW73
SHIELD PROTOCAL: 87%
29934:4:::38474
COME... NOW... PRETTY SORCERESS...
...STAND... STILL... FOR A...
...MOMENT--
--YES...
56:848484

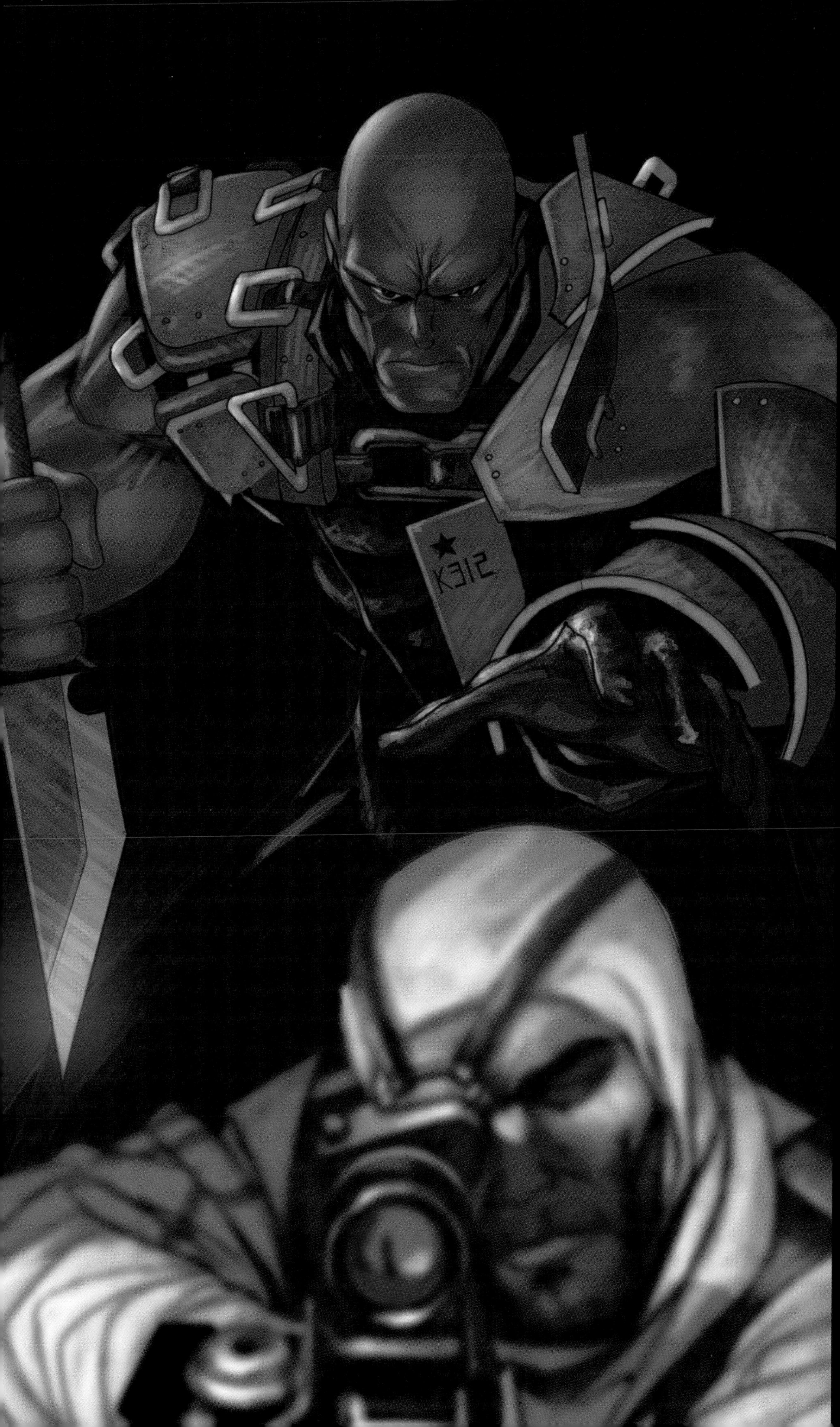

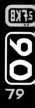

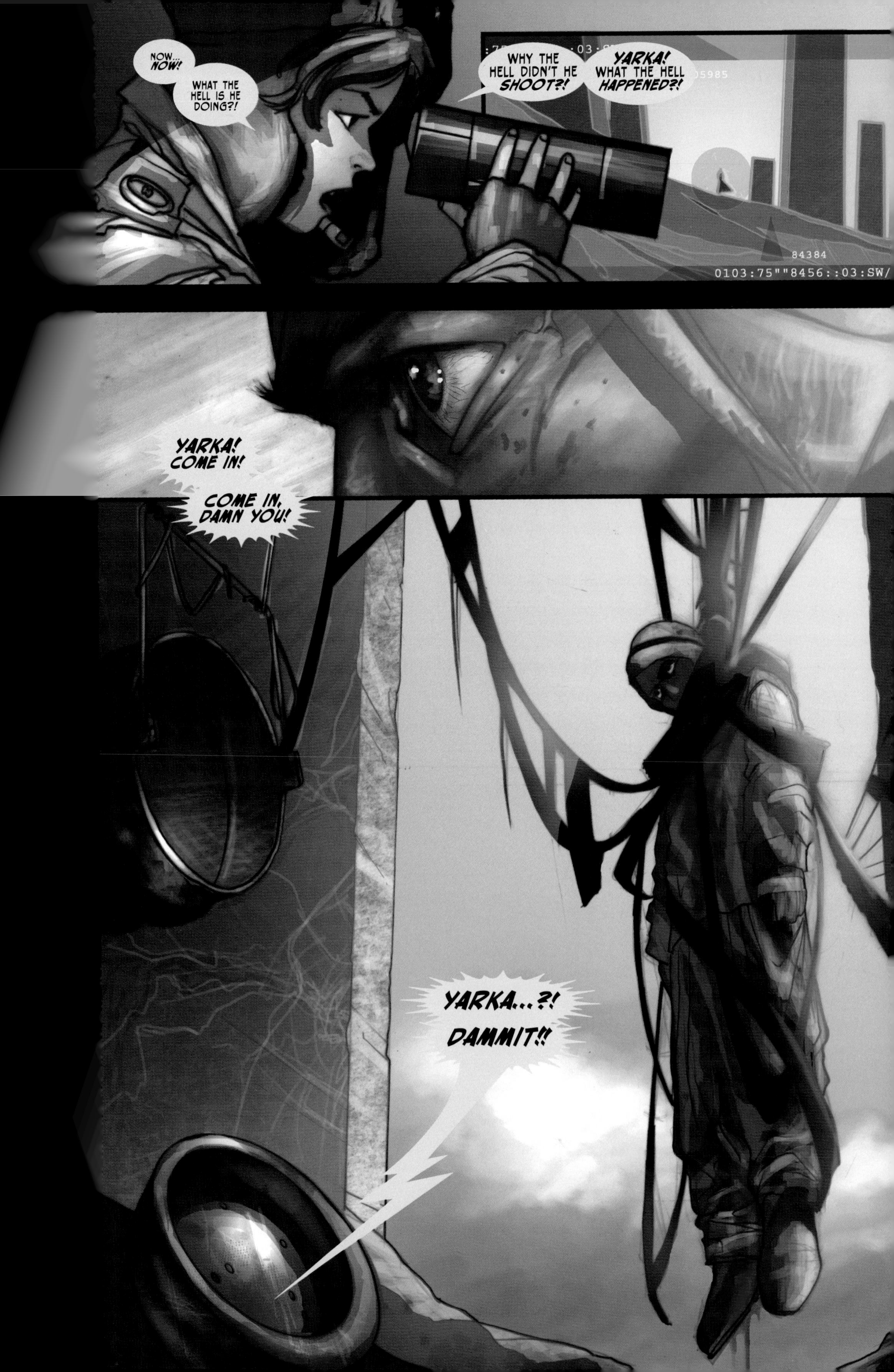
NOW... NOW!
WHAT THE HELL IS HE DOING?!
WHY THE HELL DIDN'T HE SHOOT?!
YARKA! WHAT THE HELL HAPPENED?!
84384
0103:75""8456::03:SW/
YARKA! COME IN!
COME IN, DAMN YOU!
YARKA...?! DAMMIT!!

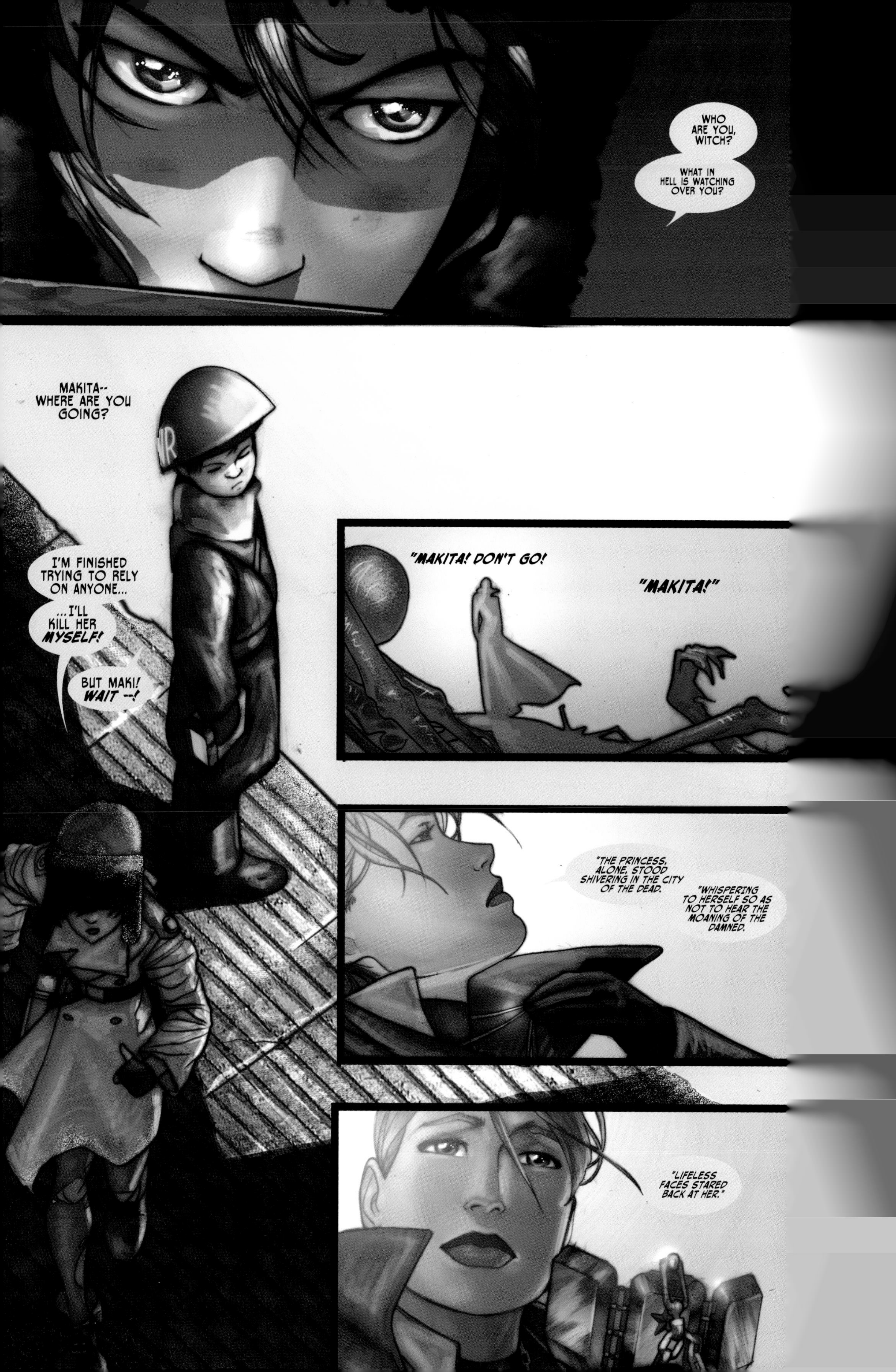

WHO ARE YOU, WITCH?
WHAT IN HELL IS WATCHING OVER YOU?
MAKITA-- WHERE ARE YOU GOING?
I'M FINISHED TRYING TO RELY ON ANYONE...
...I'LL KILL HER MYSELF!
BUT MAKI! WAIT --!
"MAKITA! DON'T GO!
"MAKITA!"
"THE PRINCESS, ALONE, STOOD SHIVERING IN THE CITY OF THE DEAD.
"WHISPERING TO HERSELF SO AS NOT TO HEAR THE MOANING OF THE DAMNED.
"LIFELESS FACES STARED BACK AT HER."

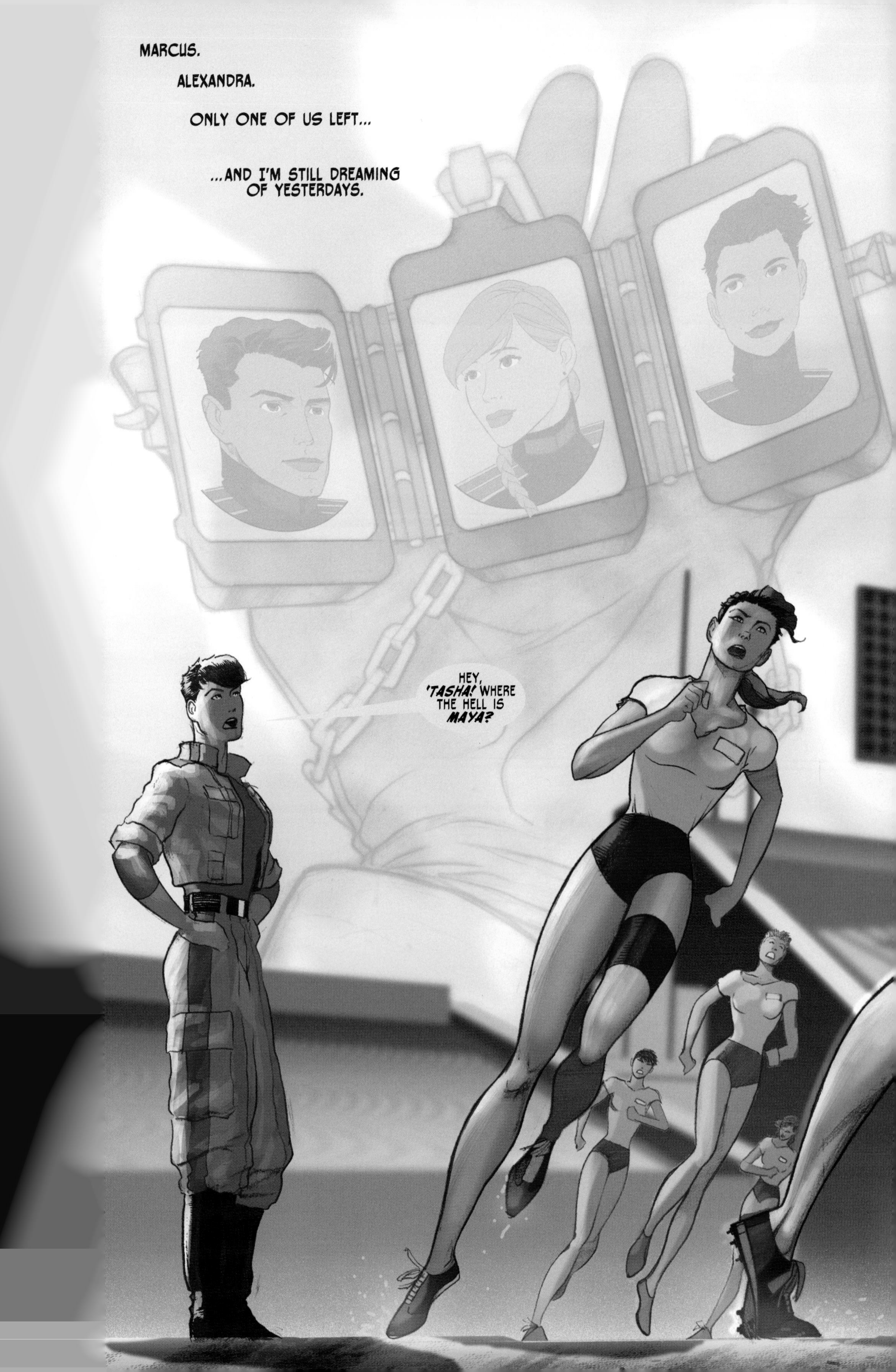
MARCUS.
ALEXANDRA.
ONLY ONE OF US LEFT...
...AND I'M STILL DREAMING OF YESTERDAYS.
HEY, 'TASHA! WHERE THE HELL IS MAYA?

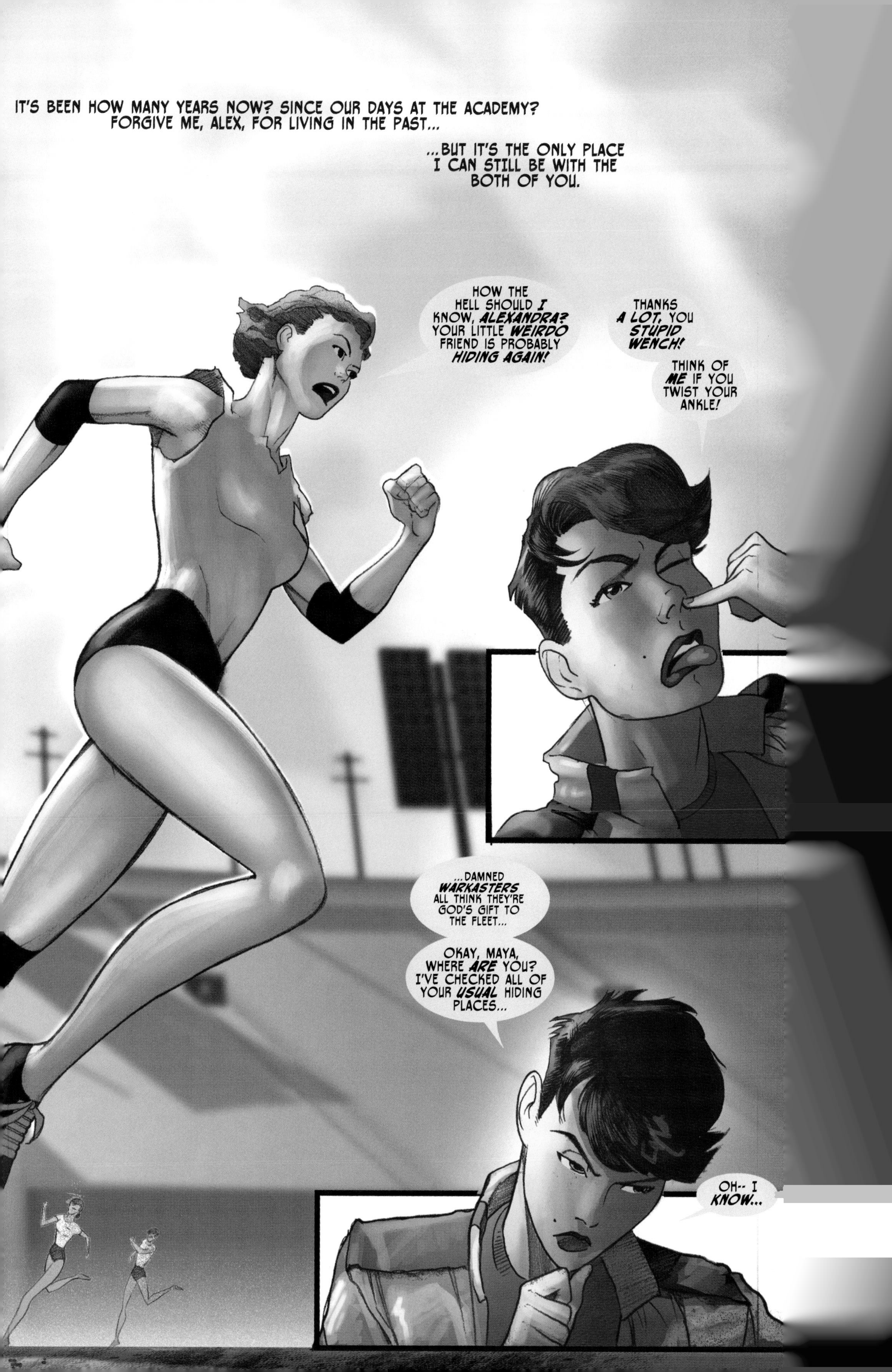
IT'S BEEN HOW MANY YEARS NOW? SINCE OUR DAYS AT THE ACADEMY? FORGIVE ME, ALEX, FOR LIVING IN THE PAST...
...BUT IT'S THE ONLY PLACE I CAN STILL BE WITH THE BOTH OF YOU.
HOW THE HELL SHOULD I KNOW, ALEXANDRA? YOUR LITTLE WEIRDO FRIEND IS PROBABLY HIDING AGAIN!
THANKS A LOT, YOU STUPID WENCH!
THINK OF ME IF YOU TWIST YOUR ANKLE!
...DAMNED WARKASTERS ALL THINK THEY'RE GOD'S GIFT TO THE FLEET...
OKAY, MAYA, WHERE ARE YOU? I'VE CHECKED ALL OF YOUR USUAL HIDING PLACES...
OH-- I KNOW...

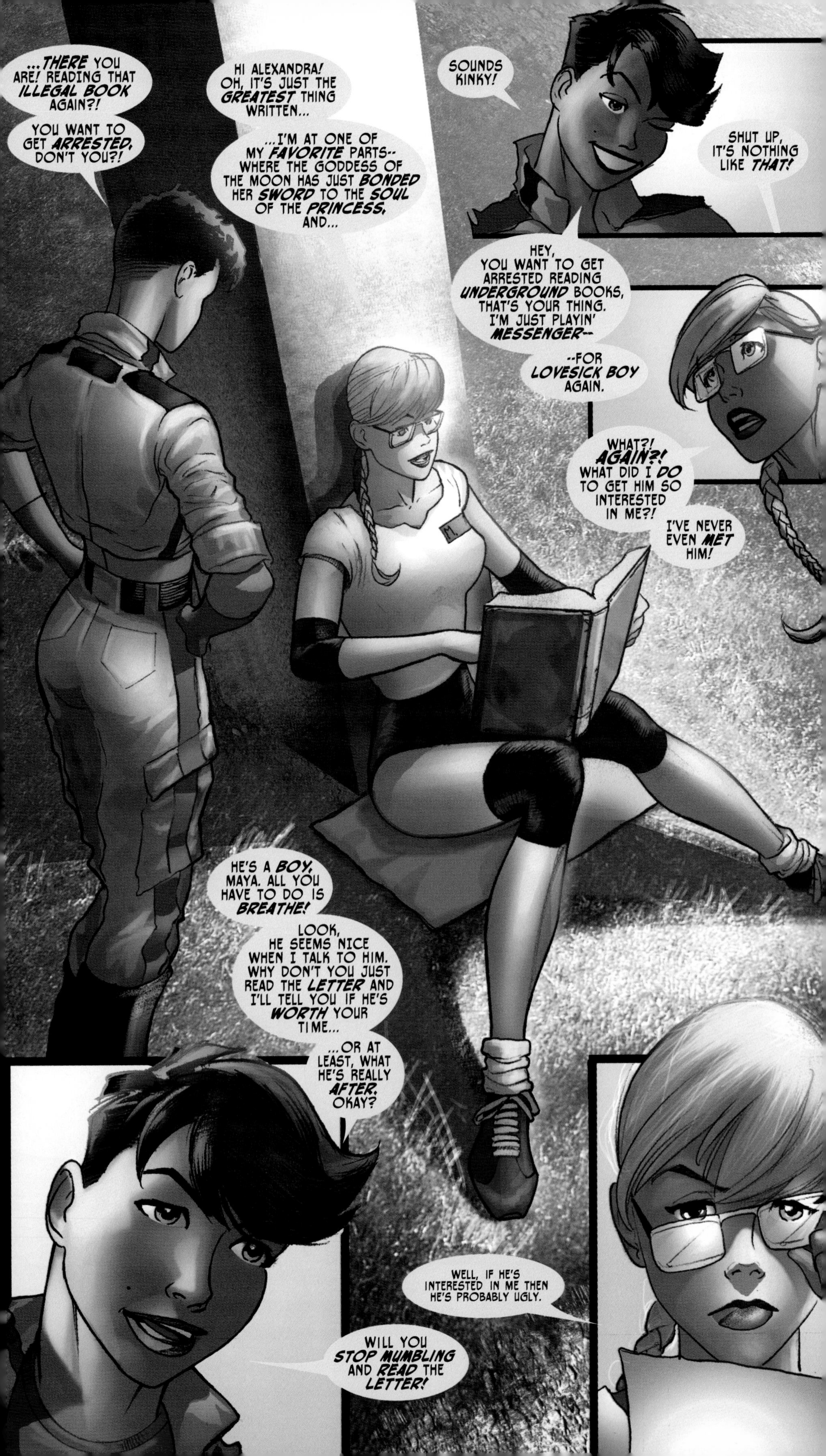
...THERE YOU ARE! READING THAT ILLEGAL BOOK AGAIN?!
YOU WANT TO GET ARRESTED, DON'T YOU?!
HI ALEXANDRA! OH, IT'S JUST THE GREATEST THING WRITTEN...
...I'M AT ONE OF MY FAVORITE PARTS-- WHERE THE GODDESS OF THE MOON HAS JUST BONDED HER SWORD TO THE SOUL OF THE PRINCESS, AND...
SOUNDS KINKY!
SHUT UP, IT'S NOTHING LIKE THAT!
HEY, YOU WANT TO GET ARRESTED READING UNDERGROUND BOOKS, THAT'S YOUR THING. I'M JUST PLAYIN' MESSENGER--
--FOR LOVESICK BOY AGAIN.
WHAT?! AGAIN?! WHAT DID I DO TO GET HIM SO INTERESTED IN ME?!
I'VE NEVER EVEN MET HIM!
HE'S A BOY, MAYA. ALL YOU HAVE TO DO IS BREATHE!
LOOK, HE SEEMS NICE WHEN I TALK TO HIM. WHY DON'T YOU JUST READ THE LETTER AND I'LL TELL YOU IF HE'S WORTH YOUR TIME...
...OR AT LEAST, WHAT HE'S REALLY AFTER. OKAY?
WELL, IF HE'S INTERESTED IN ME THEN HE'S PROBABLY UGLY.
WILL YOU STOP MUMBLING AND READ THE LETTER!

"DEAR MAYA VLASOVA, I AM A SOLDIER, NOT A WRITER, SO PLEASE FORGIVE MY USE OF ANOTHER MAN'S WORDS..."

"...IT WERE NOT MERELY AS IF THE WORLD HAD STOPPED, DIED AND BEEN REBORN ANEW, BUT THAT THERE HAD BEEN NO WORLD AT ALL UNTIL HE FIRST SAW HER..."

...

WHAT DOES IT SAY?! KEEP READING!

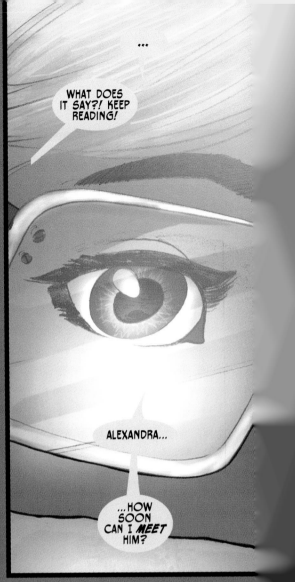

"...I PROMISE IF YOU ALLOW ME THE PRIVILEGE OF MEETING YOU, THAT YOU WILL HEAR THOUGHTS OTHER THAN THOSE YOU HAVE INSPIRED IN ME. UNTIL THEN, HERE IS A PASSAGE FROM MY FAVORITE POET, I HOPE YOU ENJOY IT..."

ALEXANDRA...

...HOW SOON CAN I *MEET* HIM?

OH-HO-HOOO! WHAT IS THIS!? LITTLE "MS. STORYBOOKLAND" IS SUDDENLY "*ACTION GIRL*"! TAKE IT FROM ME, KID-- THE ONES THAT ARE GOOD WITH *WORDS* ARE THE MOST *DEADLY!*

BUT HE'S *READ THIS BOOK!* "CAASTLE JUSTICE"! HE *QUOTES* ONE OF MY *FAVORITE* PASSAGES!

SO? YOU'RE *TWO* CRIMINALS WHO BUY UNDERGROUND BOOKS? *THAT'S* LOVE?

OH, DON'T BE SUCH A HAG, ALEX! JUST BRING ME TO HIM, *WILL* YOU?

HAG!? NOW I'M A *HAG!?* WHO THE HELL *BROUGHT YOU* THIS *LETTER*, WITCH!?

YOUR HEAD'S SO *FAR* IN THE CLOUDS YOU *DIDN'T EVEN ASK ABOUT MY TEST* THIS MORNING!

--!

...I'M *SO SORRY*, ALEX!

HRMPH! WHO'S THE HAG *NOW?!*

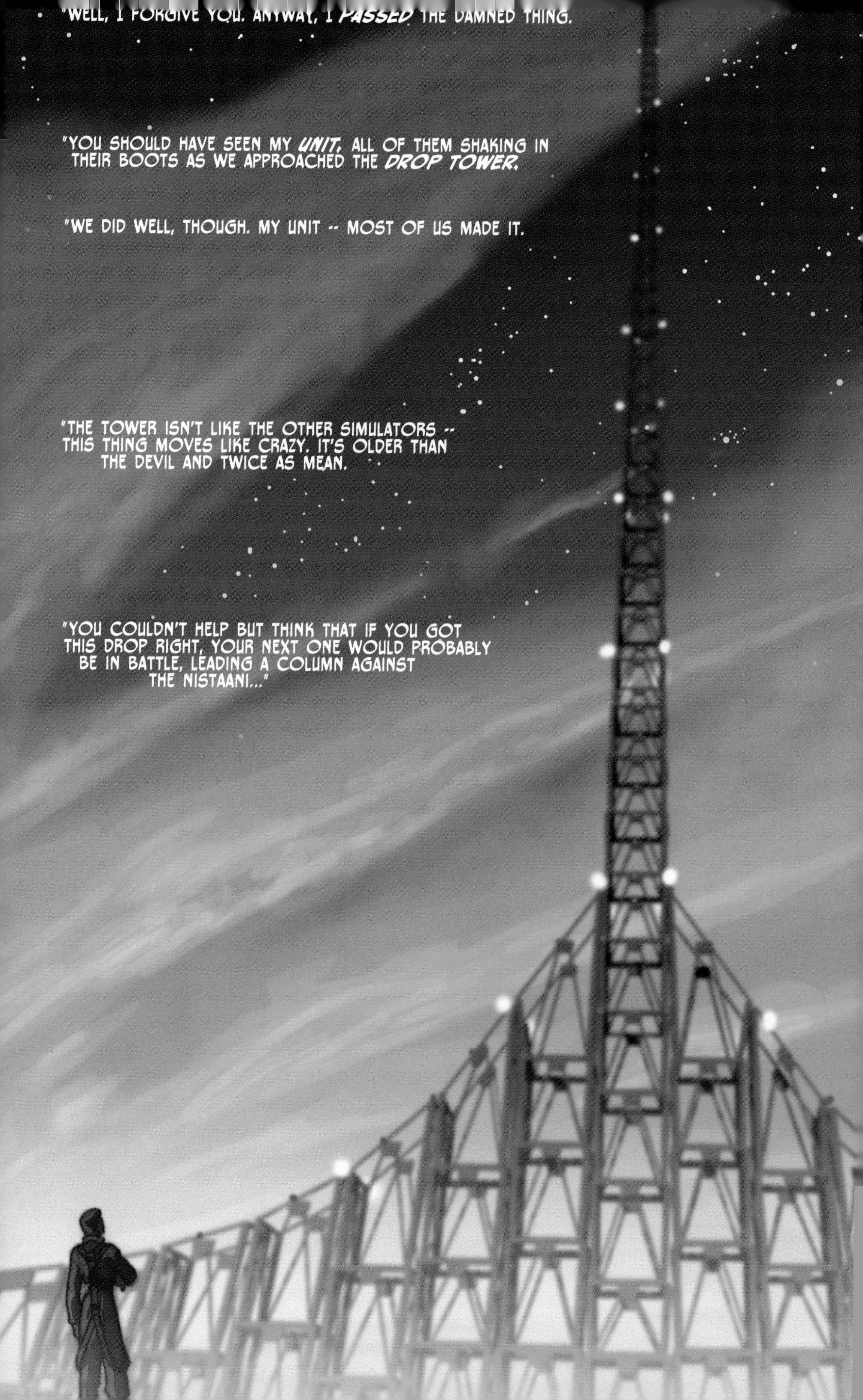
"WELL, I FORGIVE YOU. ANYWAY, I *PASSED* THE DAMNED THING.
"YOU SHOULD HAVE SEEN MY *UNIT,* ALL OF THEM SHAKING IN THEIR BOOTS AS WE APPROACHED THE *DROP TOWER.*
"WE DID WELL, THOUGH. MY UNIT -- MOST OF US MADE IT.
"THE TOWER ISN'T LIKE THE OTHER SIMULATORS -- THIS THING MOVES LIKE CRAZY. IT'S OLDER THAN THE DEVIL AND TWICE AS MEAN.
"YOU COULDN'T HELP BUT THINK THAT IF YOU GOT THIS DROP RIGHT, YOUR NEXT ONE WOULD PROBABLY BE IN BATTLE, LEADING A COLUMN AGAINST THE NISTAANI..."

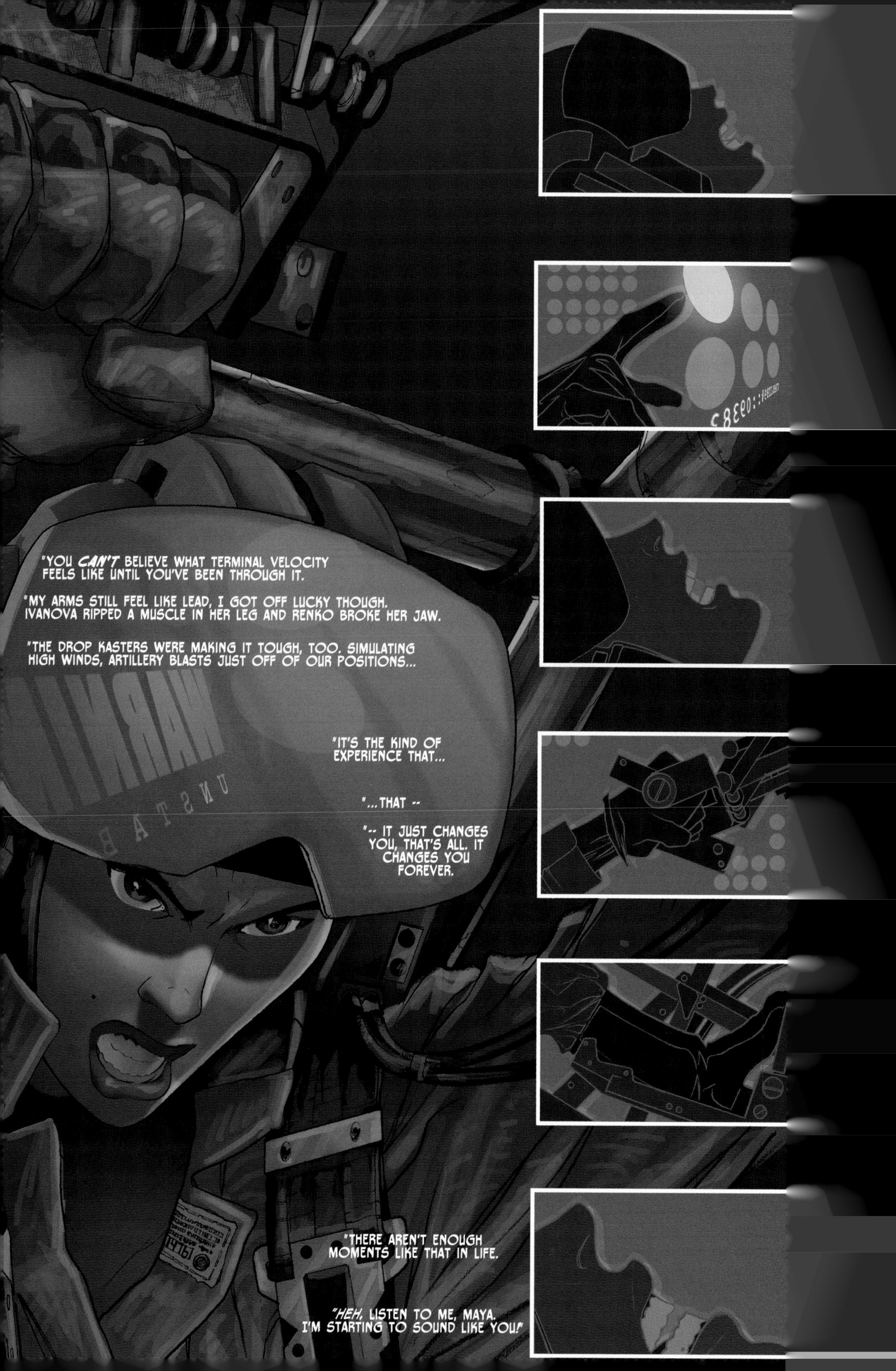
"YOU CAN'T BELIEVE WHAT TERMINAL VELOCITY FEELS LIKE UNTIL YOU'VE BEEN THROUGH IT.
"MY ARMS STILL FEEL LIKE LEAD, I GOT OFF LUCKY THOUGH. IVANOVA RIPPED A MUSCLE IN HER LEG AND RENKO BROKE HER JAW.
"THE DROP KASTERS WERE MAKING IT TOUGH, TOO. SIMULATING HIGH WINDS, ARTILLERY BLASTS JUST OFF OF OUR POSITIONS...
"IT'S THE KIND OF EXPERIENCE THAT...
"...THAT --
"-- IT JUST CHANGES YOU, THAT'S ALL. IT CHANGES YOU FOREVER.
"THERE AREN'T ENOUGH MOMENTS LIKE THAT IN LIFE.
"HEH, LISTEN TO ME, MAYA. I'M STARTING TO SOUND LIKE YOU."

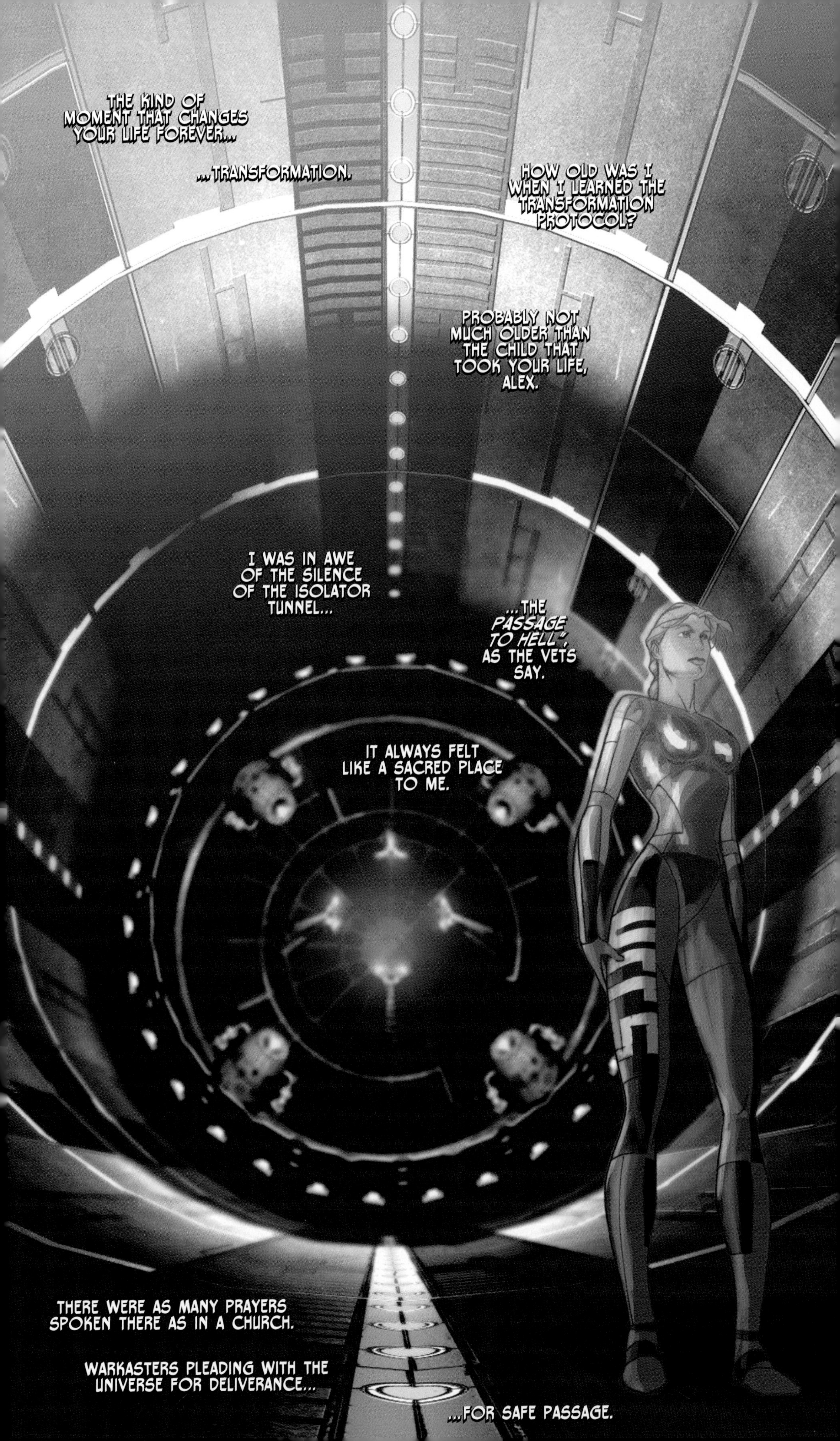
THE KIND OF MOMENT THAT CHANGES YOUR LIFE FOREVER...
...TRANSFORMATION.
HOW OLD WAS I WHEN I LEARNED THE TRANSFORMATION PROTOCOL?
PROBABLY NOT MUCH OLDER THAN THE CHILD THAT TOOK YOUR LIFE, ALEX.
I WAS IN AWE OF THE SILENCE OF THE ISOLATOR TUNNEL...
...THE *PASSAGE TO HELL"*, AS THE VETS SAY.
IT ALWAYS FELT LIKE A SACRED PLACE TO ME.
THERE WERE AS MANY PRAYERS SPOKEN THERE AS IN A CHURCH.
WARKASTERS PLEADING WITH THE UNIVERSE FOR DELIVERANCE...
...FOR SAFE PASSAGE.

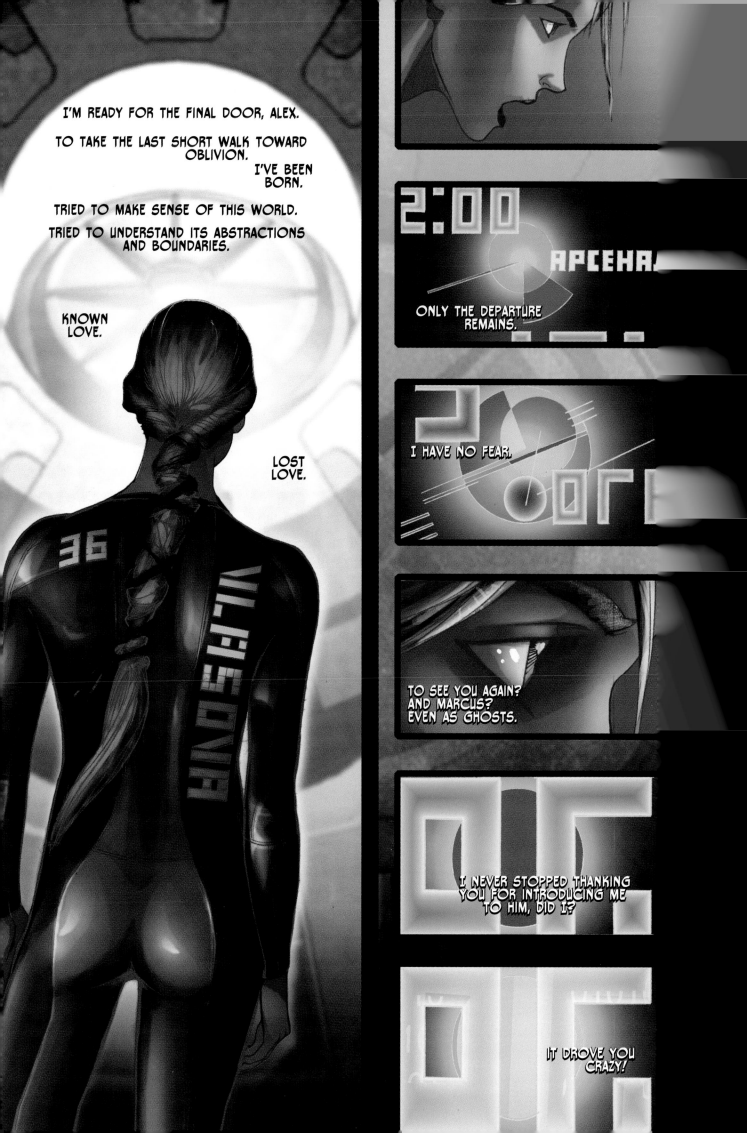

I'M READY FOR THE FINAL DOOR, ALEX.

TO TAKE THE LAST SHORT WALK TOWARD OBLIVION.

I'VE BEEN BORN.

TRIED TO MAKE SENSE OF THIS WORLD.

TRIED TO UNDERSTAND ITS ABSTRACTIONS AND BOUNDARIES.

KNOWN LOVE.

LOST LOVE.

2:00

APCEHA

ONLY THE DEPARTURE REMAINS.

I HAVE NO FEAR.

TO SEE YOU AGAIN? AND MARCUS? EVEN AS GHOSTS.

I NEVER STOPPED THANKING YOU FOR INTRODUCING ME TO HIM, DID I?

IT DROVE YOU CRAZY!

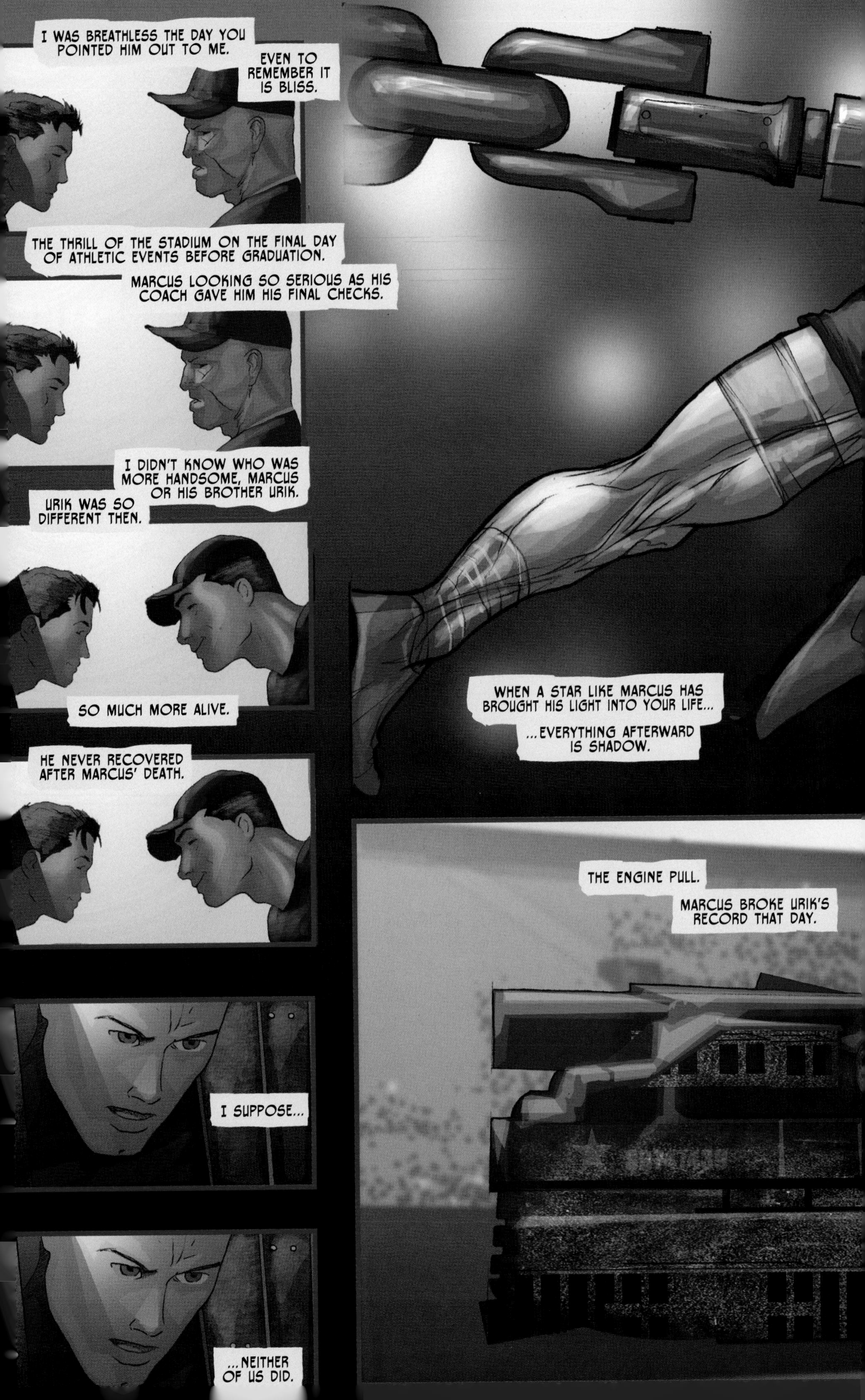
I WAS BREATHLESS THE DAY YOU POINTED HIM OUT TO ME.
EVEN TO REMEMBER IT IS BLISS.
THE THRILL OF THE STADIUM ON THE FINAL DAY OF ATHLETIC EVENTS BEFORE GRADUATION.
MARCUS LOOKING SO SERIOUS AS HIS COACH GAVE HIM HIS FINAL CHECKS.
I DIDN'T KNOW WHO WAS MORE HANDSOME, MARCUS OR HIS BROTHER URIK.
URIK WAS SO DIFFERENT THEN.
SO MUCH MORE ALIVE.
HE NEVER RECOVERED AFTER MARCUS' DEATH.
I SUPPOSE...
...NEITHER OF US DID.
WHEN A STAR LIKE MARCUS HAS BROUGHT HIS LIGHT INTO YOUR LIFE...
...EVERYTHING AFTERWARD IS SHADOW.
THE ENGINE PULL.
MARCUS BROKE URIK'S RECORD THAT DAY.

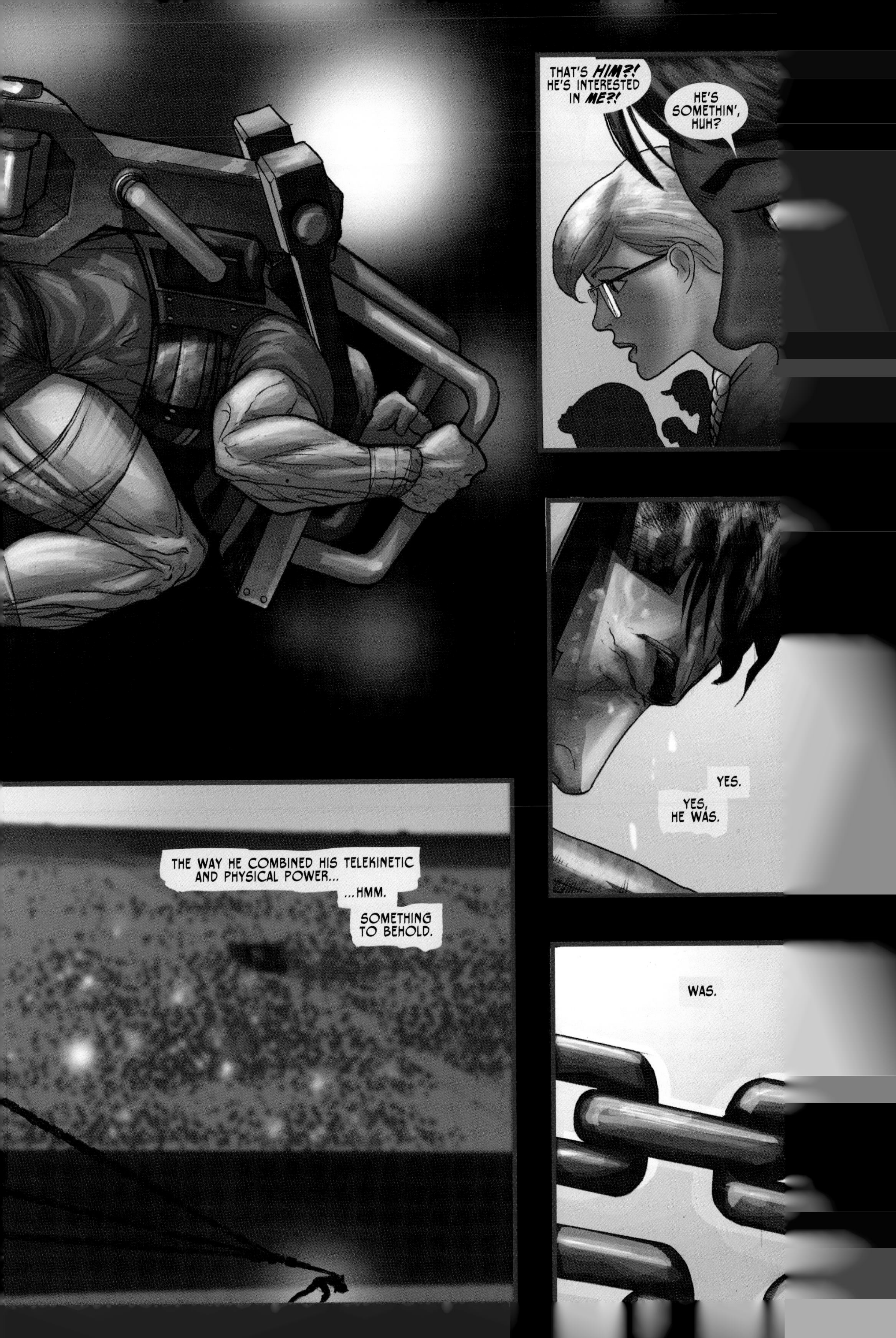
THAT'S HIM?! HE'S INTERESTED IN ME?!
HE'S SOMETHIN', HUH?
YES.
YES, HE WAS.
THE WAY HE COMBINED HIS TELEKINETIC AND PHYSICAL POWER...
...HMM.
SOMETHING TO BEHOLD.
WAS.

NATIONS...

WAS.

...DON'T FIGHT AGAINST NATIONS.

NO MORE.

THEY FEED ON OUR LIVES, DRINK OUR OBEDIENT BLOOD.

LET HIM GO, MAYA...

PLEASE LET HIM GO...

THEY LIVE AND WE PERISH.

WHO WERE THESE LOVERS THAT HELD EACH OTHER UNTIL THE BITTER END?

WHOSE FINAL MOMENT TOGETHER WAS SPENT IN THE BLAZING HORROR OF THEIR LOVED ONE'S DYING SCREAMS?

THE HEAT FROM A SKYFURNACE RAINED DOWN...

...TOOK THEM FROM EACH OTHER.

FOREVER.

I CAN'T LET HIM GO.

I'LL NEVER LET HIM GO.

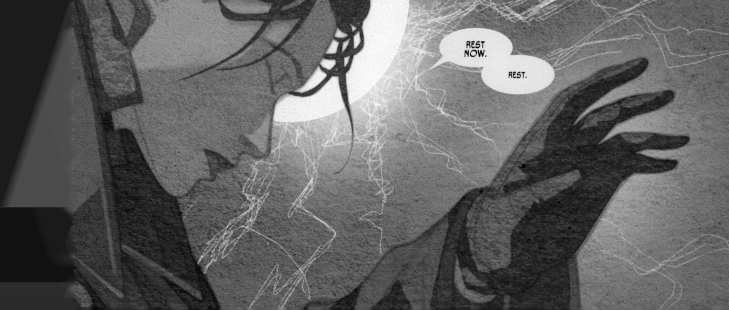

REST NOW.

REST.

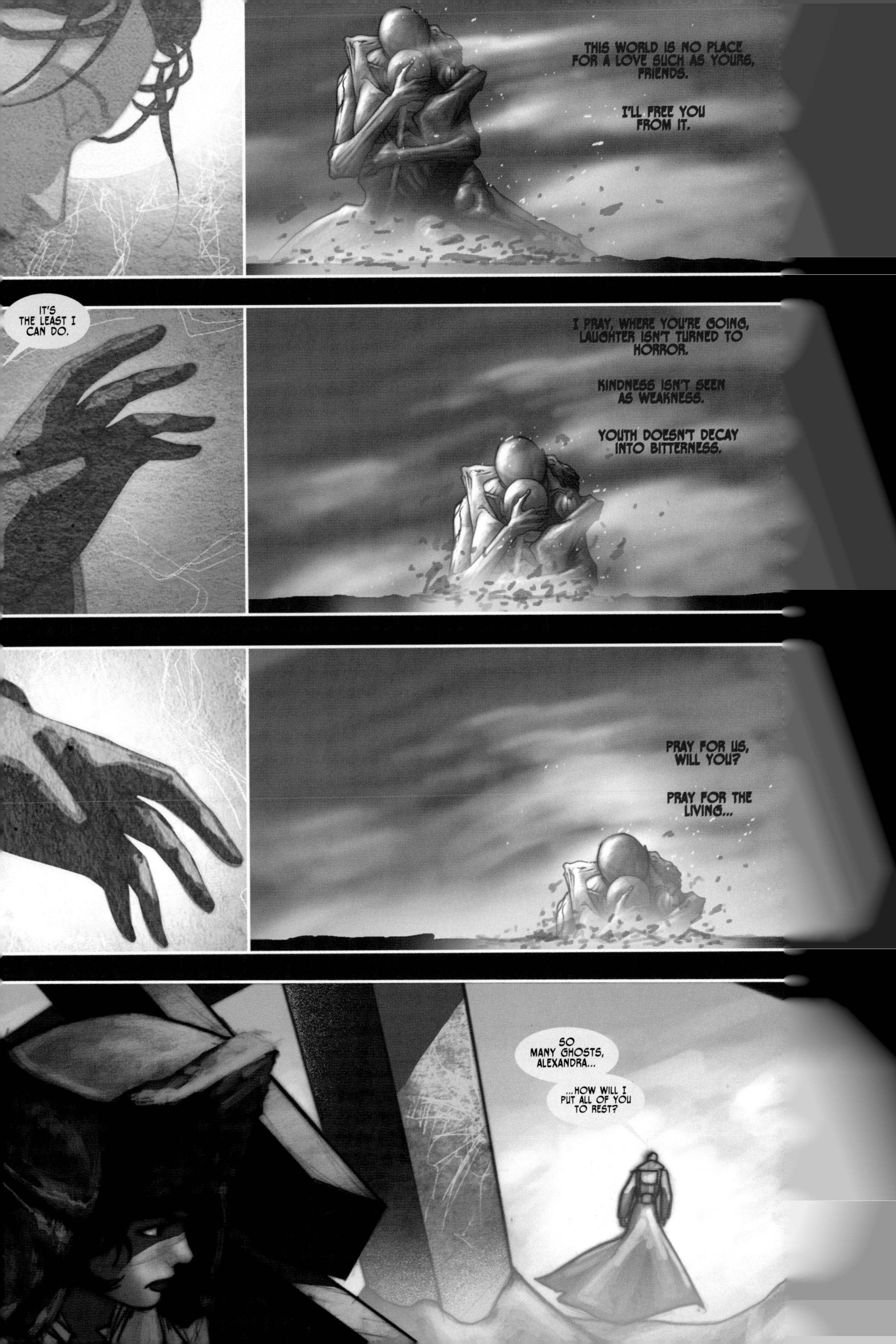
THIS WORLD IS NO PLACE FOR A LOVE SUCH AS YOURS, FRIENDS.
I'LL FREE YOU FROM IT.
IT'S THE LEAST I CAN DO.
I PRAY, WHERE YOU'RE GOING, LAUGHTER ISN'T TURNED TO HORROR.
KINDNESS ISN'T SEEN AS WEAKNESS.
YOUTH DOESN'T DECAY INTO BITTERNESS.
PRAY FOR US, WILL YOU?
PRAY FOR THE LIVING...
SO MANY GHOSTS, ALEXANDRA...
...HOW WILL I PUT ALL OF YOU TO REST?

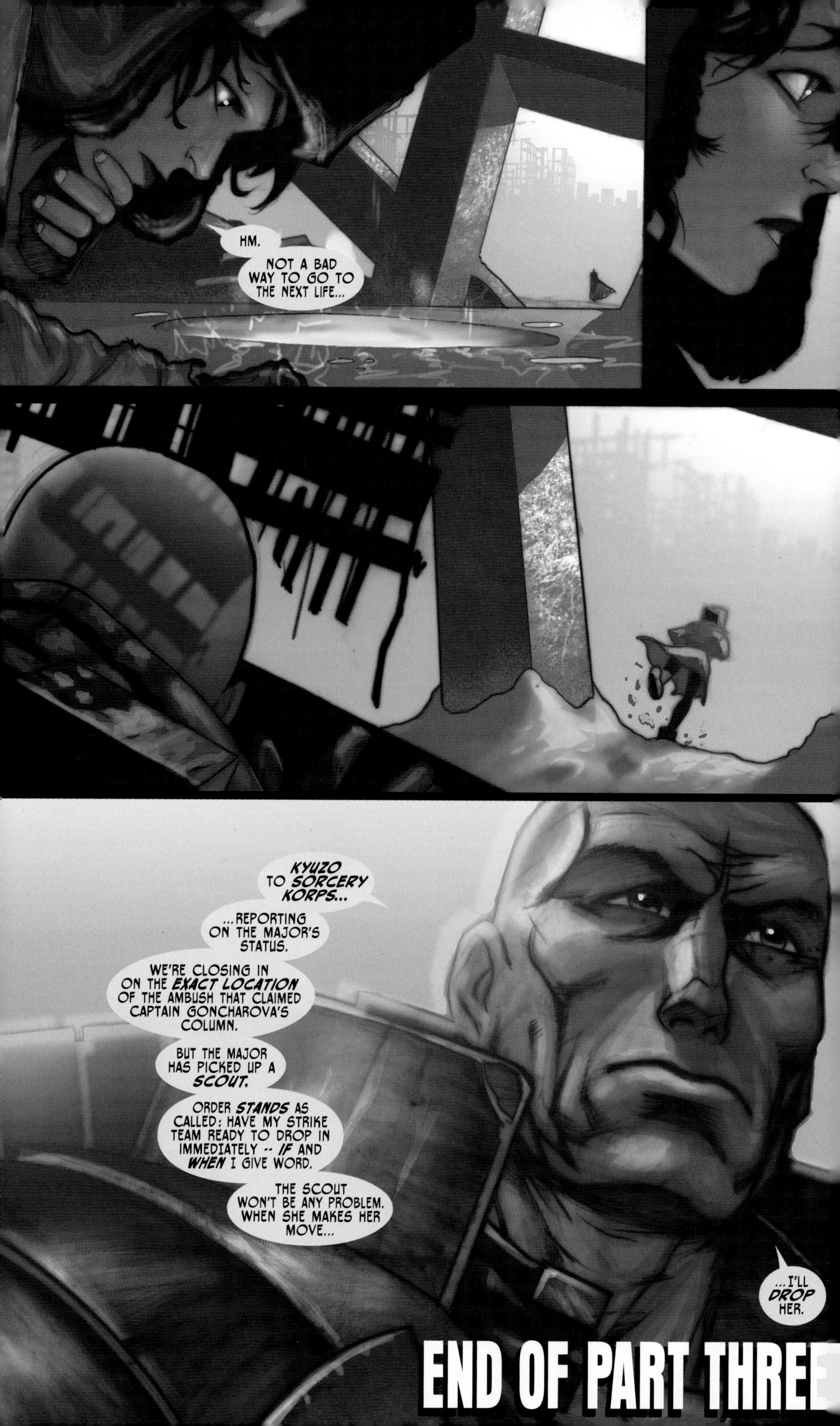
HM.
NOT A BAD WAY TO GO TO THE NEXT LIFE...
KYUZO TO SORCERY KORPS...
...REPORTING ON THE MAJOR'S STATUS.
WE'RE CLOSING IN ON THE EXACT LOCATION OF THE AMBUSH THAT CLAIMED CAPTAIN GONCHAROVA'S COLUMN.
BUT THE MAJOR HAS PICKED UP A SCOUT.
ORDER STANDS AS CALLED: HAVE MY STRIKE TEAM READY TO DROP IN IMMEDIATELY -- IF AND WHEN I GIVE WORD.
THE SCOUT WON'T BE ANY PROBLEM. WHEN SHE MAKES HER MOVE...
...I'LL DROP HER.
END OF PART THREE

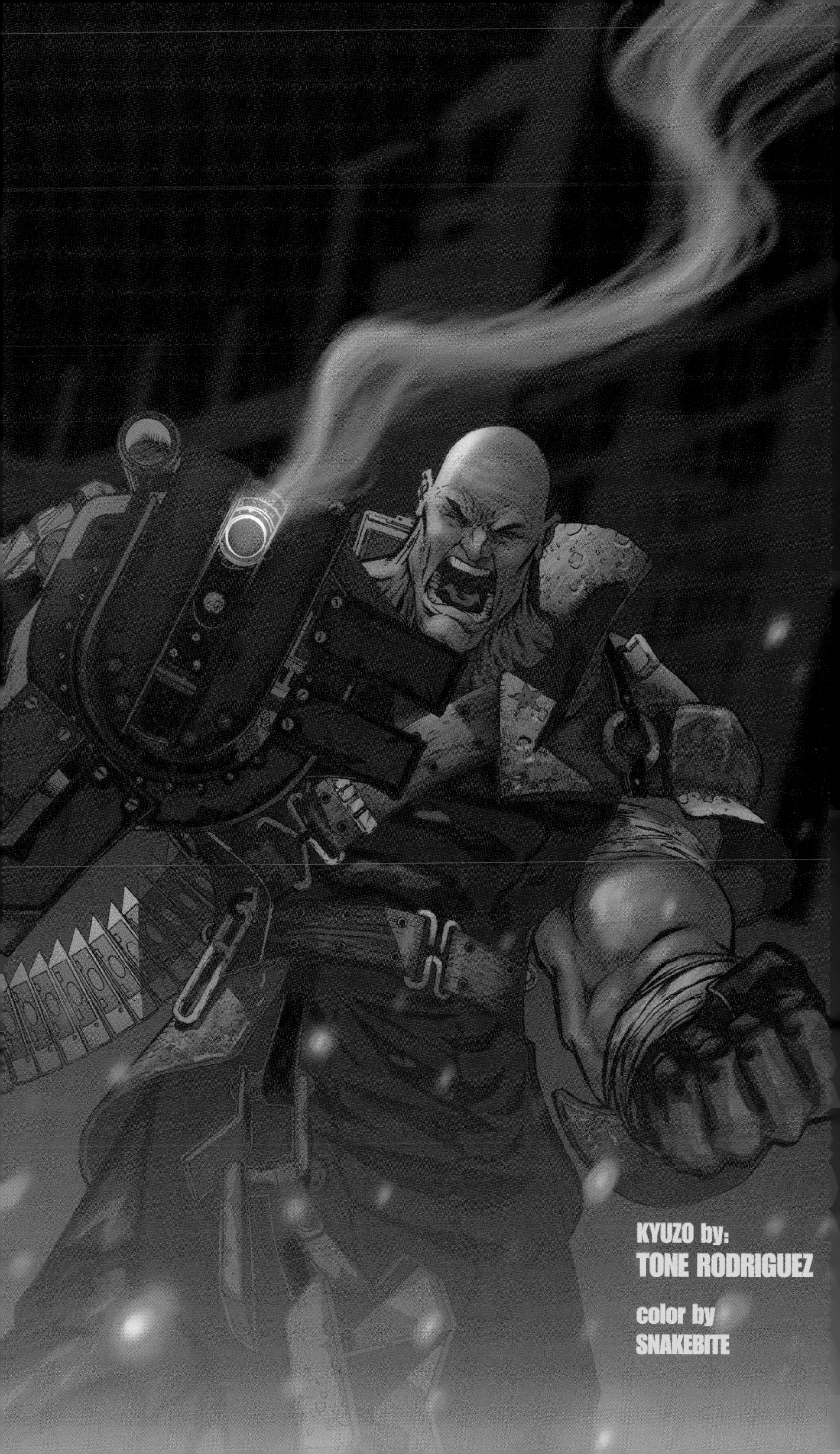

KYUZO by:
TONE RODRIGUEZ

color by
SNAKEBITE

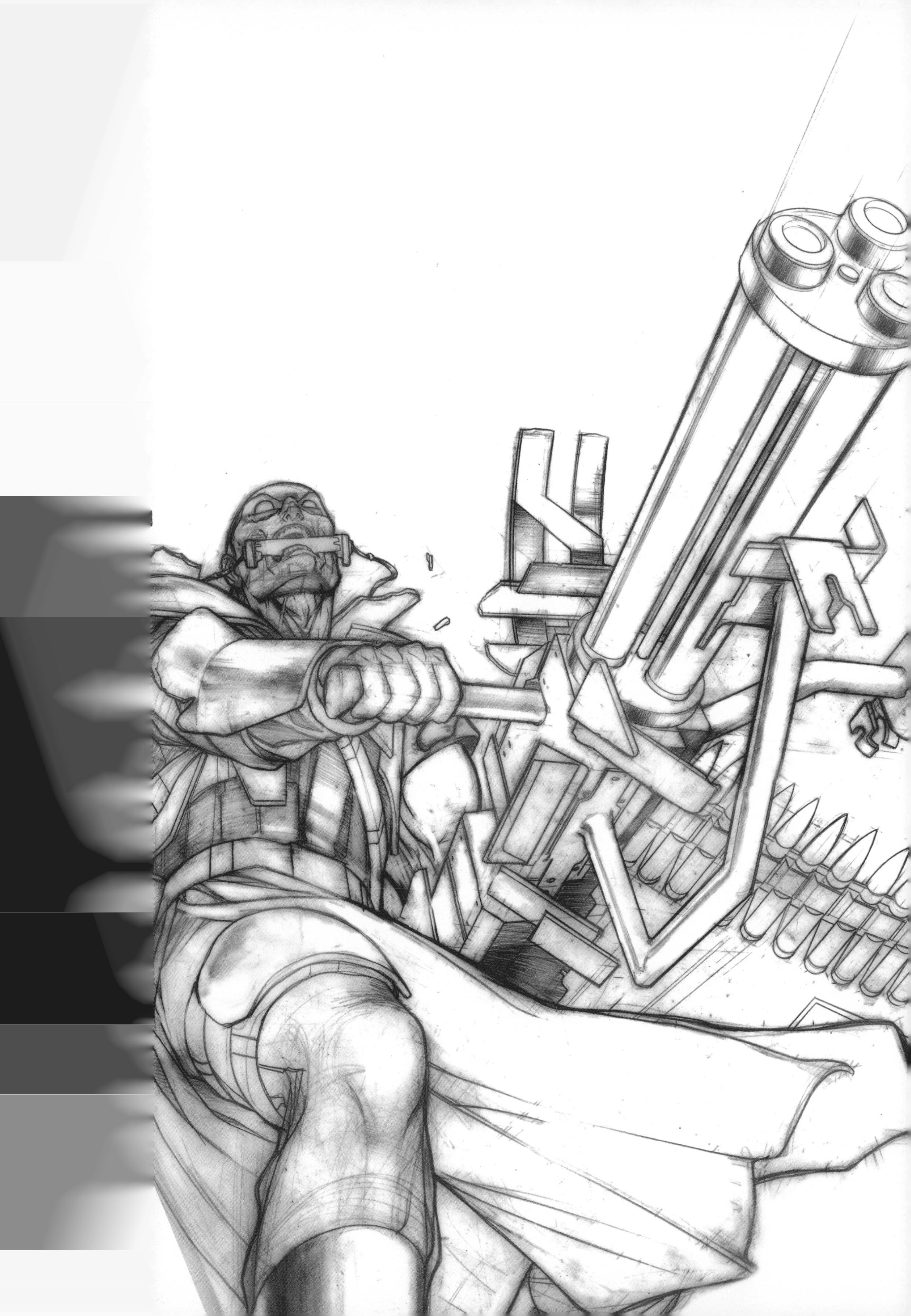

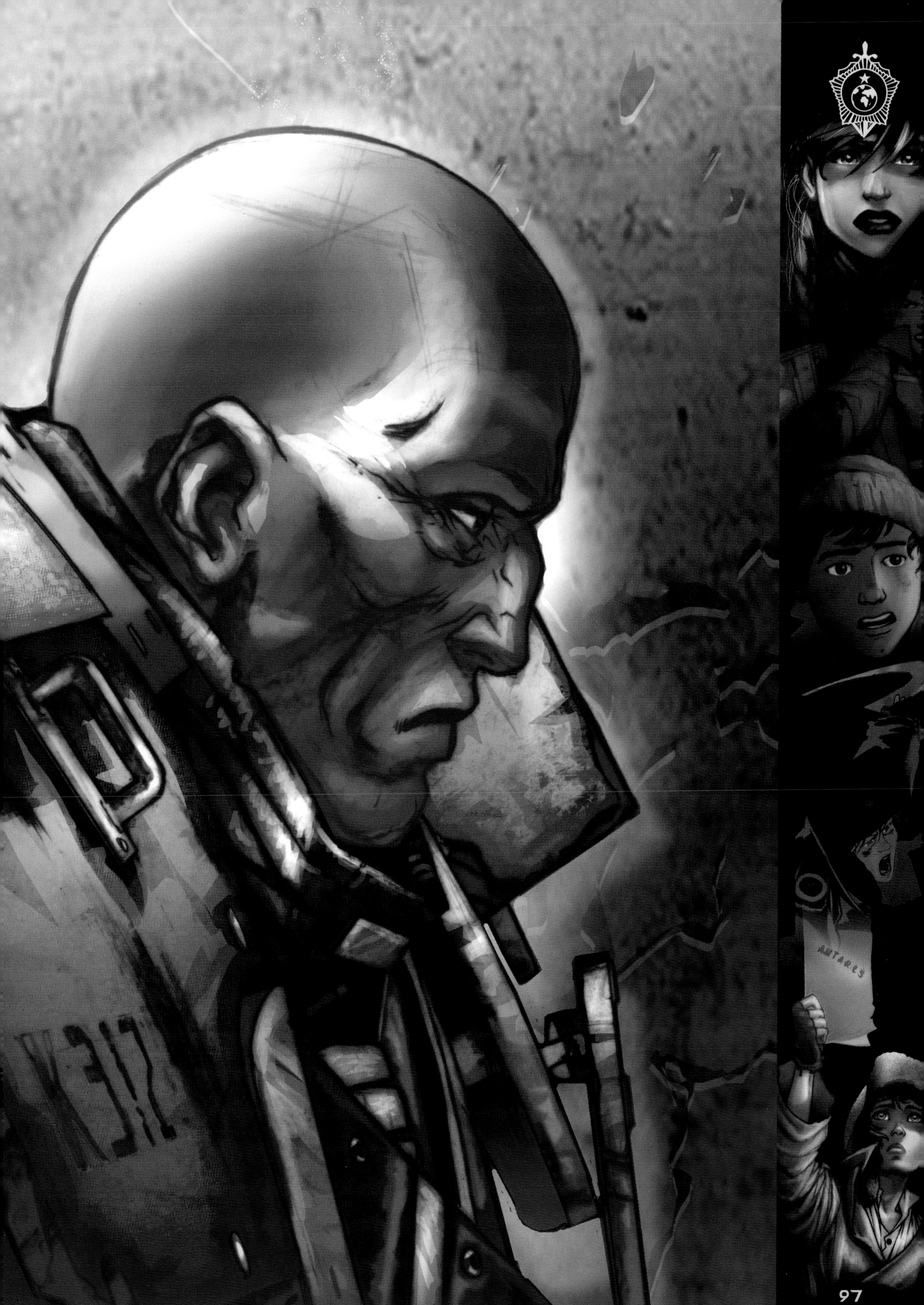
ANTARES

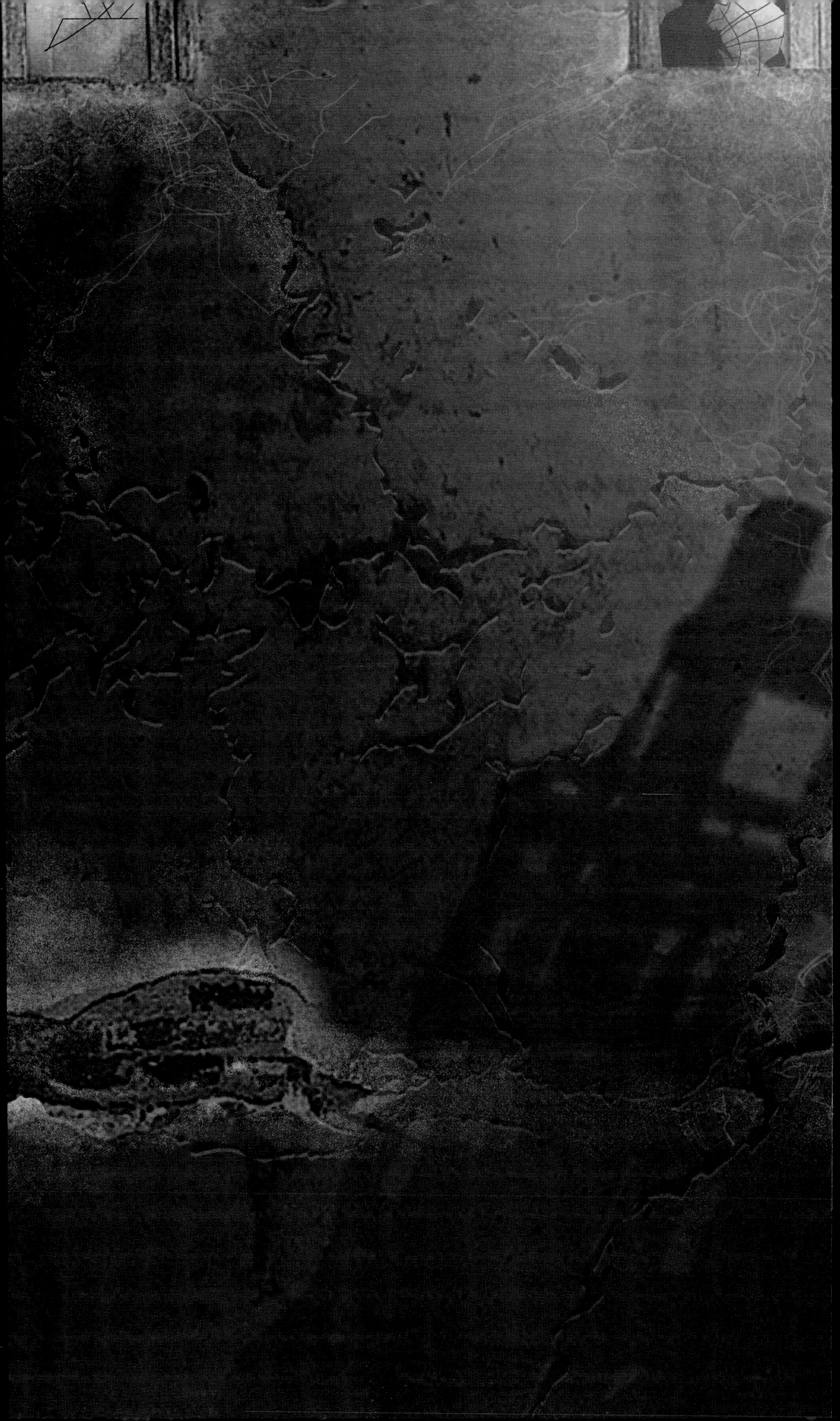

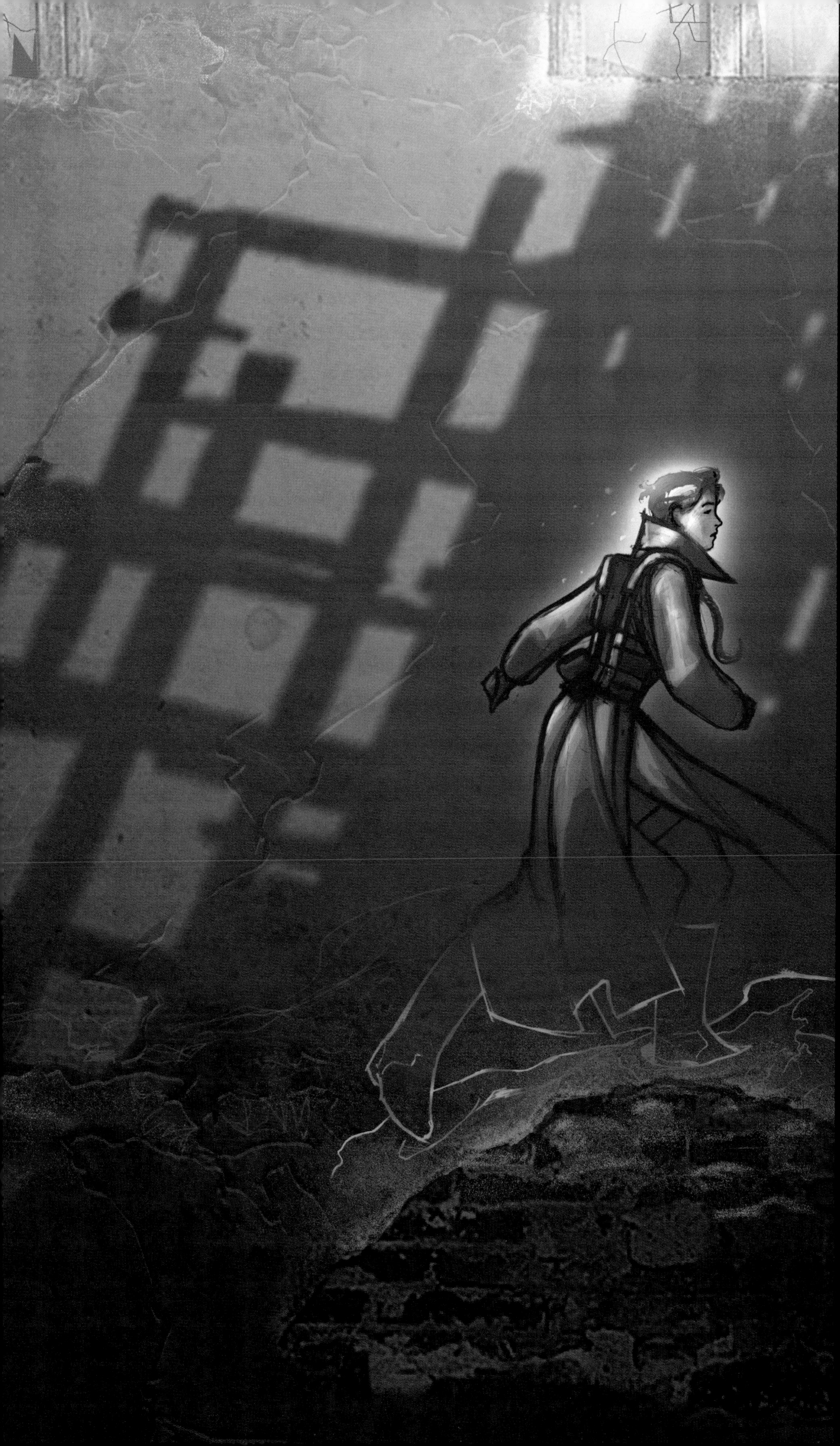

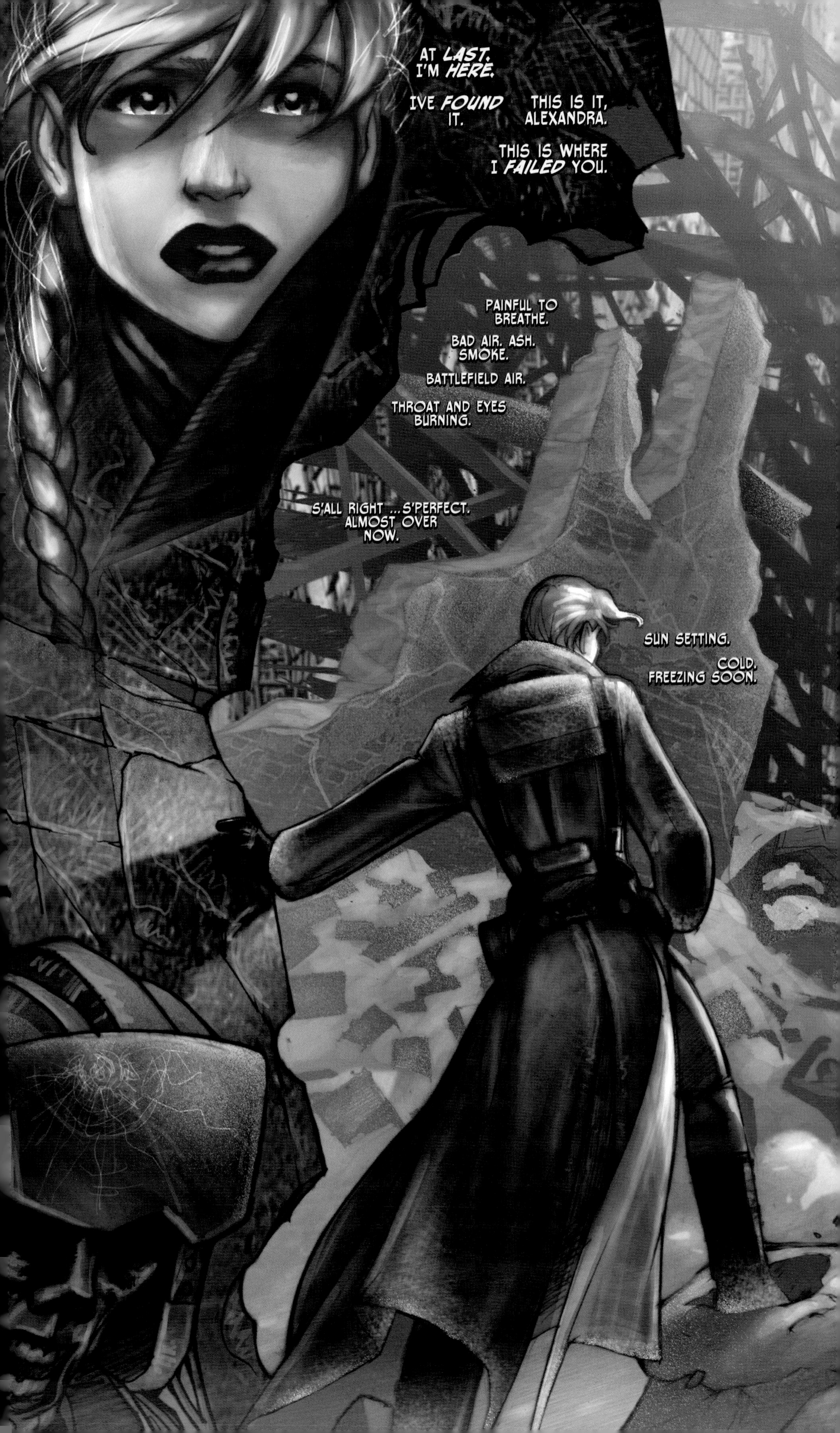
AT LAST. I'M HERE.
IVE FOUND IT.
THIS IS IT, ALEXANDRA.
THIS IS WHERE I FAILED YOU.
PAINFUL TO BREATHE.
BAD AIR. ASH. SMOKE.
BATTLEFIELD AIR.
THROAT AND EYES BURNING.
S'ALL RIGHT ...S'PERFECT. ALMOST OVER NOW.
SUN SETTING.
COLD. FREEZING SOON.

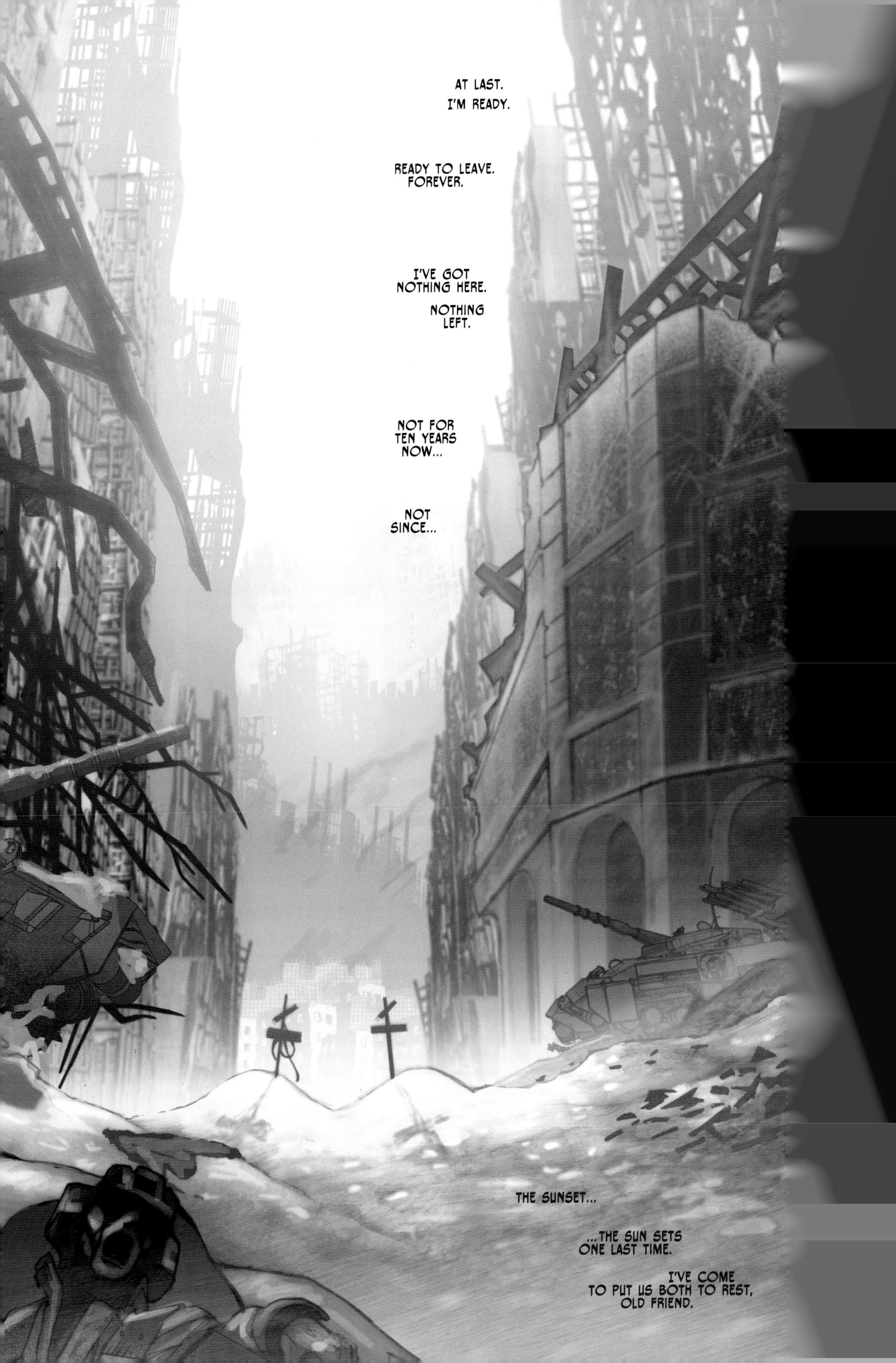
AT LAST.
I'M READY.
READY TO LEAVE.
FOREVER.
I'VE GOT
NOTHING HERE.
NOTHING
LEFT.
NOT FOR
TEN YEARS
NOW...
NOT
SINCE...
THE SUNSET...
...THE SUN SETS
ONE LAST TIME.
I'VE COME
TO PUT US BOTH TO REST,
OLD FRIEND.

THE RE

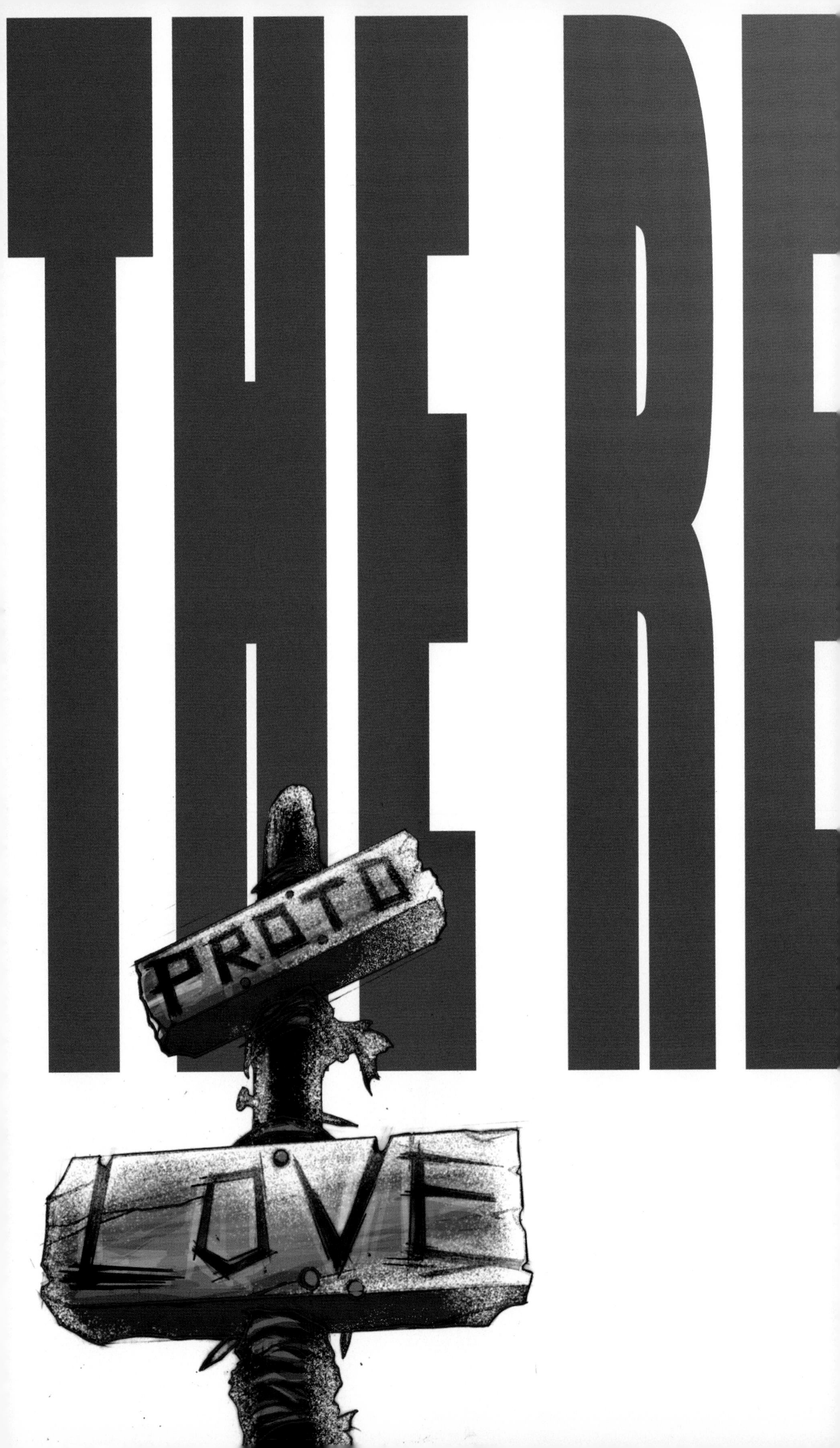
PROTO
LOVE

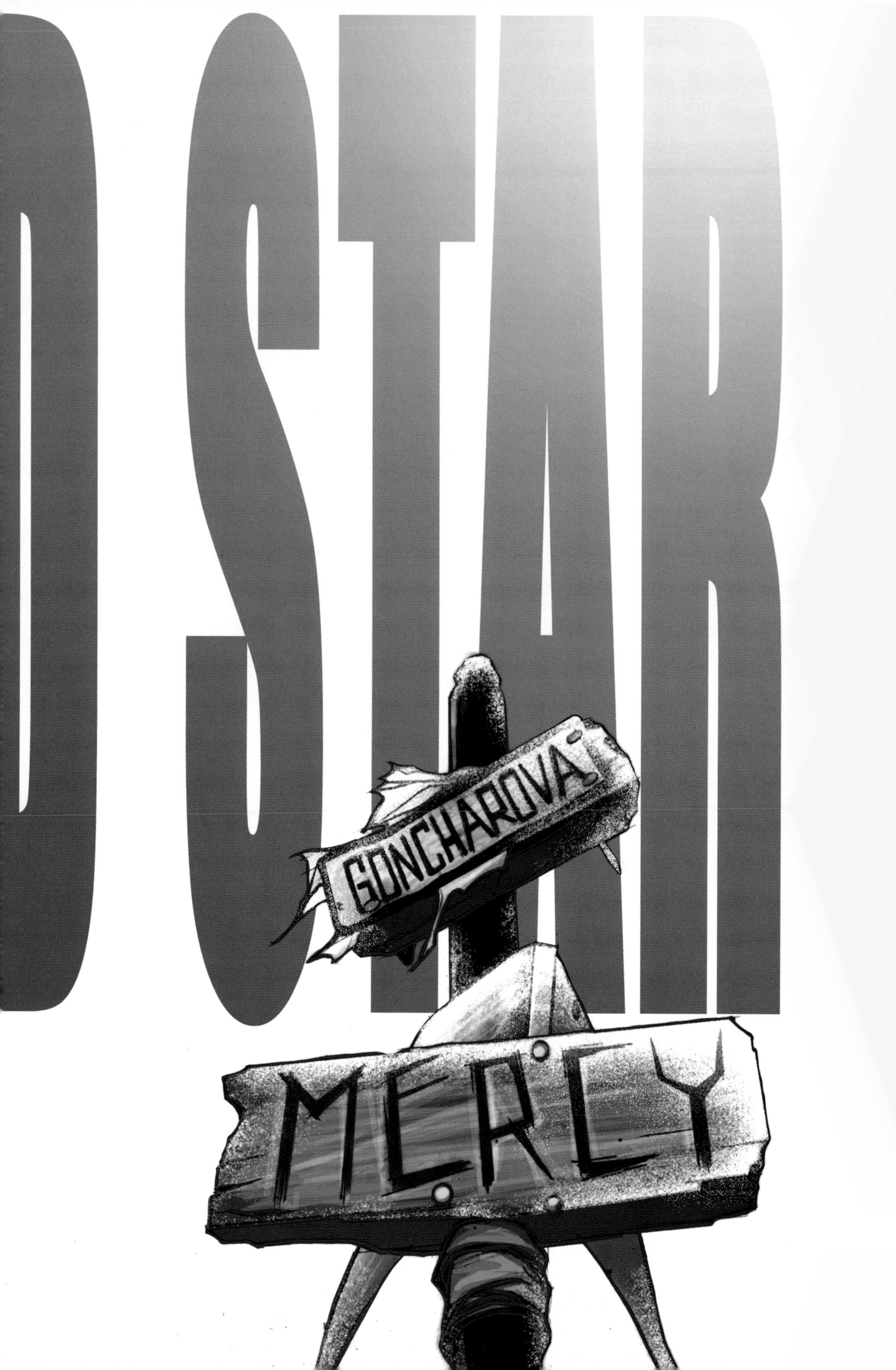
D STAR
GONCHAROVA
MERCY

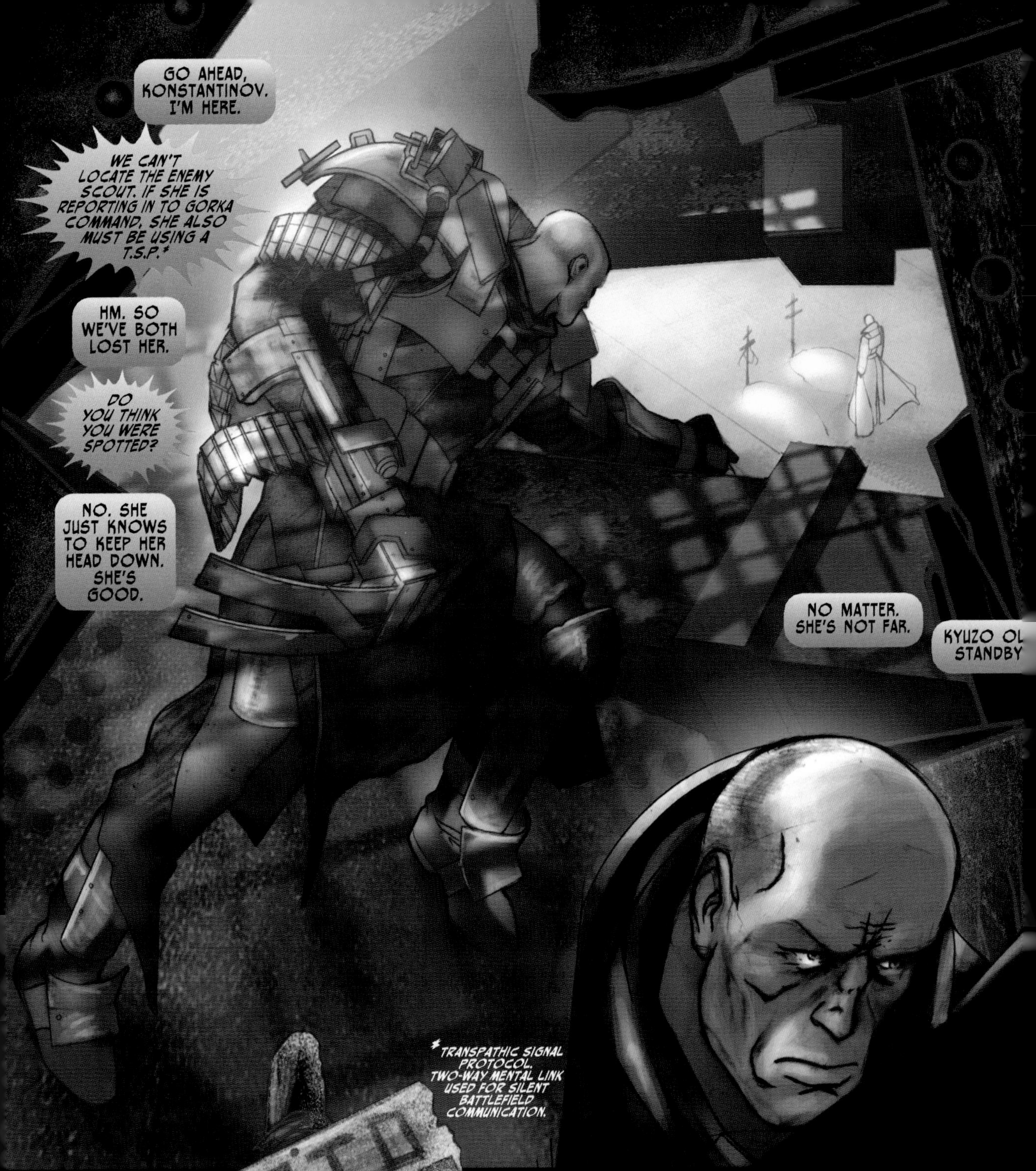
GO AHEAD, KONSTANTINOV. I'M HERE.
WE CAN'T LOCATE THE ENEMY SCOUT. IF SHE IS REPORTING IN TO GORKA COMMAND, SHE ALSO MUST BE USING A T.S.P.*
HM. SO WE'VE BOTH LOST HER.
DO YOU THINK YOU WERE SPOTTED?
NO. SHE JUST KNOWS TO KEEP HER HEAD DOWN. SHE'S GOOD.
NO MATTER. SHE'S NOT FAR.
KYUZO OL STANDBY
* TRANSPATHIC SIGNAL PROTOCOL. TWO-WAY MENTAL LINK USED FOR SILENT BATTLEFIELD COMMUNICATION.

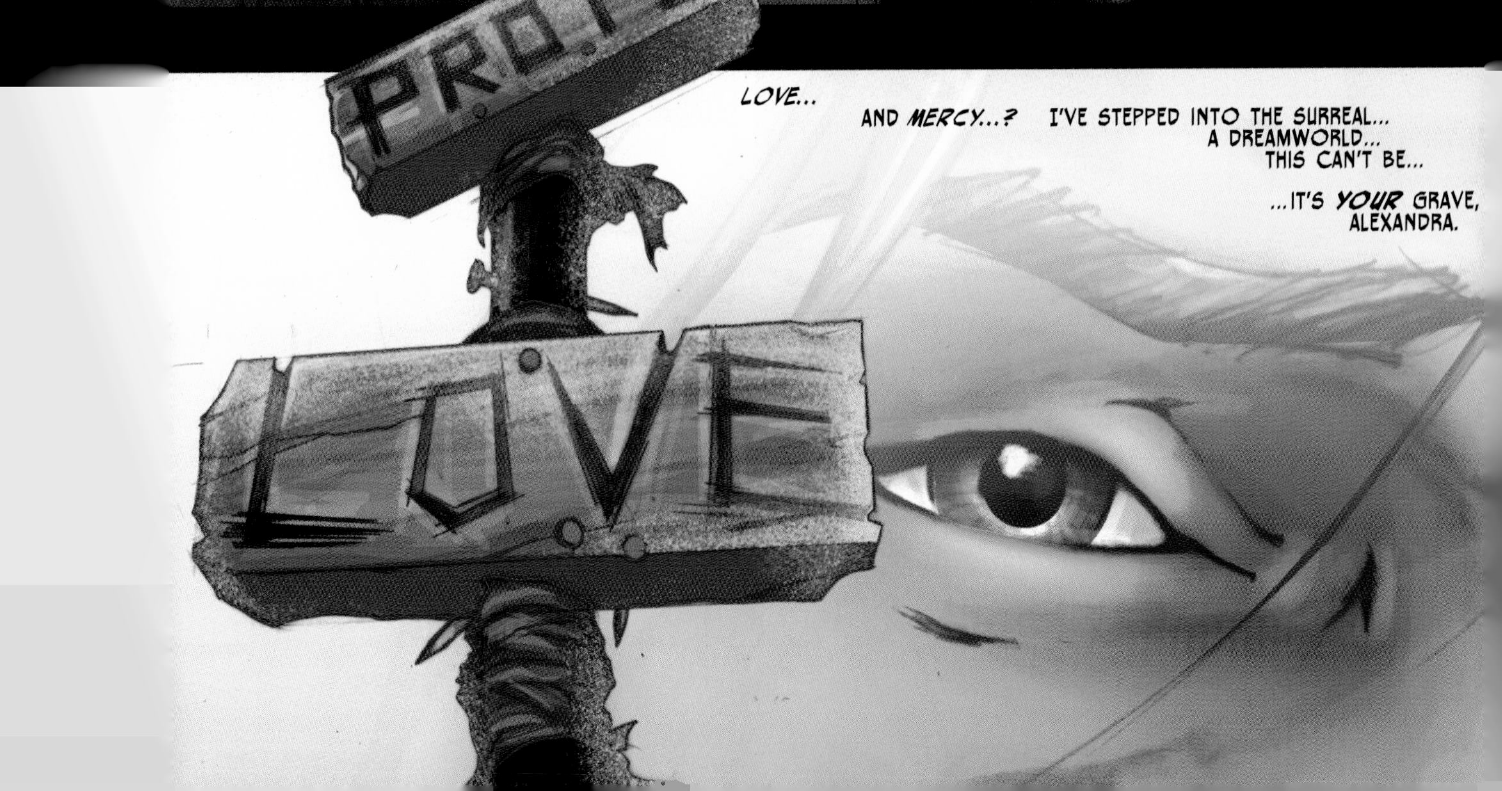
PROTO
LOVE
LOVE...
AND MERCY...?
I'VE STEPPED INTO THE SURREAL... A DREAMWORLD... THIS CAN'T BE...
...IT'S YOUR GRAVE, ALEXANDRA.

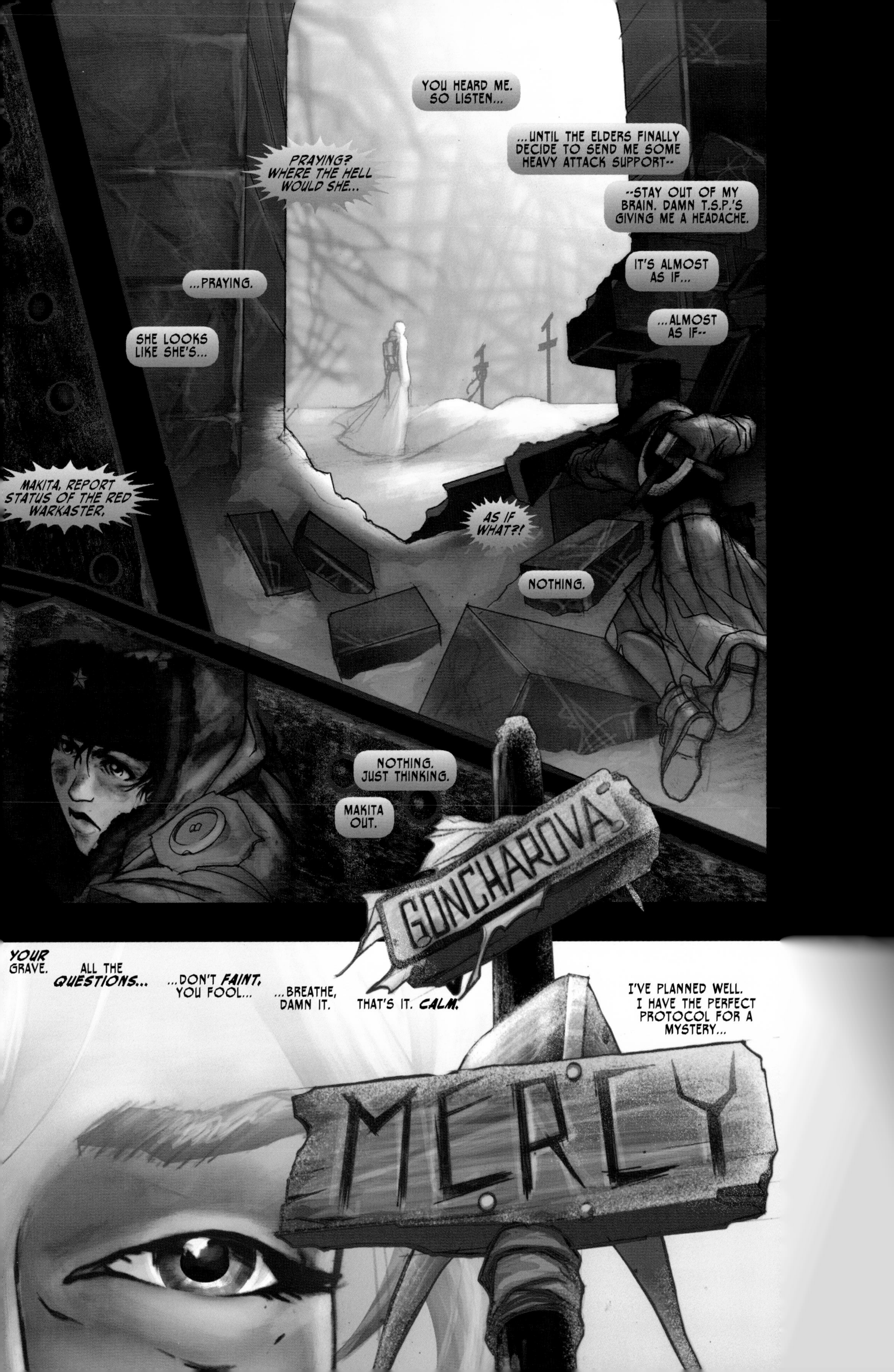
YOU HEARD ME. SO LISTEN...
...UNTIL THE ELDERS FINALLY DECIDE TO SEND ME SOME HEAVY ATTACK SUPPORT--
--STAY OUT OF MY BRAIN. DAMN T.S.P.'S GIVING ME A HEADACHE.
IT'S ALMOST AS IF...
...ALMOST AS IF--
PRAYING? WHERE THE HELL WOULD SHE...
...PRAYING.
SHE LOOKS LIKE SHE'S...
MAKITA, REPORT STATUS OF THE RED WARKASTER.
AS IF WHAT?!
NOTHING.
NOTHING. JUST THINKING.
MAKITA OUT.
GONCHAROVA
YOUR GRAVE.
ALL THE QUESTIONS...
...DON'T FAINT, YOU FOOL...
...BREATHE, DAMN IT.
THAT'S IT. CALM.
I'VE PLANNED WELL. I HAVE THE PERFECT PROTOCOL FOR A MYSTERY...
MERCY

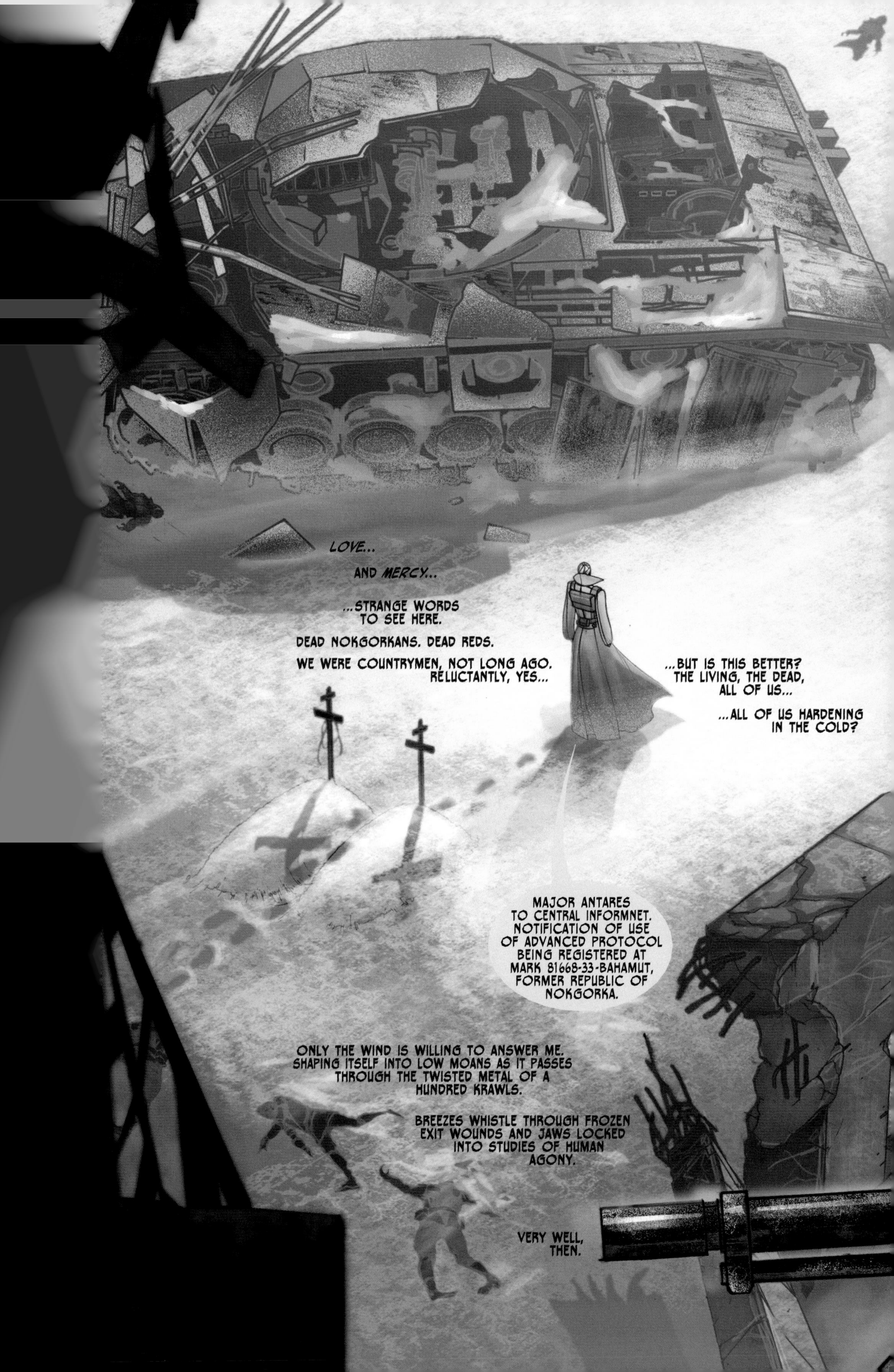
LOVE...
AND MERCY...
...STRANGE WORDS TO SEE HERE.
DEAD NOKGORKANS. DEAD REDS.
WE WERE COUNTRYMEN, NOT LONG AGO. RELUCTANTLY, YES...
...BUT IS THIS BETTER? THE LIVING, THE DEAD, ALL OF US...
...ALL OF US HARDENING IN THE COLD?
MAJOR ANTARES TO CENTRAL INFORMNET. NOTIFICATION OF USE OF ADVANCED PROTOCOL BEING REGISTERED AT MARK 81668-33-BAHAMUT, FORMER REPUBLIC OF NOKGORKA.
ONLY THE WIND IS WILLING TO ANSWER ME. SHAPING ITSELF INTO LOW MOANS AS IT PASSES THROUGH THE TWISTED METAL OF A HUNDRED KRAWLS.
BREEZES WHISTLE THROUGH FROZEN EXIT WOUNDS AND JAWS LOCKED INTO STUDIES OF HUMAN AGONY.
VERY WELL, THEN.

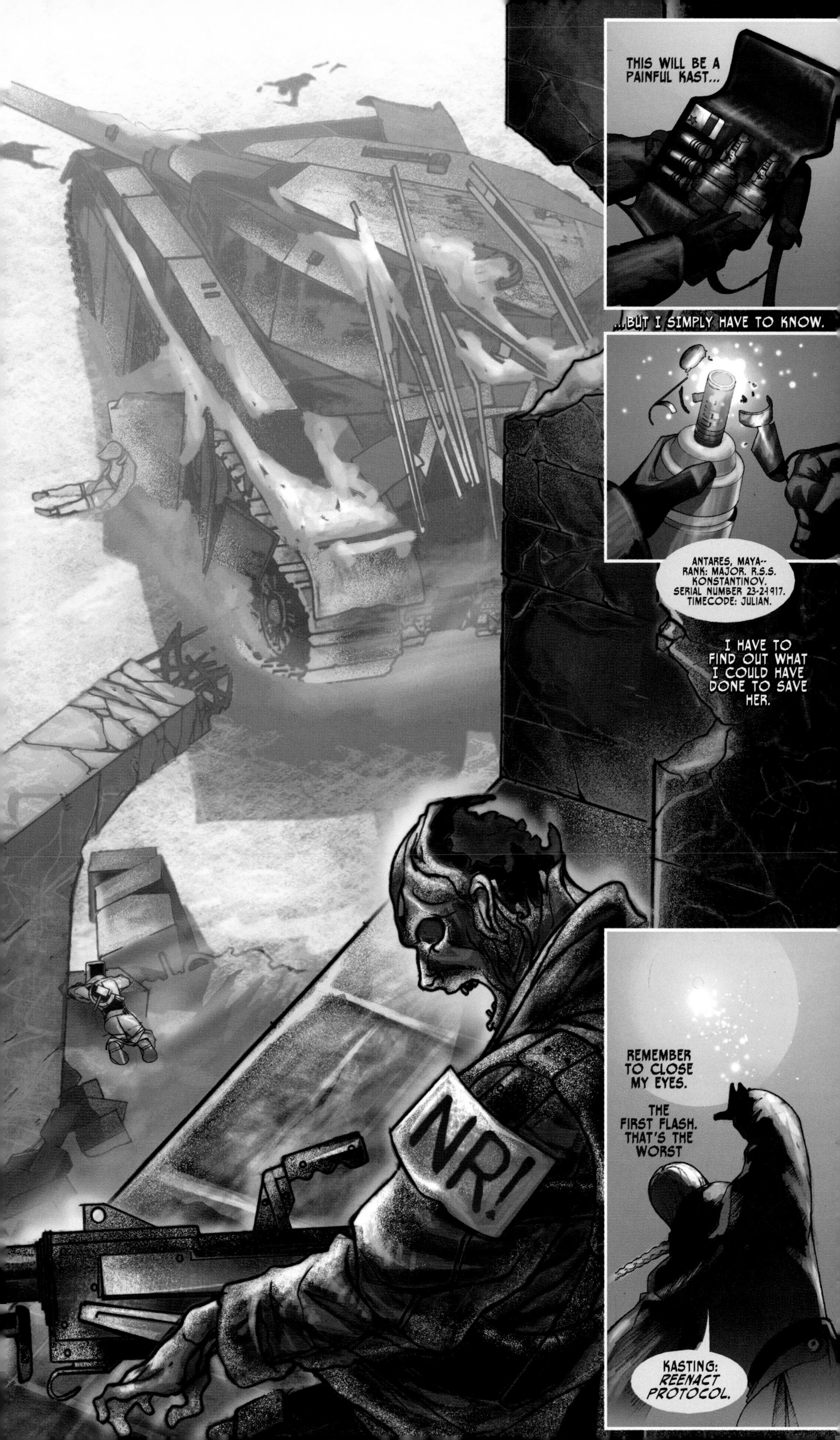
THIS WILL BE A PAINFUL KAST...
...BUT I SIMPLY HAVE TO KNOW.
ANTARES, MAYA-- RANK: MAJOR. R.S.S. KONSTANTINOV. SERIAL NUMBER 23-21917. TIMECODE: JULIAN.
I HAVE TO FIND OUT WHAT I COULD HAVE DONE TO SAVE HER.
NR!
REMEMBER TO CLOSE MY EYES.
THE FIRST FLASH. THAT'S THE WORST
KASTING: REENACT PROTOCOL.

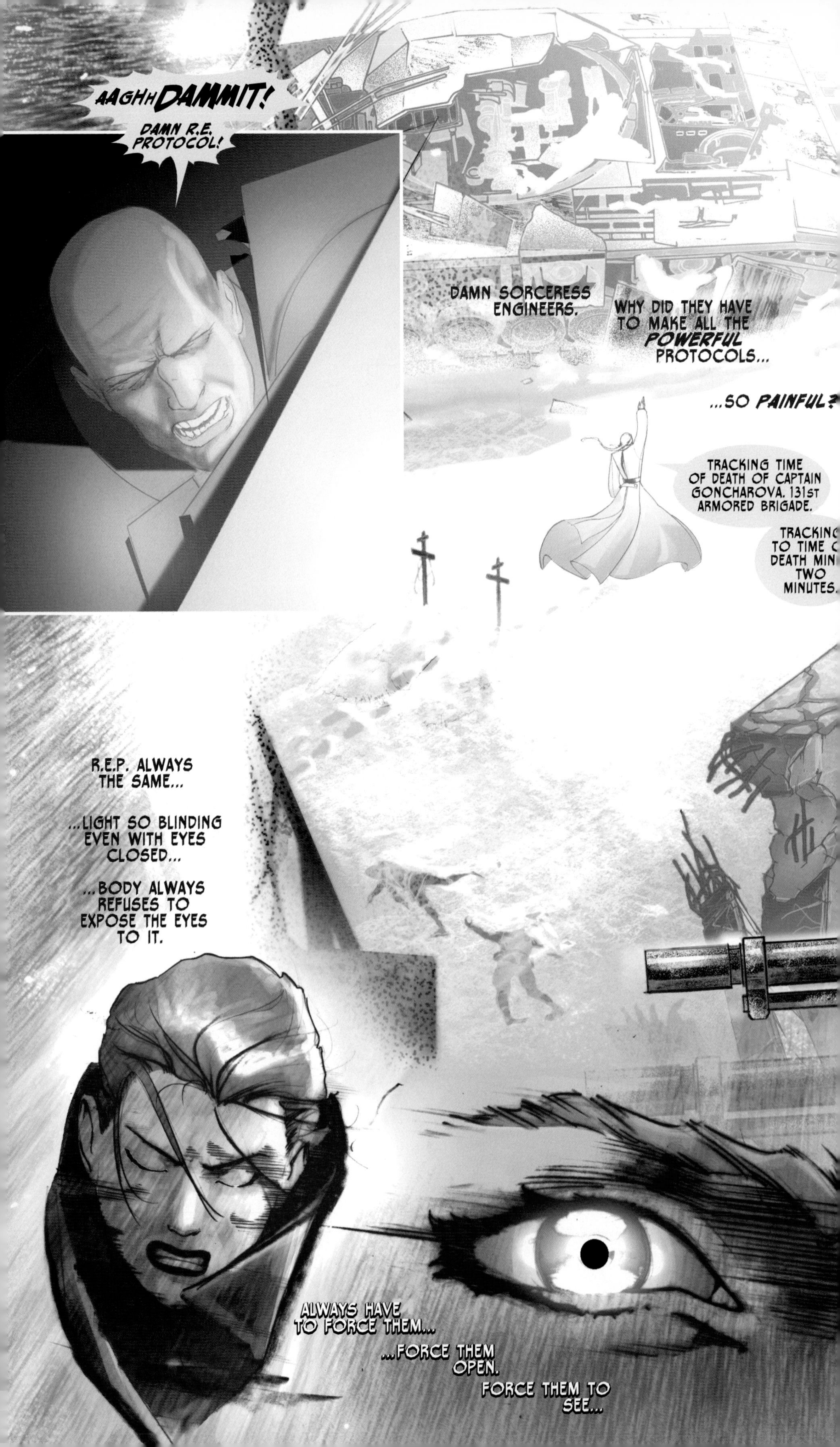
AAGHH DAMMIT!
DAMN R.E. PROTOCOL!
DAMN SORCERESS ENGINEERS.
WHY DID THEY HAVE TO MAKE ALL THE *POWERFUL* PROTOCOLS...
...SO *PAINFUL?*
TRACKING TIME OF DEATH OF CAPTAIN GONCHAROVA. 131ST ARMORED BRIGADE.
R.E.P. ALWAYS THE SAME...
...LIGHT SO BLINDING EVEN WITH EYES CLOSED...
...BODY ALWAYS REFUSES TO EXPOSE THE EYES TO IT.
ALWAYS HAVE TO FORCE THEM...
...FORCE THEM OPEN.
FORCE THEM TO SEE...

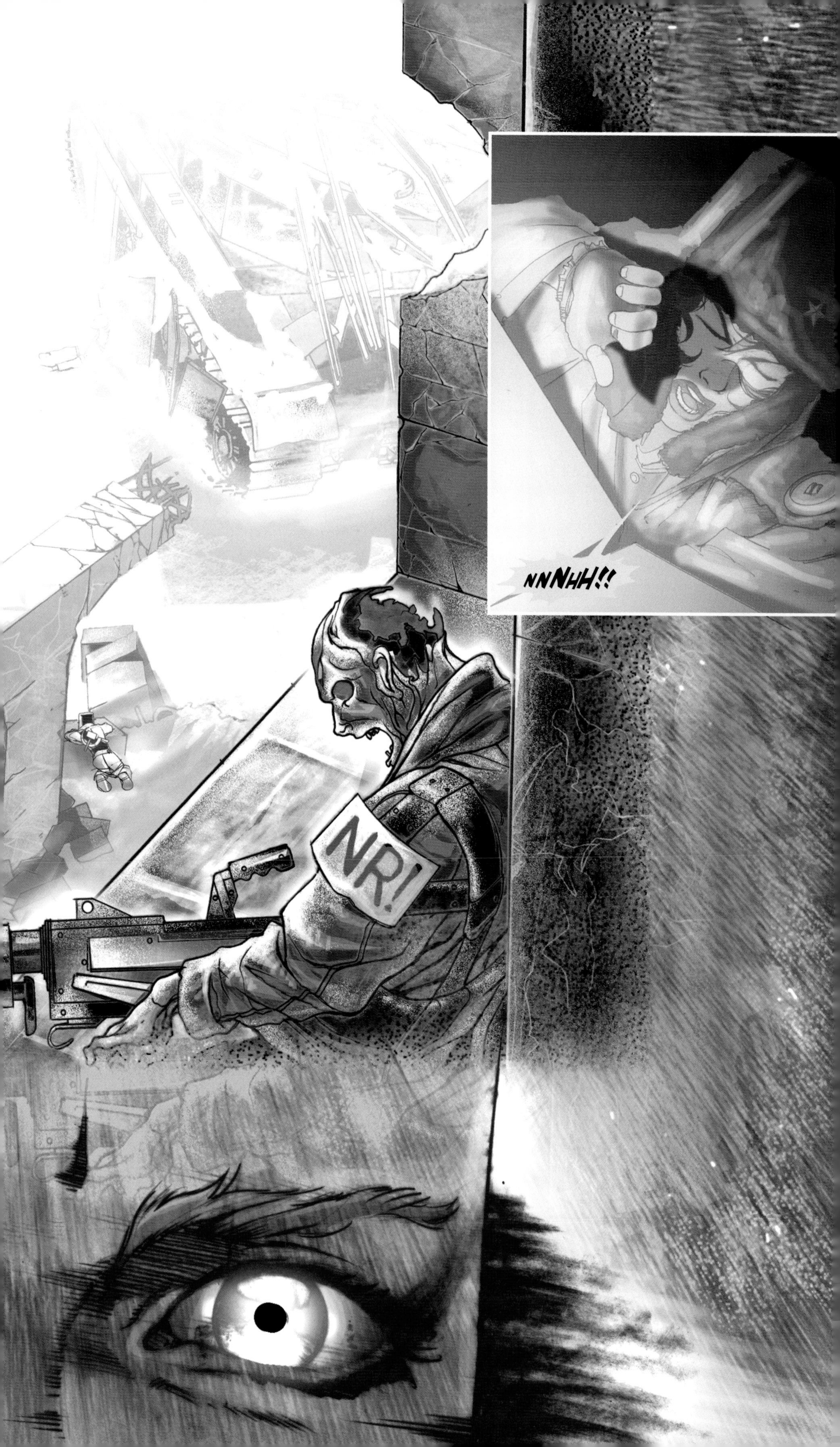
NNNHH!!
NR!

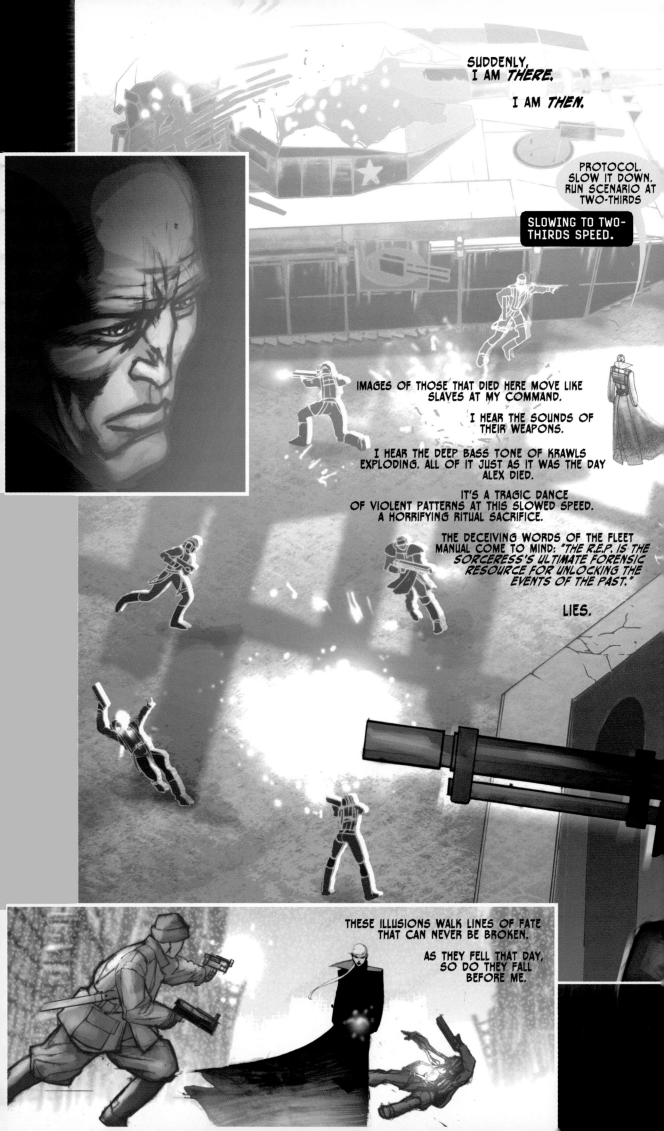

SUDDENLY,
I AM *THERE*.

I AM *THEN*.

PROTOCOL.
SLOW IT DOWN.
RUN SCENARIO AT
TWO-THIRDS

SLOWING TO TWO-
THIRDS SPEED.

IMAGES OF THOSE THAT DIED HERE MOVE LIKE
SLAVES AT MY COMMAND.

I HEAR THE SOUNDS OF
THEIR WEAPONS.

I HEAR THE DEEP BASS TONE OF KRAWLS
EXPLODING. ALL OF IT JUST AS IT WAS THE DAY
ALEX DIED.

IT'S A TRAGIC DANCE
OF VIOLENT PATTERNS AT THIS SLOWED SPEED.
A HORRIFYING RITUAL SACRIFICE.

THE DECEIVING WORDS OF THE FLEET
MANUAL COME TO MIND: *"THE R.E.P. IS THE
SORCERESS'S ULTIMATE FORENSIC
RESOURCE FOR UNLOCKING THE
EVENTS OF THE PAST."*

LIES.

THESE ILLUSIONS WALK LINES OF FATE
THAT CAN NEVER BE BROKEN.

AS THEY FELL THAT DAY,
SO DO THEY FALL
BEFORE ME.

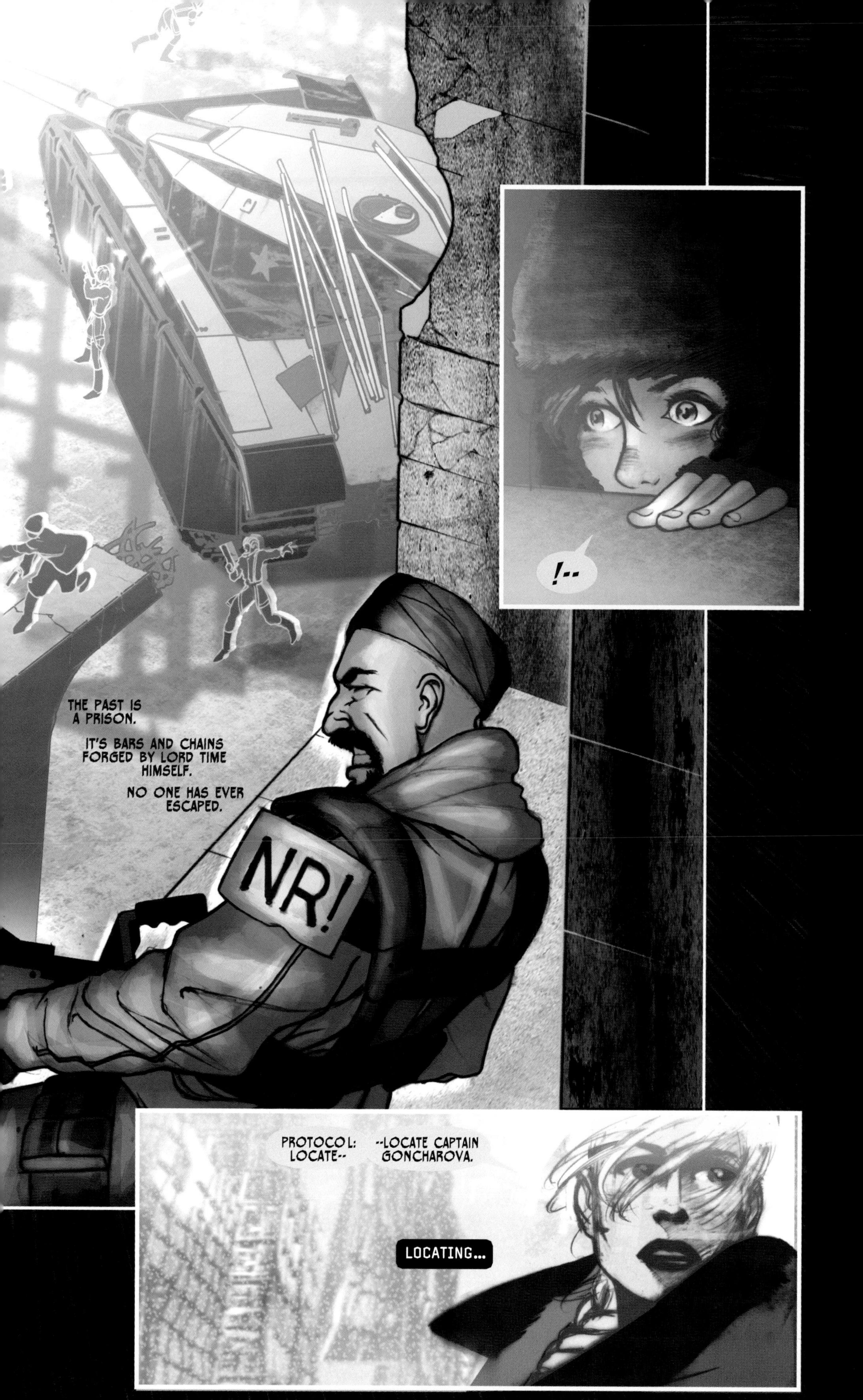
THE PAST IS A PRISON.
IT'S BARS AND CHAINS FORGED BY LORD TIME HIMSELF.
NO ONE HAS EVER ESCAPED.
NR!
!--
PROTOCOL: LOCATE--
--LOCATE CAPTAIN GONCHAROVA.
LOCATING...

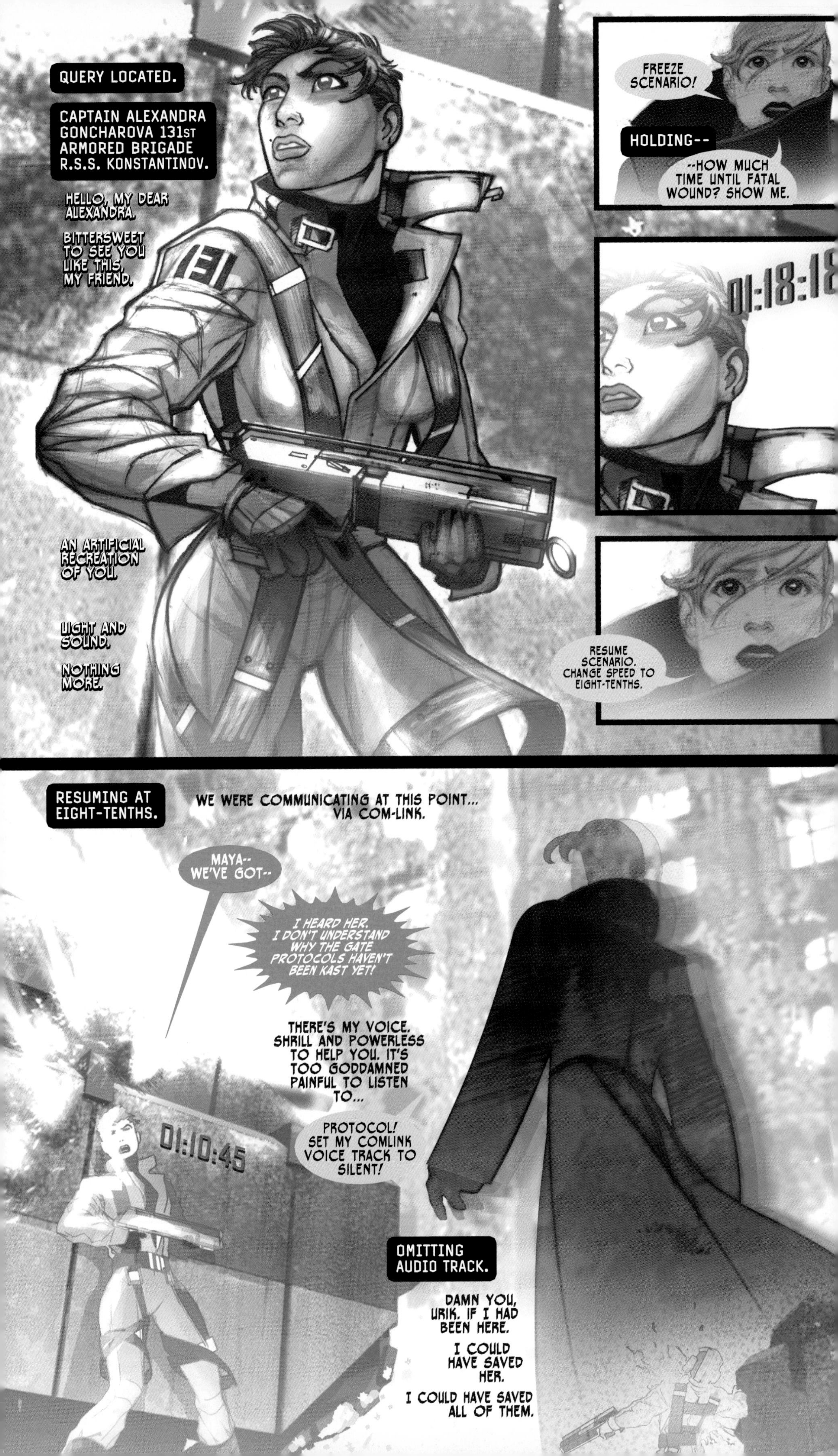
QUERY LOCATED.
CAPTAIN ALEXANDRA GONCHAROVA 131ST ARMORED BRIGADE R.S.S. KONSTANTINOV.
HELLO, MY DEAR ALEXANDRA.
BITTERSWEET TO SEE YOU LIKE THIS, MY FRIEND.
AN ARTIFICIAL RECREATION OF YOU.
LIGHT AND SOUND.
NOTHING MORE.
131
FREEZE SCENARIO!
HOLDING--
--HOW MUCH TIME UNTIL FATAL WOUND? SHOW ME.
01:18:18
RESUME SCENARIO. CHANGE SPEED TO EIGHT-TENTHS.
RESUMING AT EIGHT-TENTHS.
WE WERE COMMUNICATING AT THIS POINT... VIA COM-LINK.
MAYA-- WE'VE GOT--
I HEARD HER. I DON'T UNDERSTAND WHY THE GATE PROTOCOLS HAVEN'T BEEN KAST YET!
THERE'S MY VOICE. SHRILL AND POWERLESS TO HELP YOU. IT'S TOO GODDAMNED PAINFUL TO LISTEN TO...
01:10:45
PROTOCOL! SET MY COMLINK VOICE TRACK TO SILENT!
OMITTING AUDIO TRACK.
DAMN YOU, URIK. IF I HAD BEEN HERE.
I COULD HAVE SAVED HER.
I COULD HAVE SAVED ALL OF THEM.

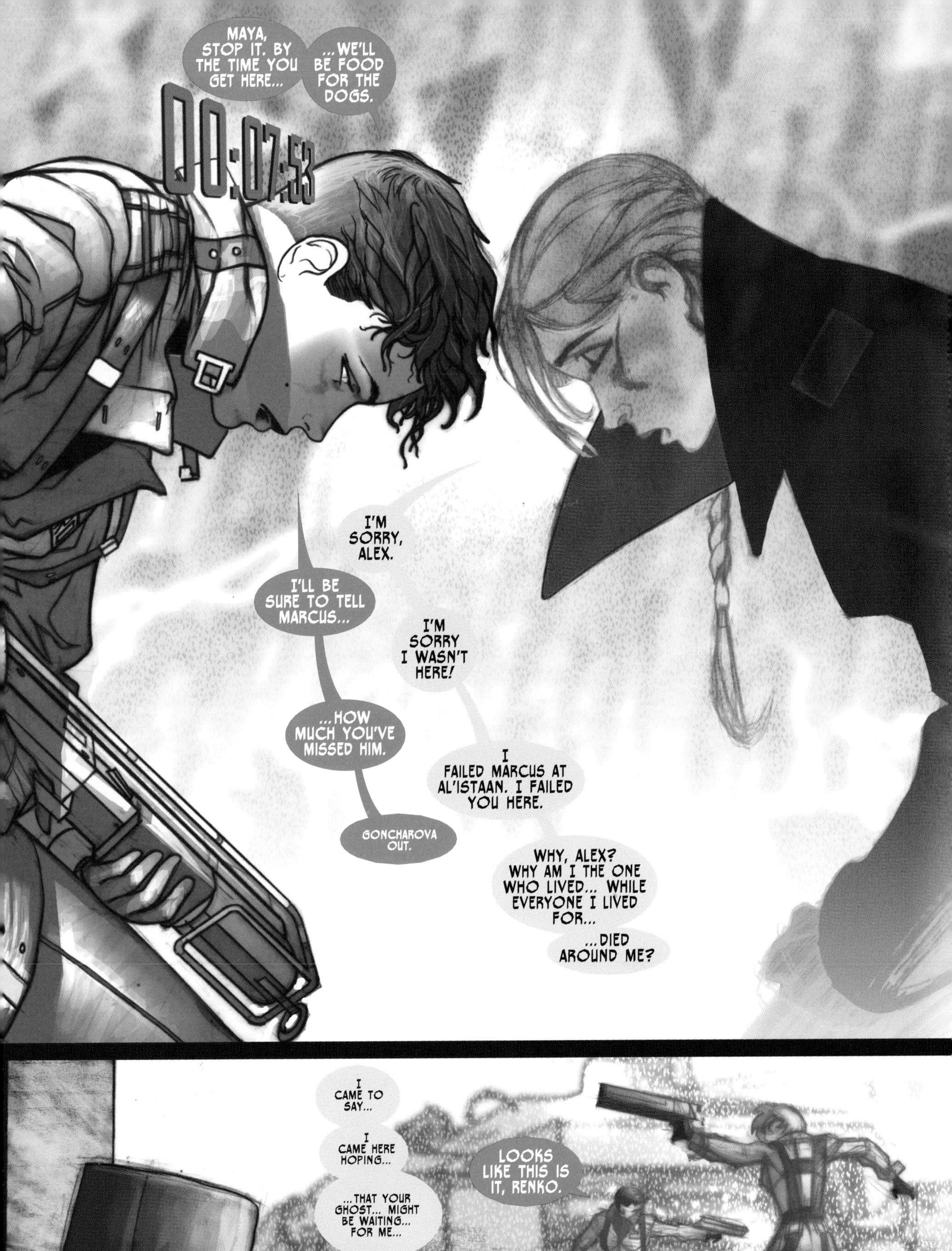
MAYA, STOP IT. BY THE TIME YOU GET HERE...
...WE'LL BE FOOD FOR THE DOGS.
00:07:53
I'M SORRY, ALEX.
I'LL BE SURE TO TELL MARCUS...
I'M SORRY I WASN'T HERE!
...HOW MUCH YOU'VE MISSED HIM.
I FAILED MARCUS AT AL'ISTAAN. I FAILED YOU HERE.
GONCHAROVA OUT.
WHY, ALEX? WHY AM I THE ONE WHO LIVED... WHILE EVERYONE I LIVED FOR...
...DIED AROUND ME?

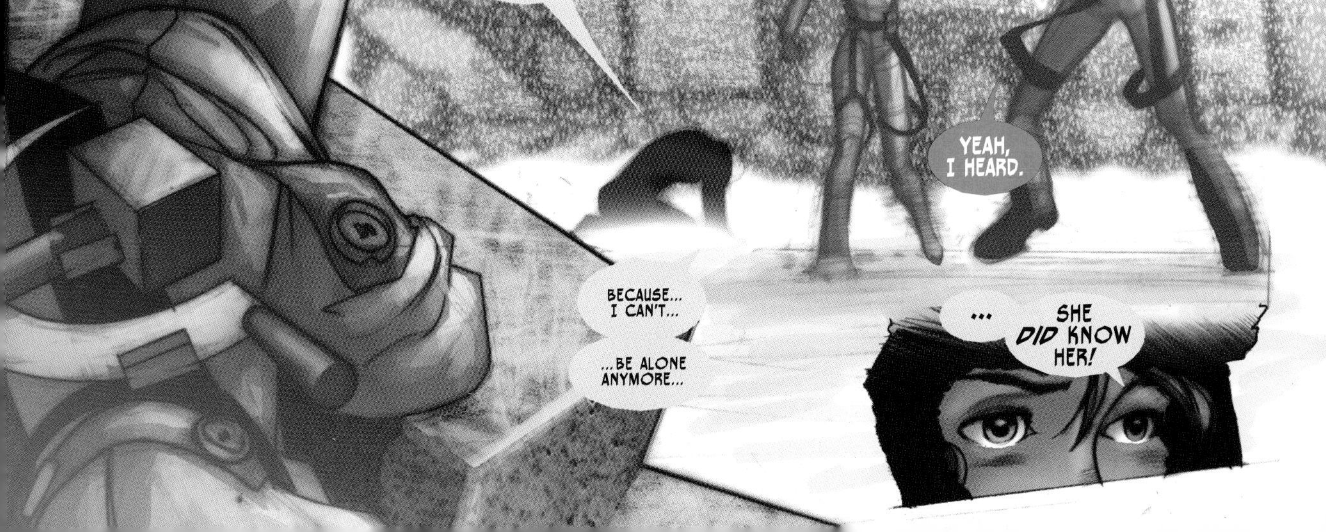
I CAME TO SAY...
I CAME HERE HOPING...
...THAT YOUR GHOST... MIGHT BE WAITING... FOR ME...
LOOKS LIKE THIS IS IT, RENKO.
YEAH, I HEARD.
BECAUSE... I CAN'T...
...BE ALONE ANYMORE...
...
SHE *DID* KNOW HER!

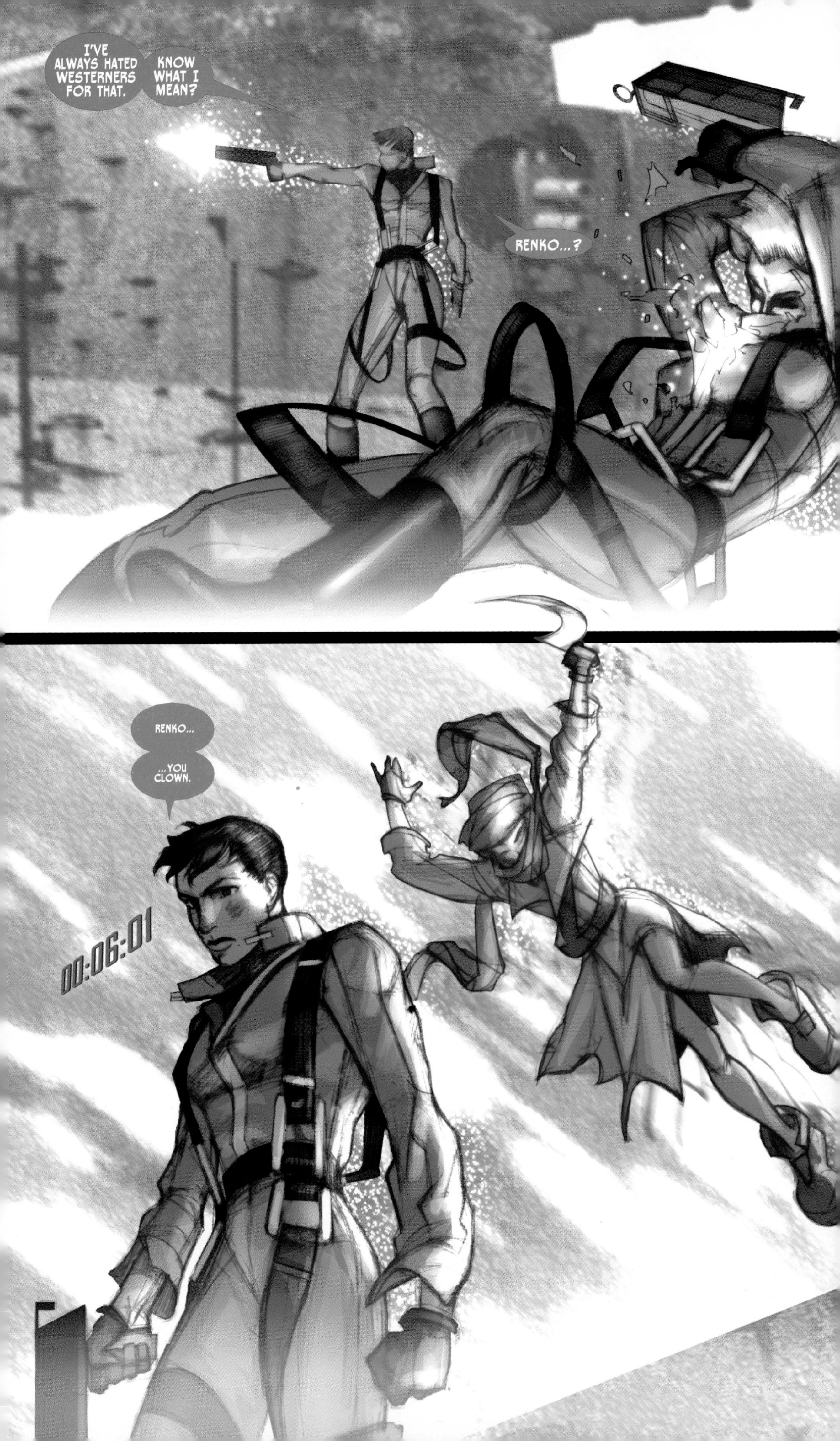
I'VE ALWAYS HATED WESTERNERS FOR THAT.
KNOW WHAT I MEAN?
RENKO...?
RENKO...
...YOU CLOWN.
00:06:01

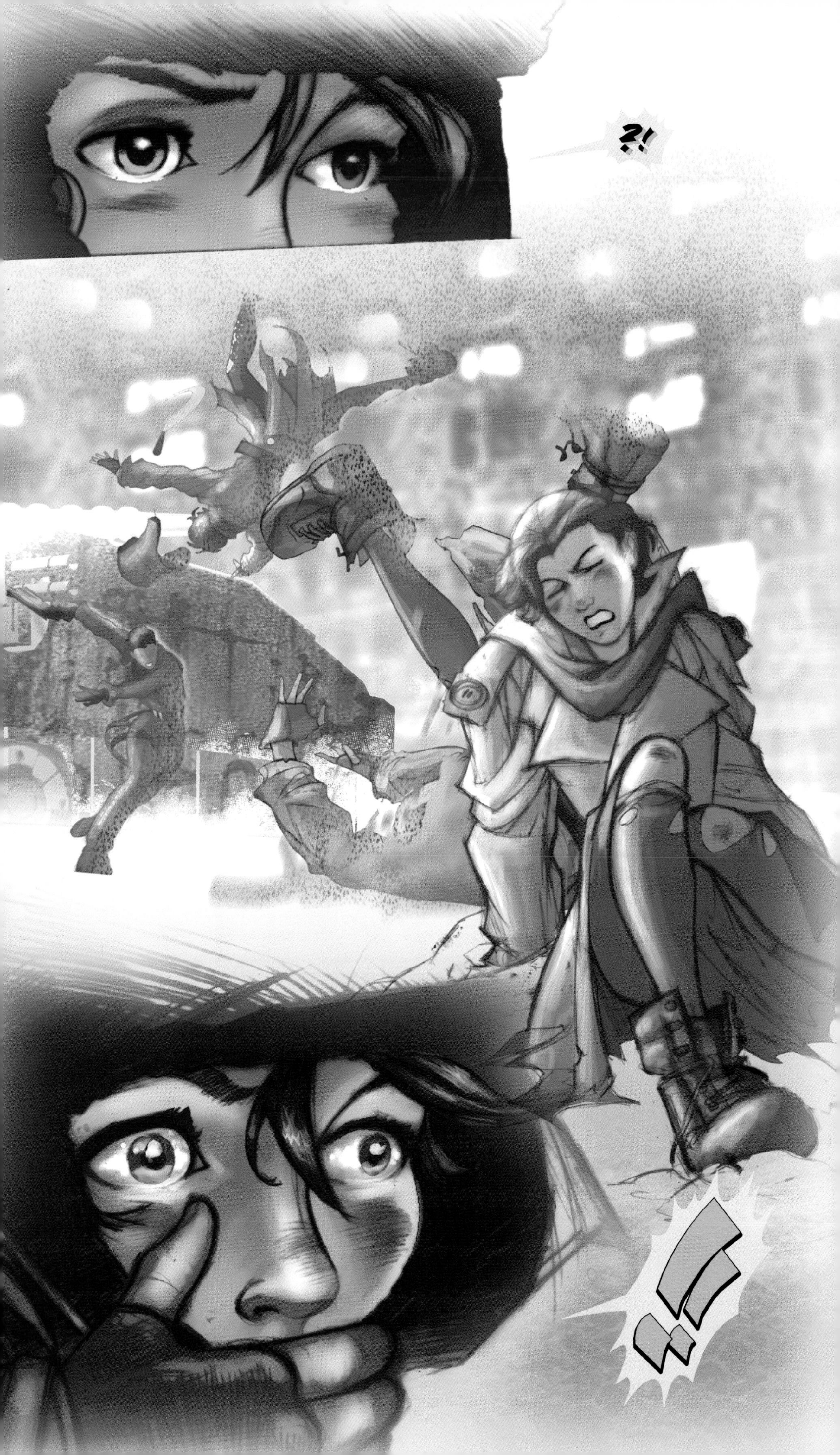
?!
!!

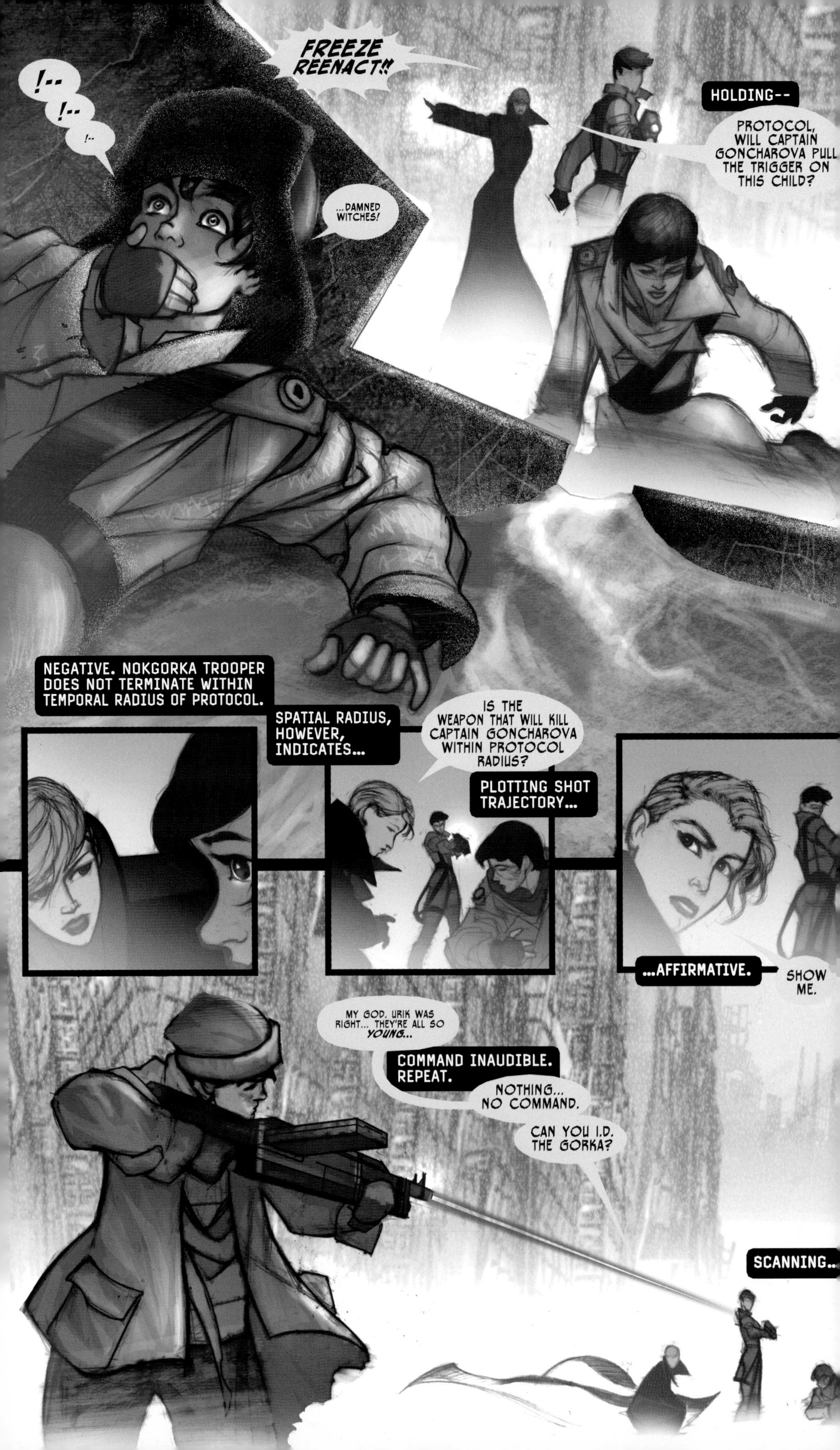
!--
!--
!--
FREEZE REENACT!!
...DAMNED WITCHES!
HOLDING--
PROTOCOL, WILL CAPTAIN GONCHAROVA PULL THE TRIGGER ON THIS CHILD?
NEGATIVE. NOKGORKA TROOPER DOES NOT TERMINATE WITHIN TEMPORAL RADIUS OF PROTOCOL.
SPATIAL RADIUS, HOWEVER, INDICATES...
IS THE WEAPON THAT WILL KILL CAPTAIN GONCHAROVA WITHIN PROTOCOL RADIUS?
PLOTTING SHOT TRAJECTORY...
...AFFIRMATIVE.
SHOW ME.
MY GOD. URIK WAS RIGHT... THEY'RE ALL SO YOUNG...
COMMAND INAUDIBLE. REPEAT.
NOTHING... NO COMMAND.
CAN YOU I.D. THE GORKA?
SCANNING...

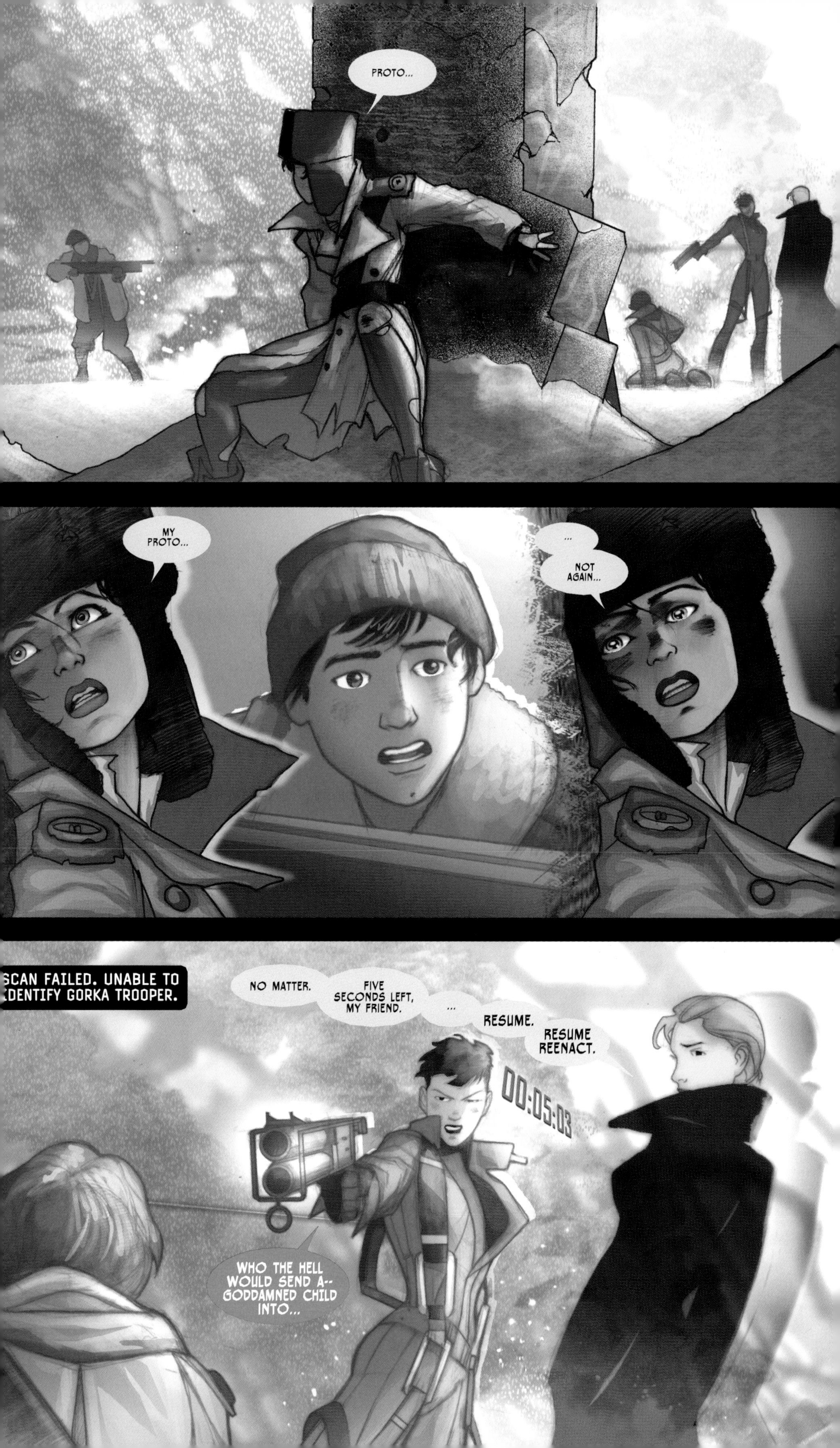
PROTO...
MY PROTO...
...
NOT AGAIN...
SCAN FAILED. UNABLE TO IDENTIFY GORKA TROOPER.
NO MATTER.
FIVE SECONDS LEFT, MY FRIEND.
...
RESUME.
RESUME REENACT.
00:05:03
WHO THE HELL WOULD SEND A-- GODDAMNED CHILD INTO...

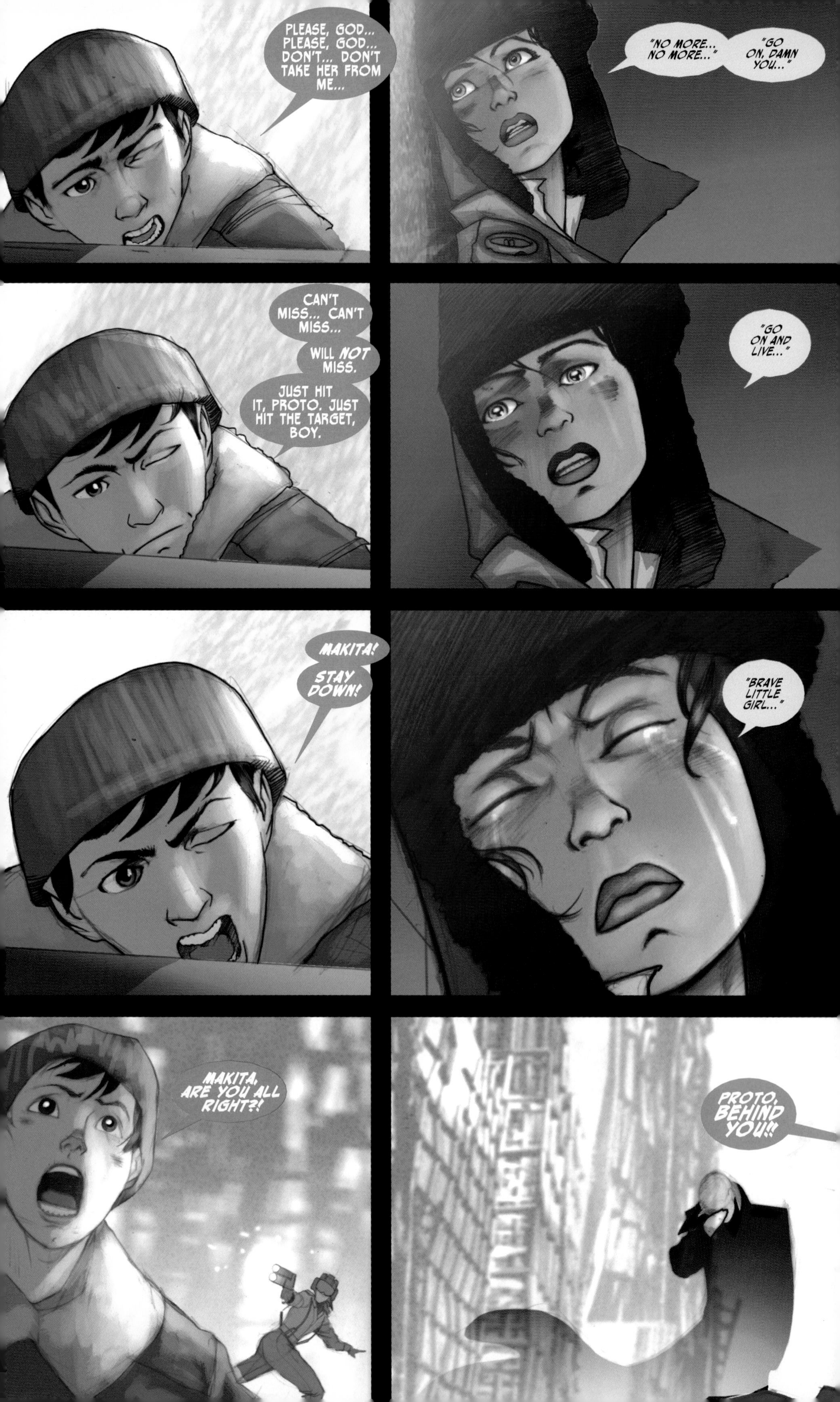
PLEASE, GOD... PLEASE, GOD... DON'T... DON'T TAKE HER FROM ME...
"NO MORE... NO MORE..."
"GO ON, DAMN YOU..."
CAN'T MISS... CAN'T MISS...
WILL *NOT* MISS.
JUST HIT IT, PROTO. JUST HIT THE TARGET, BOY.
"GO ON AND LIVE..."
MAKITA!
STAY DOWN!
"BRAVE LITTLE GIRL..."
MAKITA, ARE YOU ALL RIGHT?!
PROTO, BEHIND YOU!!

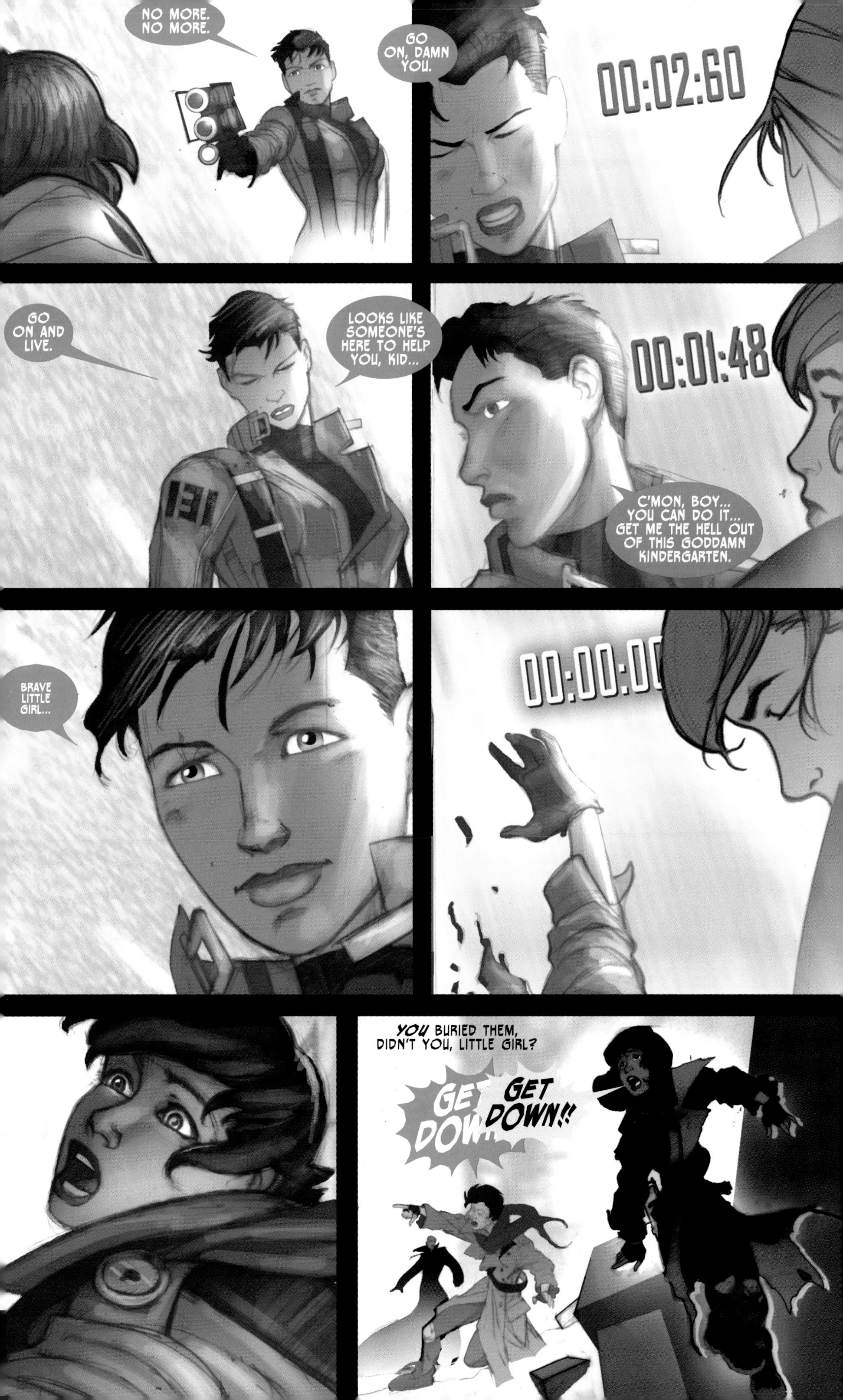
NO MORE. NO MORE.
GO ON, DAMN YOU.
00:02:60
GO ON AND LIVE.
LOOKS LIKE SOMEONE'S HERE TO HELP YOU, KID...
00:01:48
C'MON, BOY... YOU CAN DO IT... GET ME THE HELL OUT OF THIS GODDAMN KINDERGARTEN.
BRAVE LITTLE GIRL...
00:00:00
YOU BURIED THEM, DIDN'T YOU, LITTLE GIRL?
GET DOWN!!
GET DOWN!!

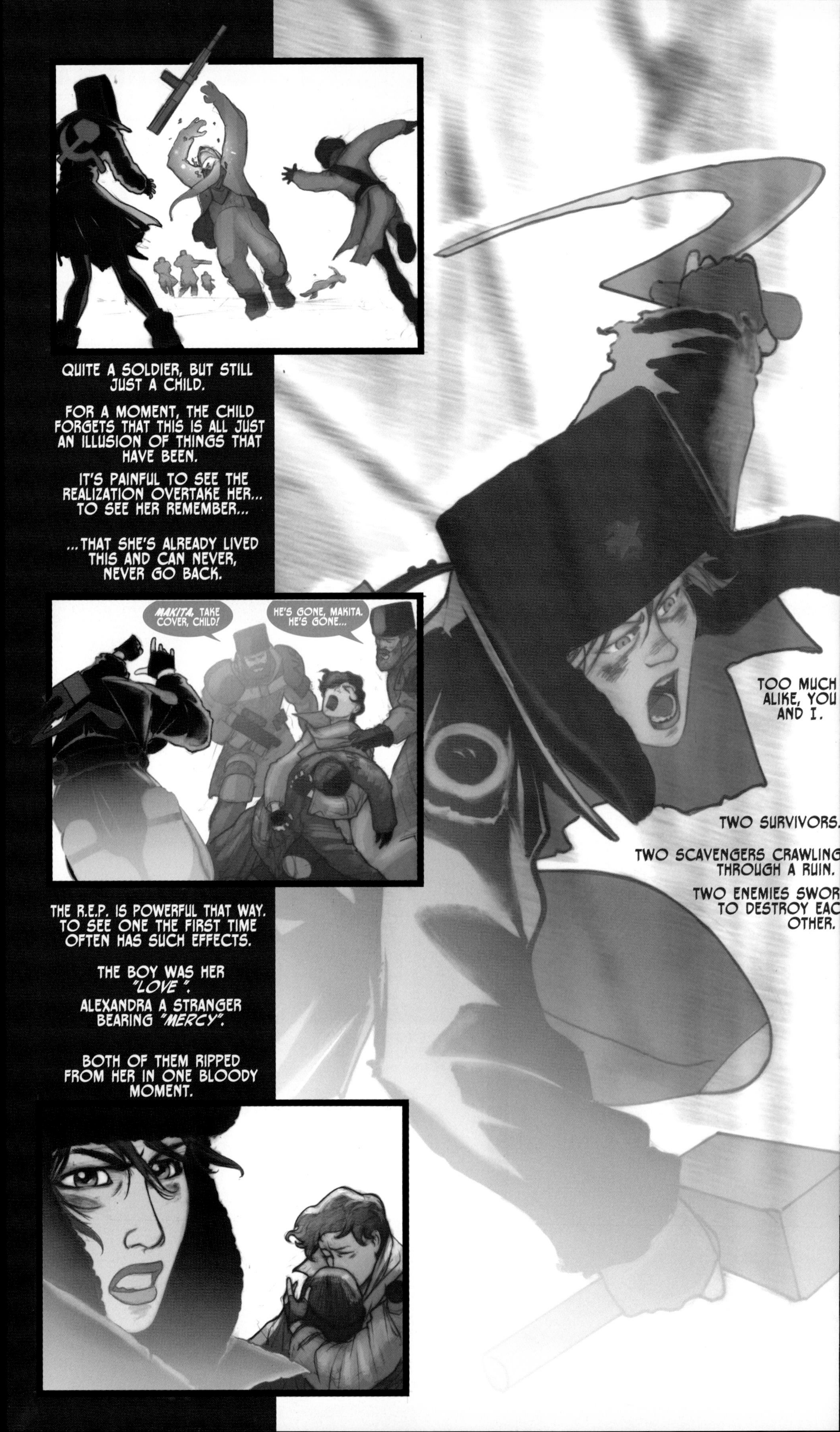
QUITE A SOLDIER, BUT STILL JUST A CHILD.
FOR A MOMENT, THE CHILD FORGETS THAT THIS IS ALL JUST AN ILLUSION OF THINGS THAT HAVE BEEN.
IT'S PAINFUL TO SEE THE REALIZATION OVERTAKE HER... TO SEE HER REMEMBER...
...THAT SHE'S ALREADY LIVED THIS AND CAN NEVER, NEVER GO BACK.
MAKITA, TAKE COVER, CHILD!
HE'S GONE, MAKITA. HE'S GONE...
THE R.E.P. IS POWERFUL THAT WAY. TO SEE ONE THE FIRST TIME OFTEN HAS SUCH EFFECTS.
THE BOY WAS HER "LOVE".
ALEXANDRA A STRANGER BEARING "MERCY".
BOTH OF THEM RIPPED FROM HER IN ONE BLOODY MOMENT.
TOO MUCH ALIKE, YOU AND I.
TWO SURVIVORS.
TWO SCAVENGERS CRAWLING THROUGH A RUIN.
TWO ENEMIES SWOR TO DESTROY EAC OTHER.

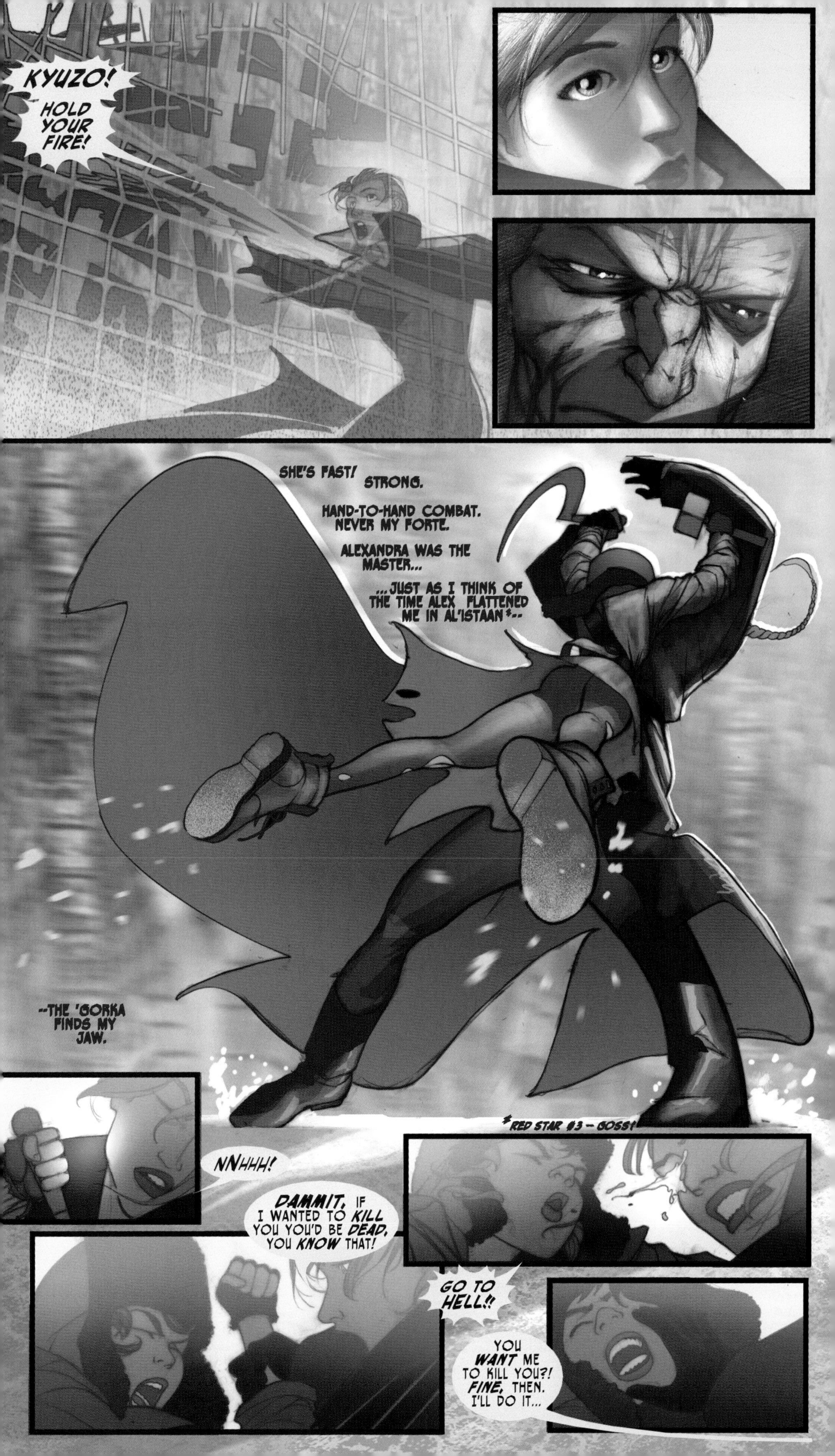
KYUZO!
HOLD YOUR FIRE!
SHE'S FAST! STRONG.
HAND-TO-HAND COMBAT. NEVER MY FORTE.
ALEXANDRA WAS THE MASTER...
...JUST AS I THINK OF THE TIME ALEX FLATTENED ME IN AL'ISTAAN*--
--THE 'GORKA FINDS MY JAW.
*RED STAR #3 – GOSS!
NNHHH!
DAMMIT, IF I WANTED TO KILL YOU YOU'D BE DEAD, YOU KNOW THAT!
GO TO HELL!!
YOU WANT ME TO KILL YOU?! FINE, THEN. I'LL DO IT...

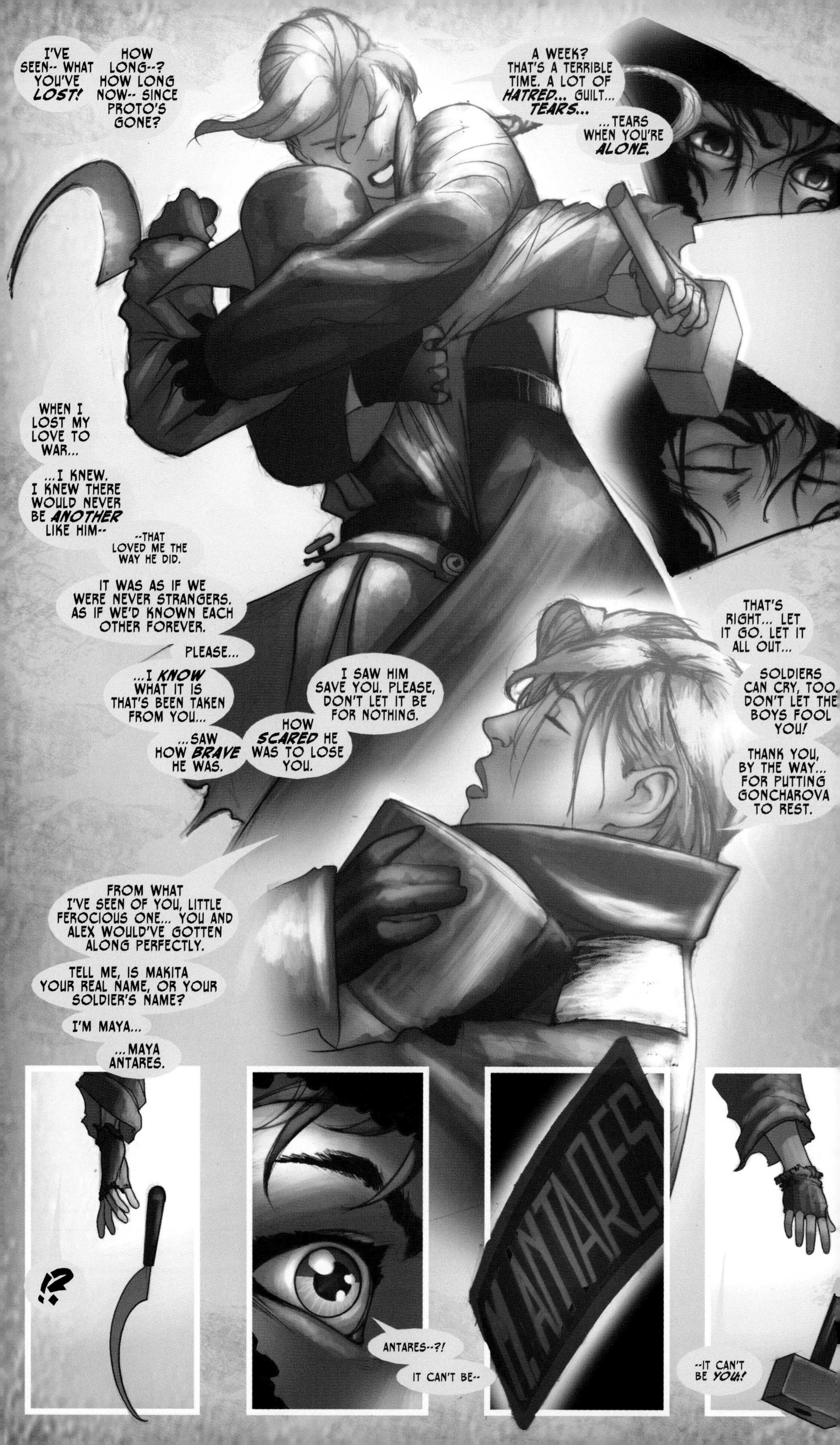

I'VE SEEN-- WHAT YOU'VE LOST!
HOW LONG--? HOW LONG NOW-- SINCE PROTO'S GONE?
A WEEK? THAT'S A TERRIBLE TIME. A LOT OF HATRED... GUILT... TEARS...
...TEARS WHEN YOU'RE ALONE.
WHEN I LOST MY LOVE TO WAR...
...I KNEW. I KNEW THERE WOULD NEVER BE ANOTHER LIKE HIM--
--THAT LOVED ME THE WAY HE DID.
IT WAS AS IF WE WERE NEVER STRANGERS. AS IF WE'D KNOWN EACH OTHER FOREVER.
PLEASE...
...I KNOW WHAT IT IS THAT'S BEEN TAKEN FROM YOU...
...SAW HOW BRAVE HE WAS.
I SAW HIM SAVE YOU. PLEASE, DON'T LET IT BE FOR NOTHING.
HOW SCARED HE WAS TO LOSE YOU.
THAT'S RIGHT... LET IT GO. LET IT ALL OUT...
SOLDIERS CAN CRY, TOO. DON'T LET THE BOYS FOOL YOU!
THANK YOU, BY THE WAY... FOR PUTTING GONCHAROVA TO REST.
FROM WHAT I'VE SEEN OF YOU, LITTLE FEROCIOUS ONE... YOU AND ALEX WOULD'VE GOTTEN ALONG PERFECTLY.
TELL ME, IS MAKITA YOUR REAL NAME, OR YOUR SOLDIER'S NAME?
I'M MAYA...
...MAYA ANTARES.
!?
ANTARES--?!
IT CAN'T BE--
ANTARES
--IT CAN'T BE YOU!

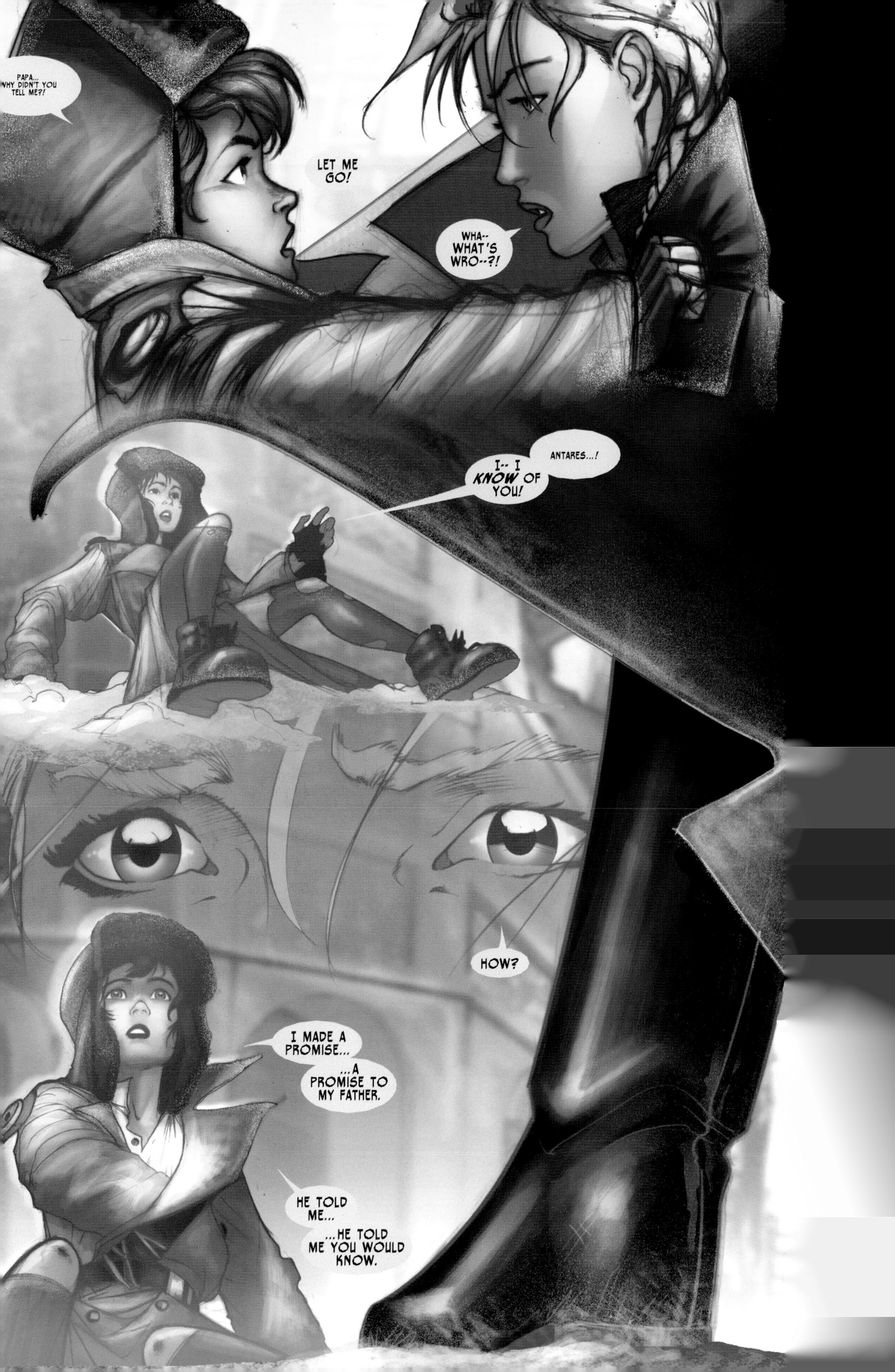
PAPA... WHY DIDN'T YOU TELL ME?!
LET ME GO!
WHA-- WHAT'S WRO--?!
ANTARES...!
I-- I KNOW OF YOU!
HOW?
I MADE A PROMISE...
...A PROMISE TO MY FATHER.
HE TOLD ME...
...HE TOLD ME YOU WOULD KNOW.

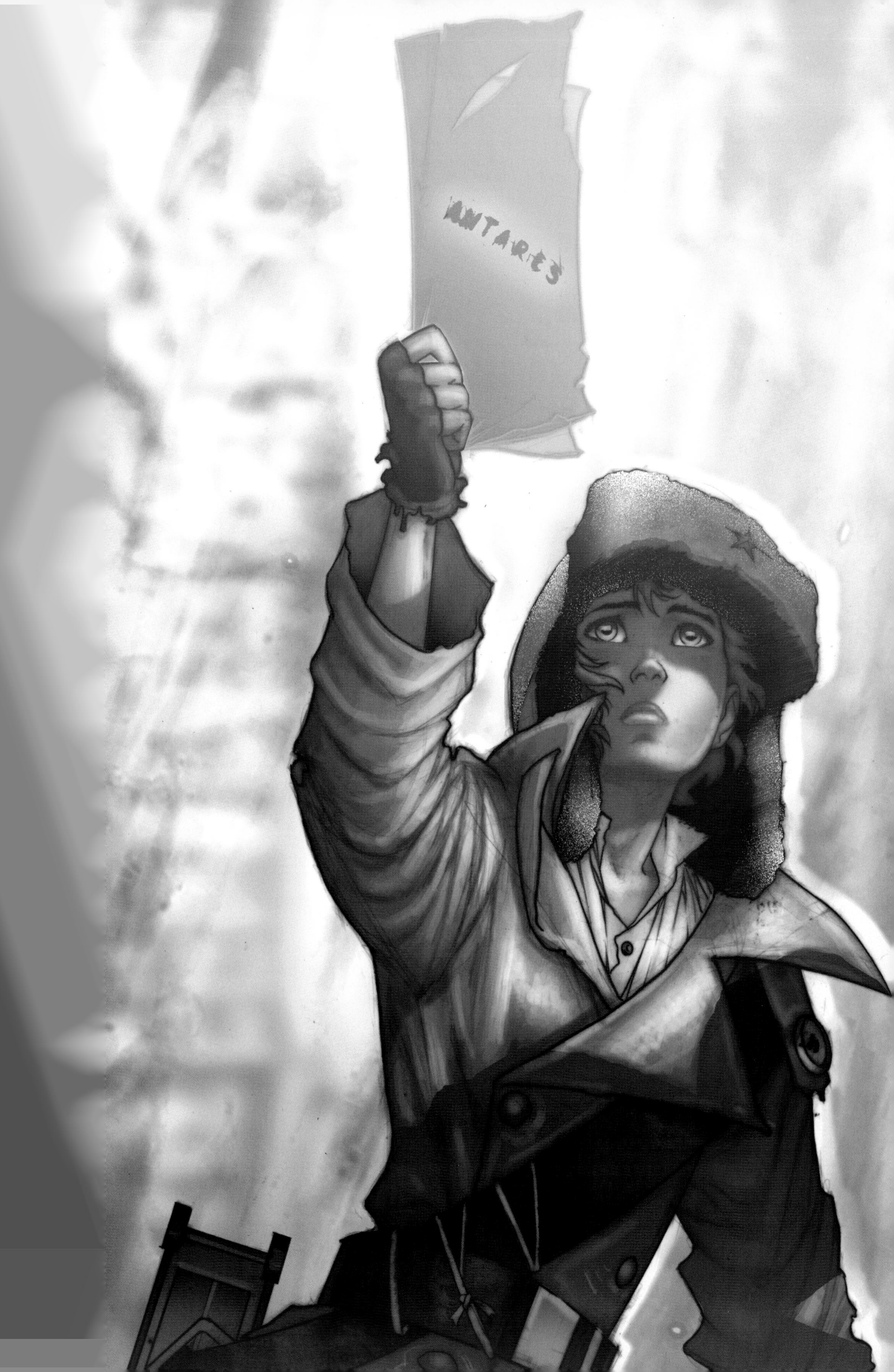
ANTARES

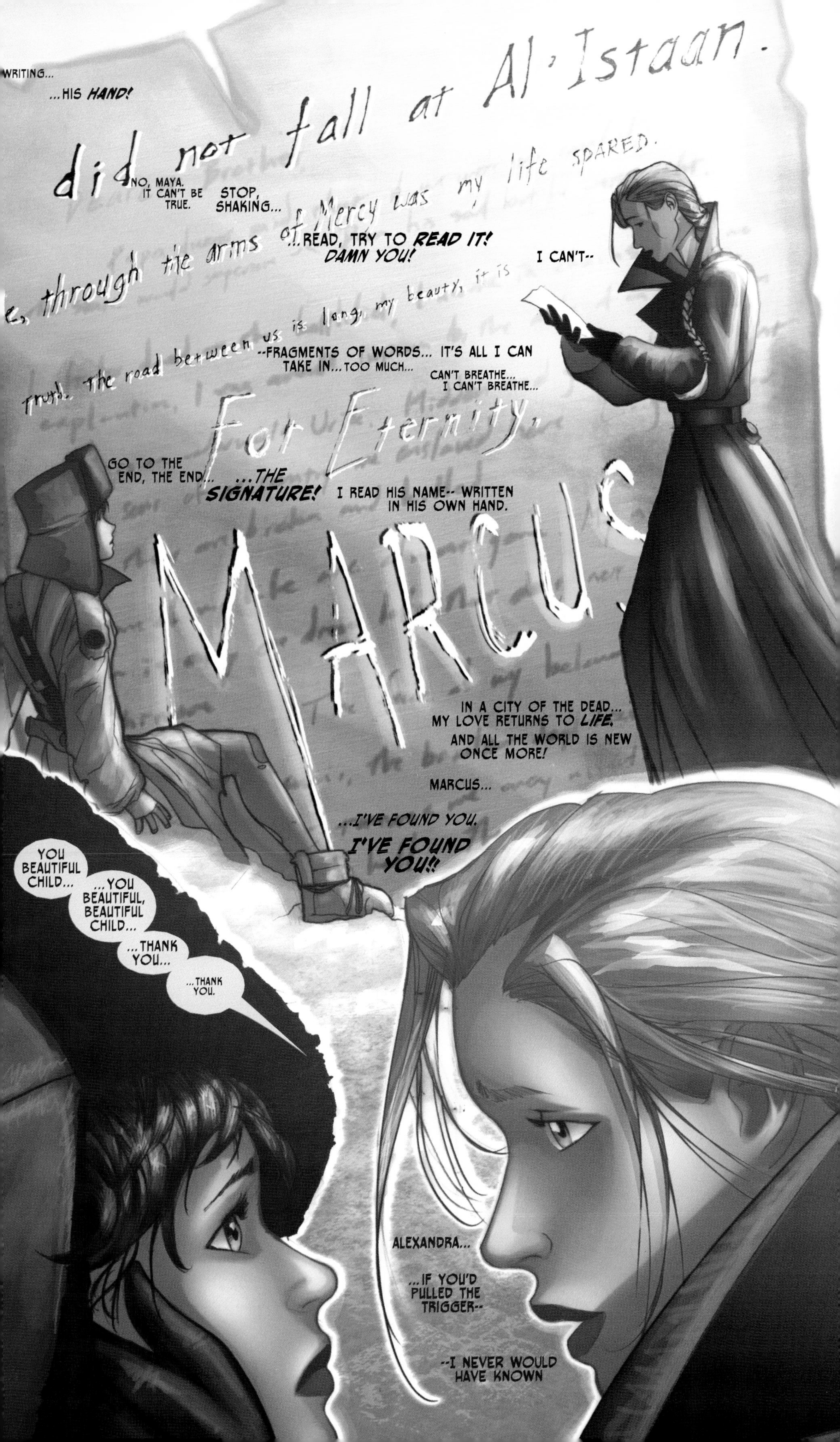

WRITING...
...HIS HAND!
did not fall at Al-Istaan.
NO, MAYA. IT CAN'T BE TRUE.
STOP, SHAKING...
e, through the arms of Mercy was my life spared.
...READ, TRY TO READ IT! DAMN YOU!
I CAN'T--
truth. The road between us is long, my beauty, it is
--FRAGMENTS OF WORDS... IT'S ALL I CAN TAKE IN...TOO MUCH...
CAN'T BREATHE... I CAN'T BREATHE...
For Eternity,
GO TO THE END, THE END...
...THE SIGNATURE!
I READ HIS NAME-- WRITTEN IN HIS OWN HAND.
MARCUS
IN A CITY OF THE DEAD... MY LOVE RETURNS TO LIFE.
AND ALL THE WORLD IS NEW ONCE MORE!
MARCUS...
...I'VE FOUND YOU.
I'VE FOUND YOU!!
YOU BEAUTIFUL CHILD...
...YOU BEAUTIFUL, BEAUTIFUL CHILD...
...THANK YOU...
...THANK YOU.
ALEXANDRA...
...IF YOU'D PULLED THE TRIGGER--
--I NEVER WOULD HAVE KNOWN

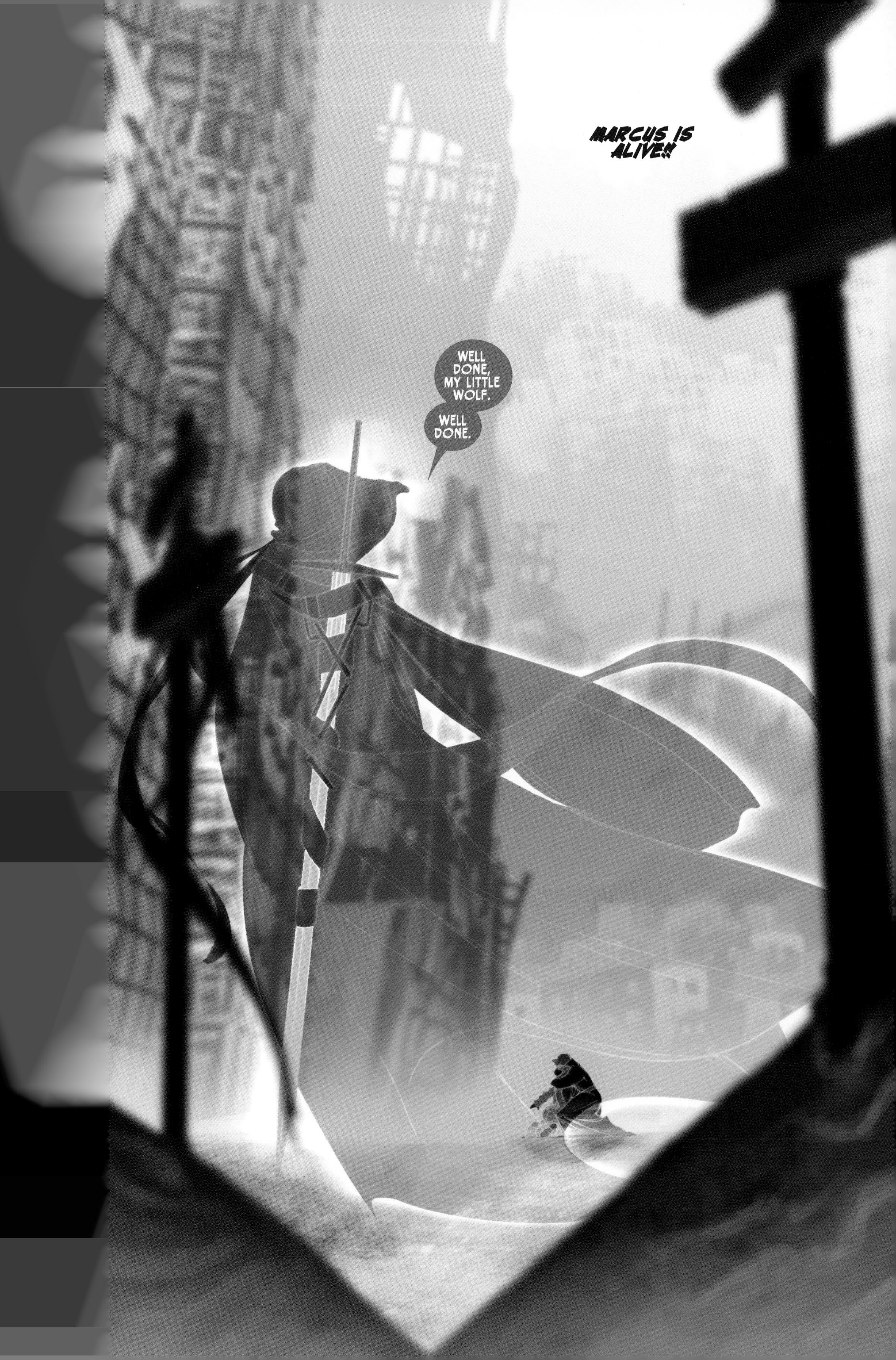
MARCUS IS ALIVE!!
WELL DONE, MY LITTLE WOLF.
WELL DONE.

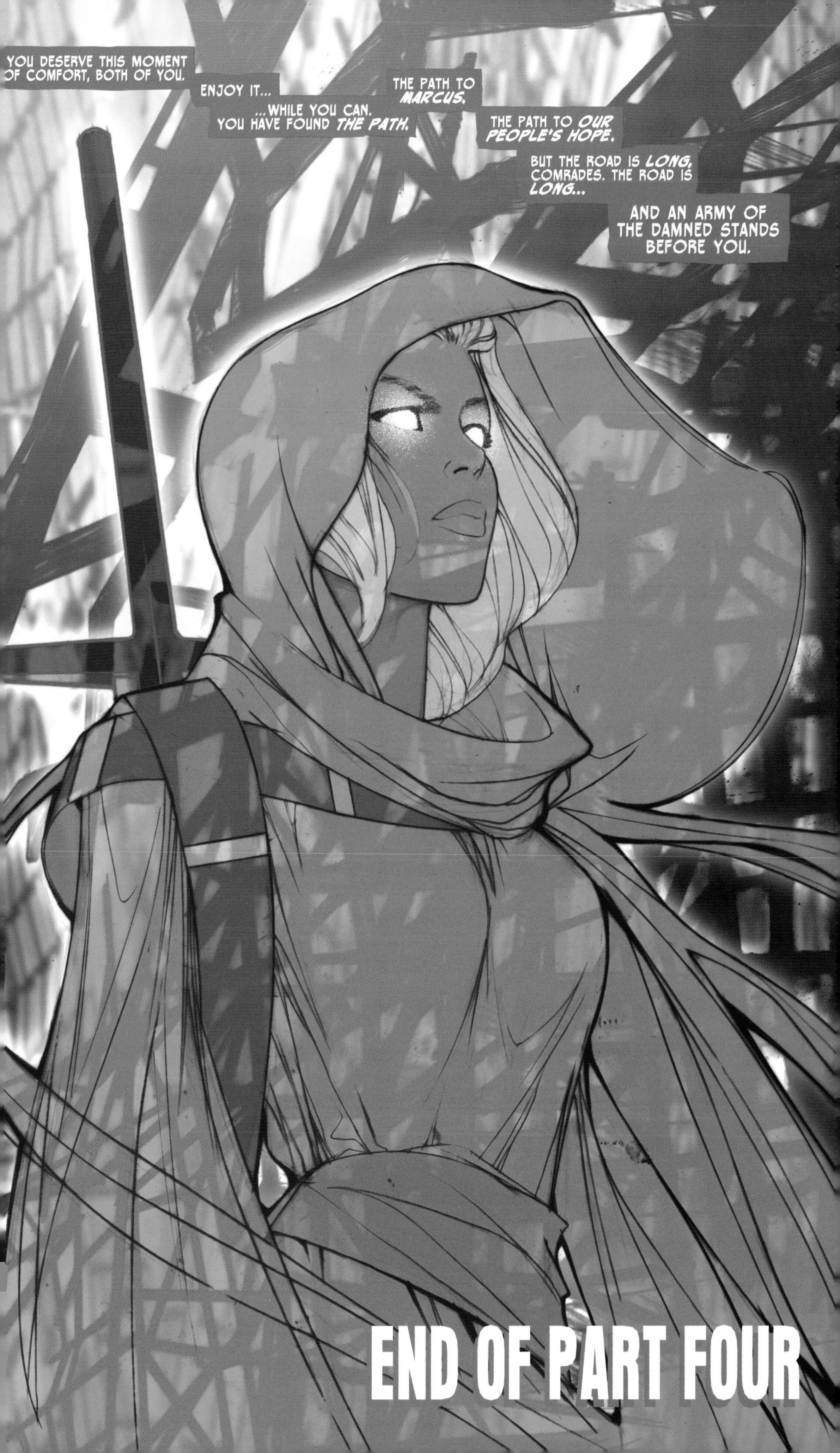

YOU DESERVE THIS MOMENT OF COMFORT, BOTH OF YOU.
ENJOY IT...
...WHILE YOU CAN. YOU HAVE FOUND *THE PATH.*
THE PATH TO *MARCUS.*
THE PATH TO *OUR PEOPLE'S HOPE.*
BUT THE ROAD IS *LONG,* COMRADES. THE ROAD IS *LONG...*
AND AN ARMY OF THE DAMNED STANDS BEFORE YOU.
END OF PART FOUR

BOOK NINE

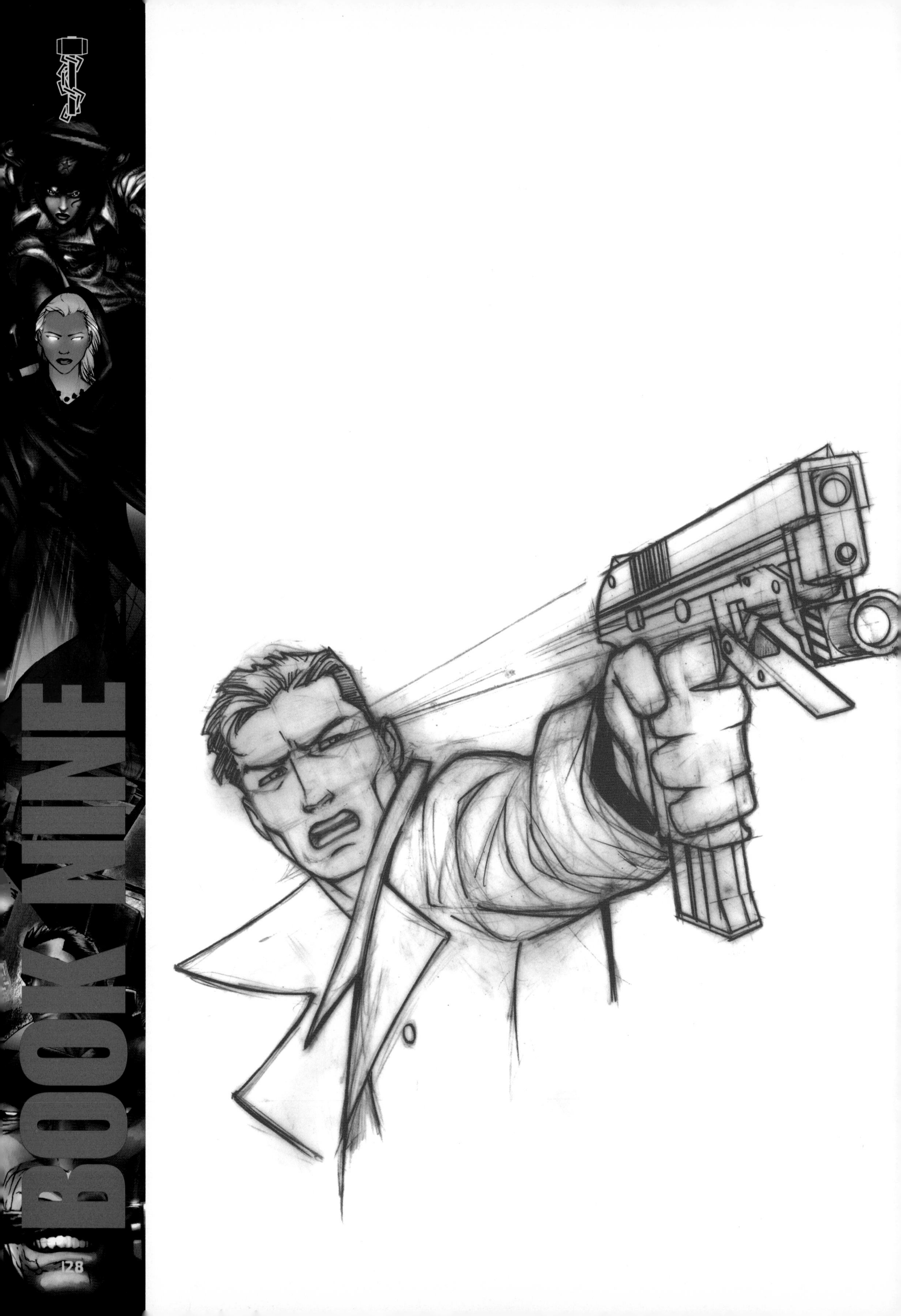

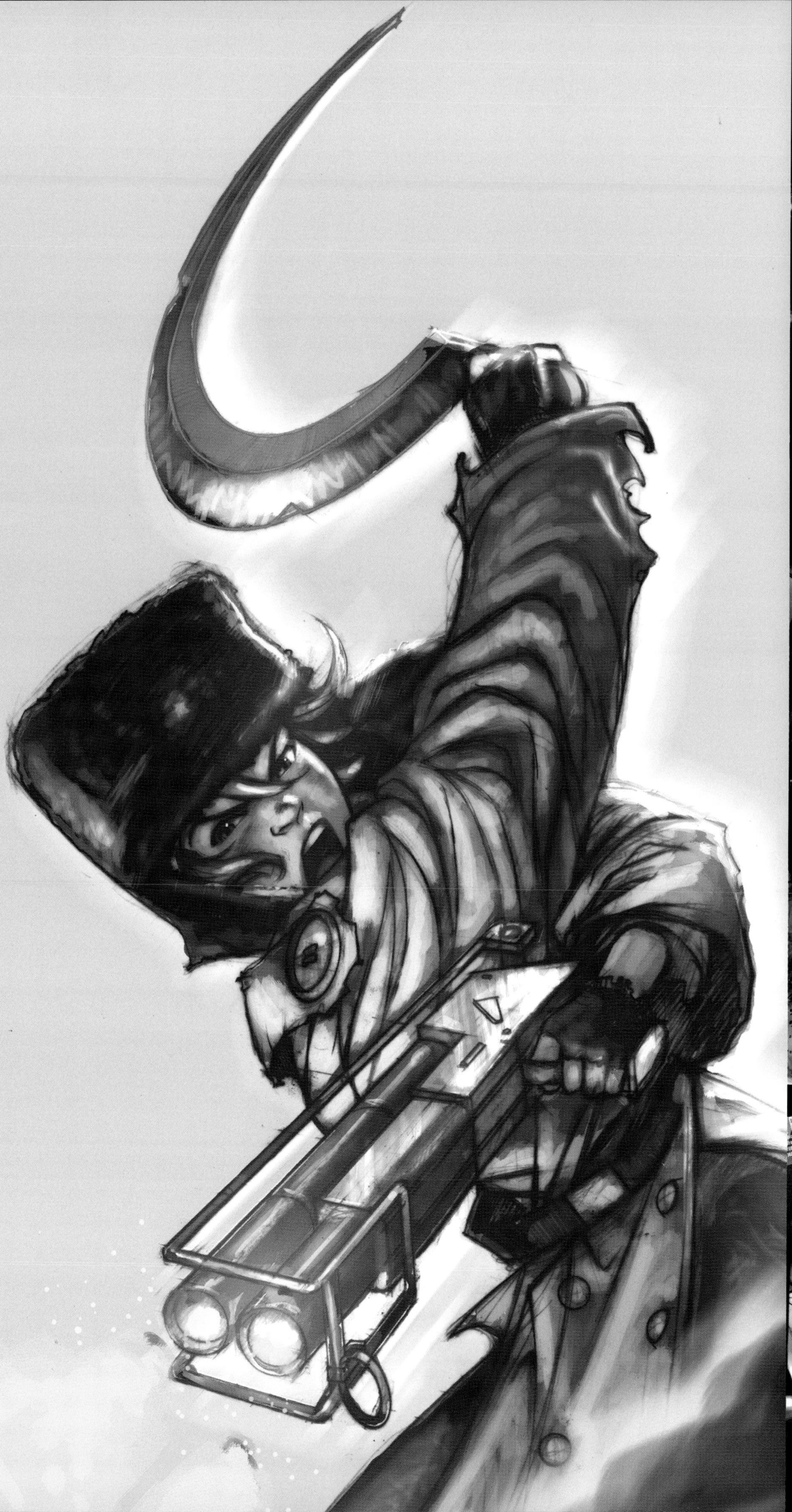

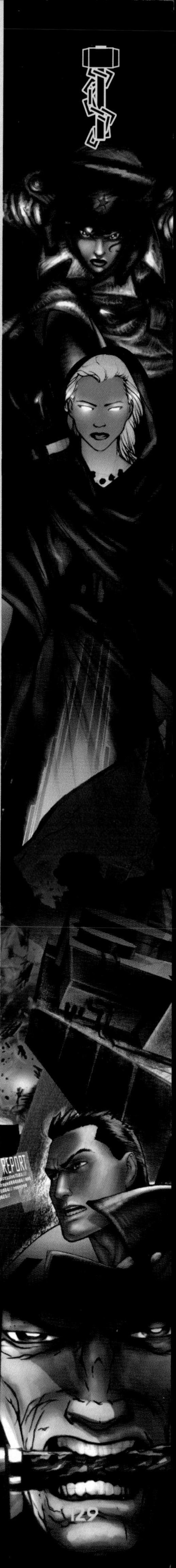
REPORT

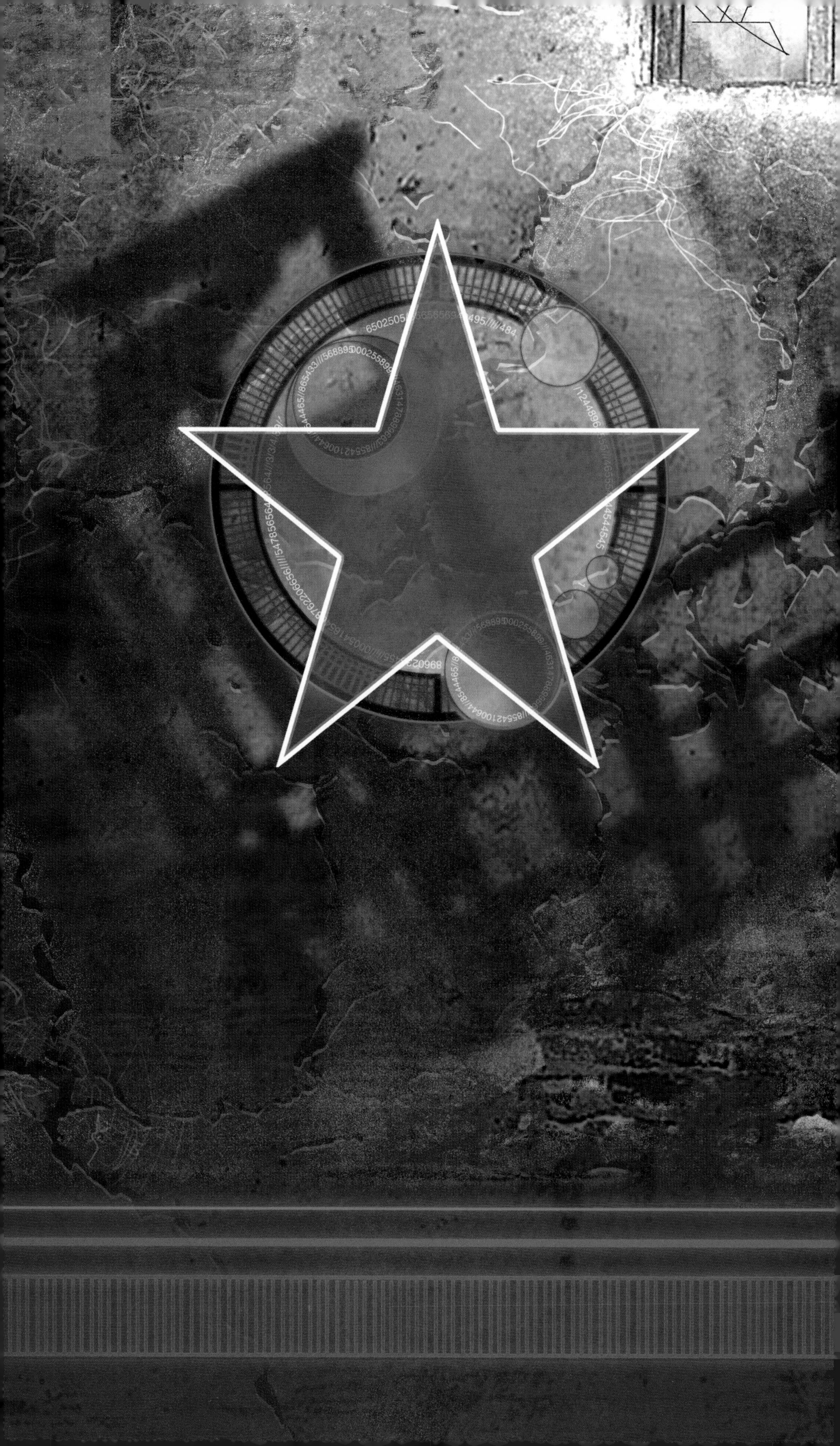

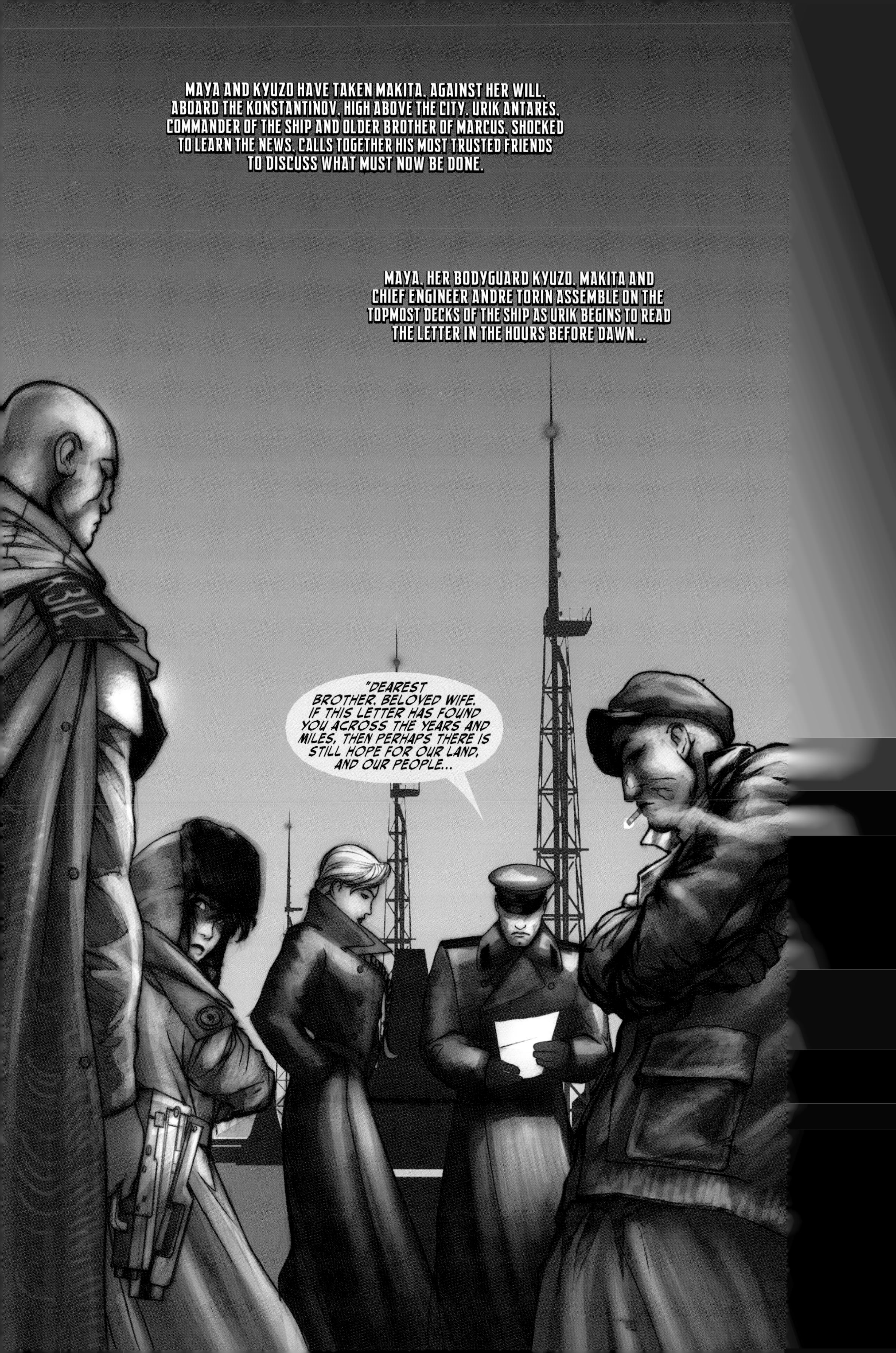
MAYA AND KYUZO HAVE TAKEN MAKITA, AGAINST HER WILL, ABOARD THE KONSTANTINOV, HIGH ABOVE THE CITY. URIK ANTARES, COMMANDER OF THE SHIP AND OLDER BROTHER OF MARCUS, SHOCKED TO LEARN THE NEWS, CALLS TOGETHER HIS MOST TRUSTED FRIENDS TO DISCUSS WHAT MUST NOW BE DONE.
MAYA, HER BODYGUARD KYUZO, MAKITA AND CHIEF ENGINEER ANDRE TORIN ASSEMBLE ON THE TOPMOST DECKS OF THE SHIP AS URIK BEGINS TO READ THE LETTER IN THE HOURS BEFORE DAWN...
"DEAREST BROTHER, BELOVED WIFE. IF THIS LETTER HAS FOUND YOU ACROSS THE YEARS AND MILES, THEN PERHAPS THERE IS STILL HOPE FOR OUR LAND, AND OUR PEOPLE...
K312

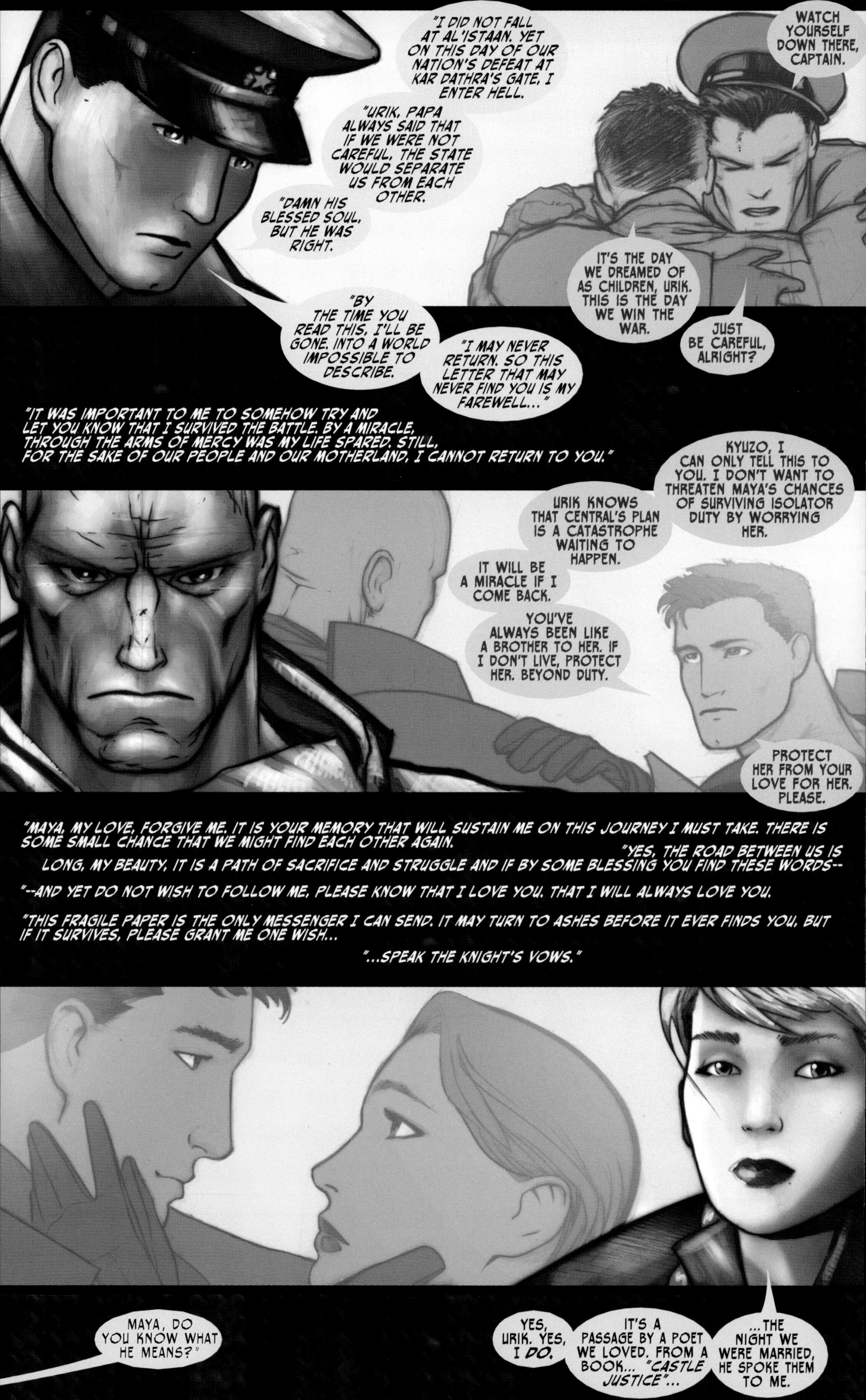
"I DID NOT FALL AT AL'ISTAAN. YET ON THIS DAY OF OUR NATION'S DEFEAT AT KAR DATHRA'S GATE, I ENTER HELL.
"URIK, PAPA ALWAYS SAID THAT IF WE WERE NOT CAREFUL, THE STATE WOULD SEPARATE US FROM EACH OTHER.
"DAMN HIS BLESSED SOUL, BUT HE WAS RIGHT.
WATCH YOURSELF DOWN THERE, CAPTAIN.
IT'S THE DAY WE DREAMED OF AS CHILDREN, URIK. THIS IS THE DAY WE WIN THE WAR.
JUST BE CAREFUL, ALRIGHT?
"BY THE TIME YOU READ THIS, I'LL BE GONE. INTO A WORLD IMPOSSIBLE TO DESCRIBE.
"I MAY NEVER RETURN. SO THIS LETTER THAT MAY NEVER FIND YOU IS MY FAREWELL..."
"IT WAS IMPORTANT TO ME TO SOMEHOW TRY AND LET YOU KNOW THAT I SURVIVED THE BATTLE. BY A MIRACLE, THROUGH THE ARMS OF MERCY WAS MY LIFE SPARED. STILL, FOR THE SAKE OF OUR PEOPLE AND OUR MOTHERLAND, I CANNOT RETURN TO YOU."
KYUZO, I CAN ONLY TELL THIS TO YOU. I DON'T WANT TO THREATEN MAYA'S CHANCES OF SURVIVING ISOLATOR DUTY BY WORRYING HER.
URIK KNOWS THAT CENTRAL'S PLAN IS A CATASTROPHE WAITING TO HAPPEN.
IT WILL BE A MIRACLE IF I COME BACK.
YOU'VE ALWAYS BEEN LIKE A BROTHER TO HER. IF I DON'T LIVE, PROTECT HER. BEYOND DUTY.
PROTECT HER FROM YOUR LOVE FOR HER. PLEASE.
"MAYA, MY LOVE, FORGIVE ME. IT IS YOUR MEMORY THAT WILL SUSTAIN ME ON THIS JOURNEY I MUST TAKE. THERE IS SOME SMALL CHANCE THAT WE MIGHT FIND EACH OTHER AGAIN.
"YES, THE ROAD BETWEEN US IS LONG, MY BEAUTY. IT IS A PATH OF SACRIFICE AND STRUGGLE AND IF BY SOME BLESSING YOU FIND THESE WORDS--
"--AND YET DO NOT WISH TO FOLLOW ME, PLEASE KNOW THAT I LOVE YOU. THAT I WILL ALWAYS LOVE YOU.
"THIS FRAGILE PAPER IS THE ONLY MESSENGER I CAN SEND. IT MAY TURN TO ASHES BEFORE IT EVER FINDS YOU, BUT IF IT SURVIVES, PLEASE GRANT ME ONE WISH...
"...SPEAK THE KNIGHT'S VOWS."
MAYA, DO YOU KNOW WHAT HE MEANS?"
YES, URIK. YES, I *DO*.
IT'S A PASSAGE BY A POET WE LOVED. FROM A BOOK... "CASTLE JUSTICE"...
...THE NIGHT WE WERE MARRIED, HE SPOKE THEM TO ME.

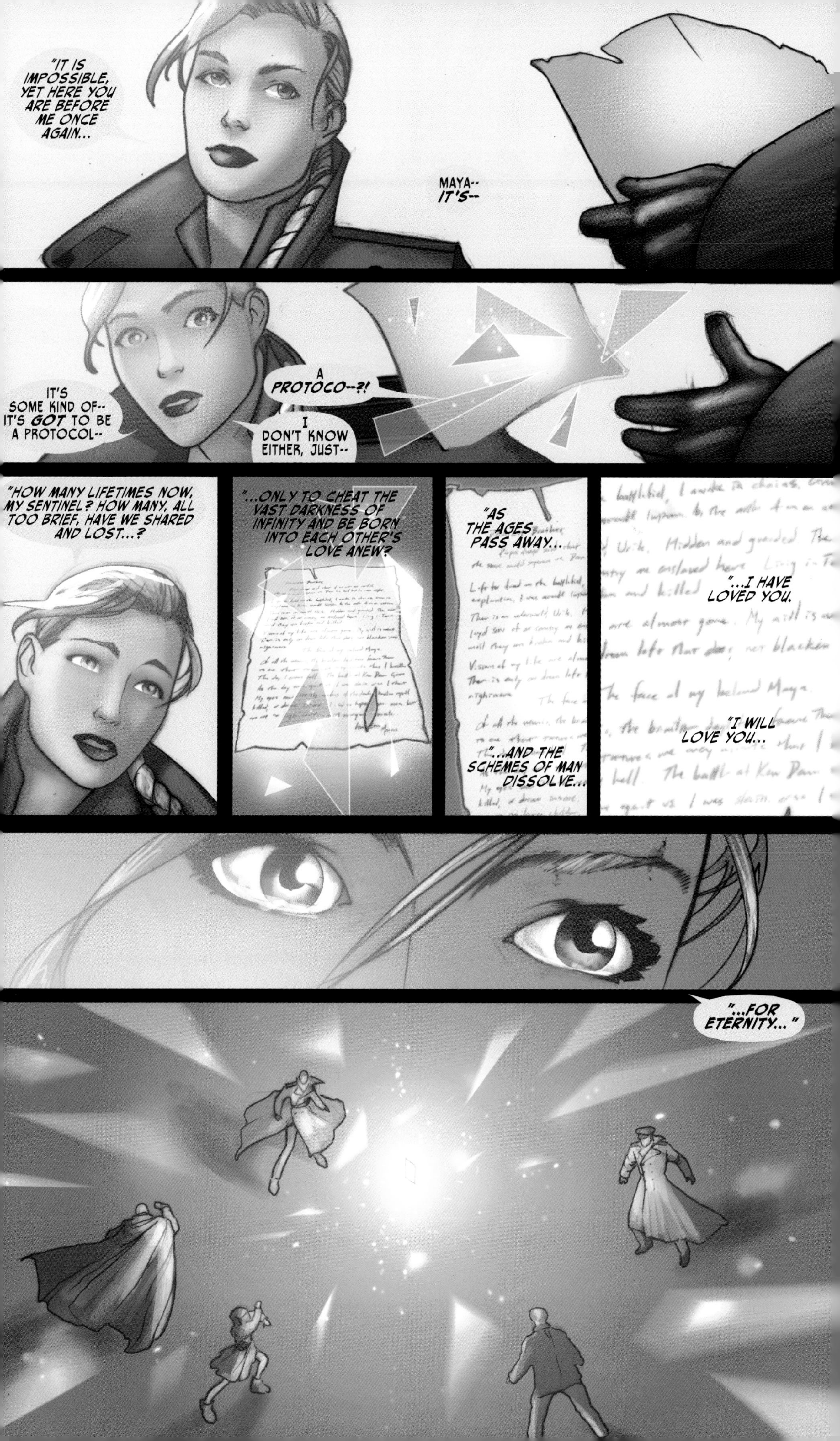
"IT IS IMPOSSIBLE, YET HERE YOU ARE BEFORE ME ONCE AGAIN...
MAYA-- IT'S--
IT'S SOME KIND OF-- IT'S GOT TO BE A PROTOCOL--
A PROTOCO--?!
I DON'T KNOW EITHER, JUST--
"HOW MANY LIFETIMES NOW, MY SENTINEL? HOW MANY, ALL TOO BRIEF, HAVE WE SHARED AND LOST...?
"...ONLY TO CHEAT THE VAST DARKNESS OF INFINITY AND BE BORN INTO EACH OTHER'S LOVE ANEW?
"AS THE AGES PASS AWAY...
"...AND THE SCHEMES OF MAN DISSOLVE...
"...I HAVE LOVED YOU.
"I WILL LOVE YOU...
"...FOR ETERNITY..."

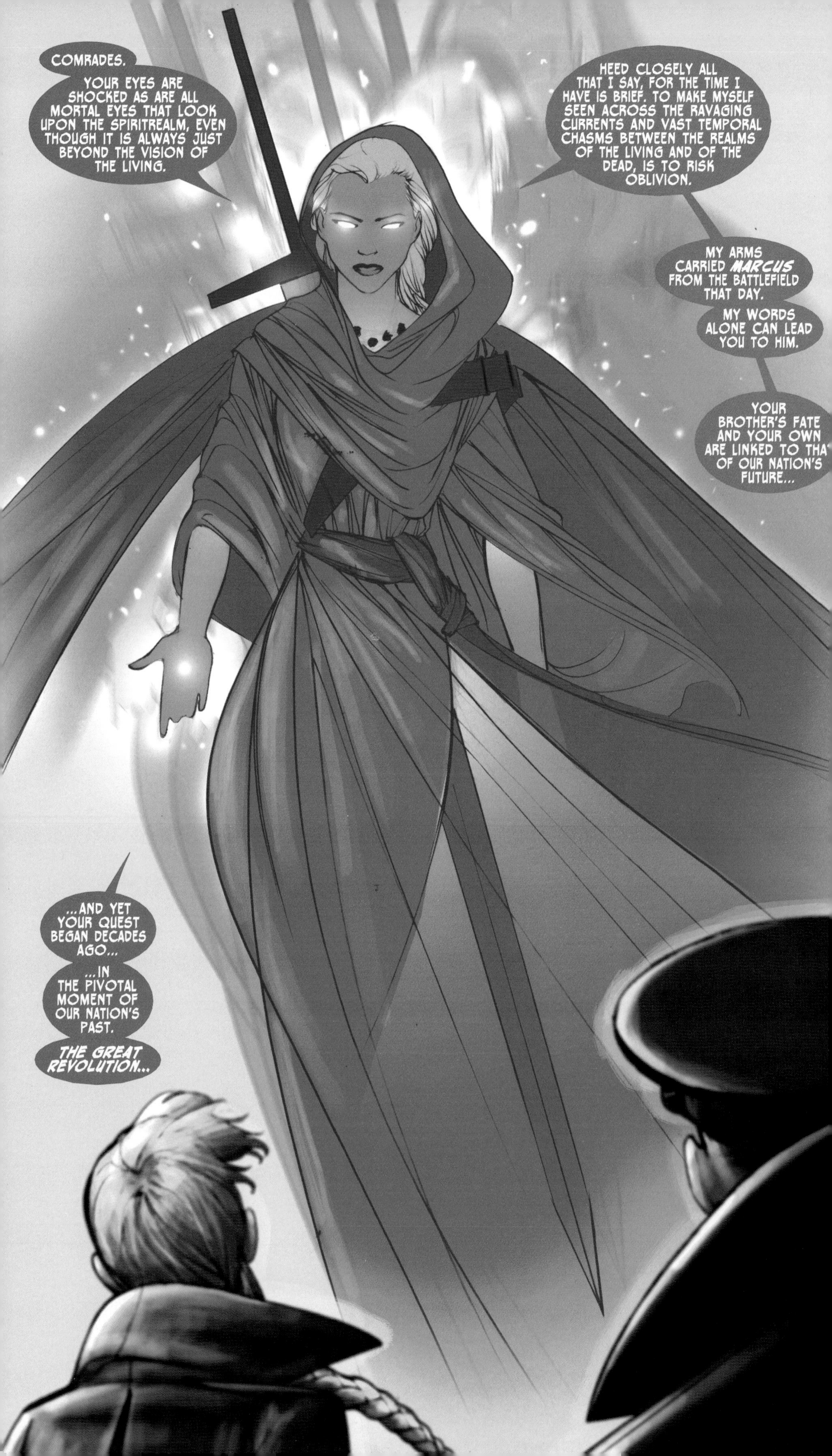
COMRADES.
YOUR EYES ARE SHOCKED AS ARE ALL MORTAL EYES THAT LOOK UPON THE SPIRITREALM, EVEN THOUGH IT IS ALWAYS JUST BEYOND THE VISION OF THE LIVING.
HEED CLOSELY ALL THAT I SAY, FOR THE TIME I HAVE IS BRIEF. TO MAKE MYSELF SEEN ACROSS THE RAVAGING CURRENTS AND VAST TEMPORAL CHASMS BETWEEN THE REALMS OF THE LIVING AND OF THE DEAD, IS TO RISK OBLIVION.
MY ARMS CARRIED *MARCUS* FROM THE BATTLEFIELD THAT DAY.
MY WORDS ALONE CAN LEAD YOU TO HIM.
YOUR BROTHER'S FATE AND YOUR OWN ARE LINKED TO THA OF OUR NATION'S FUTURE...
...AND YET YOUR QUEST BEGAN DECADES AGO...
...IN THE PIVOTAL MOMENT OF OUR NATION'S PAST.
THE GREAT REVOLUTION...

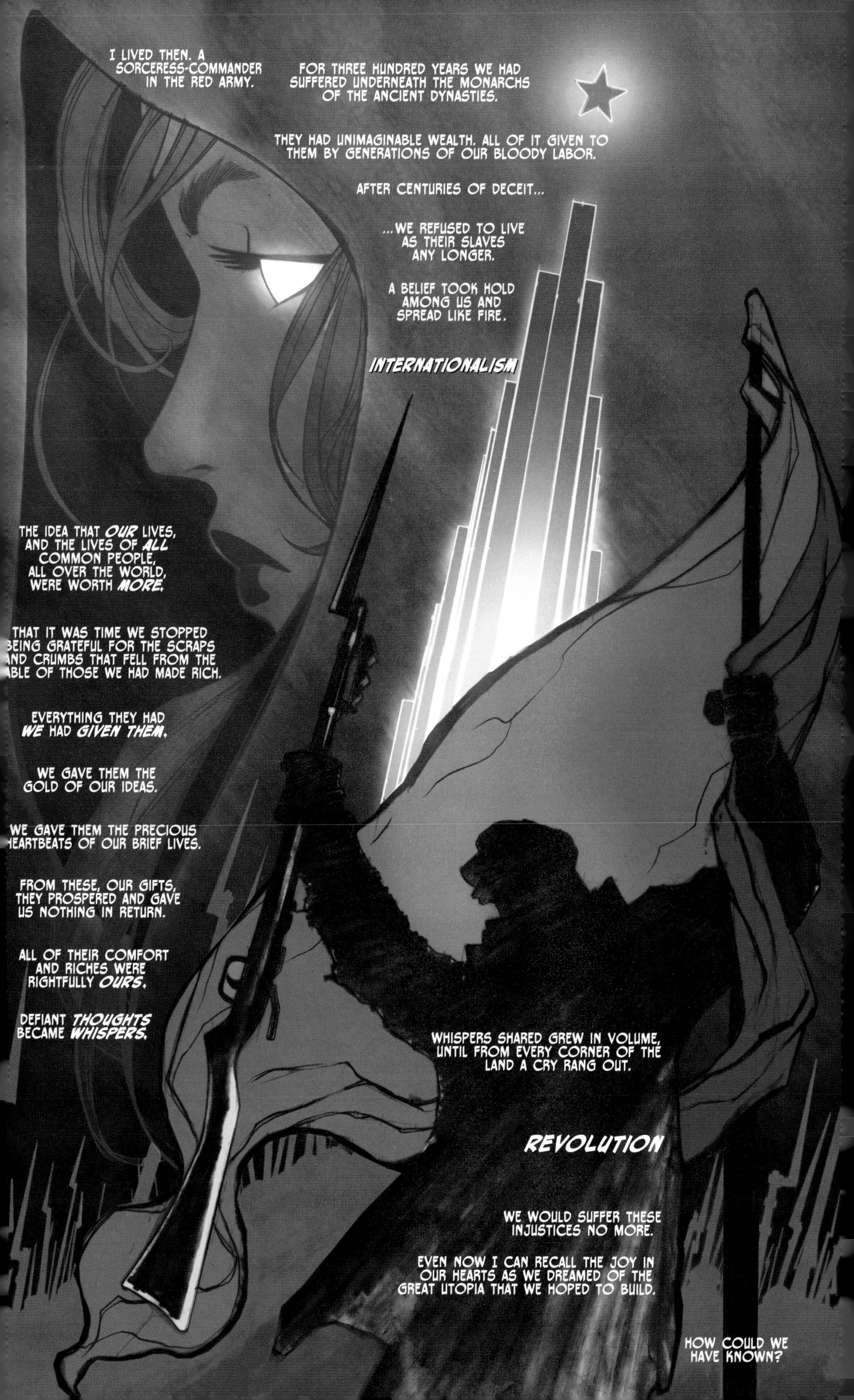
I LIVED THEN. A SORCERESS-COMMANDER IN THE RED ARMY.
FOR THREE HUNDRED YEARS WE HAD SUFFERED UNDERNEATH THE MONARCHS OF THE ANCIENT DYNASTIES.
THEY HAD UNIMAGINABLE WEALTH, ALL OF IT GIVEN TO THEM BY GENERATIONS OF OUR BLOODY LABOR.
AFTER CENTURIES OF DECEIT...
...WE REFUSED TO LIVE AS THEIR SLAVES ANY LONGER.
A BELIEF TOOK HOLD AMONG US AND SPREAD LIKE FIRE.
INTERNATIONALISM
THE IDEA THAT OUR LIVES, AND THE LIVES OF ALL COMMON PEOPLE, ALL OVER THE WORLD, WERE WORTH MORE.
THAT IT WAS TIME WE STOPPED BEING GRATEFUL FOR THE SCRAPS AND CRUMBS THAT FELL FROM THE TABLE OF THOSE WE HAD MADE RICH.
EVERYTHING THEY HAD WE HAD GIVEN THEM.
WE GAVE THEM THE GOLD OF OUR IDEAS.
WE GAVE THEM THE PRECIOUS HEARTBEATS OF OUR BRIEF LIVES.
FROM THESE, OUR GIFTS, THEY PROSPERED AND GAVE US NOTHING IN RETURN.
ALL OF THEIR COMFORT AND RICHES WERE RIGHTFULLY OURS.
DEFIANT THOUGHTS BECAME WHISPERS.
WHISPERS SHARED GREW IN VOLUME, UNTIL FROM EVERY CORNER OF THE LAND A CRY RANG OUT.
REVOLUTION
WE WOULD SUFFER THESE INJUSTICES NO MORE.
EVEN NOW I CAN RECALL THE JOY IN OUR HEARTS AS WE DREAMED OF THE GREAT UTOPIA THAT WE HOPED TO BUILD.
HOW COULD WE HAVE KNOWN?

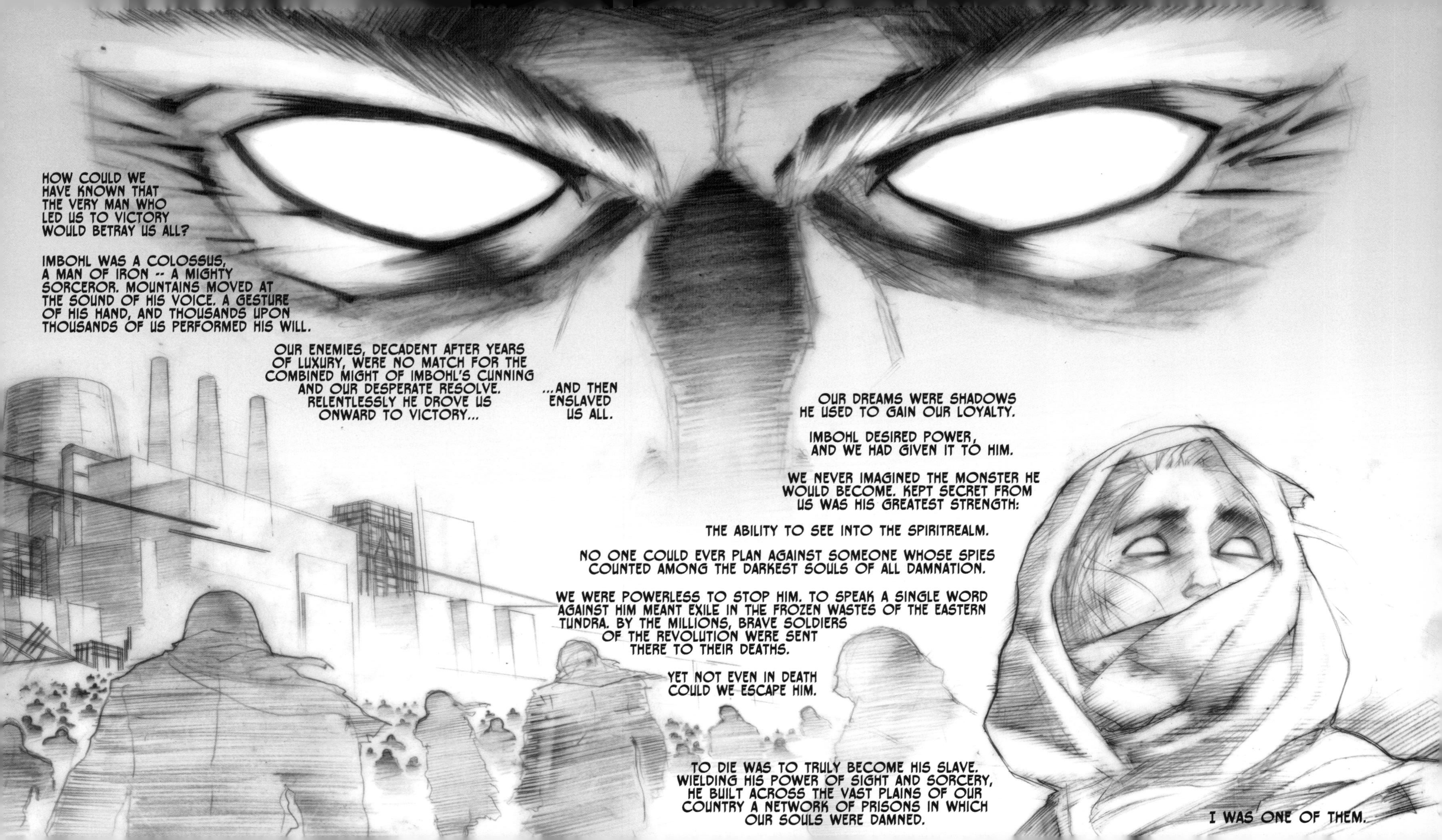
HOW COULD WE HAVE KNOWN THAT THE VERY MAN WHO LED US TO VICTORY WOULD BETRAY US ALL?
IMBOHL WAS A COLOSSUS, A MAN OF IRON -- A MIGHTY SORCEROR. MOUNTAINS MOVED AT THE SOUND OF HIS VOICE. A GESTURE OF HIS HAND, AND THOUSANDS UPON THOUSANDS OF US PERFORMED HIS WILL.
OUR ENEMIES, DECADENT AFTER YEARS OF LUXURY, WERE NO MATCH FOR THE COMBINED MIGHT OF IMBOHL'S CUNNING AND OUR DESPERATE RESOLVE. RELENTLESSLY HE DROVE US ONWARD TO VICTORY...
...AND THEN ENSLAVED US ALL.
OUR DREAMS WERE SHADOWS HE USED TO GAIN OUR LOYALTY.
IMBOHL DESIRED POWER, AND WE HAD GIVEN IT TO HIM.
WE NEVER IMAGINED THE MONSTER HE WOULD BECOME. KEPT SECRET FROM US WAS HIS GREATEST STRENGTH:
THE ABILITY TO SEE INTO THE SPIRITREALM.
NO ONE COULD EVER PLAN AGAINST SOMEONE WHOSE SPIES COUNTED AMONG THE DARKEST SOULS OF ALL DAMNATION.
WE WERE POWERLESS TO STOP HIM. TO SPEAK A SINGLE WORD AGAINST HIM MEANT EXILE IN THE FROZEN WASTES OF THE EASTERN TUNDRA. BY THE MILLIONS, BRAVE SOLDIERS OF THE REVOLUTION WERE SENT THERE TO THEIR DEATHS.
YET NOT EVEN IN DEATH COULD WE ESCAPE HIM.
TO DIE WAS TO TRULY BECOME HIS SLAVE. WIELDING HIS POWER OF SIGHT AND SORCERY, HE BUILT ACROSS THE VAST PLAINS OF OUR COUNTRY A NETWORK OF PRISONS IN WHICH OUR SOULS WERE DAMNED.
I WAS ONE OF THEM.

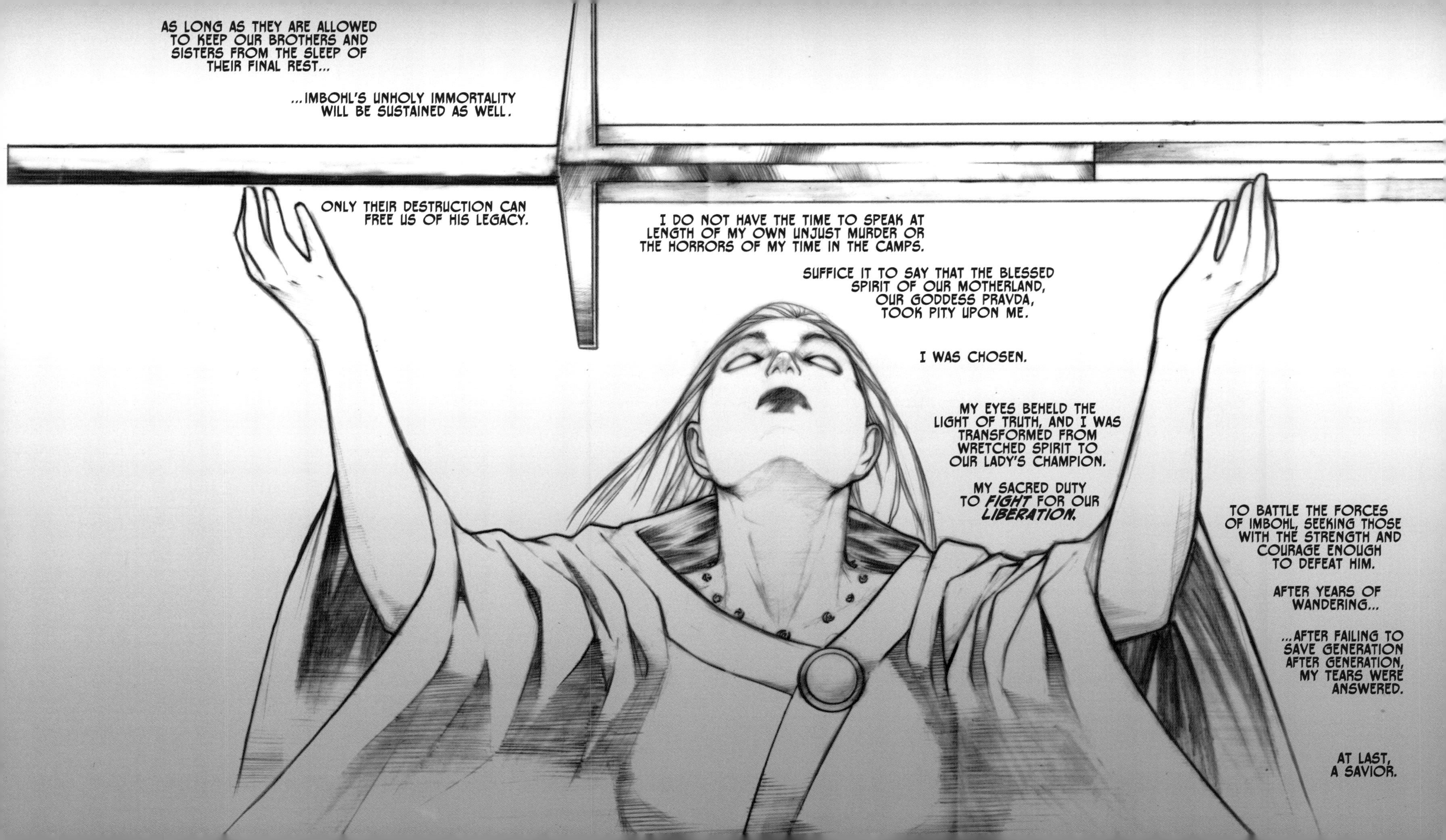
AS LONG AS THEY ARE ALLOWED TO KEEP OUR BROTHERS AND SISTERS FROM THE SLEEP OF THEIR FINAL REST...
...IMBOHL'S UNHOLY IMMORTALITY WILL BE SUSTAINED AS WELL.
ONLY THEIR DESTRUCTION CAN FREE US OF HIS LEGACY.
I DO NOT HAVE THE TIME TO SPEAK AT LENGTH OF MY OWN UNJUST MURDER OR THE HORRORS OF MY TIME IN THE CAMPS.
SUFFICE IT TO SAY THAT THE BLESSED SPIRIT OF OUR MOTHERLAND, OUR GODDESS PRAVDA, TOOK PITY UPON ME.
I WAS CHOSEN.
MY EYES BEHELD THE LIGHT OF TRUTH, AND I WAS TRANSFORMED FROM WRETCHED SPIRIT TO OUR LADY'S CHAMPION.
MY SACRED DUTY TO ***FIGHT*** FOR OUR ***LIBERATION.***
TO BATTLE THE FORCES OF IMBOHL, SEEKING THOSE WITH THE STRENGTH AND COURAGE ENOUGH TO DEFEAT HIM.
AFTER YEARS OF WANDERING...
...AFTER FAILING TO SAVE GENERATION AFTER GENERATION, MY TEARS WERE ANSWERED.
AT LAST, A SAVIOR.

AT THE BATTLE OF KAR DATHRA'S GATE, YOUR BROTHER, WOUNDED AND NEAR DEATH, LOOKED INTO THE SPIRITREALM.

AND THE AGENTS OF IMBOHL LOOKED BACK.

HARVESTING SOULS ON THE BATTLEFIELD FOR THEIR DREAD LORD, THEY WITNESSED A MORTAL PERCEIVING THEM. ONLY IMBOHL HIMSELF HAD EVER DONE SO BEFORE.

WHETHER OR NOT THEY SOUGHT TO DESTROY HIM, OR SOMEHOW DELIVER HIM FOR THEIR MASTER'S JUDGEMENT AND DARK PURPOSES IS A MYSTERY I CARED NOT TO EXPLORE.

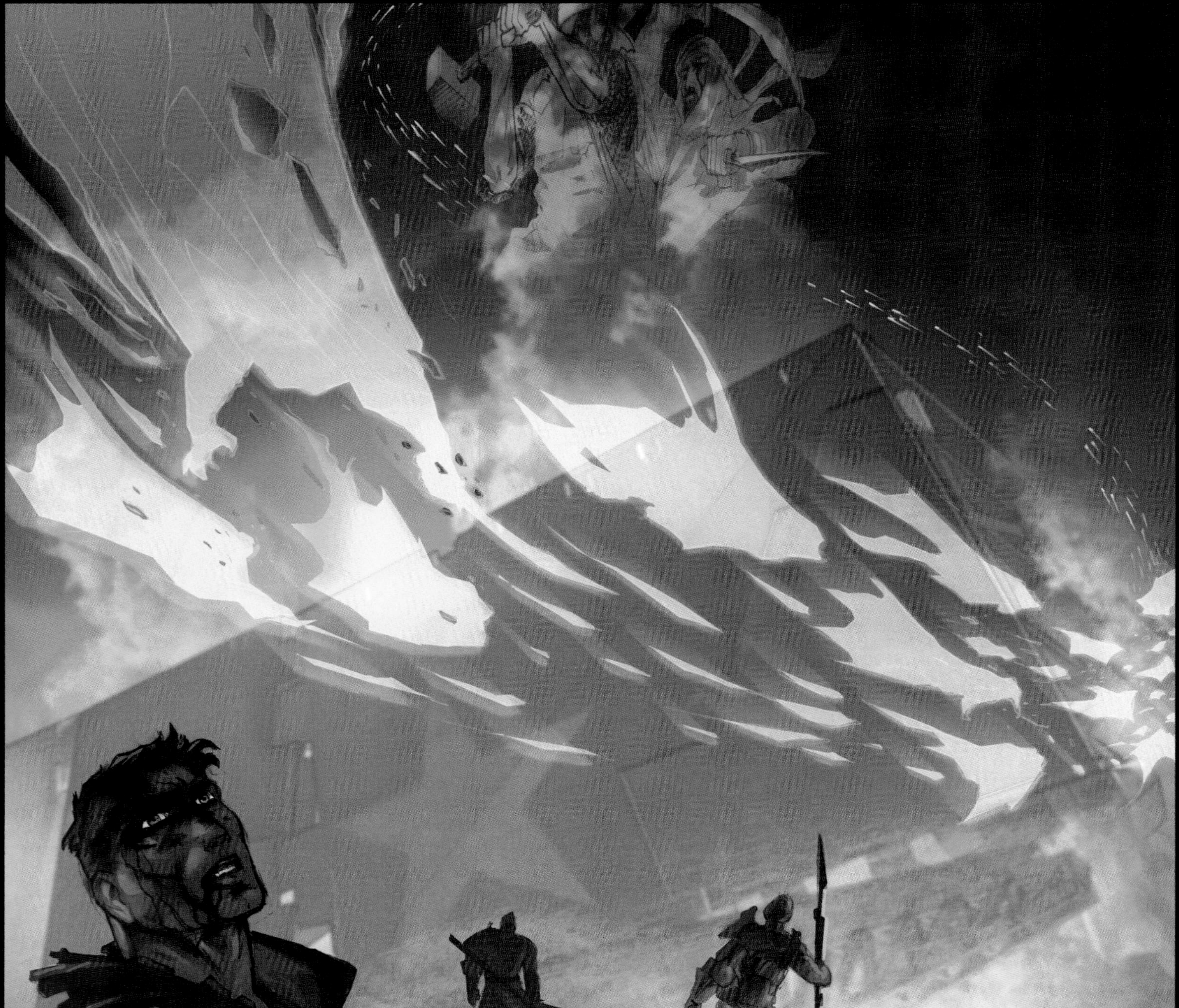

I HAD TO SAVE HIM FROM THEM.

I COULD NOT HELP BUT WONDER, AS IMBOHL'S EYES HAD BEEN USED TO IMPRISON OUR COUNTRY, COULD MARCUS' VISION NOW BE USED TO FREE IT?

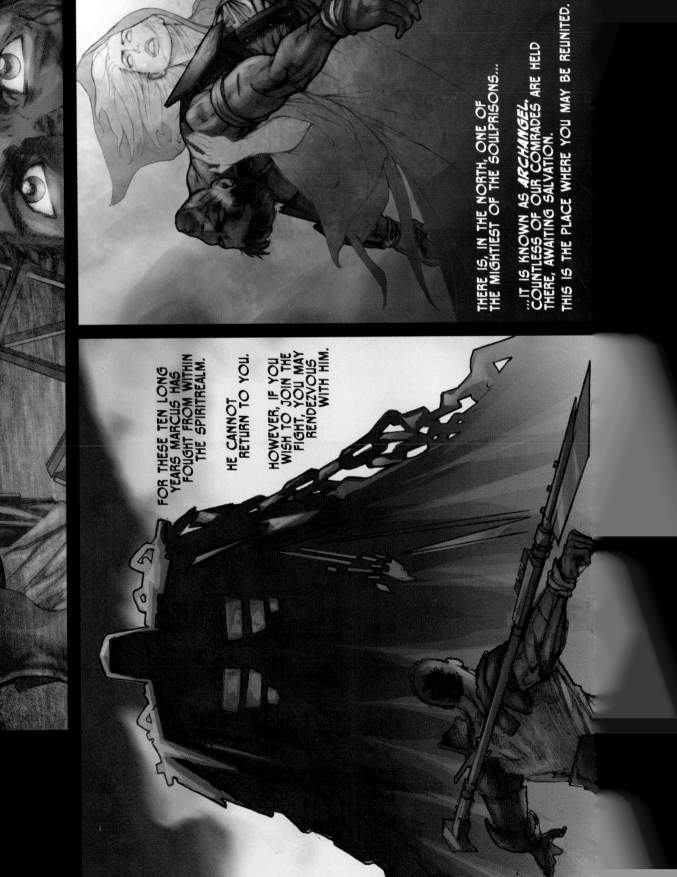

AFTER IMBOHL'S SLAVES HAD TASTED THE ANGER OF MY WEAPON, I DESCRIBED FOR HIM THE PLAGUE OF THE *SOULPRISONS*.

THERE IS, IN THE NORTH, ONE OF THE MIGHTIEST OF THE SOULPRISONS...

...IT IS KNOWN AS *ARCHANGEL*. COUNTLESS OF OUR COMRADES ARE HELD THERE, AWAITING SALVATION.

THIS IS THE PLACE WHERE YOU MAY BE REUNITED.

FOR THESE TEN LONG YEARS MARCUS HAS FOUGHT FROM WITHIN THE SPIRITREALM.

HE CANNOT RETURN TO YOU.

HOWEVER, IF YOU WISH TO JOIN THE FIGHT, YOU MAY RENDEZVOUS WITH HIM.

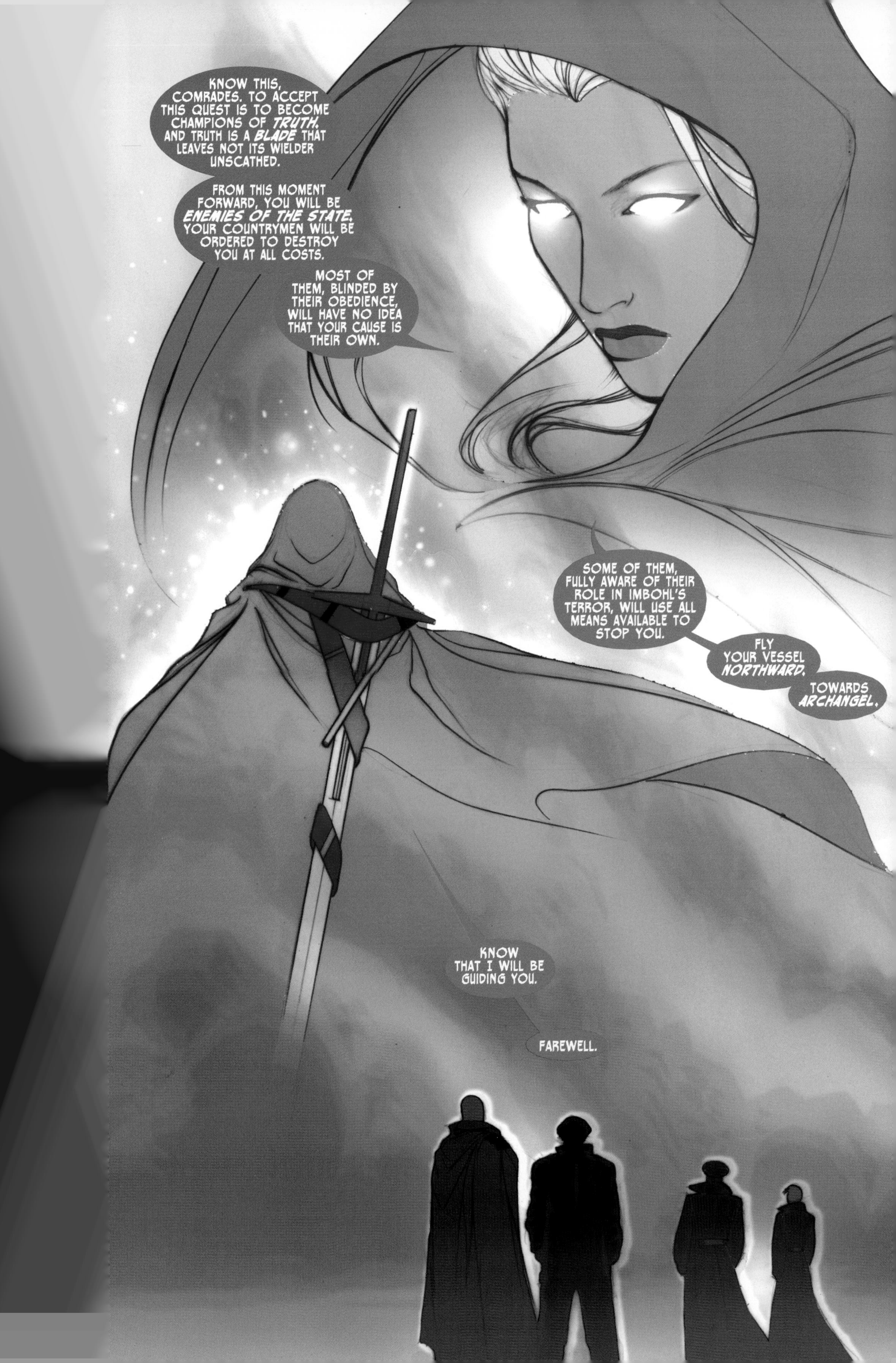
KNOW THIS, COMRADES. TO ACCEPT THIS QUEST IS TO BECOME CHAMPIONS OF TRUTH. AND TRUTH IS A BLADE THAT LEAVES NOT ITS WIELDER UNSCATHED.
FROM THIS MOMENT FORWARD, YOU WILL BE ENEMIES OF THE STATE. YOUR COUNTRYMEN WILL BE ORDERED TO DESTROY YOU AT ALL COSTS.
MOST OF THEM, BLINDED BY THEIR OBEDIENCE, WILL HAVE NO IDEA THAT YOUR CAUSE IS THEIR OWN.
SOME OF THEM, FULLY AWARE OF THEIR ROLE IN IMBOHL'S TERROR, WILL USE ALL MEANS AVAILABLE TO STOP YOU.
FLY YOUR VESSEL NORTHWARD.
TOWARDS ARCHANGEL.
KNOW THAT I WILL BE GUIDING YOU.
FAREWELL.

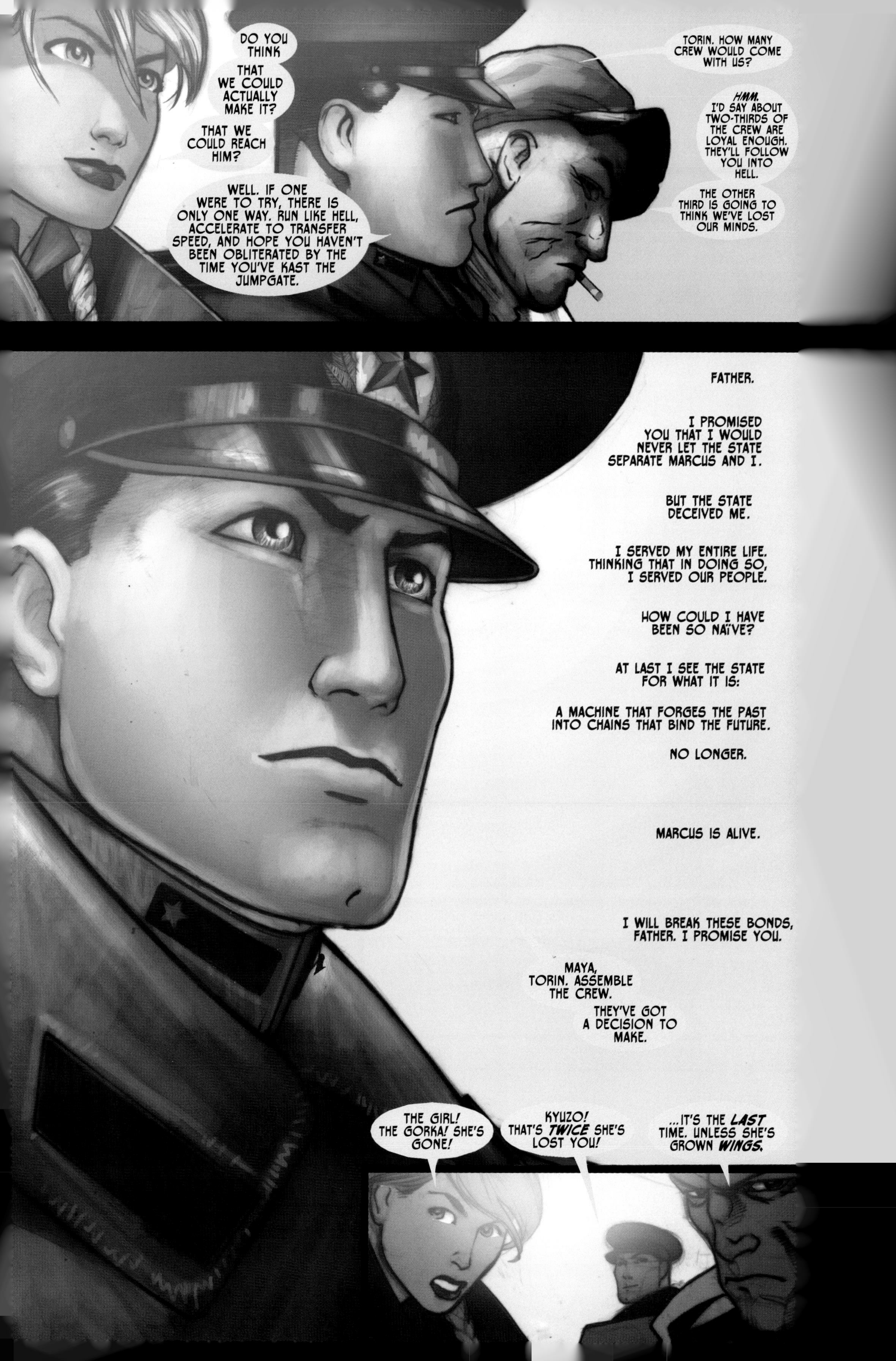
DO YOU THINK THAT WE COULD ACTUALLY MAKE IT?
THAT WE COULD REACH HIM?
WELL. IF ONE WERE TO TRY, THERE IS ONLY ONE WAY. RUN LIKE HELL, ACCELERATE TO TRANSFER SPEED, AND HOPE YOU HAVEN'T BEEN OBLITERATED BY THE TIME YOU'VE KAST THE JUMPGATE.
TORIN. HOW MANY CREW WOULD COME WITH US?
HMM. I'D SAY ABOUT TWO-THIRDS OF THE CREW ARE LOYAL ENOUGH. THEY'LL FOLLOW YOU INTO HELL.
THE OTHER THIRD IS GOING TO THINK WE'VE LOST OUR MINDS.
FATHER.
I PROMISED YOU THAT I WOULD NEVER LET THE STATE SEPARATE MARCUS AND I.
BUT THE STATE DECEIVED ME.
I SERVED MY ENTIRE LIFE. THINKING THAT IN DOING SO, I SERVED OUR PEOPLE.
HOW COULD I HAVE BEEN SO NAÏVE?
AT LAST I SEE THE STATE FOR WHAT IT IS:
A MACHINE THAT FORGES THE PAST INTO CHAINS THAT BIND THE FUTURE.
NO LONGER.
MARCUS IS ALIVE.
I WILL BREAK THESE BONDS, FATHER. I PROMISE YOU.
MAYA, TORIN. ASSEMBLE THE CREW.
THEY'VE GOT A DECISION TO MAKE.
THE GIRL! THE GORKA! SHE'S GONE!
KYUZO! THAT'S *TWICE* SHE'S LOST YOU!
...IT'S THE *LAST* TIME. UNLESS SHE'S GROWN *WINGS*.

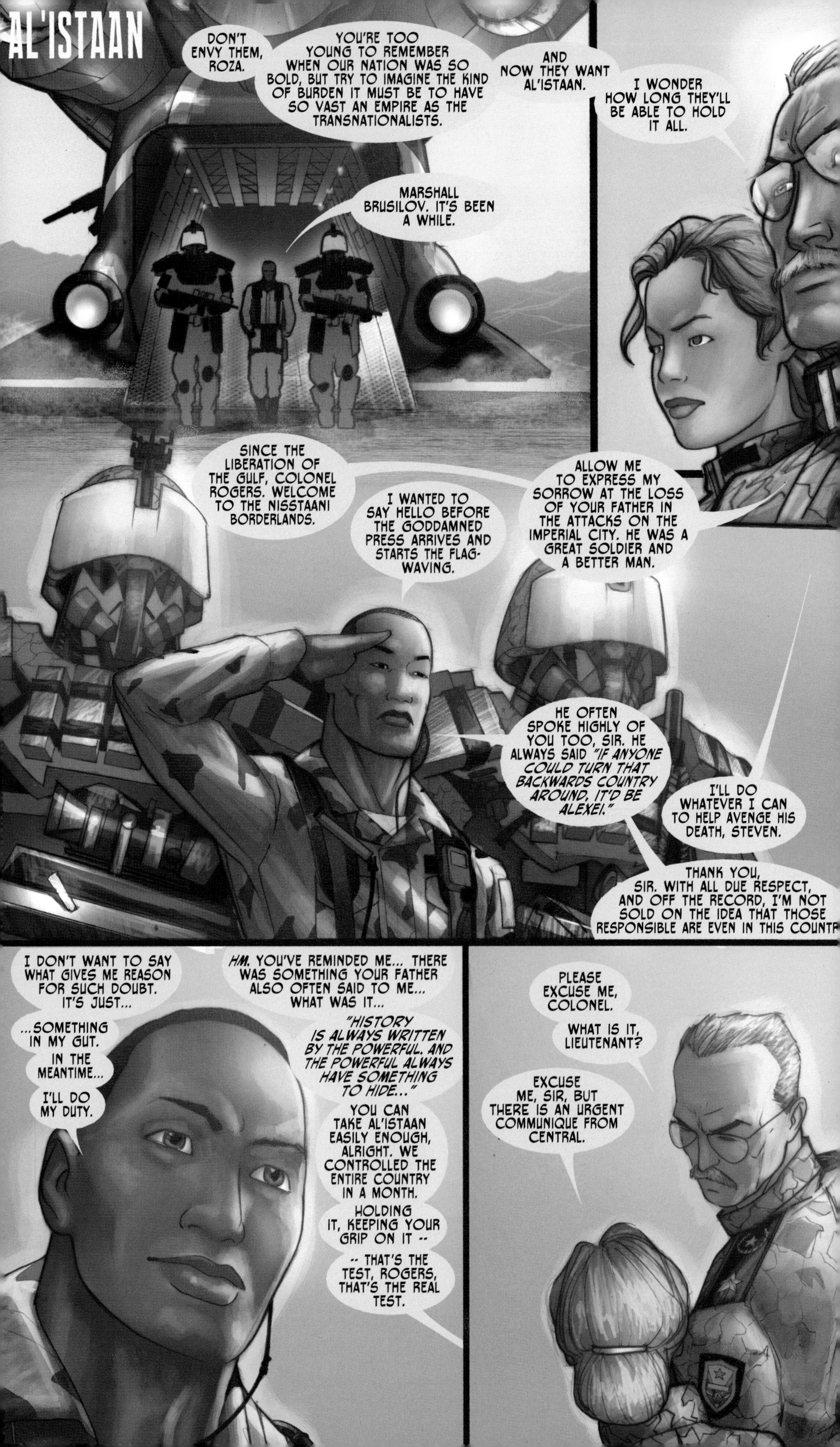
AL'ISTAAN
DON'T ENVY THEM, ROZA.
YOU'RE TOO YOUNG TO REMEMBER WHEN OUR NATION WAS SO BOLD, BUT TRY TO IMAGINE THE KIND OF BURDEN IT MUST BE TO HAVE SO VAST AN EMPIRE AS THE TRANSNATIONALISTS.
AND NOW THEY WANT AL'ISTAAN.
I WONDER HOW LONG THEY'LL BE ABLE TO HOLD IT ALL.
MARSHALL BRUSILOV. IT'S BEEN A WHILE.
SINCE THE LIBERATION OF THE GULF, COLONEL ROGERS. WELCOME TO THE NISSTAANI BORDERLANDS.
I WANTED TO SAY HELLO BEFORE THE GODDAMNED PRESS ARRIVES AND STARTS THE FLAG-WAVING.
ALLOW ME TO EXPRESS MY SORROW AT THE LOSS OF YOUR FATHER IN THE ATTACKS ON THE IMPERIAL CITY. HE WAS A GREAT SOLDIER AND A BETTER MAN.
HE OFTEN SPOKE HIGHLY OF YOU TOO, SIR. HE ALWAYS SAID *"IF ANYONE COULD TURN THAT BACKWARDS COUNTRY AROUND, IT'D BE ALEXEI."*
I'LL DO WHATEVER I CAN TO HELP AVENGE HIS DEATH, STEVEN.
THANK YOU, SIR. WITH ALL DUE RESPECT, AND OFF THE RECORD, I'M NOT SOLD ON THE IDEA THAT THOSE RESPONSIBLE ARE EVEN IN THIS COUNTR
I DON'T WANT TO SAY WHAT GIVES ME REASON FOR SUCH DOUBT. IT'S JUST...
...SOMETHING IN MY GUT.
IN THE MEANTIME...
I'LL DO MY DUTY.
HM. YOU'VE REMINDED ME... THERE WAS SOMETHING YOUR FATHER ALSO OFTEN SAID TO ME... WHAT WAS IT...
"HISTORY IS ALWAYS WRITTEN BY THE POWERFUL. AND THE POWERFUL ALWAYS HAVE SOMETHING TO HIDE..."
YOU CAN TAKE AL'ISTAAN EASILY ENOUGH, ALRIGHT. WE CONTROLLED THE ENTIRE COUNTRY IN A MONTH.
HOLDING IT, KEEPING YOUR GRIP ON IT --
-- THAT'S THE TEST, ROGERS, THAT'S THE REAL TEST.
PLEASE EXCUSE ME, COLONEL.
WHAT IS IT, LIEUTENANT?
EXCUSE ME, SIR, BUT THERE IS AN URGENT COMMUNIQUE FROM CENTRAL.

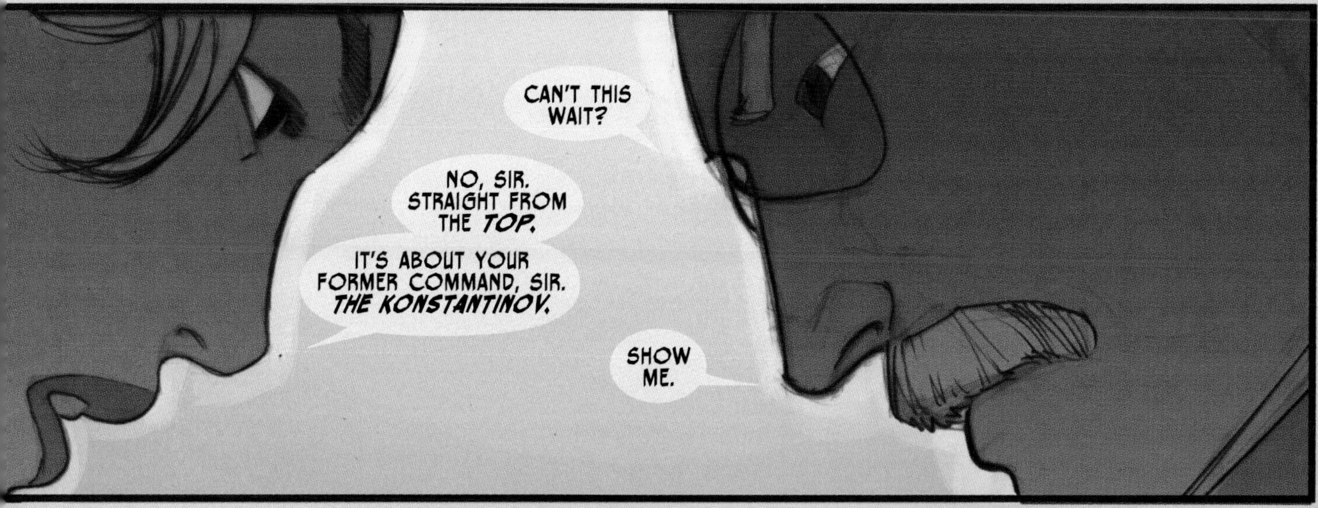
CAN'T THIS WAIT?
NO, SIR. STRAIGHT FROM THE *TOP.*
IT'S ABOUT YOUR FORMER COMMAND, SIR. *THE KONSTANTINOV.*
SHOW ME.

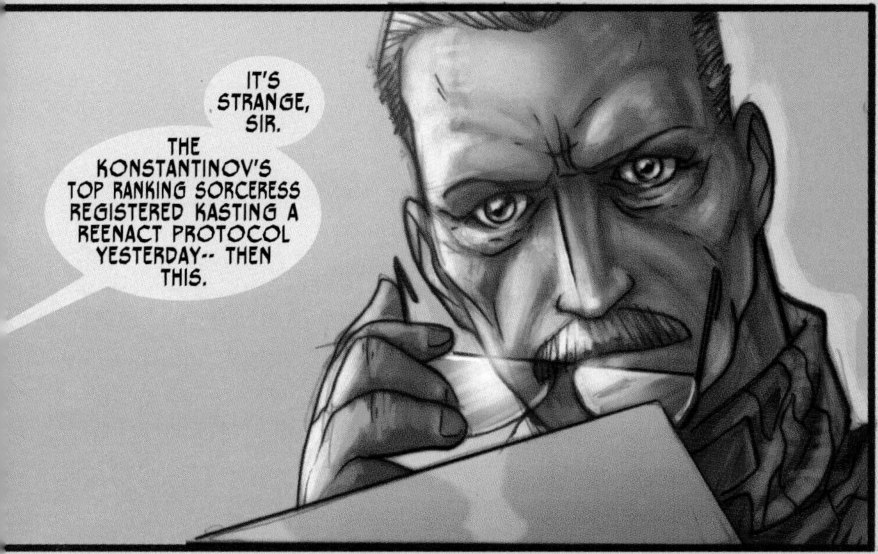
IT'S STRANGE, SIR.
THE KONSTANTINOV'S TOP RANKING SORCERESS REGISTERED KASTING A REENACT PROTOCOL YESTERDAY-- THEN THIS.

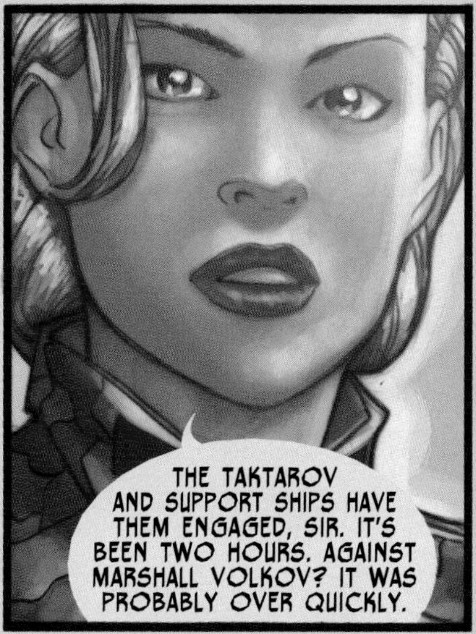
THE TAKTAROV AND SUPPORT SHIPS HAVE THEM ENGAGED, SIR. IT'S BEEN TWO HOURS. AGAINST MARSHALL VOLKOV? IT WAS PROBABLY OVER QUICKLY.

mmunique from Central Command. To all commanding officers:

ymarshall Urik Antares, Sorceress-Major Maya Antares, Chief Engineer Andre rin and a majority of the crew (est. two-thirds) have staged a mutiny and andoned their duties in Nokgorka. Remaining crew refused to join mutiny, re given safe passage groundside, and are currently under questioning.

e destination of their vessel the R.S.S. Konstantinov is unknown at this me.

ymarshall Antares has refused to surrender himself, his crew, or his ssel. The only response has been hostile reaction: The Konstantinov has red upon and immobilized the R.S.S. Firin during a brief engagement.

this treasonous insubordination, the Konstantinov ave been ripped of rank and military privileges and are from ward to considered enemies of the state.

ders Follow:

ke no further attempt at negotiation with the enemy ve

tercept and use all force necessary to subdue. If subd feasible, orders are to engage and destroy.

peat:

gage and Destroy.

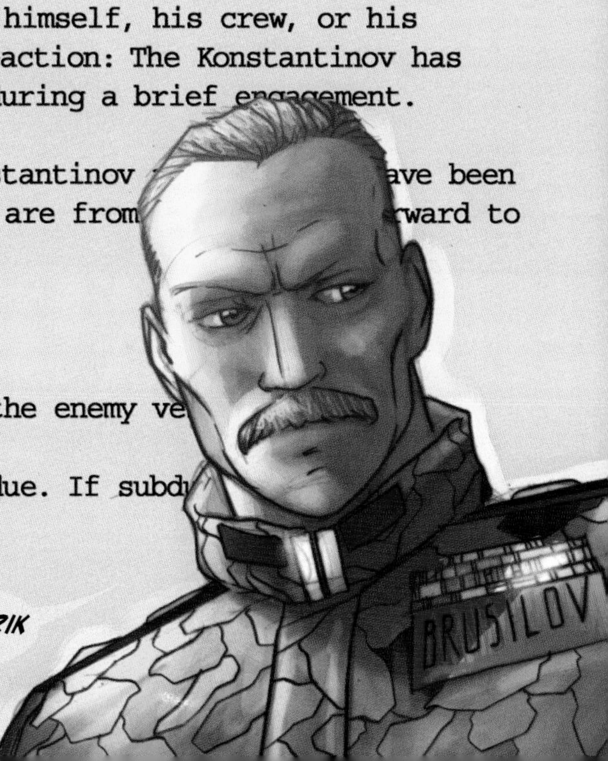
BRUSILOV
WITH ALL DUE RESPECT TO MARSHALL VOLKOV AND HIS CREW, LIEUTENANT, YOU DON'T KNOW MY OLD SHIP.
AND YOU DON'T KNOW *URIK ANTARES...*

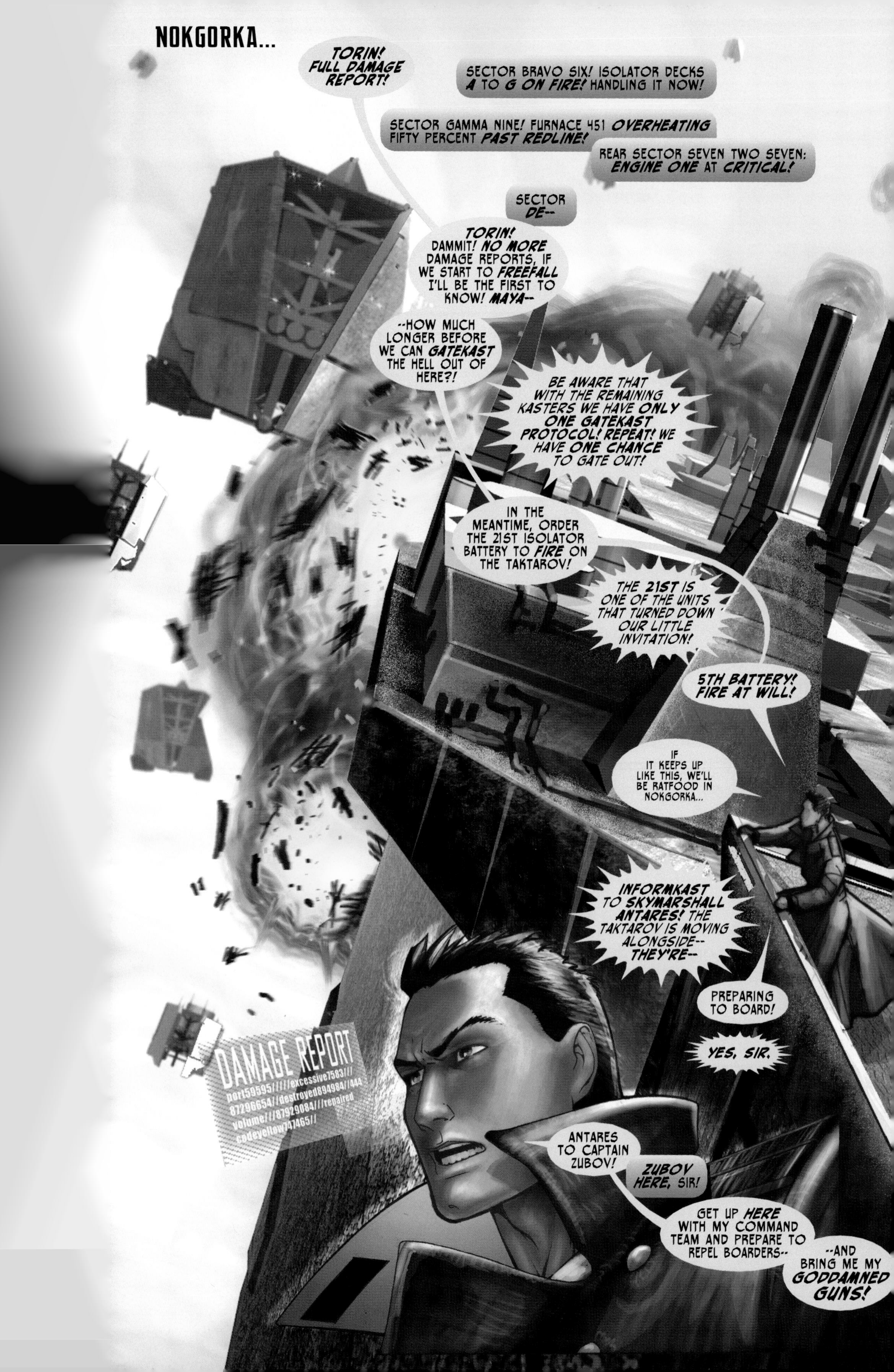
NOKGORKA...
TORIN! FULL DAMAGE REPORT!
SECTOR BRAVO SIX! ISOLATOR DECKS A TO G ON FIRE! HANDLING IT NOW!
SECTOR GAMMA NINE! FURNACE 451 OVERHEATING FIFTY PERCENT PAST REDLINE!
REAR SECTOR SEVEN TWO SEVEN: ENGINE ONE AT CRITICAL!
SECTOR DE--
TORIN! DAMMIT! NO MORE DAMAGE REPORTS, IF WE START TO FREEFALL I'LL BE THE FIRST TO KNOW! MAYA--
--HOW MUCH LONGER BEFORE WE CAN GATEKAST THE HELL OUT OF HERE?!
BE AWARE THAT WITH THE REMAINING KASTERS WE HAVE ONLY ONE GATEKAST PROTOCOL! REPEAT! WE HAVE ONE CHANCE TO GATE OUT!
IN THE MEANTIME, ORDER THE 21ST ISOLATOR BATTERY TO FIRE ON THE TAKTAROV!
THE 21ST IS ONE OF THE UNITS THAT TURNED DOWN OUR LITTLE INVITATION!
5TH BATTERY! FIRE AT WILL!
IF IT KEEPS UP LIKE THIS, WE'LL BE RATFOOD IN NOKGORKA...
INFORMKAST TO SKYMARSHALL ANTARES! THE TAKTAROV IS MOVING ALONGSIDE-- THEY'RE--
PREPARING TO BOARD!
YES, SIR.
DAMAGE REPORT
port59595/////excessive7583///
87296654//destroyed894984//444
volume///87929084///repaired
codeyellow747465//
ANTARES TO CAPTAIN ZUBOV!
ZUBOV HERE, SIR!
GET UP HERE WITH MY COMMAND TEAM AND PREPARE TO REPEL BOARDERS--
--AND BRING ME MY GODDAMNED GUNS!

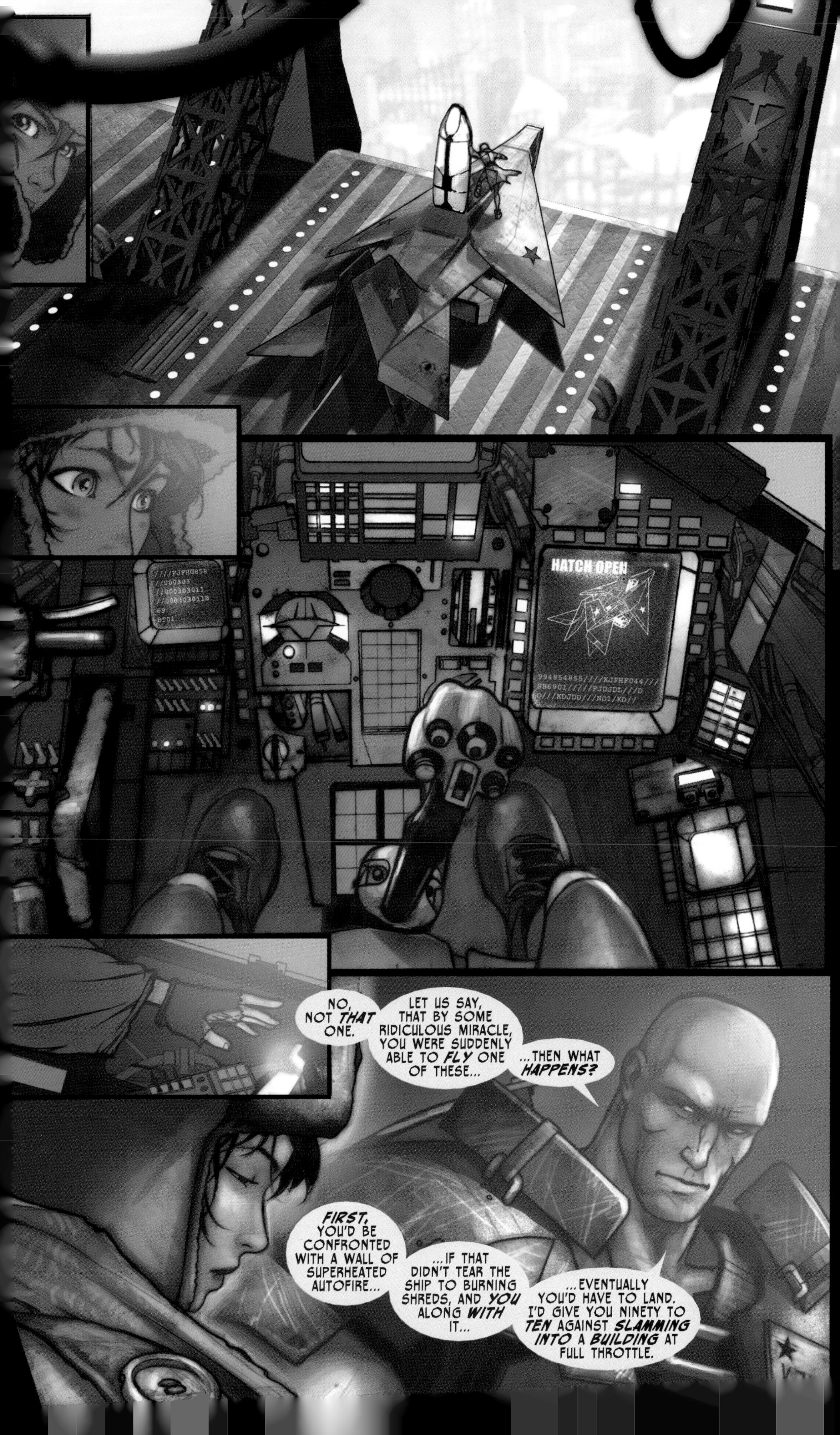
HATCH OPEN
NO, NOT *THAT* ONE.
LET US SAY, THAT BY SOME RIDICULOUS MIRACLE, YOU WERE SUDDENLY ABLE TO *FLY* ONE OF THESE...
...THEN WHAT *HAPPENS?*
FIRST, YOU'D BE CONFRONTED WITH A WALL OF SUPERHEATED AUTOFIRE...
...IF THAT DIDN'T TEAR THE SHIP TO BURNING SHREDS, AND *YOU* ALONG *WITH* IT...
...EVENTUALLY YOU'D HAVE TO LAND. I'D GIVE YOU NINETY TO *TEN* AGAINST *SLAMMING INTO* A *BUILDING* AT FULL THROTTLE.

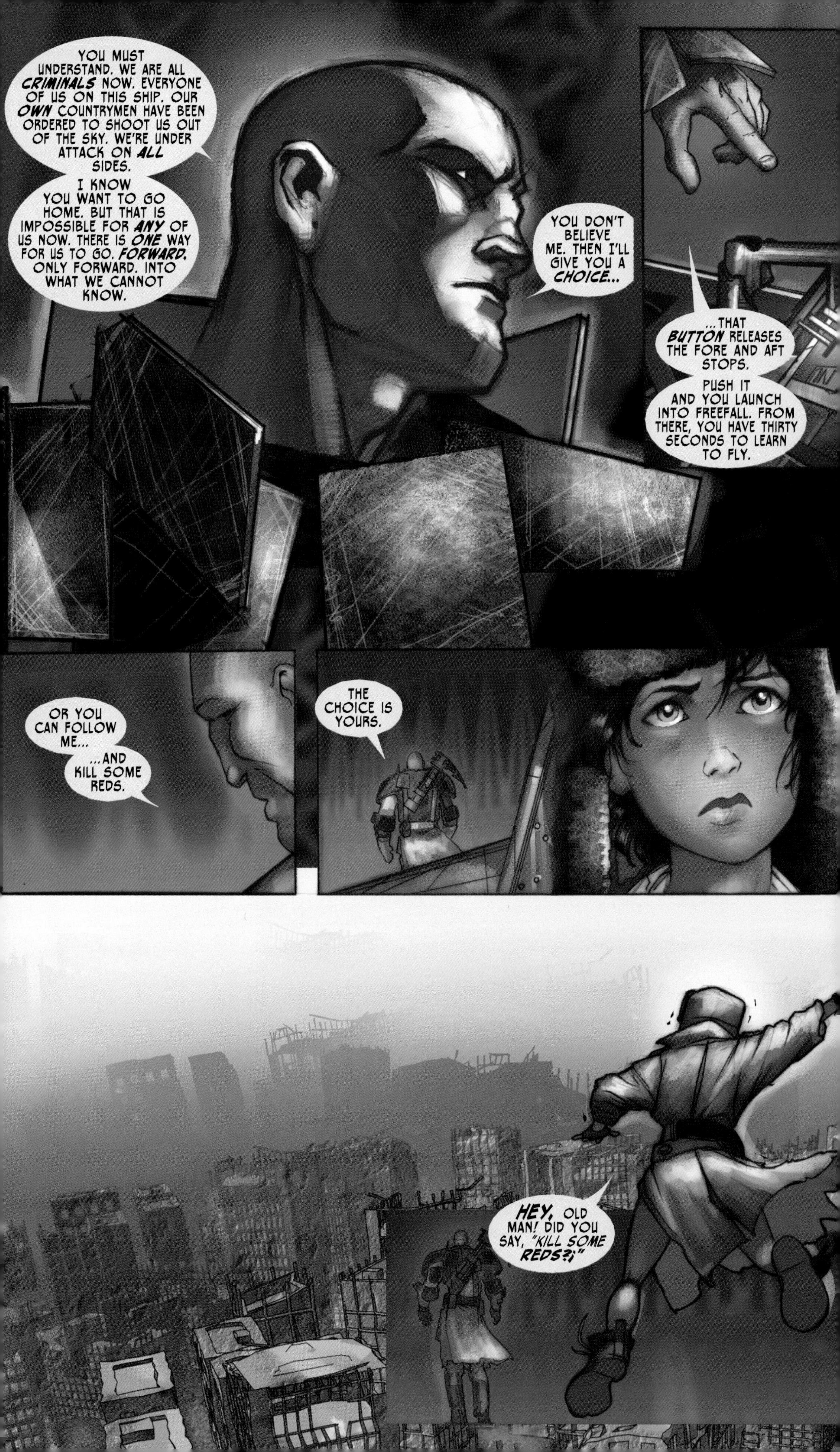
YOU MUST UNDERSTAND. WE ARE ALL CRIMINALS NOW. EVERYONE OF US ON THIS SHIP. OUR OWN COUNTRYMEN HAVE BEEN ORDERED TO SHOOT US OUT OF THE SKY. WE'RE UNDER ATTACK ON ALL SIDES.
I KNOW YOU WANT TO GO HOME. BUT THAT IS IMPOSSIBLE FOR ANY OF US NOW. THERE IS ONE WAY FOR US TO GO. FORWARD. ONLY FORWARD. INTO WHAT WE CANNOT KNOW.
YOU DON'T BELIEVE ME. THEN I'LL GIVE YOU A CHOICE...
...THAT BUTTON RELEASES THE FORE AND AFT STOPS.
PUSH IT AND YOU LAUNCH INTO FREEFALL. FROM THERE, YOU HAVE THIRTY SECONDS TO LEARN TO FLY.
OR YOU CAN FOLLOW ME...
...AND KILL SOME REDS.
THE CHOICE IS YOURS.
HEY, OLD MAN! DID YOU SAY, "KILL SOME REDS?¡"

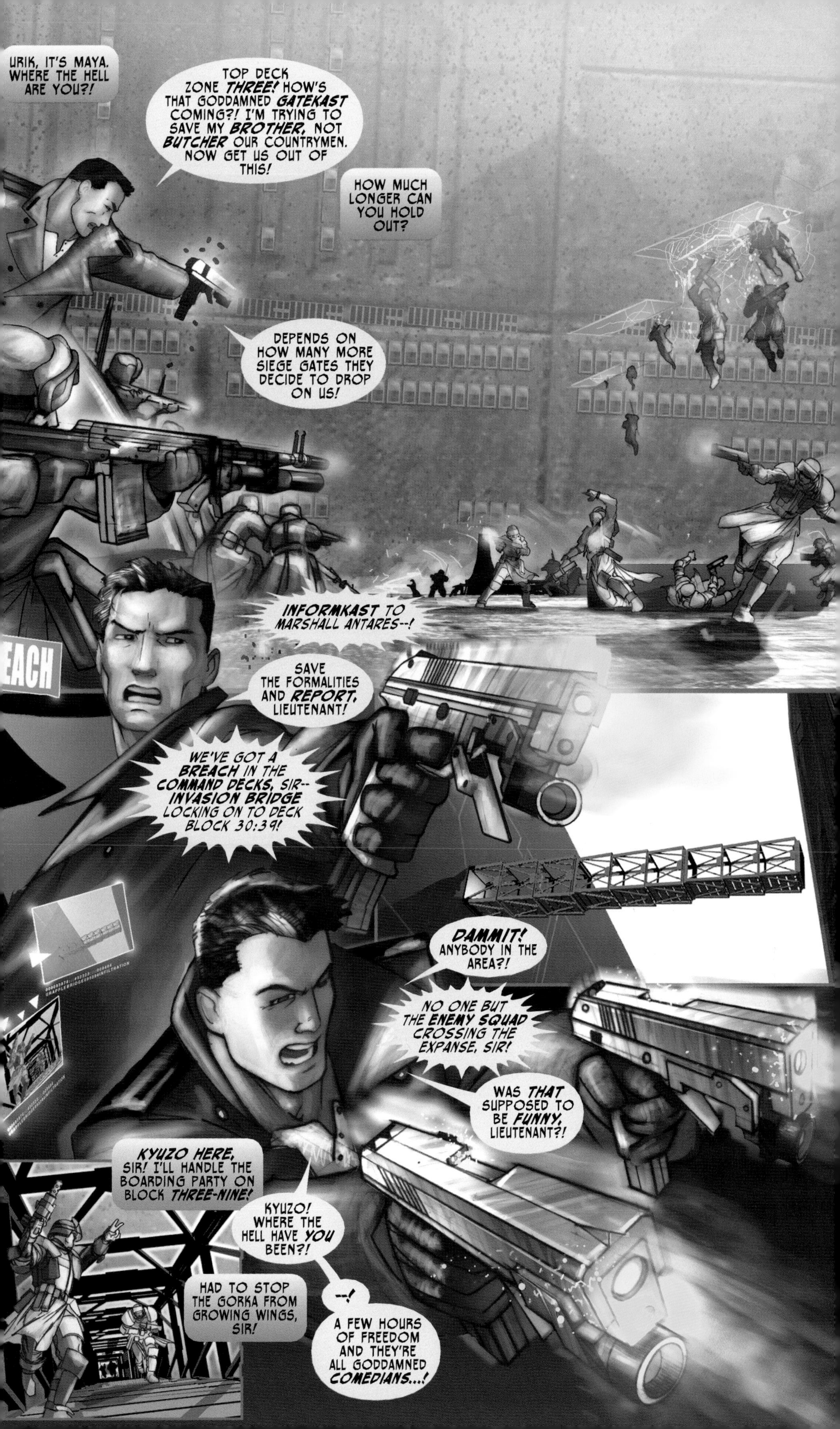
URIK, IT'S MAYA. WHERE THE HELL ARE YOU?!
TOP DECK ZONE *THREE!* HOW'S THAT GODDAMNED *GATEKAST* COMING?! I'M TRYING TO SAVE MY *BROTHER,* NOT *BUTCHER* OUR COUNTRYMEN. NOW GET US OUT OF THIS!
HOW MUCH LONGER CAN YOU HOLD OUT?
DEPENDS ON HOW MANY MORE SIEGE GATES THEY DECIDE TO DROP ON US!
EACH
INFORMKAST TO MARSHALL ANTARES--!
SAVE THE FORMALITIES AND *REPORT,* LIEUTENANT!
WE'VE GOT A *BREACH* IN THE *COMMAND DECKS,* SIR-- *INVASION BRIDGE* LOCKING ON TO DECK BLOCK 30:39!
DAMMIT! ANYBODY IN THE AREA?!
NO ONE BUT THE *ENEMY SQUAD* CROSSING THE EXPANSE, SIR!
WAS *THAT* SUPPOSED TO BE *FUNNY,* LIEUTENANT?!
KYUZO HERE, SIR! I'LL HANDLE THE BOARDING PARTY ON BLOCK *THREE-NINE!*
KYUZO! WHERE THE HELL HAVE *YOU* BEEN?!
HAD TO STOP THE GORKA FROM GROWING WINGS, SIR!
--!
A FEW HOURS OF FREEDOM AND THEY'RE ALL GODDAMNED *COMEDIANS...!*

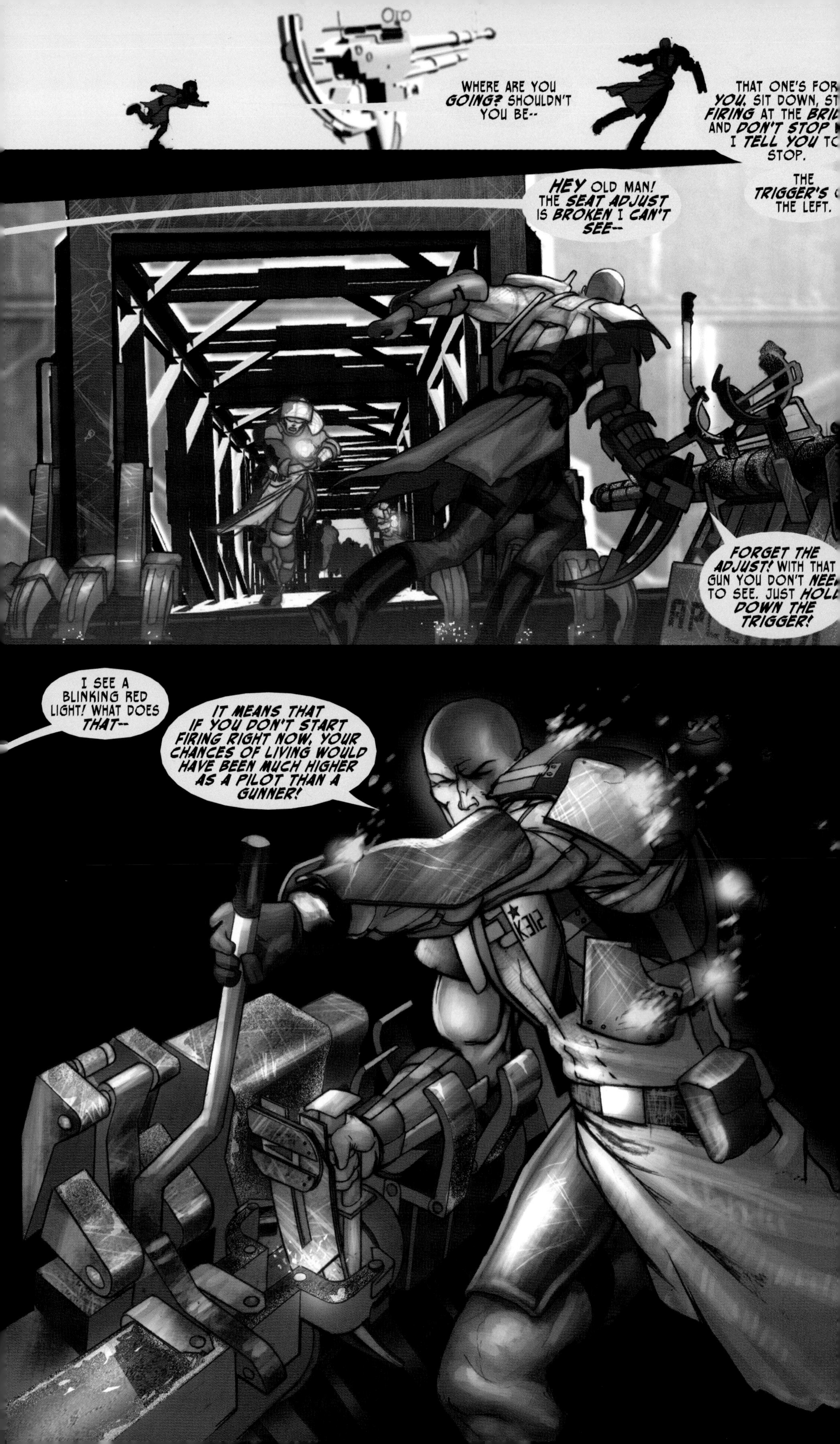
WHERE ARE YOU GOING? SHOULDN'T YOU BE--
THAT ONE'S FOR YOU. SIT DOWN, ST FIRING AT THE BRI AND DON'T STOP I TELL YOU TO STOP.
HEY OLD MAN! THE SEAT ADJUST IS BROKEN I CAN'T SEE--
THE TRIGGER'S THE LEFT.
FORGET THE ADJUST! WITH THAT GUN YOU DON'T NEE TO SEE. JUST HOL DOWN THE TRIGGER!
I SEE A BLINKING RED LIGHT! WHAT DOES THAT--
IT MEANS THAT IF YOU DON'T START FIRING RIGHT NOW, YOUR CHANCES OF LIVING WOULD HAVE BEEN MUCH HIGHER AS A PILOT THAN A GUNNER!

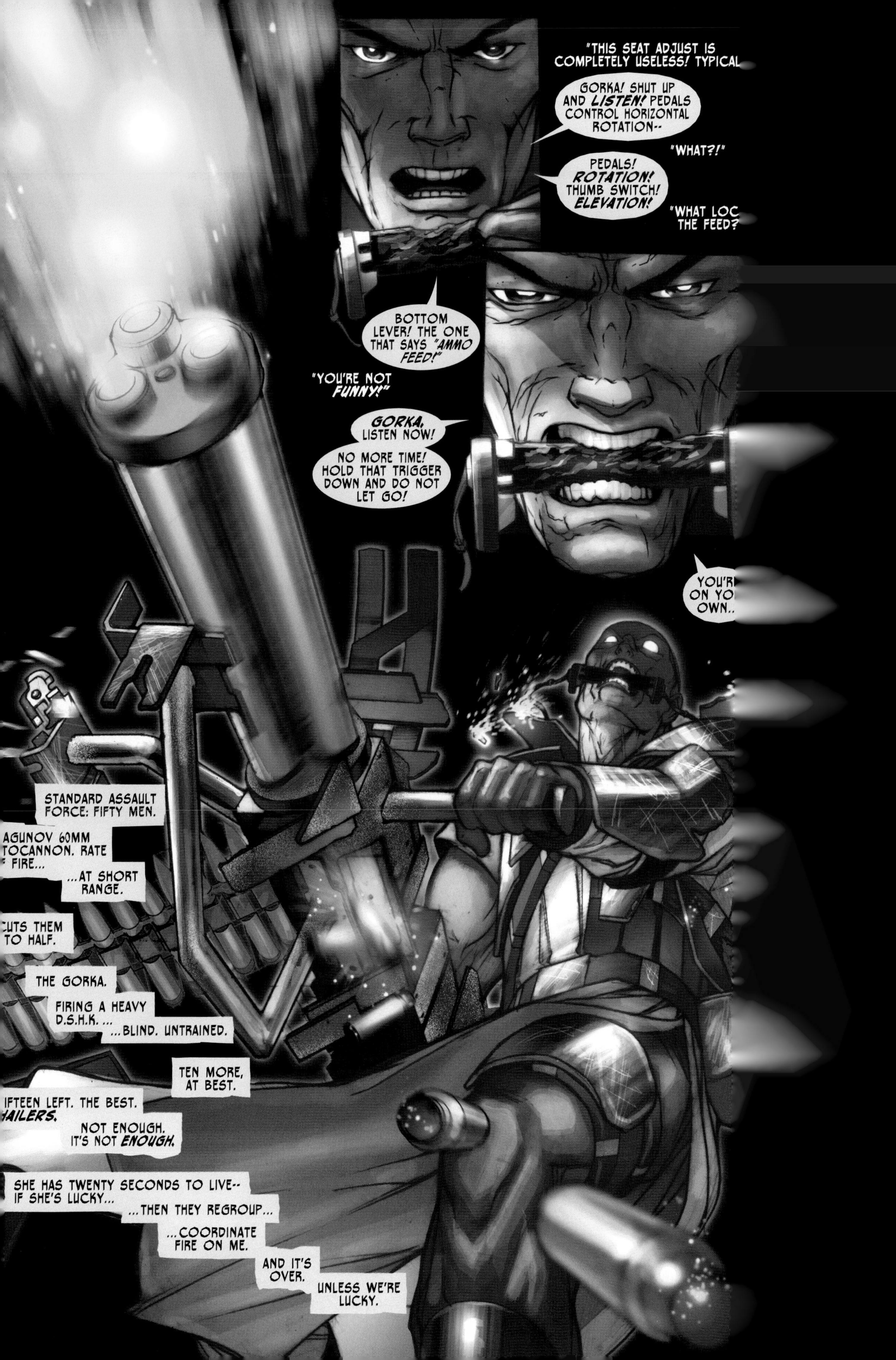
"THIS SEAT ADJUST IS COMPLETELY USELESS! TYPICAL
GORKA! SHUT UP AND LISTEN! PEDALS CONTROL HORIZONTAL ROTATION--
"WHAT?!"
PEDALS! ROTATION! THUMB SWITCH! ELEVATION!
"WHAT LOC THE FEED?
BOTTOM LEVER! THE ONE THAT SAYS "AMMO FEED!"
"YOU'RE NOT FUNNY!"
GORKA, LISTEN NOW!
NO MORE TIME! HOLD THAT TRIGGER DOWN AND DO NOT LET GO!
YOU'R ON YO OWN..
STANDARD ASSAULT FORCE: FIFTY MEN.
AGUNOV 60MM TOCANNON. RATE FIRE...
...AT SHORT RANGE.
CUTS THEM TO HALF.
THE GORKA.
FIRING A HEAVY D.S.H.K. ...
...BLIND. UNTRAINED.
TEN MORE, AT BEST.
IFTEEN LEFT. THE BEST. HAILERS.
NOT ENOUGH. IT'S NOT ENOUGH.
SHE HAS TWENTY SECONDS TO LIVE-- IF SHE'S LUCKY...
...THEN THEY REGROUP...
...COORDINATE FIRE ON ME.
AND IT'S OVER.
UNLESS WE'RE LUCKY.

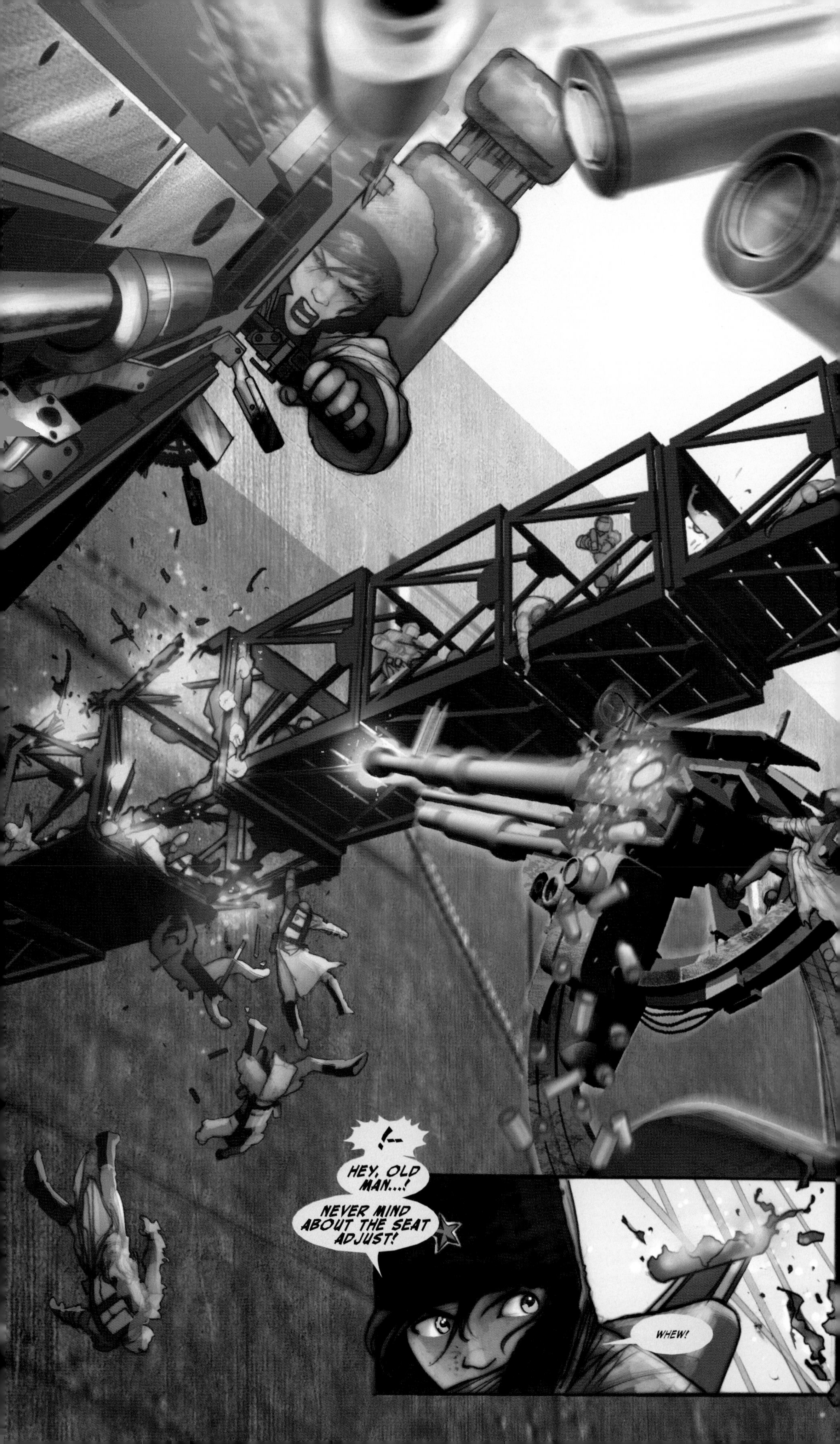
!--
HEY, OLD MAN...!
NEVER MIND ABOUT THE SEAT ADJUST!
WHEW!

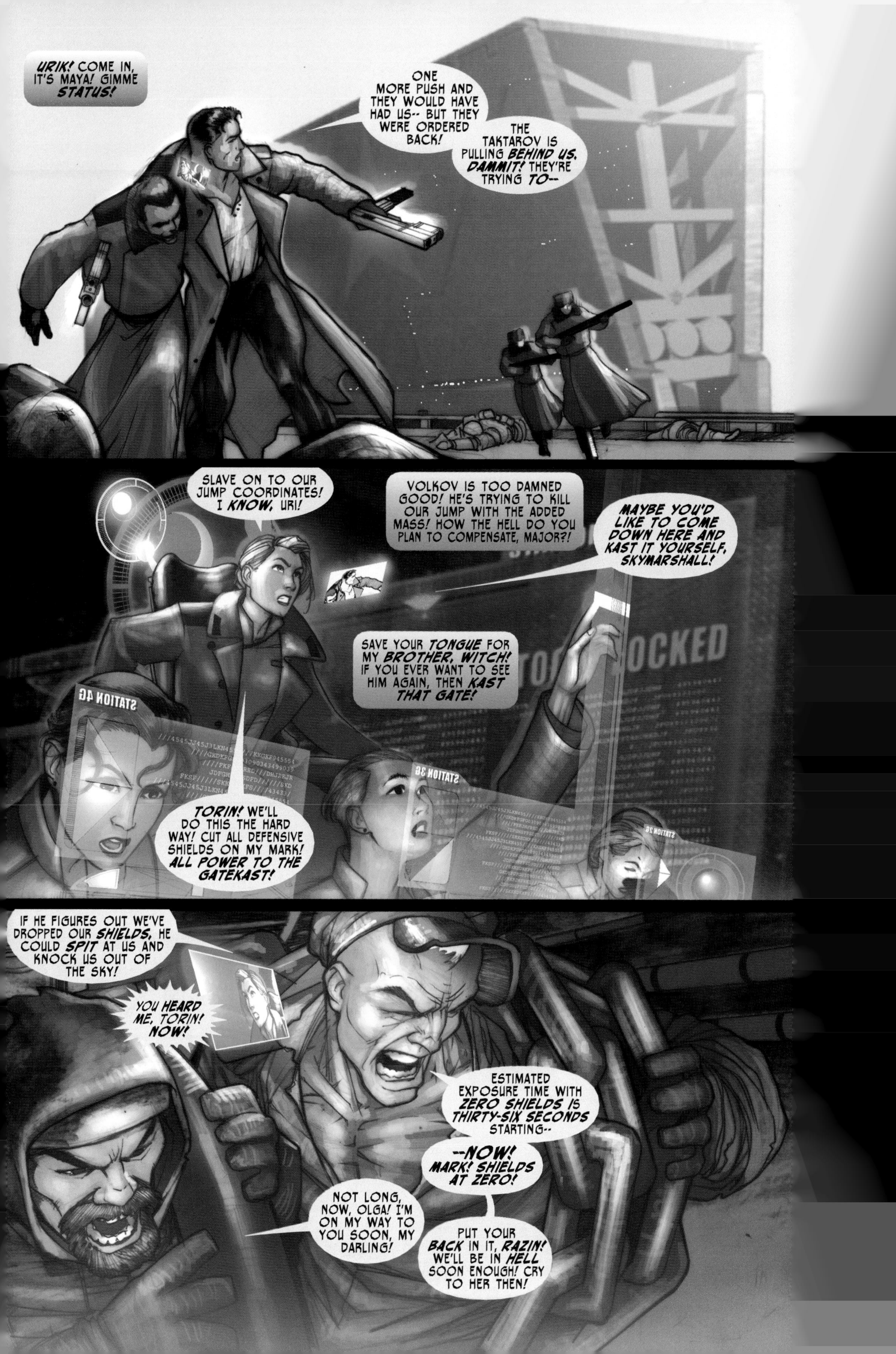
URIK! COME IN, IT'S MAYA! GIMME STATUS!
ONE MORE PUSH AND THEY WOULD HAVE HAD US-- BUT THEY WERE ORDERED BACK!
THE TAKTAROV IS PULLING BEHIND US, DAMMIT! THEY'RE TRYING TO--
SLAVE ON TO OUR JUMP COORDINATES! I KNOW, URI!
VOLKOV IS TOO DAMNED GOOD! HE'S TRYING TO KILL OUR JUMP WITH THE ADDED MASS! HOW THE HELL DO YOU PLAN TO COMPENSATE, MAJOR?!
MAYBE YOU'D LIKE TO COME DOWN HERE AND KAST IT YOURSELF, SKYMARSHALL!
SAVE YOUR TONGUE FOR MY BROTHER, WITCH! IF YOU EVER WANT TO SEE HIM AGAIN, THEN KAST THAT GATE!
TORIN! WE'LL DO THIS THE HARD WAY! CUT ALL DEFENSIVE SHIELDS ON MY MARK! ALL POWER TO THE GATEKAST!
IF HE FIGURES OUT WE'VE DROPPED OUR SHIELDS, HE COULD SPIT AT US AND KNOCK US OUT OF THE SKY!
YOU HEARD ME, TORIN! NOW!
ESTIMATED EXPOSURE TIME WITH ZERO SHIELDS IS THIRTY-SIX SECONDS STARTING--
--NOW! MARK! SHIELDS AT ZERO!
NOT LONG, NOW, OLGA! I'M ON MY WAY TO YOU SOON, MY DARLING!
PUT YOUR BACK IN IT, RAZIN! WE'LL BE IN HELL SOON ENOUGH! CRY TO HER THEN!

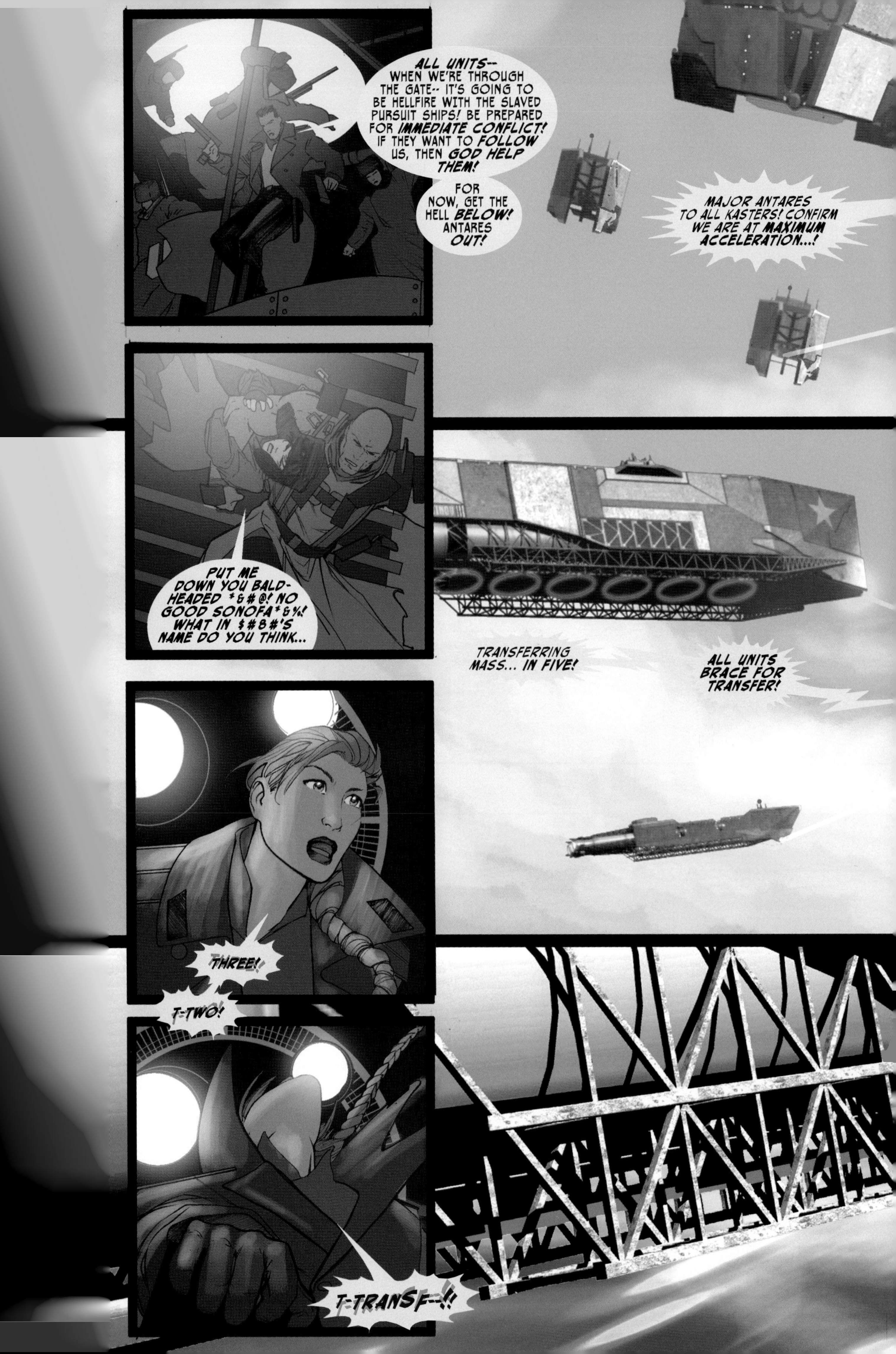
ALL UNITS-- WHEN WE'RE THROUGH THE GATE-- IT'S GOING TO BE HELLFIRE WITH THE SLAVED PURSUIT SHIPS! BE PREPARED FOR IMMEDIATE CONFLICT! IF THEY WANT TO FOLLOW US, THEN GOD HELP THEM!
FOR NOW, GET THE HELL BELOW! ANTARES OUT!
MAJOR ANTARES TO ALL KASTERS! CONFIRM WE ARE AT MAXIMUM ACCELERATION...!
PUT ME DOWN YOU BALD-HEADED *&#@! NO GOOD SONOFA*&%! WHAT IN $#8#'S NAME DO YOU THINK...
TRANSFERRING MASS... IN FIVE!
ALL UNITS BRACE FOR TRANSFER!
THREE!
T-TWO!
T-TRANSF--!!

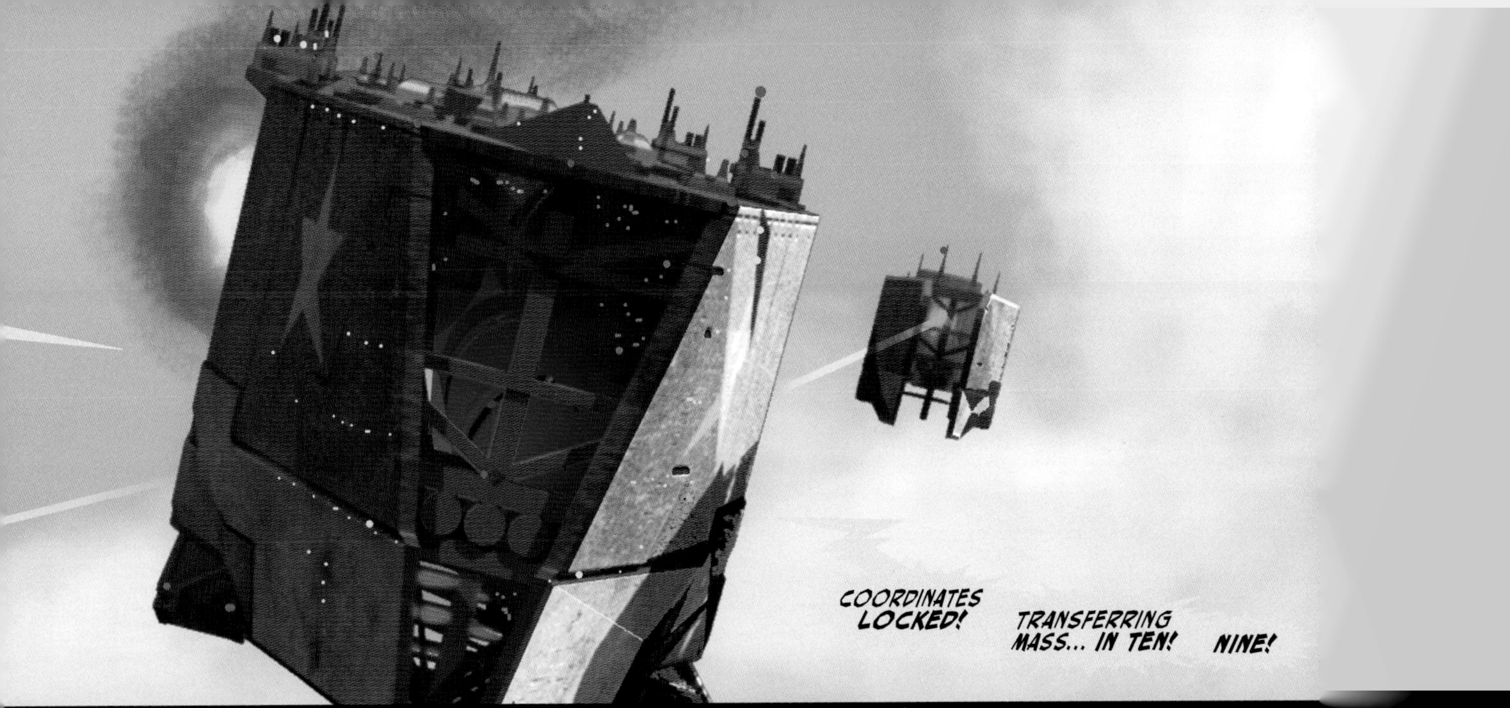
COORDINATES LOCKED!
TRANSFERRING MASS... IN TEN!
NINE!
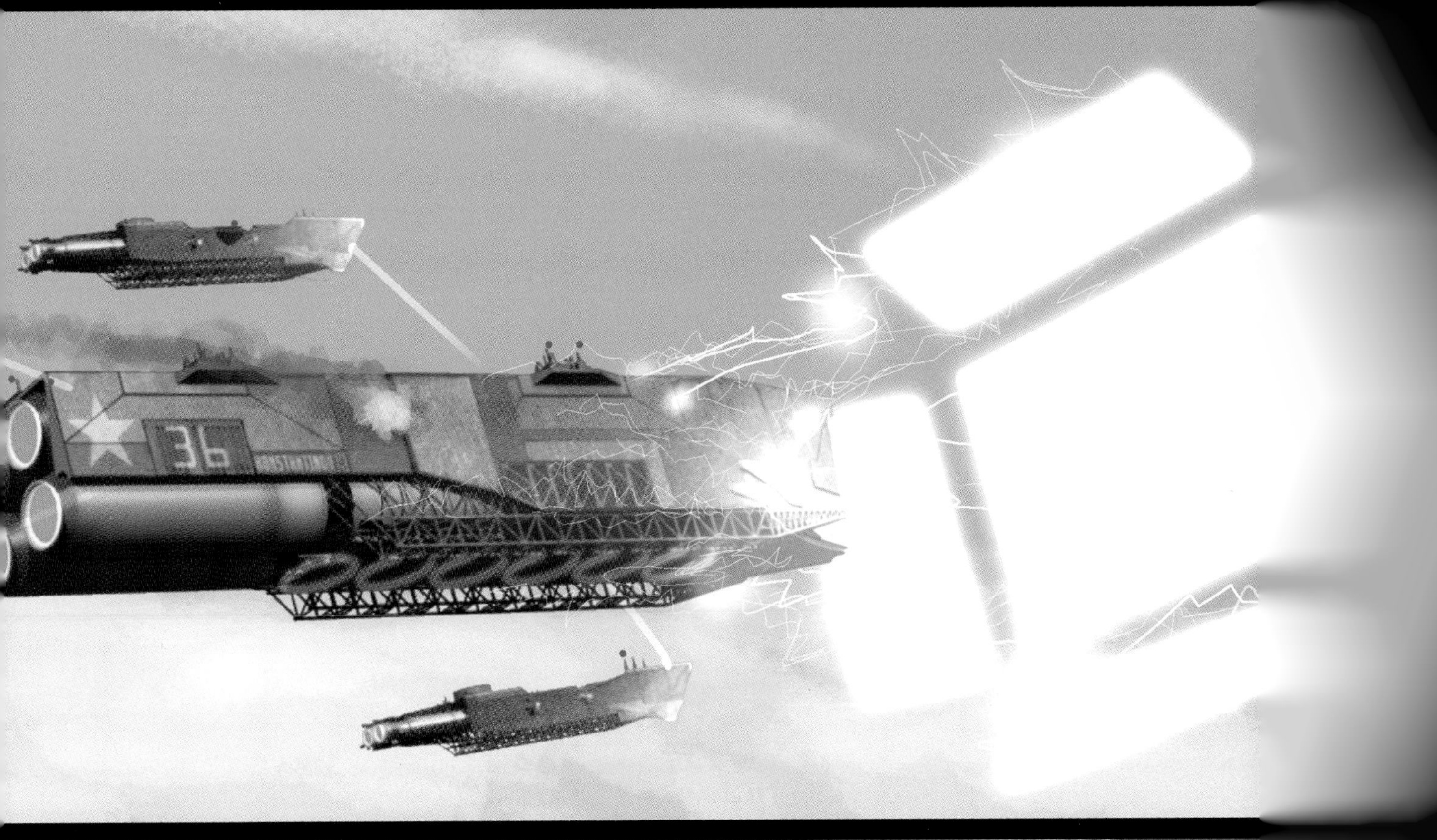
36
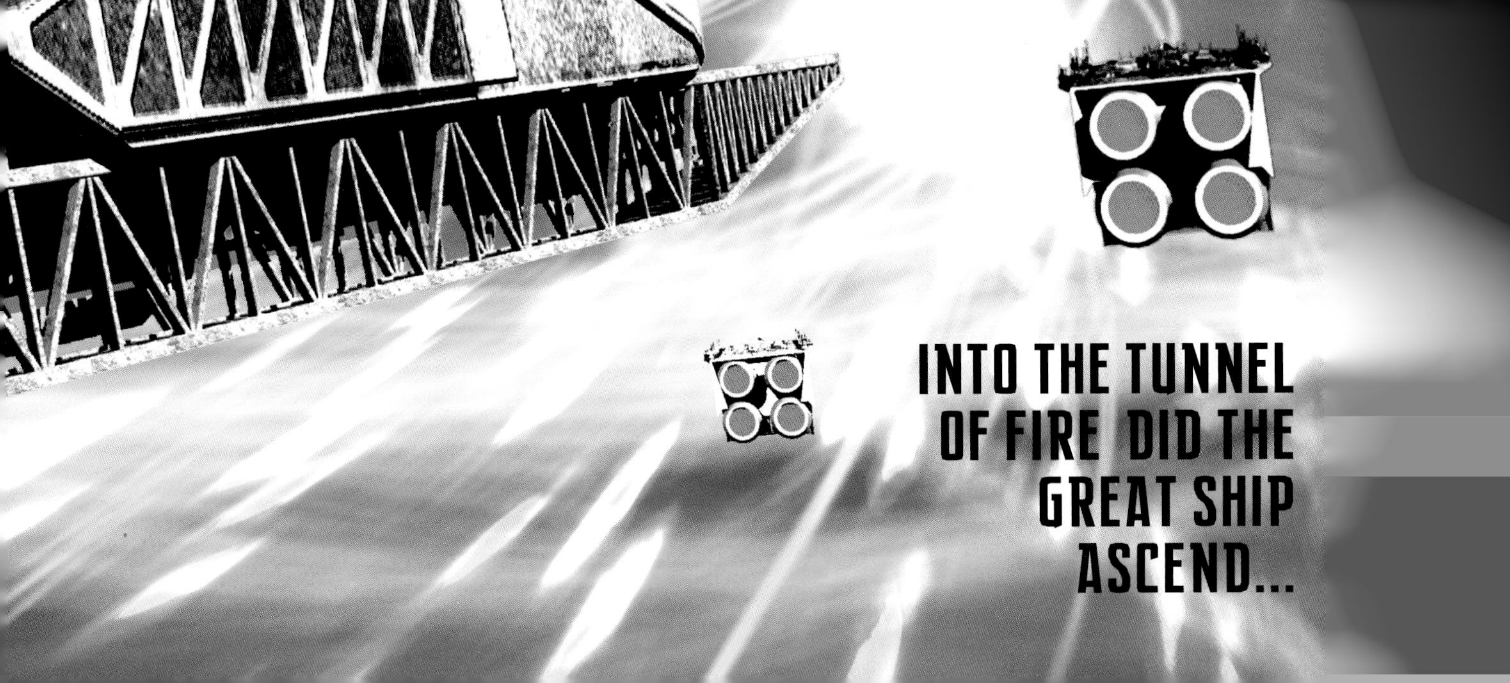
INTO THE TUNNEL OF FIRE DID THE GREAT SHIP ASCEND...

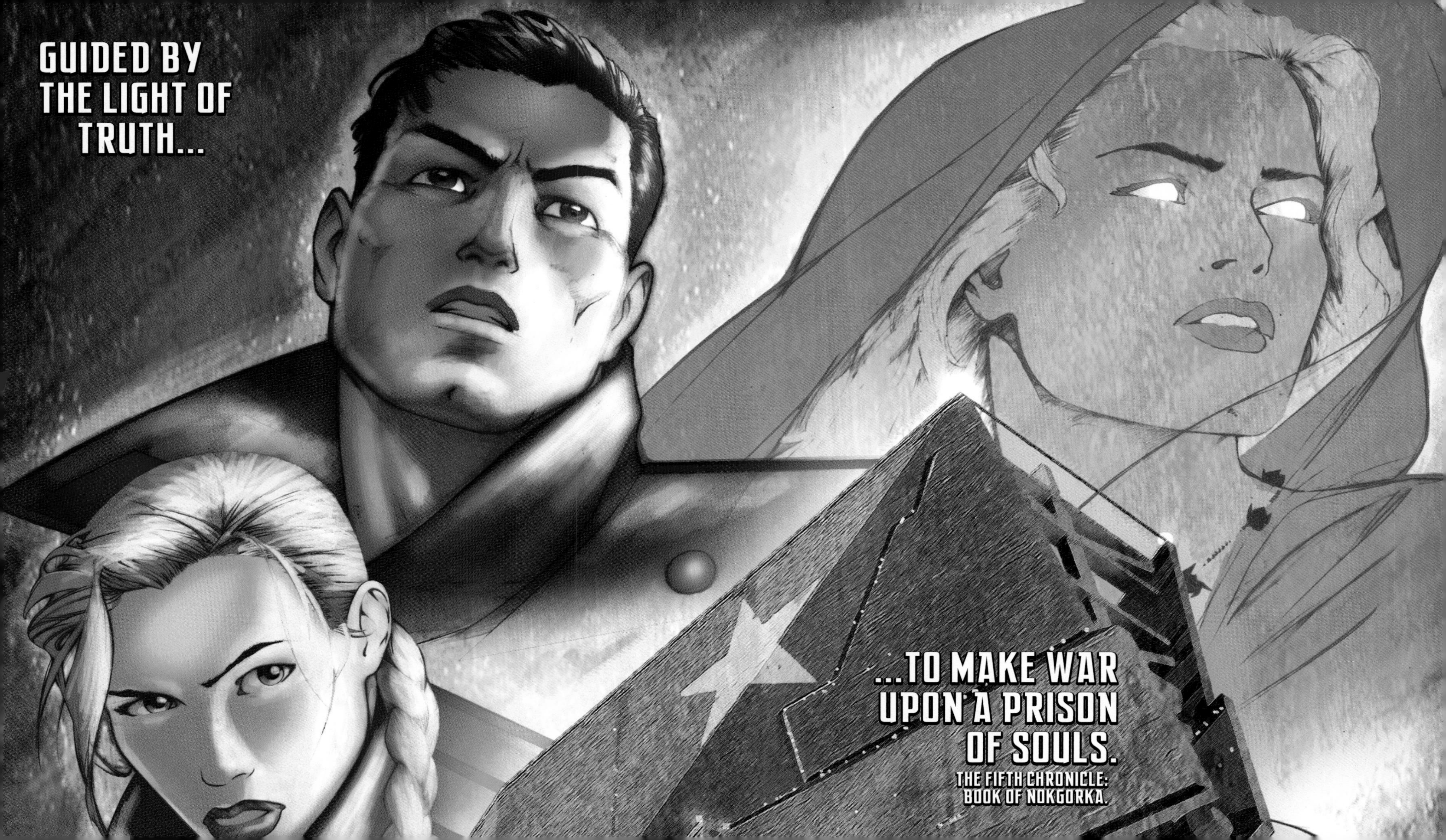
GUIDED BY THE LIGHT OF TRUTH...
...TO MAKE WAR UPON A PRISON OF SOULS.
THE FIFTH CHRONICLE: BOOK OF NOKGORKA.

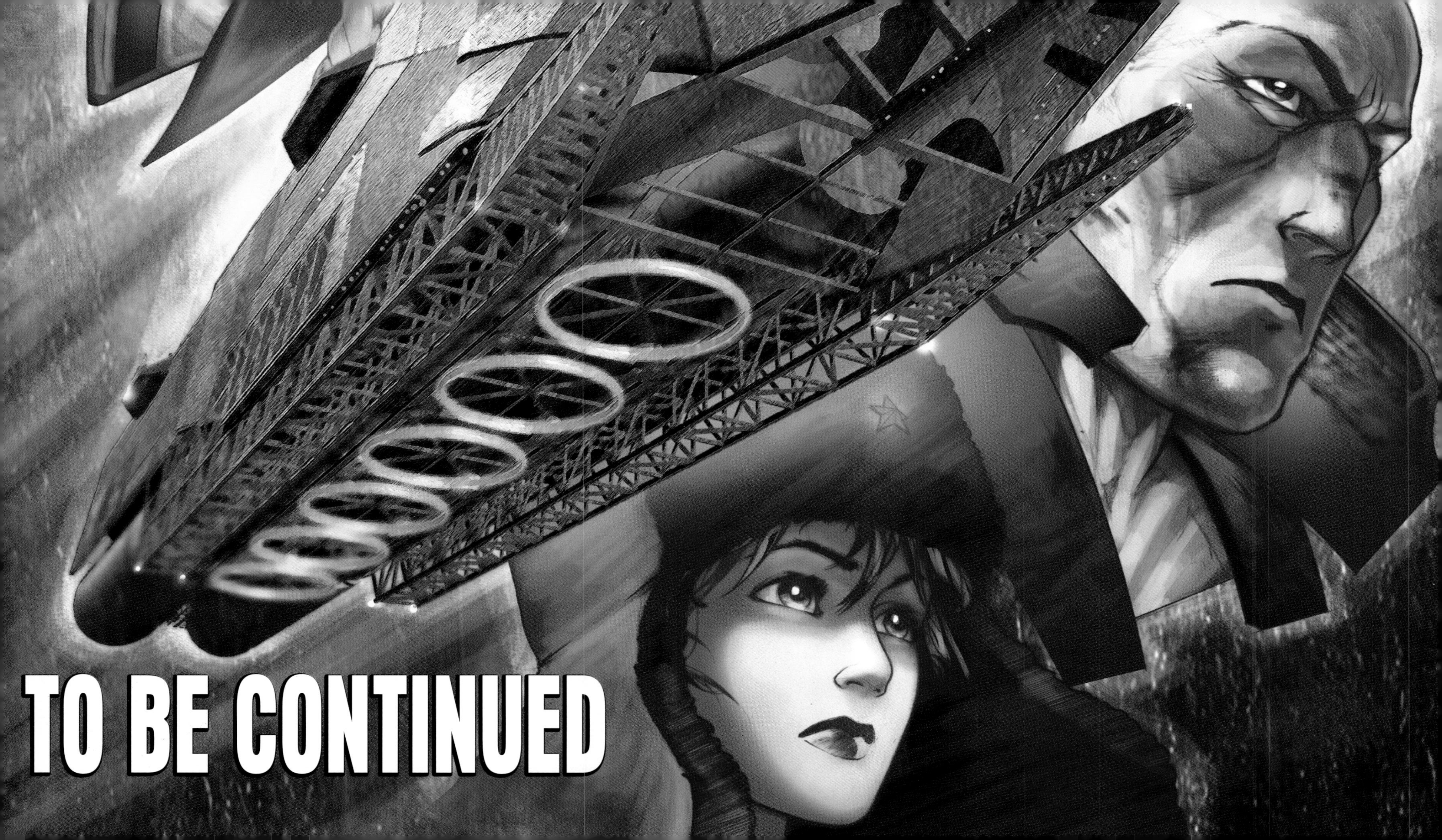
TO BE CONTINUED

DEFENDERS OF THE KONSTANTINOV

BY DAVID MICHAEL BECK

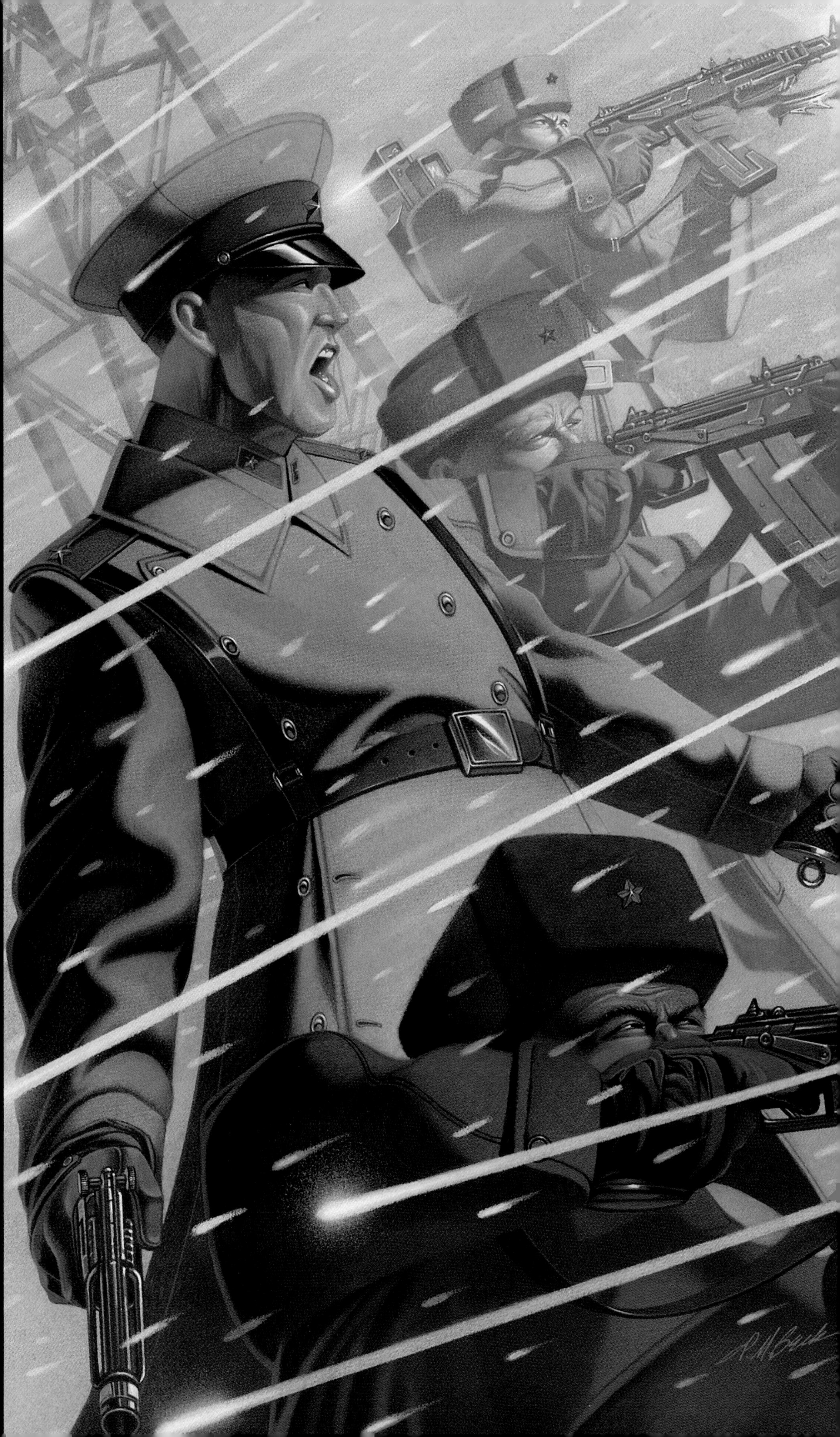

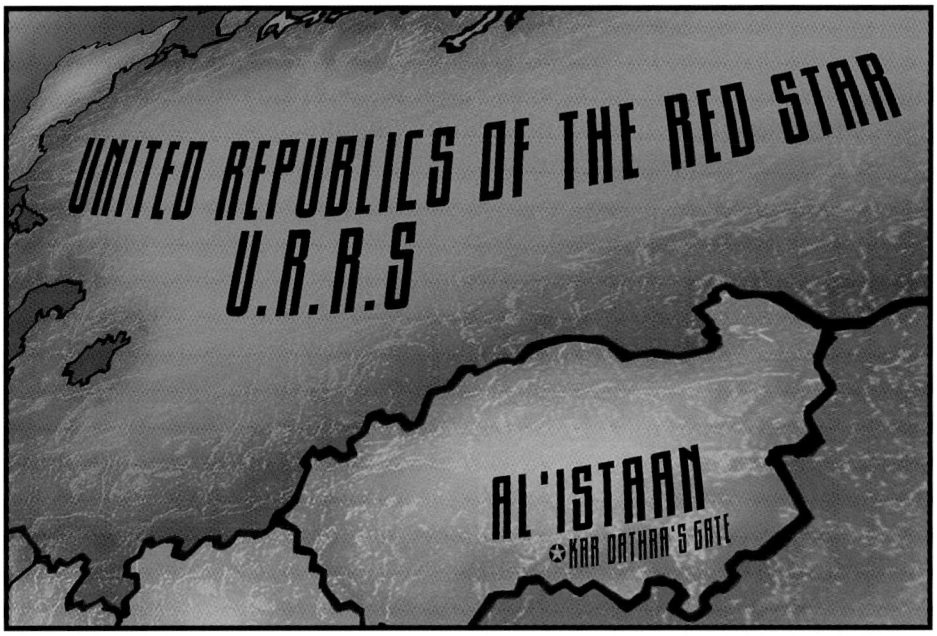
UNITED REPUBLICS OF THE RED STAR
U.R.R.S
AL'ISTAAN
KAR DATHRA'S GATE

LEXICON

A

Al' Istaan – al•is•taan (ahl_iztahn): Country south of the URRS; home of the Nistaani warrior.

Alexandra Goncharova – al•ex•an•dra gon•cha•rov•a (al ex an_ drah gohn chah rov_ ah): Krawl captain of the Red Fleet and long time friend of Maya Antares. Alexandra was one of the last people to see Marcus Antares alive.

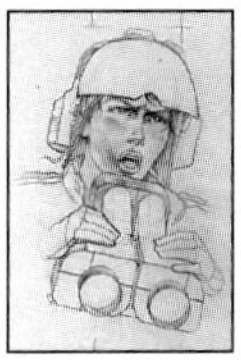

B

Brusilov, Alexei – bru•si•lov (broo_sih loff): Former Commander of the Skyfurnace RSS Konstantinov.

D

Defensive Shell Protocol - de•fen•sive shell pro•to•col (dee fen'sihv shehl proh'tah kol): Also DSP. Immobile defensive shield used during battle to protect those that are severely wounded and cannot defend themselves. This protocol is is also used during times of heavy shelling to protect vehicles and soldiers from damage. slang SL: 'Throw down a DSP!'

Dragunov 60mm – dra•gun•ov (dr_' g_n off): A heavy assault auto-cannon equipped with a rotating barrel capable of incredible rates of fire. This weapon was designed primarily as a hailer-hardpoint on specific decks of a skyfurnace to repel enemy boarding parties.

Drop Casing — drop cas•ing (drop kae_sing): Armored crate or framework used to deploy various craft, mainly krawls, from high altitudes.

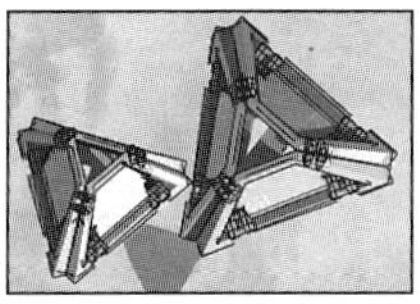

G

Gate Transfer Protocol - gate trans•fer pro•to•col (gayt trans´fur proh´tah kol): Protocol used mainly for transport of infantry and heavy equipment over long distances.

H

Hailer – hail•er (hay_ler): 1. A heavy caliber automatic weapon carried by a special class of infantryman within the Red Fleet. 2. Military term for a skilled soldier who operates a hailer weapon, and who is charged with the sole duty of defending an assigned Warkaster.

Hook – hook: Heavy infantry weapon wielded by soldiers of the Red Fleet; Infantrymen have limited mental control of the weapon, and so may hurl it long distances, or use it for an array of other offensive tasks.

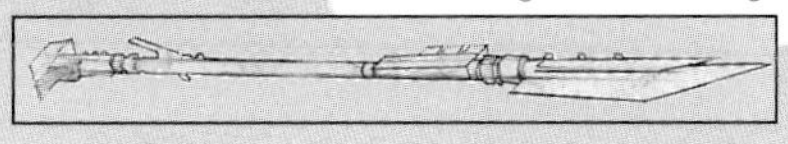

I

Isolator Tunnel – i•so•lat•or tun•nel (i_so lay tor tun_el): Structure found onboard a skyfurnace that, during battle, houses a Warkaster and allows her to kast a transformation protocol. This transformation protocol changes the Warkaster into a large pillar of energy which, when kast correctly, can deliver grave amounts of damage to enemy craft.

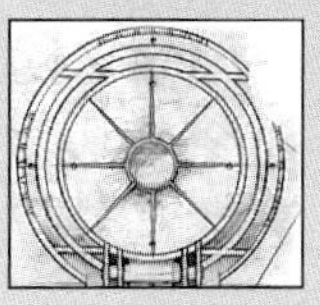

K

Kar Dathra's Gate – kar dath•ras gate (kar_ da_ thruhs gayt): 1. Area named after Kar Dathra the Eternal Defender, a holy icon revered by the Nistaani people. This region is one of the most sacred within Al' Istaan. 2. Battle site where the Red Fleet met with heavy defeat at the hands of the Nistaani.

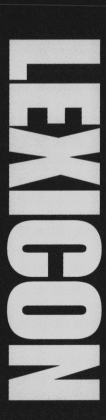

Konstantinov – kon•stan•tin•ov (kahn stan teen_ off): Skyfurnace flagship of The Red Fleet; currently commanded by Skymarshall Urik Antares.

Krawl – krawl (krahl): Heavy offensive combat vehicle of the Red Fleet armed with cannons and machine guns which moves on caterpillar tread. Krawls are deployed into battle via strategic Skyfurnace drop at an RDA or rapid deployment altitude.

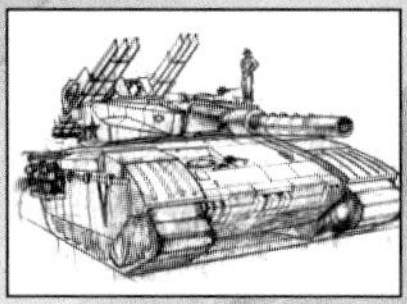

M

Marcus Antares - mar•cus an•tar•es (mar'kus an tar'eez): Infantry Captain of the Red Fleet; husband to Maya Antares.

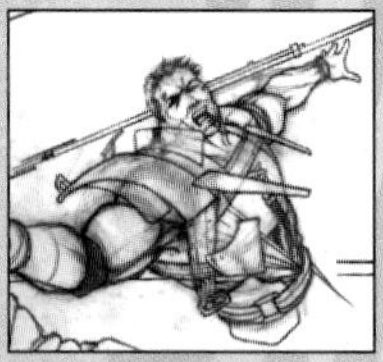

Makita – ma•ki•ta (mah ki'tah): A fierce young soldier of the Nokgorkan Resistance Army (NRA). Makita lost her only love, Proto, in an ambush of Captain Goncharova's Krawl Column. She delivered to Maya a letter that would change the fate of the Antares family forever; for this, in the annals of history, she would be remembered as 'The Letter Bearer.'

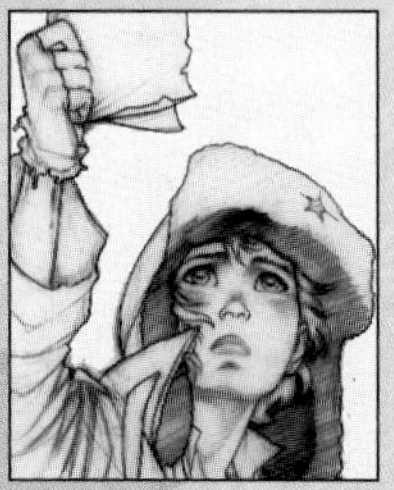

Maya Antares - ma•ya an•tar•es (ma'yah an tar'eez): Warkaster of the Red Fleet, Sorceress Major; wife to Marcus Antares.

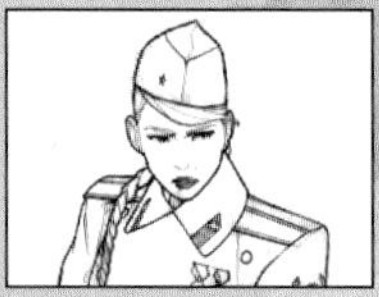

N

Nistaani – nis•taa•ni (nihs tahn_ee): Hardened desert warriors of Al' Istaan.

Nokgorka – nok•gor•ka (n_ gohr' kah): Republic province located south of the U.R.R.S. Now involved in a bitter war with the United Republics of The Red Star due to its unlikely bid for independence from said country.

P

Pravda's Gem of Judgement – prav•da's gem of judge•ment (prahv'dahz jehm uhv juhj' ment): 1. Legendary artifact of power granted to the elite sorceresses that fought for the cause of truth at the behest of their goddess, Pravda. 2. Legend states that upon the Fall of Pravda to the forces of her sister, Krivda, goddess of lies, the gems were lost within the far reaches of the multiverse. 3. Those who fall victim to the power of the gems are imprisoned by the spirits of those who had been wronged by their malevolence.

Proto - proto (pr_'t_h): A young soldier in the Nokgorkan Resistance Army, Makita's first and only love. Proto shot and killed Captain Goncharova during the ambush of the Captain's Krawl column.

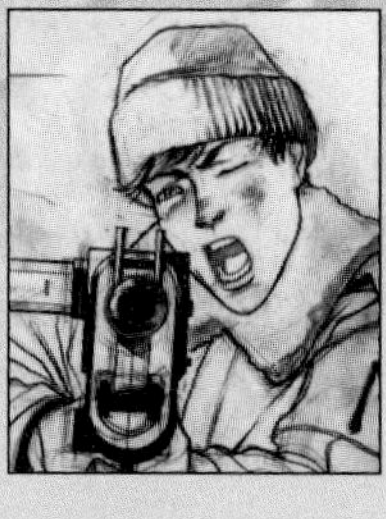

Protocol - pro•to•col (proh'tah kol): Military terminology for a spell or enchantment.

R

Razin, Sergei - ser•gei ra•zin (sehr' gae ra' zihn): Leader of the 104th prisoner squad. Sergeant Razin, after escaping capture by Nistaani warriors in an early battle in Al' Istaan was falsely accused of divulging military secrets to the Nistaani. He was stripped of rank and received a term of 25 years for suspected treason.

Reenact Protocol - re•en•act pro•to•col (ree ehn' act proh'tah kol): A powerful forensic tool, this protocol allows a sorceress to witness firsthand the events that transpired within a certain time and place as designated at the time of kasting. While the protocol is functioning a sorceress may determine numerous facts such as times of death, trajectories of fatal wounds, and identities of those present within the radius of the protocol.

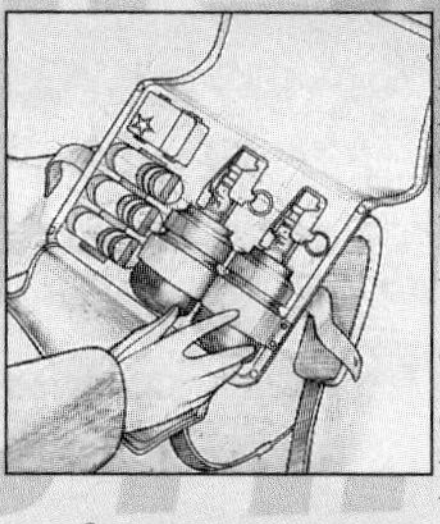

S

Siege Gates - siege gate (s_j g_t): A form of transport gate kast in a horizontal alignment instead of the traditional vertical used for evacuation purposes. Kast in such a manner the gate is used primarily for invasion and heavy assault purposes.

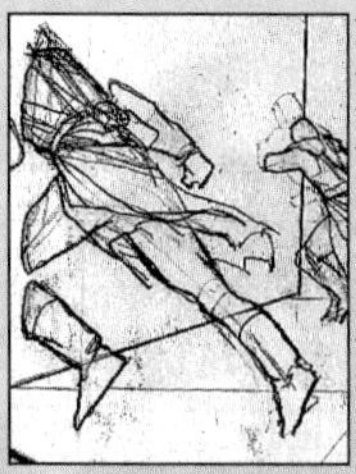

Skyfurnace – sky•fur•nace (sky_fuhr_nus): A 1.5 mile long heavily armored warship designed mainly for rapid deployment of infantry and various craft, and massive siege operations.

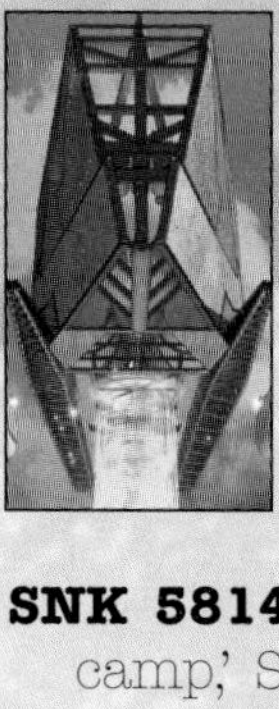

SNK 5814 – Designated as a 'special labor camp,' SNK 5814 is but one of many such prisons. Collectively, they are called the GULAG system of labor camps, and hold millions of forced labor prisoners.

Squad – squad (skwod): A small number of prisoners, commonly 20 men, led usually by a squad leader; the smallest prisoner unit.

Sword of Truth, The – sword of truth (sôrd uv trooth): After choosing The Red Woman to be her champion of justice, Pravda, Goddess of Truth bestowed upon her this sacred weapon to carry out her war against those that would enslave her nation.

T

The Red Woman - the red wo•man (the rehd woom'muhn): The mysterious image of the red woman has seldom been witnessed. Testimony of those that have seen this enigmantic figure often report noticing her weep at the graves of fallen soldiers. She is also Troika's sworn arch-enemy and works for the day that she might see him destroyed.

Torin, Andre – to•rin an•dre (to'rehn, ahn' dray): Chief Engineer of the Konstantinov. Before his arrest, Torin was a professor of Heavy Weapons systems at the Korolev Complex of Skyship Design. His essays on restructuring the Red Fleet, and his criticisms of contemporary military strategy, earned him a 10 year prison sentence as a political offender.

Troika - troi•ka (troy'ka): 1. Traditionally a group or association of three operatives or interrogators. 2. The name of Imbohl's main lieutenant and feared assassin. Legend speaks of Troika's heinous ability to harvest the souls of the fallen and deliver them to his liege lord for judgement.

U

Urik Antares - ur•ik an•tar•es (yur'ik an tar'eez): Commanding officer of the Skyfurnace R.S.S Konstantinov. Brother to Marcus Antares.

U.R.R.S. – U•R•R•S: United Republics of The Red Star.

V

Vanya – van•ya (vahn_yah): An old war veteran of The Great Patriotic Wars.

Volkov – vol•kov (vohl' koff): Current Skymarshall of the Skyfurnace R.S.S. Taktorov. Volkov is most known for his impeccable and often ruthless strategies in combat.

W

Warkaster – war•kas•ter (wohr_kas tur): Red Fleet military terminology for a sorceress, or someone trained in the sorcery corp. capable of kasting protocols of a mainly destructive nature.

Work Lift – work lift (werk lihft): Elevator shafts that transport zeks to their duties aboard their assigned skyfurnaces. These shafts are able to extend to a maximum length of approx. 800 meters. Multi-level, open-air elevator cars, known as 'cages' to the zeks, hold a capacity of up to three squads.

Z

Zek – zek (zehk): 1. Sl. derogative. Guard terminology for 'prisoner.' Many zeks are trained during imprisonment for the harshest of duties aboard a skyfurnace. Some of these duties include, but are not limited to, ventral blast furnace maintenance and operation, and engine maintenance and repair. Many of those unfortunate enough to be chosen to work the blast furnaces have an extremely short life expectancy.

MAYA'S DREAM

THE RE...

3Konstantinov

GOSS

3D

RICH

SCRIP

STAR SKETCHBOOK

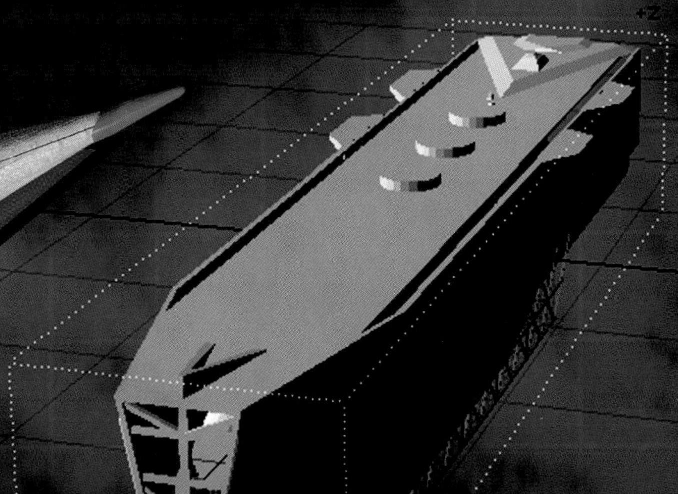

conception to integration

The many faces of the ferocious child of war, Makita.

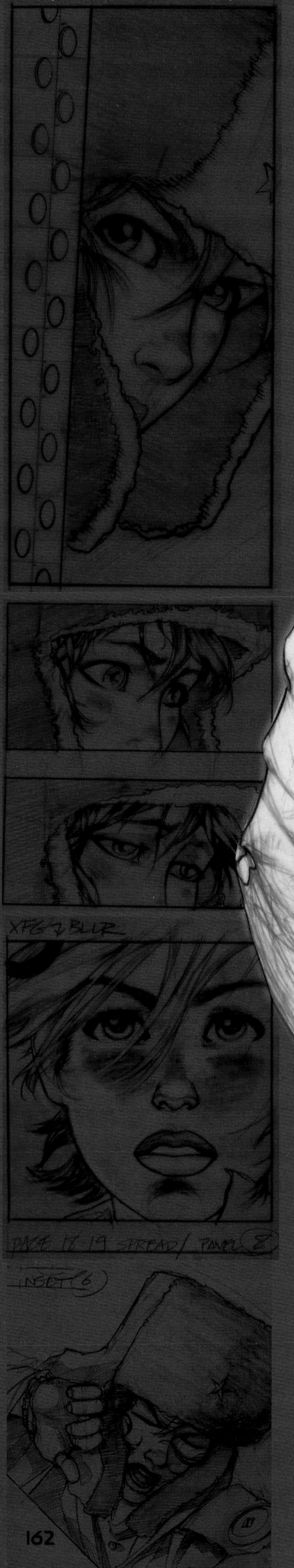
PAGE 18-19 SPREAD/ PANEL 8

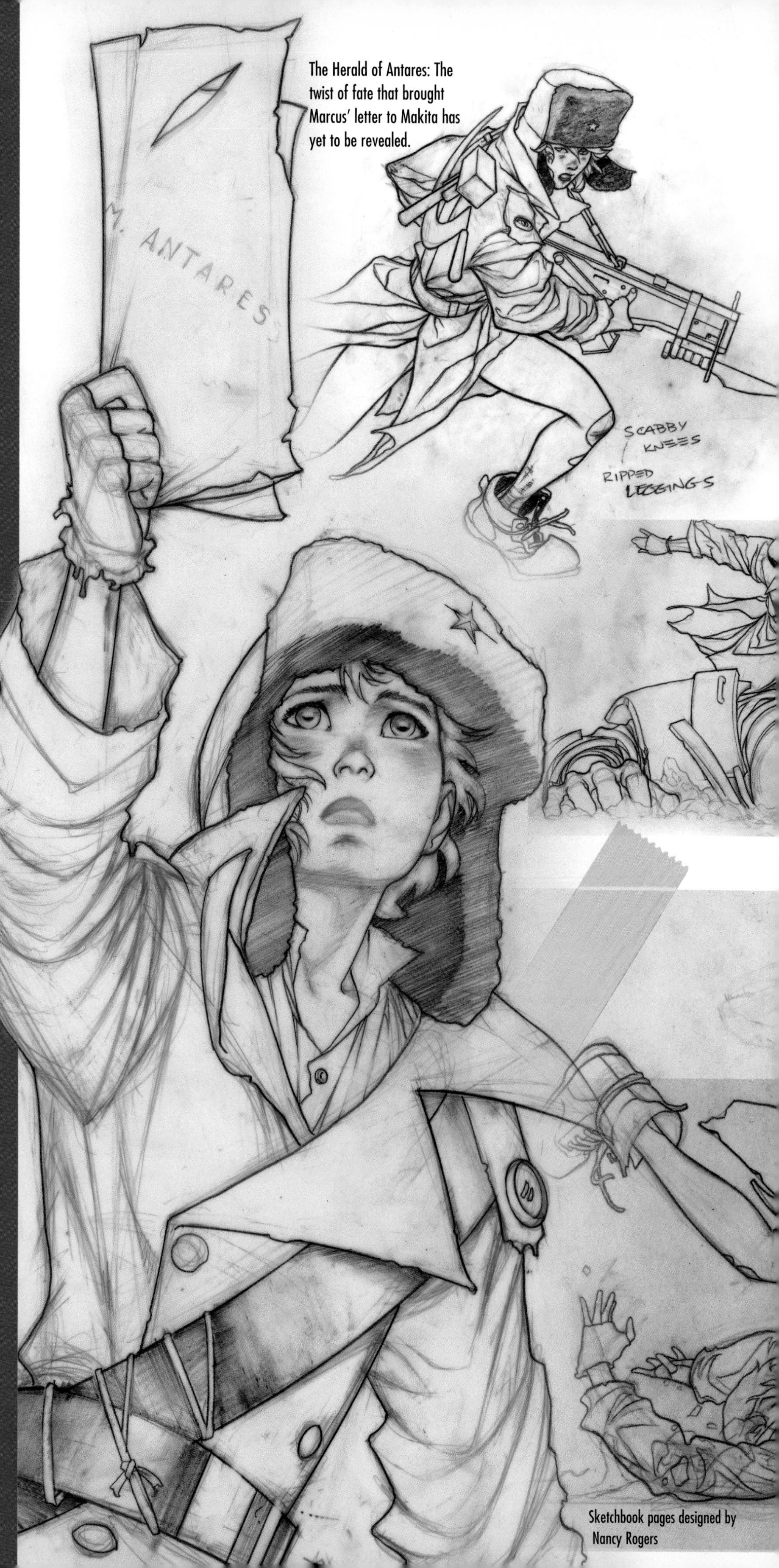
M. ANTARES
SCABBY KNEES
RIPPED LEGGINGS

The Herald of Antares: The twist of fate that brought Marcus' letter to Makita has yet to be revealed.

Sketchbook pages designed by Nancy Rogers

A symbol of irrepressible youth, defiant against all odds, Makita's physical prowess was inspired by the bold movements of Soviet female gymnasts.

Goss: "To use a real world analogy, the Soviet sports machine was famous for identifying its most talented athletes throughout their vast territories and committing these children to careers of arduous training and often, great triumph. Like Olga Korbut or Nadia Comenici, Makita would have been an Olympic champion many times over."

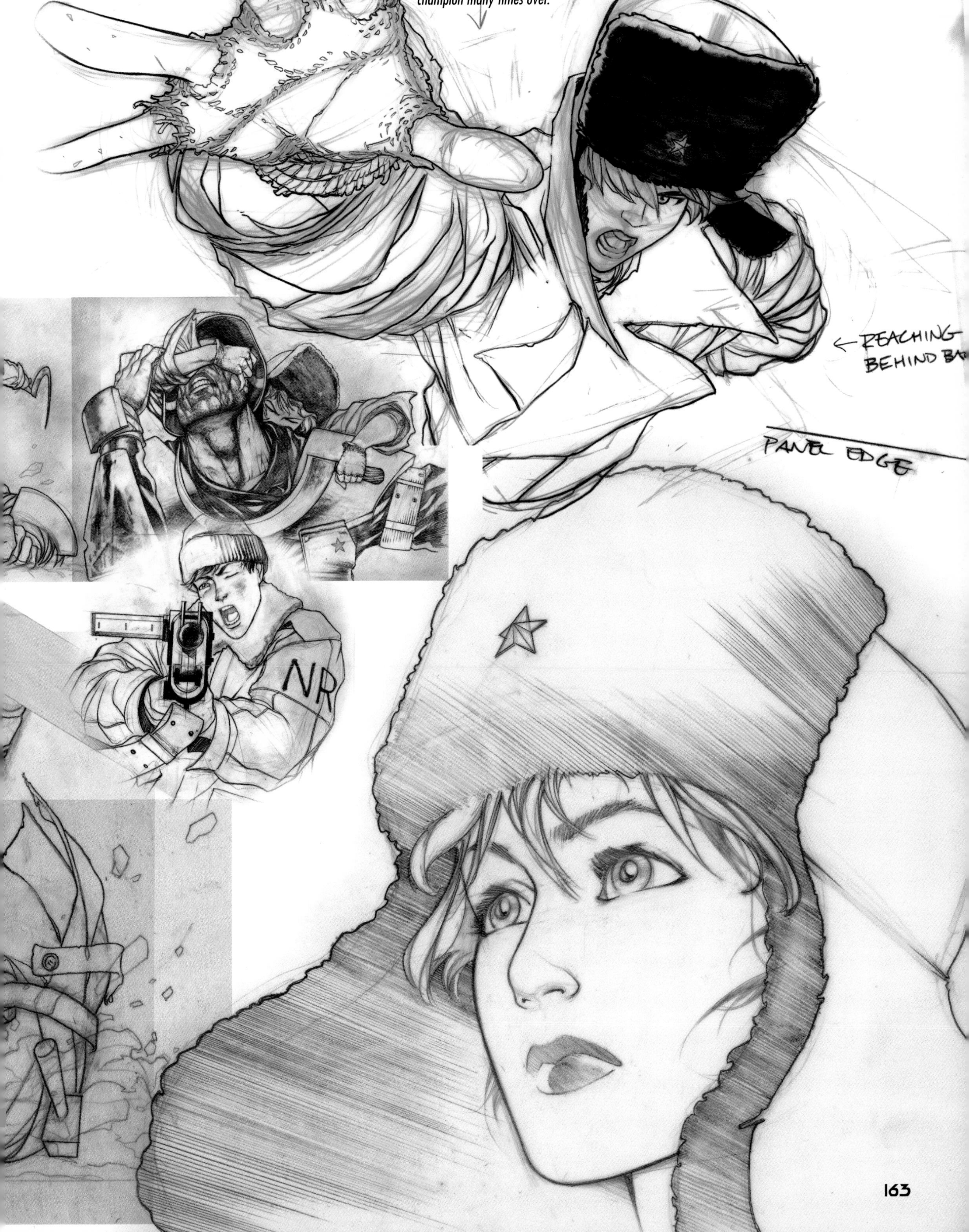
GLASS SPLINTERS
FINGERS
← REACHING BEHIND BA
PANEL EDGE
NR

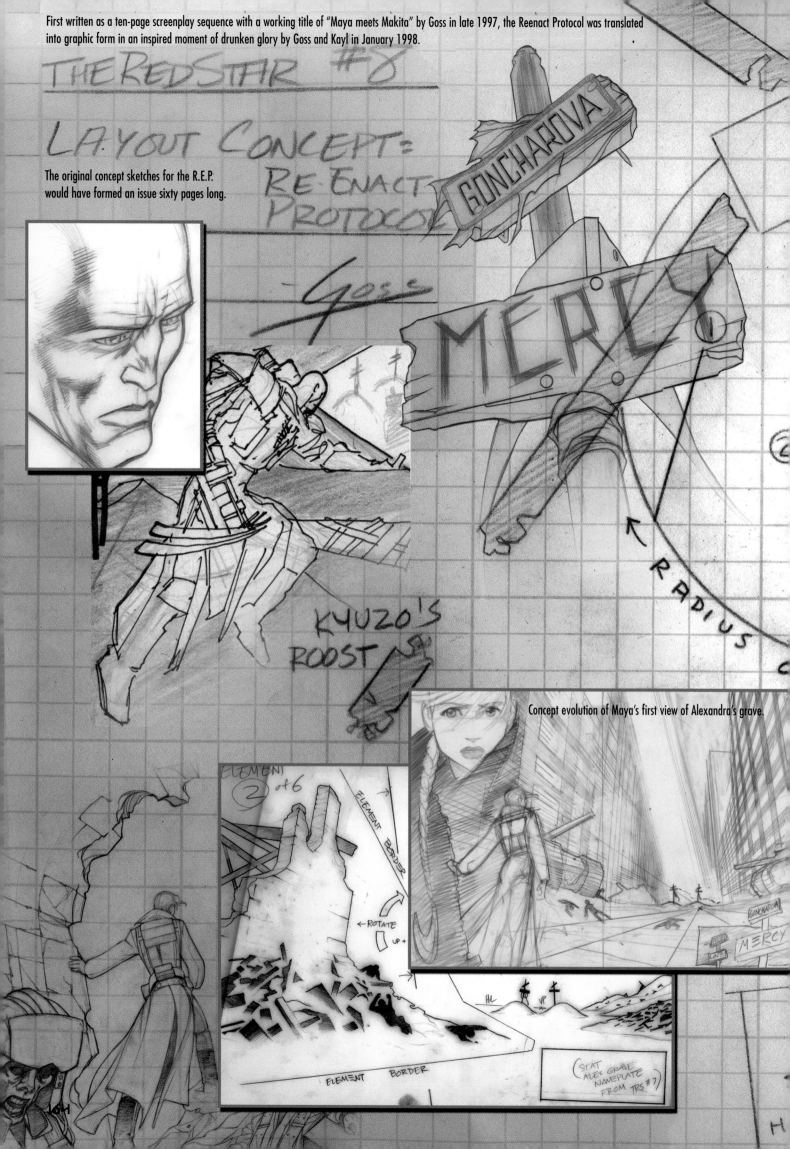

First written as a ten-page screenplay sequence with a working title of "Maya meets Makita" by Goss in late 1997, the Reenact Protocol was translated into graphic form in an inspired moment of drunken glory by Goss and Kayl in January 1998.

THE RED STAR #8

LAYOUT CONCEPT:
RE-ENACT
PROTOCOL

The original concept sketches for the R.E.P. would have formed an issue sixty pages long.

—Goss

GONCHAROVA

MERCY

← RADIUS

KYUZO'S ROOST

Concept evolution of Maya's first view of Alexandra's grave.

ELEMENT 3 of 6

ELEMENT BORDER

← ROTATE

UP +

ELEMENT BORDER

HL   VP

(STAT 'ALEX GRAVE' NAMEPLATE FROM TRS #7)

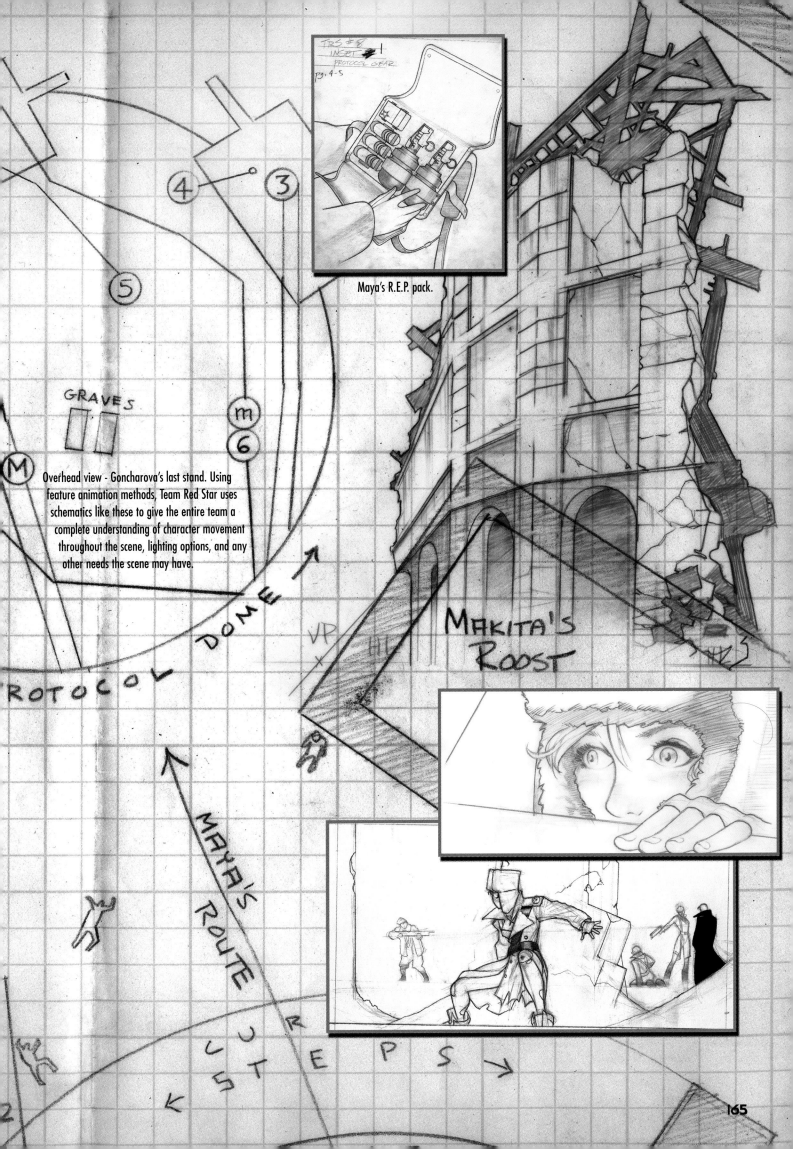

TRS #8 1
INSET 1
PROTOCOL GEAR
pg. 4-5

Maya's R.E.P. pack.

GRAVES

Overhead view - Goncharova's last stand. Using feature animation methods, Team Red Star uses schematics like these to give the entire team a complete understanding of character movement throughout the scene, lighting options, and any other needs the scene may have.

PROTOCOL DOME →

MAKITA'S ROOST

MAYA'S ROUTE

STEPS →

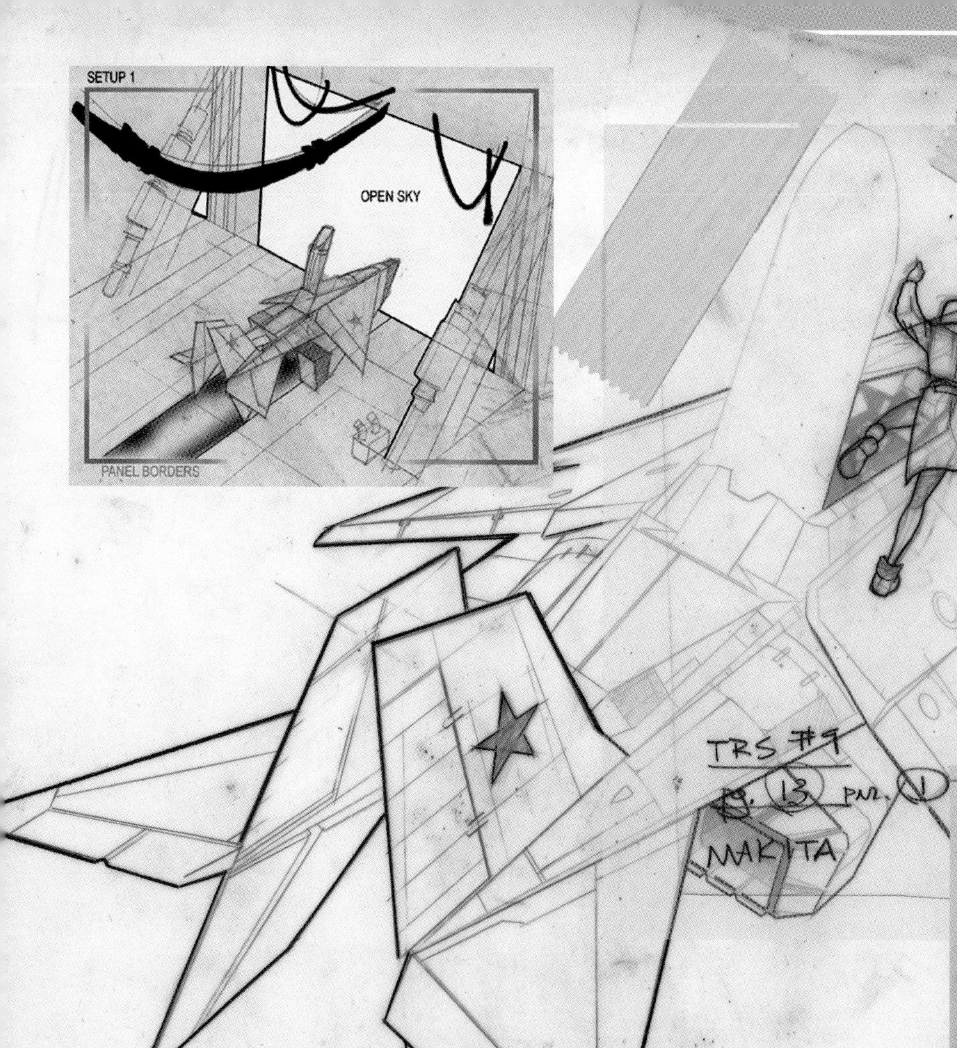
SETUP 1
OPEN SKY
PANEL BORDERS
TRS #9
P. 13 PNL. 1
MAKITA

The cockpit was based on a Mig-29, and altered to fit the Red Star universe.

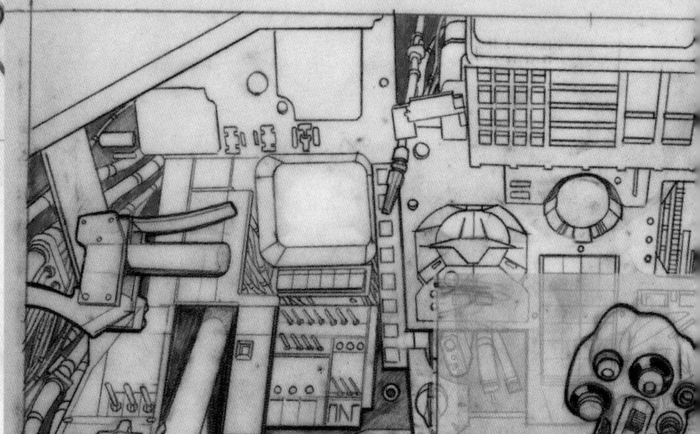

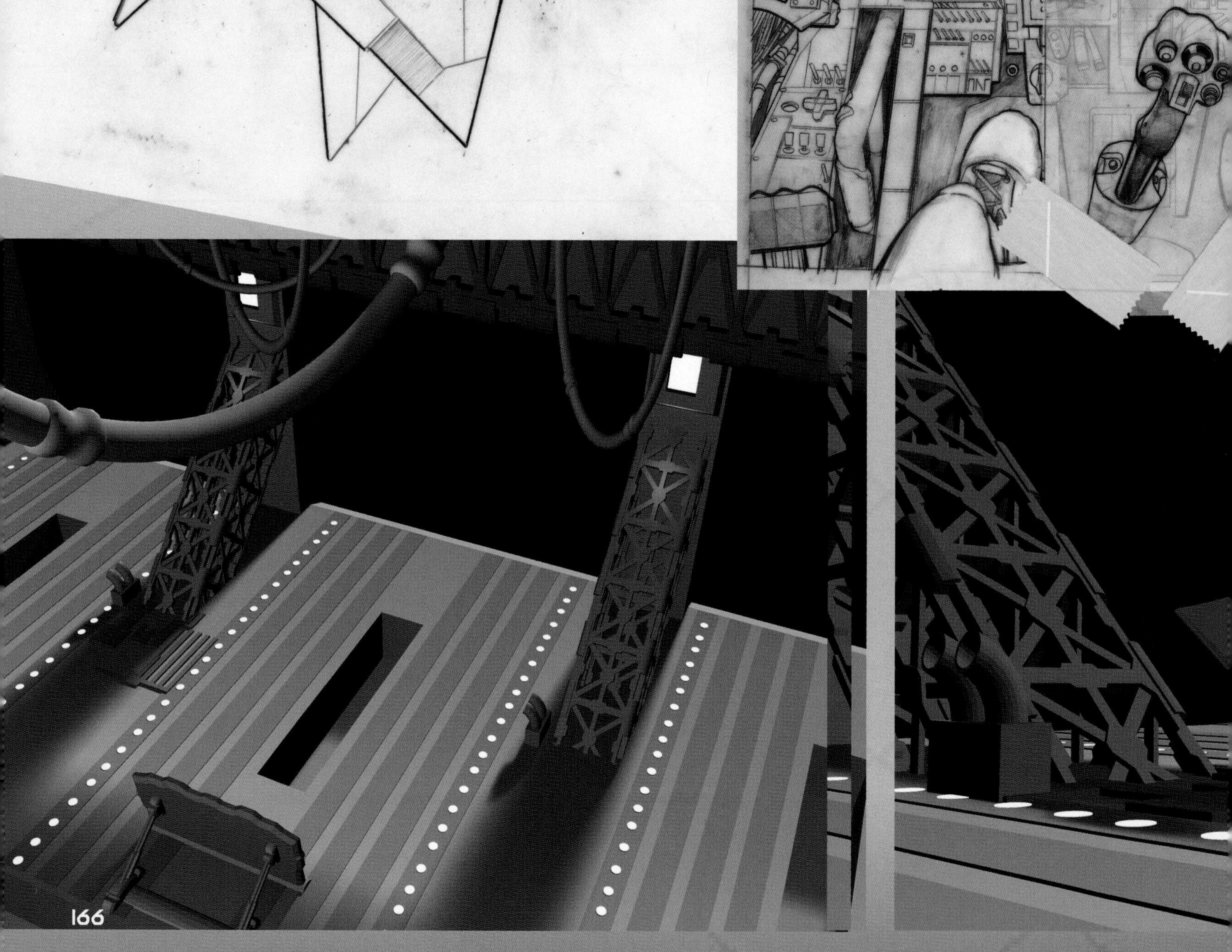

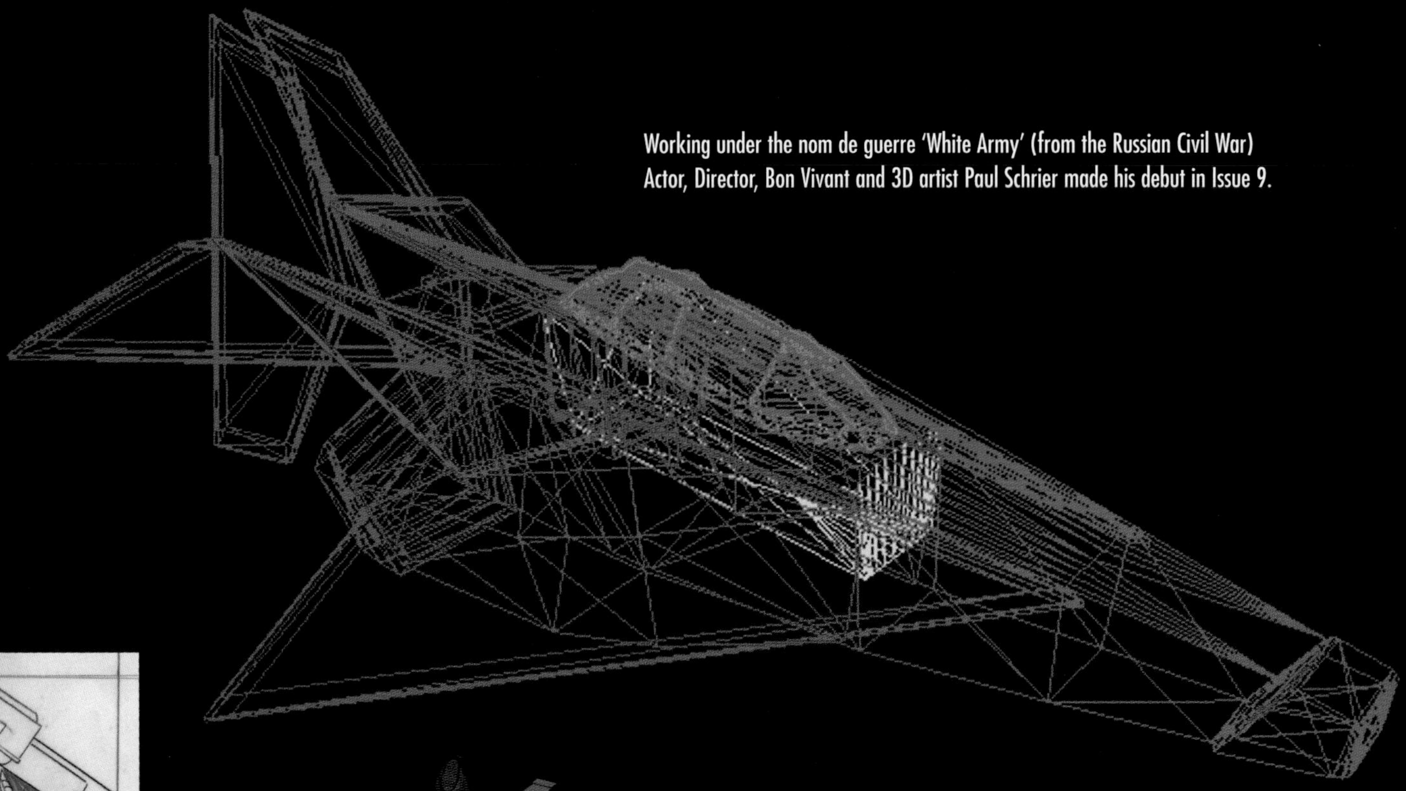

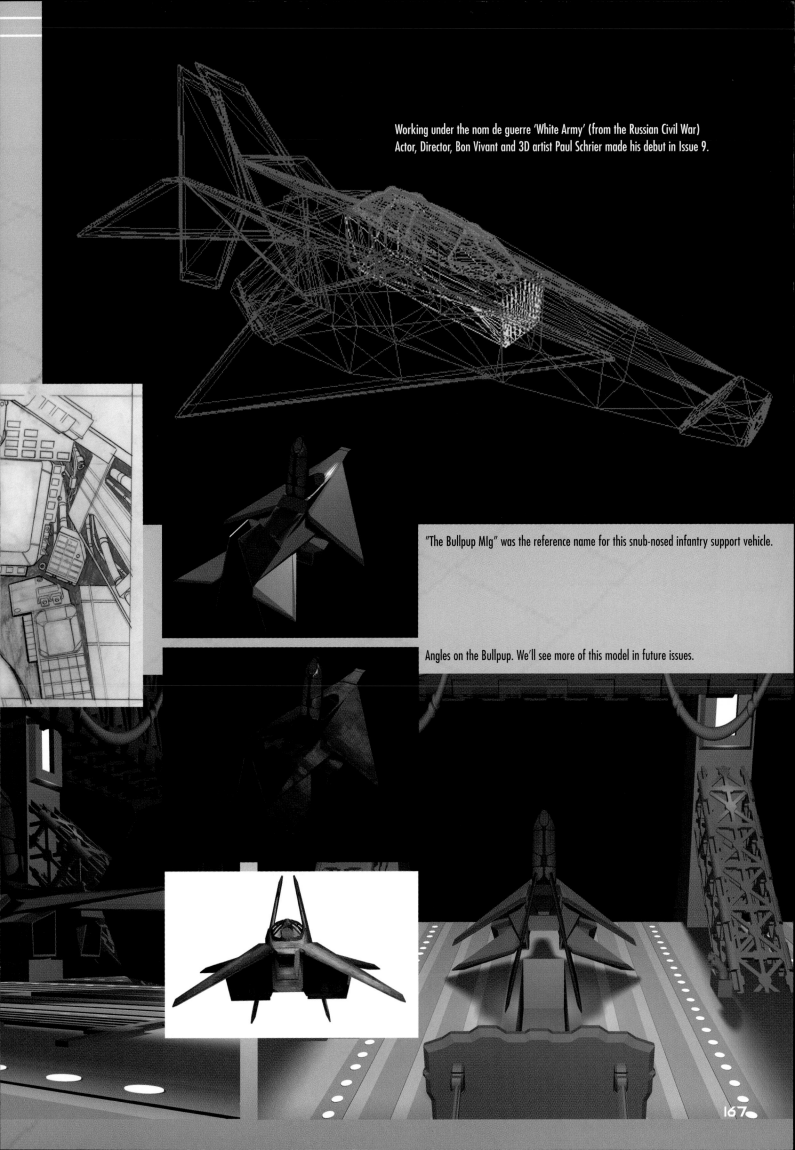

Working under the nom de guerre 'White Army' (from the Russian Civil War) Actor, Director, Bon Vivant and 3D artist Paul Schrier made his debut in Issue 9.

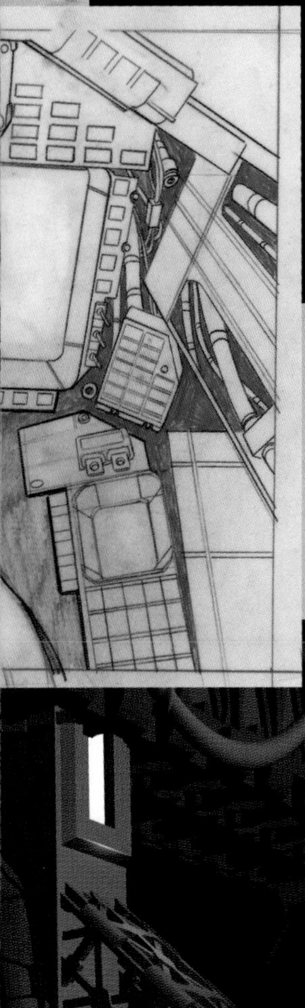

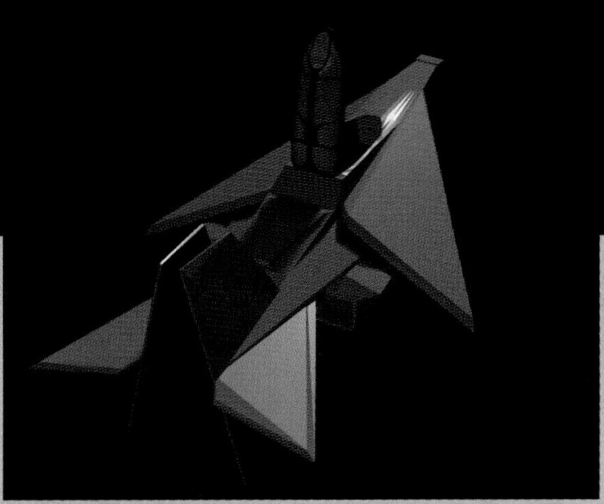

"The Bullpup MIg" was the reference name for this snub-nosed infantry support vehicle.

Angles on the Bullpup. We'll see more of this model in future issues.

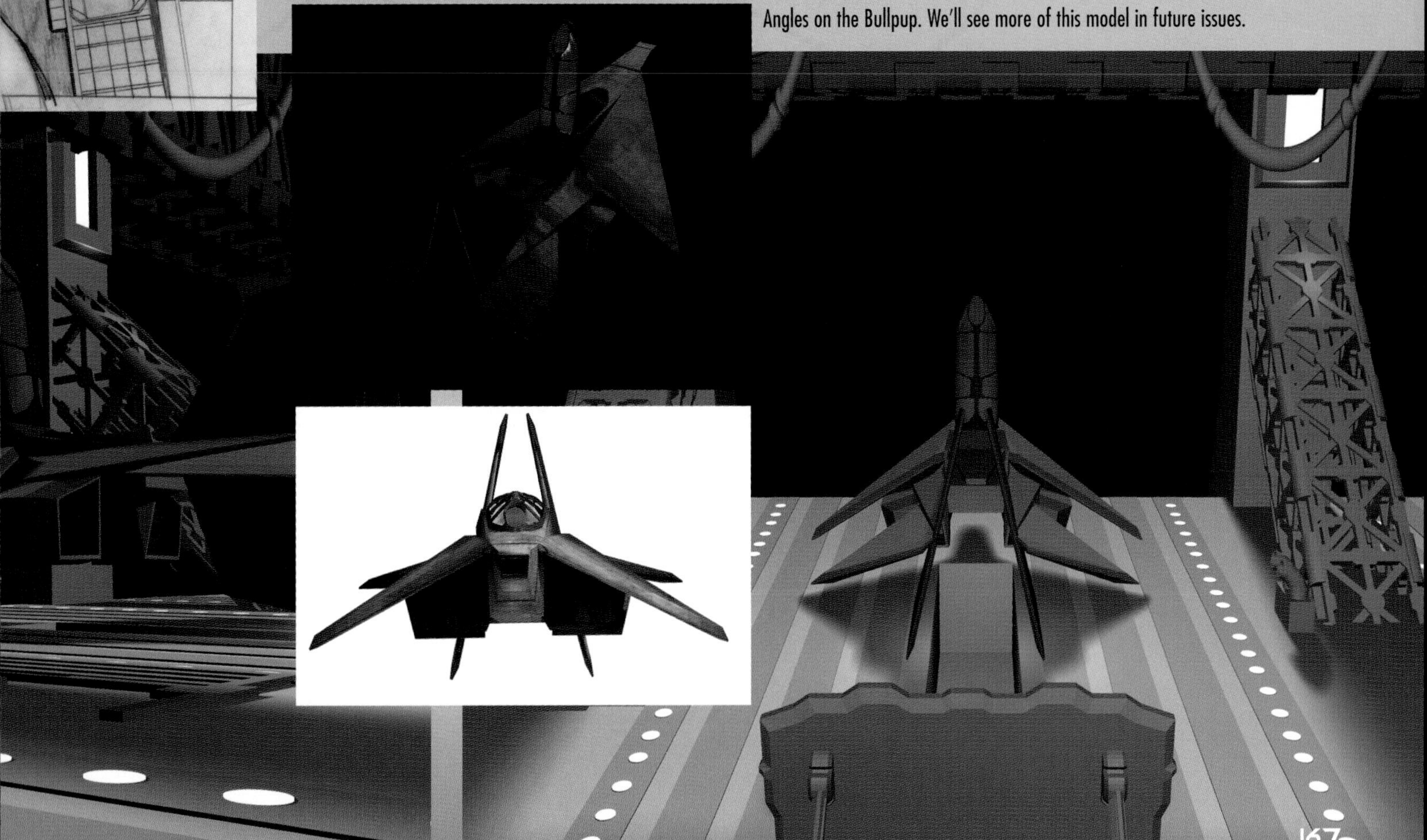

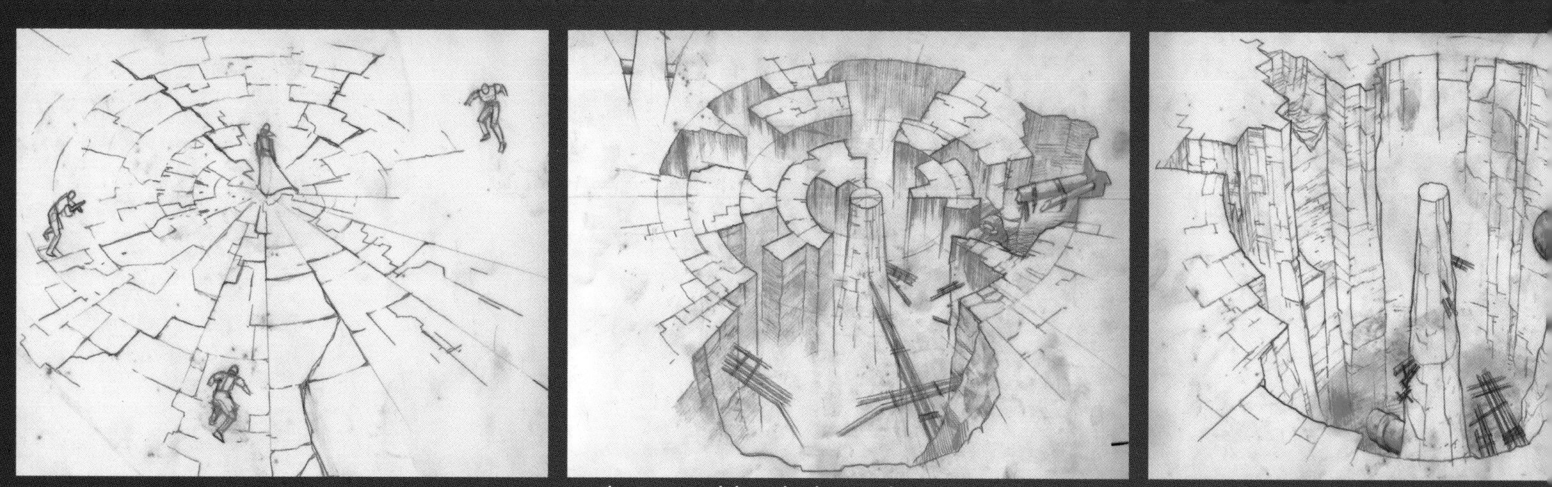

The KGB turned these sketches into the Drop Protocol (Issue 7)

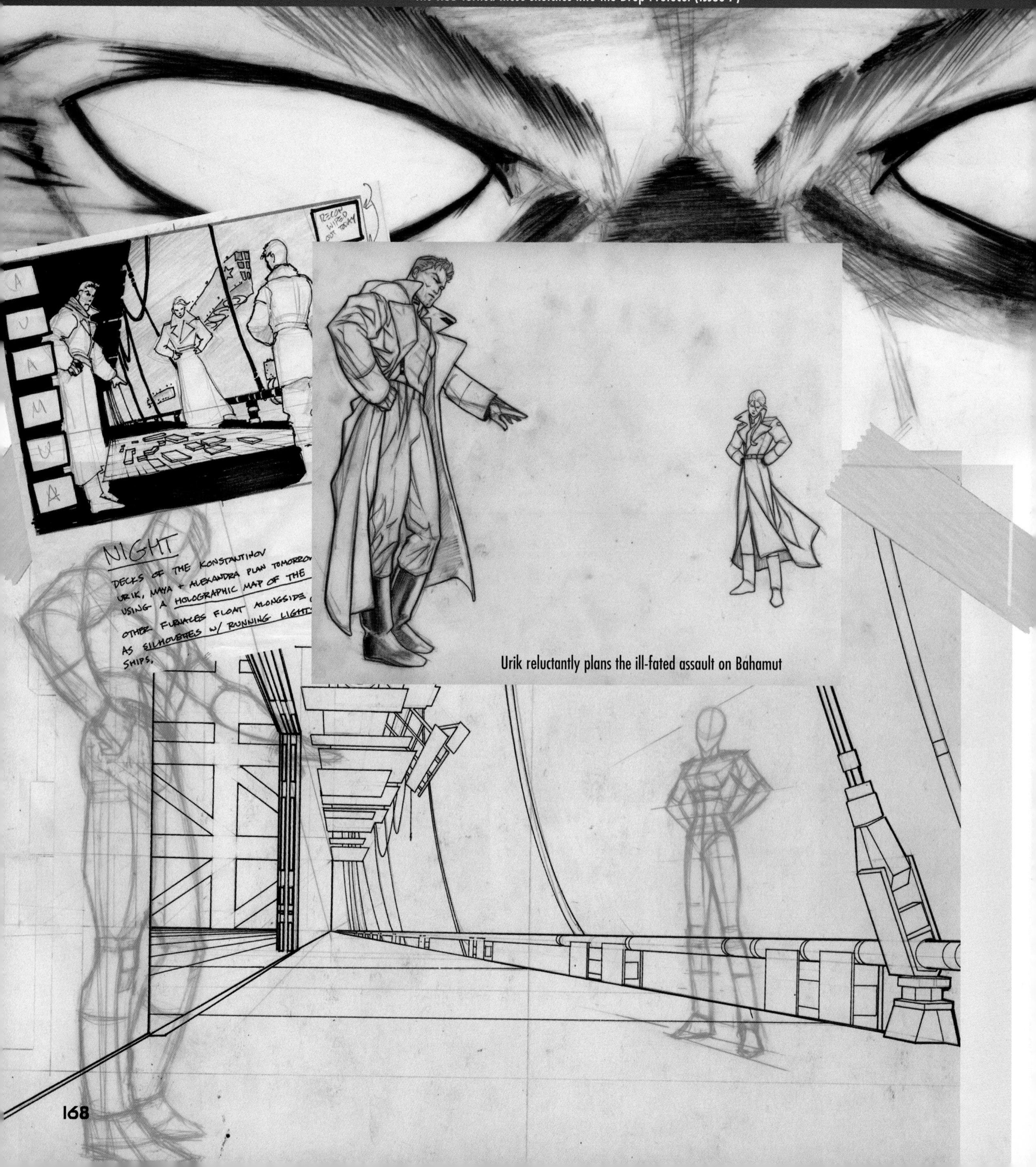

NIGHT
DECKS OF THE KONSTANTINOV
URIK, MAYA + ALEXANDRA PLAN TOMORRO
USING A HOLOGRAPHIC MAP OF THE
OTHER FURNACES FLOAT ALONGSIDE
AS SILHOUETTES W/ RUNNING LIGHT
SHIPS.

Urik reluctantly plans the ill-fated assault on Bahamut

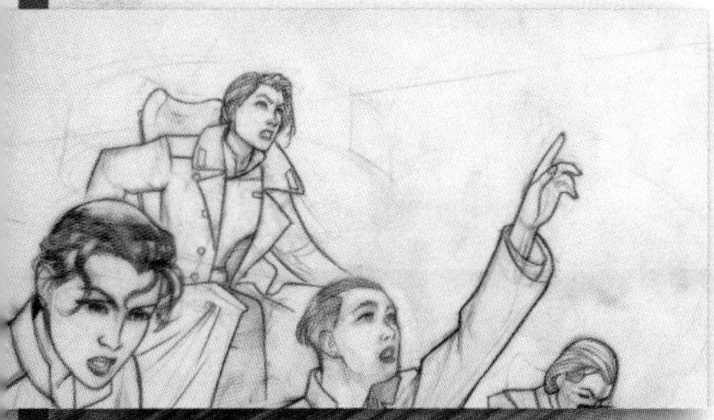

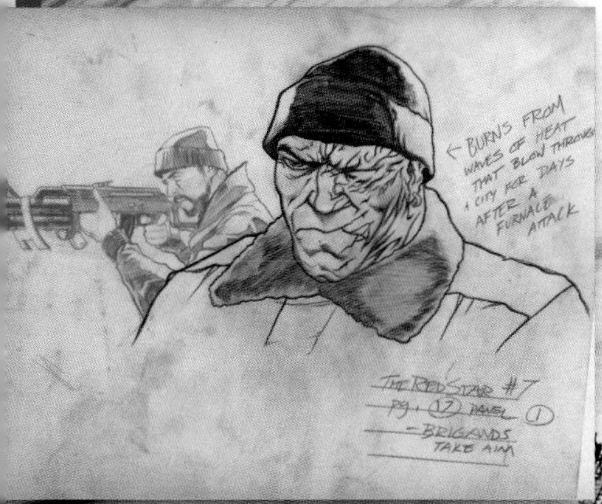

← BURNS FROM WAVES OF HEAT THAT BLOW THROUGH CITY FOR DAYS AFTER A FURNACE ATTACK
THE RED STAR #7
PG. 17 PANEL 1
— BRIGANDS TAKE AIM

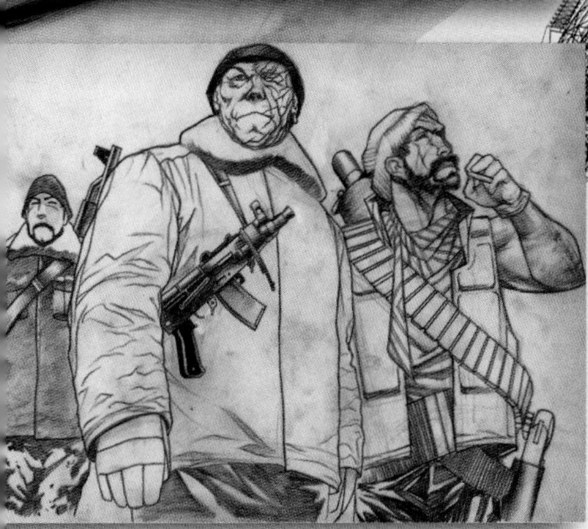

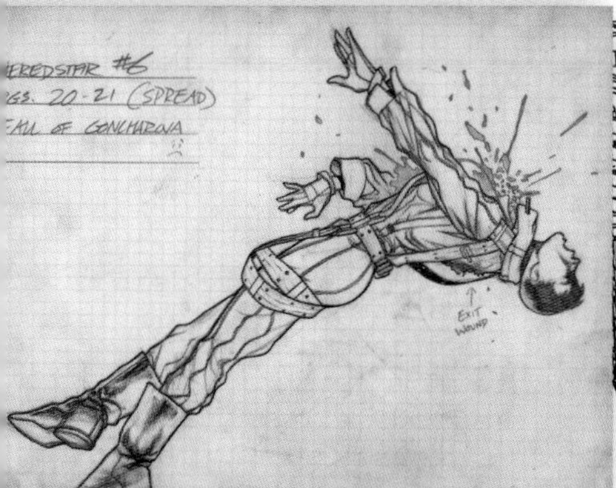

EREDSTAR #6
GS. 20-21 (SPREAD)
ALL OF GONCHAROVA
EXIT WOUND

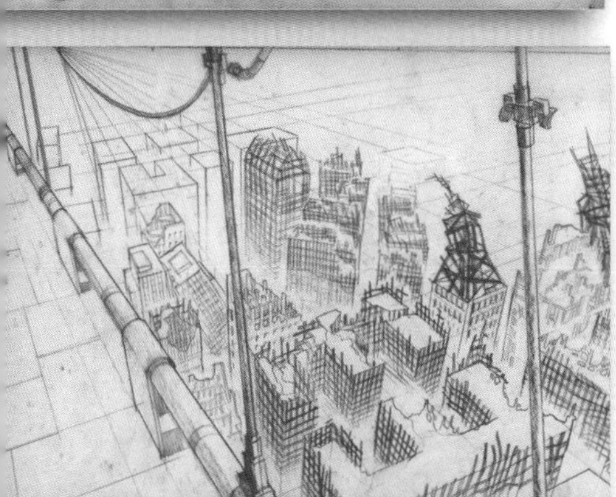

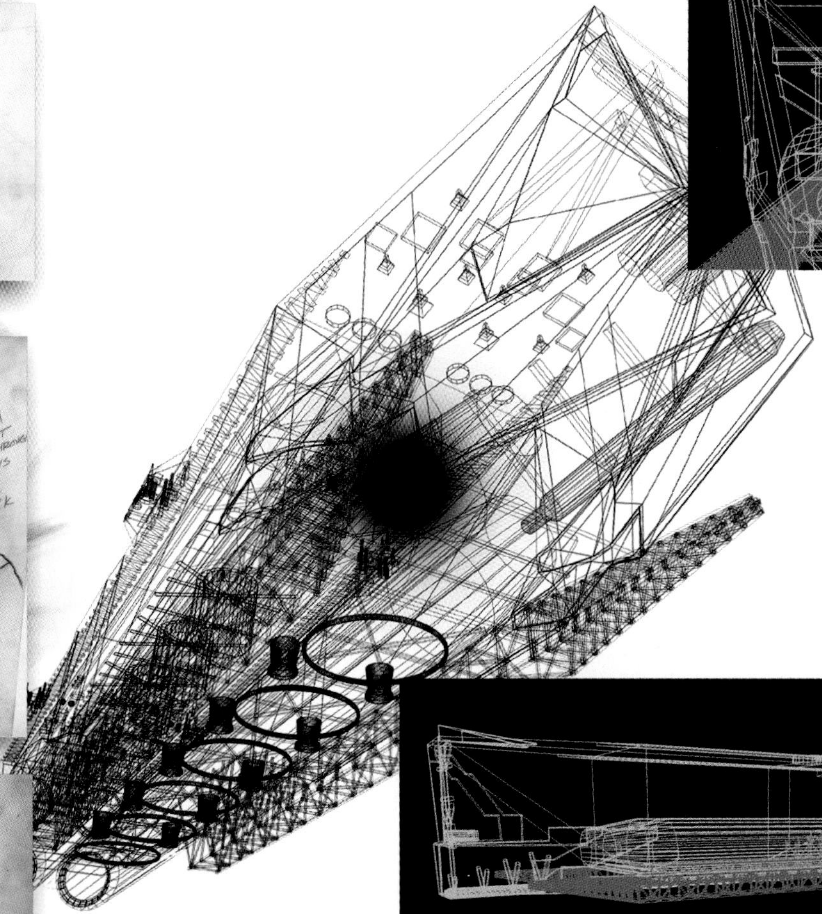

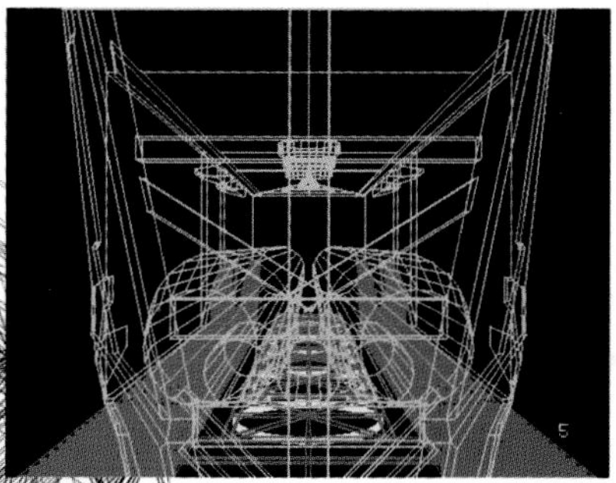

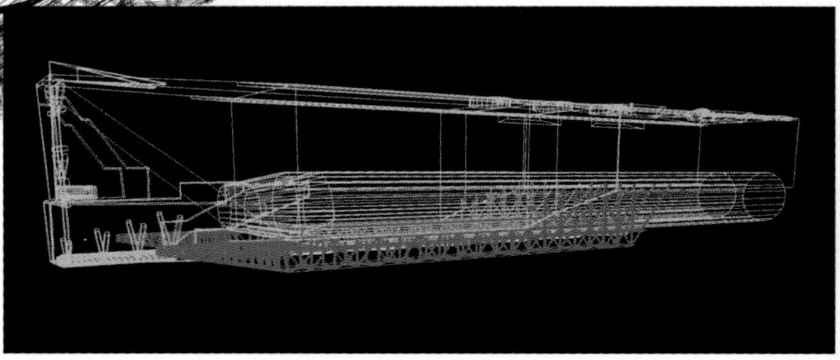

Cold war era battleship,
Viking Longship,
The clean lines of the RSS Konstantinov

Bahamat in ruins by the Komputer Graphiks Bureau

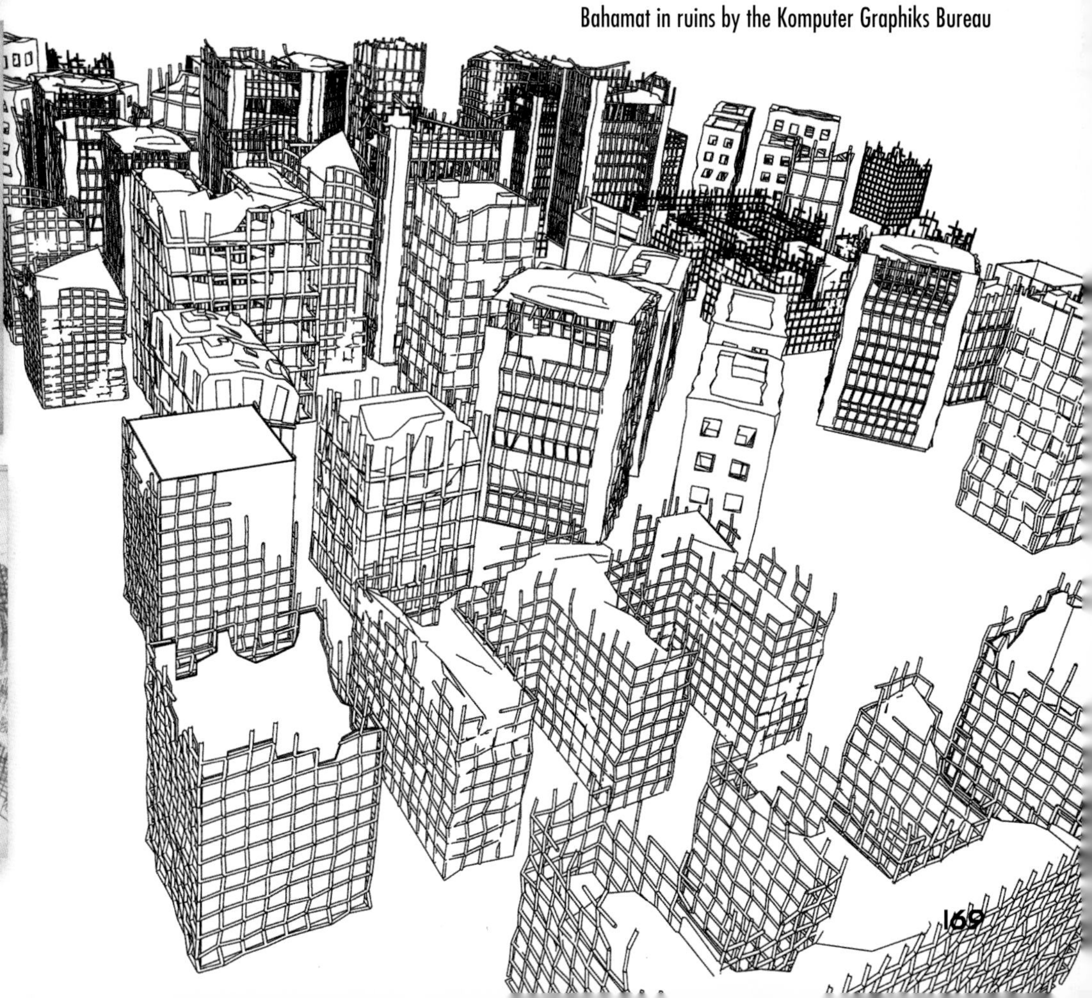

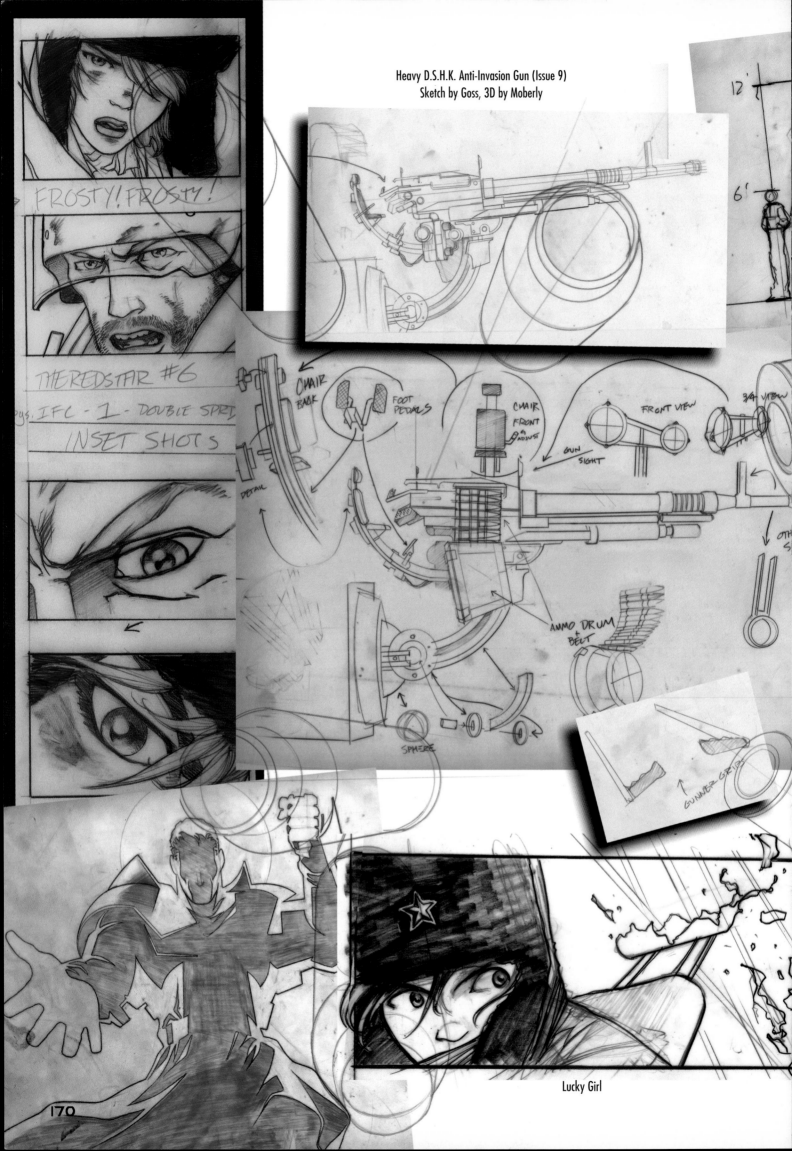

Heavy D.S.H.K. Anti-Invasion Gun (Issue 9)
Sketch by Goss, 3D by Moberly

FROSTY! FROSTY!

THE RED STAR #6
Pys. IFC - 1 - DOUBLE SPRD
INSET SHOTS

CHAIR BACK

FOOT PEDALS

CHAIR FRONT
4 ADJUST

DETAIL

GUN SIGHT

FRONT VIEW

3/4 VIEW

OTH S

AMMO DRUM + BELT

SPHERE

GUNNER GRIPS

Lucky Girl

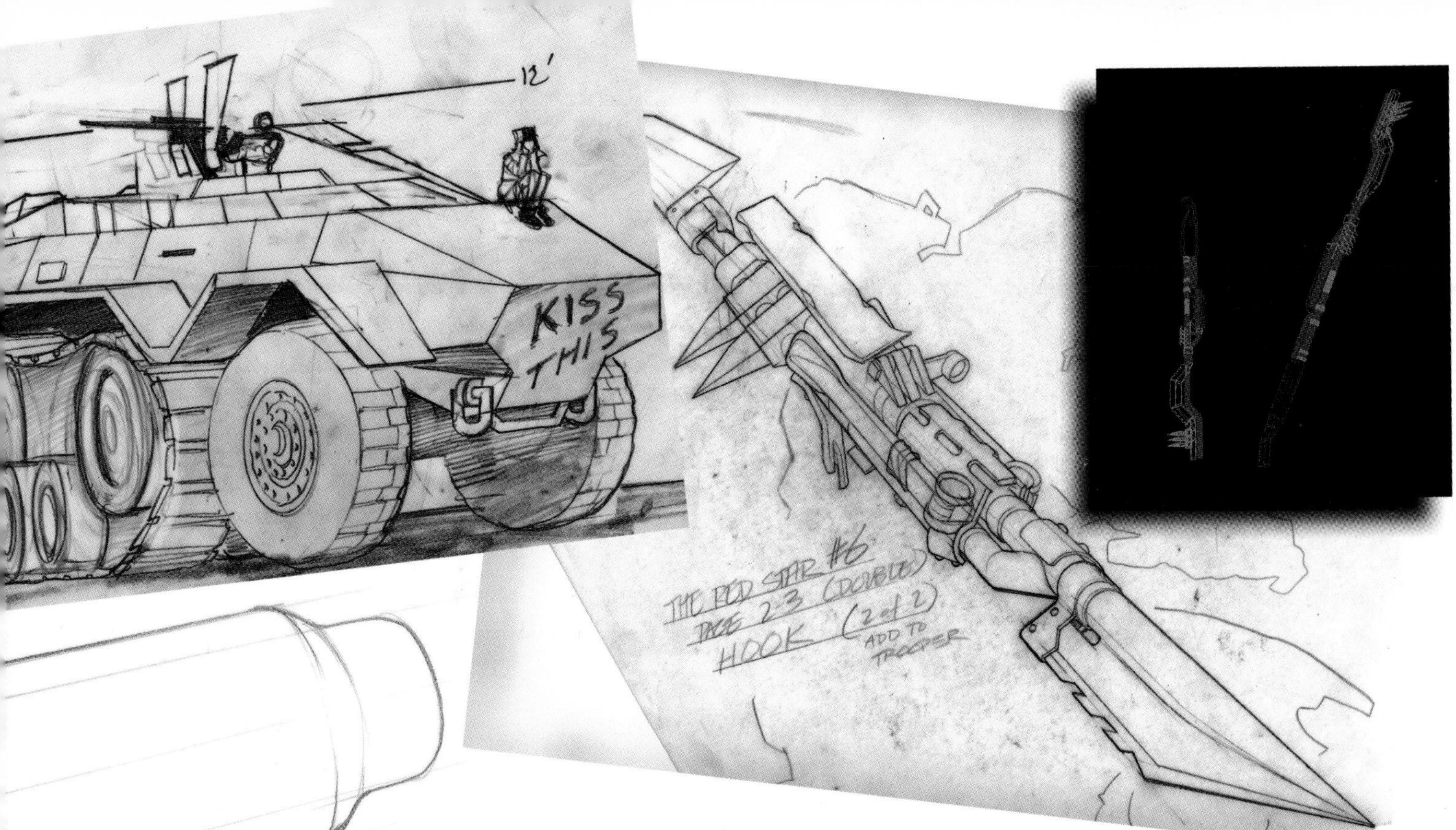
12'
KISS
THIS
THE RED STAR #6
PAGE 23 (DOUBLE)
HOOK (2 of 2)
ADD TO
TROOPER

Overlays!
Overlays!
Overlays!

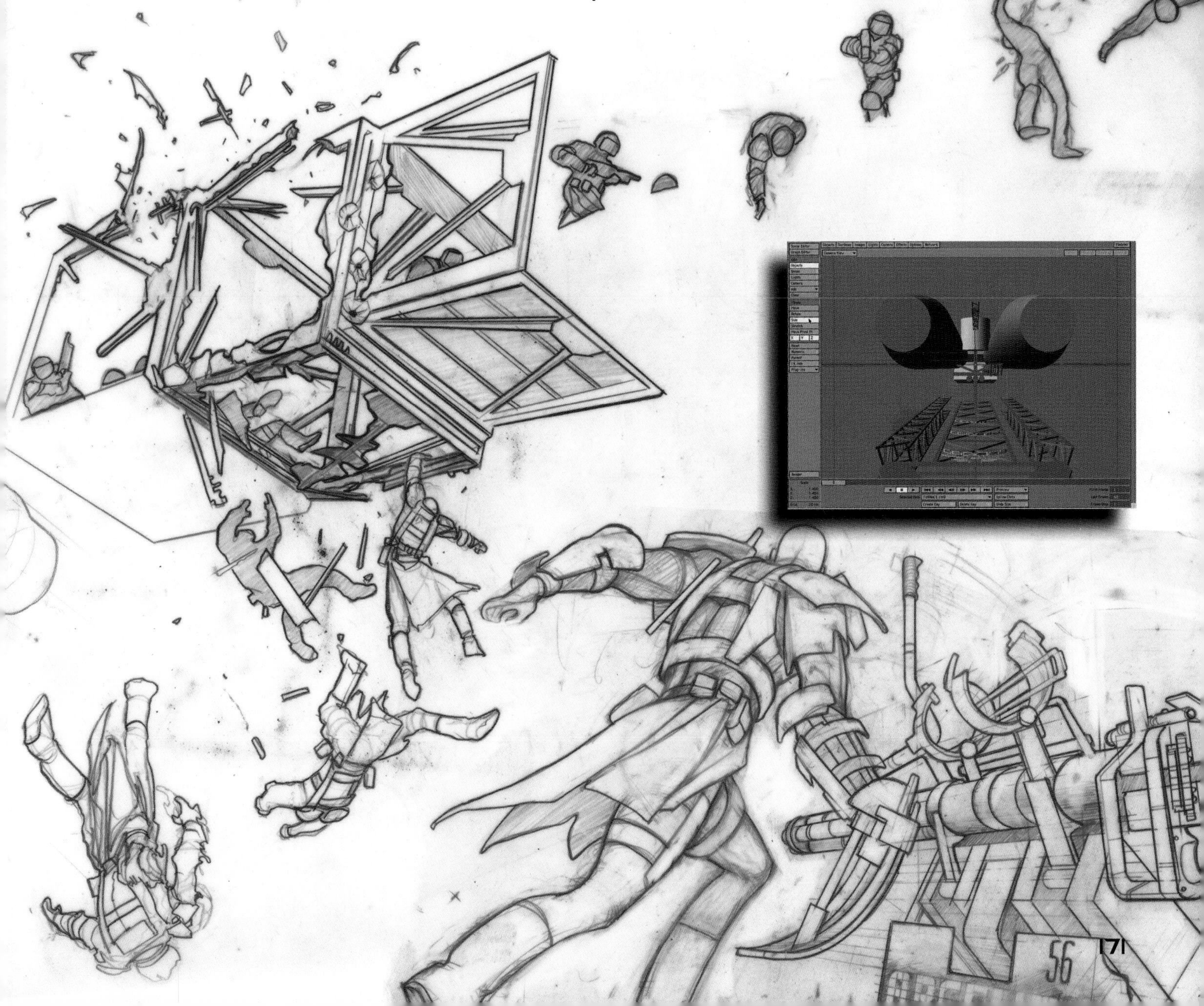
56

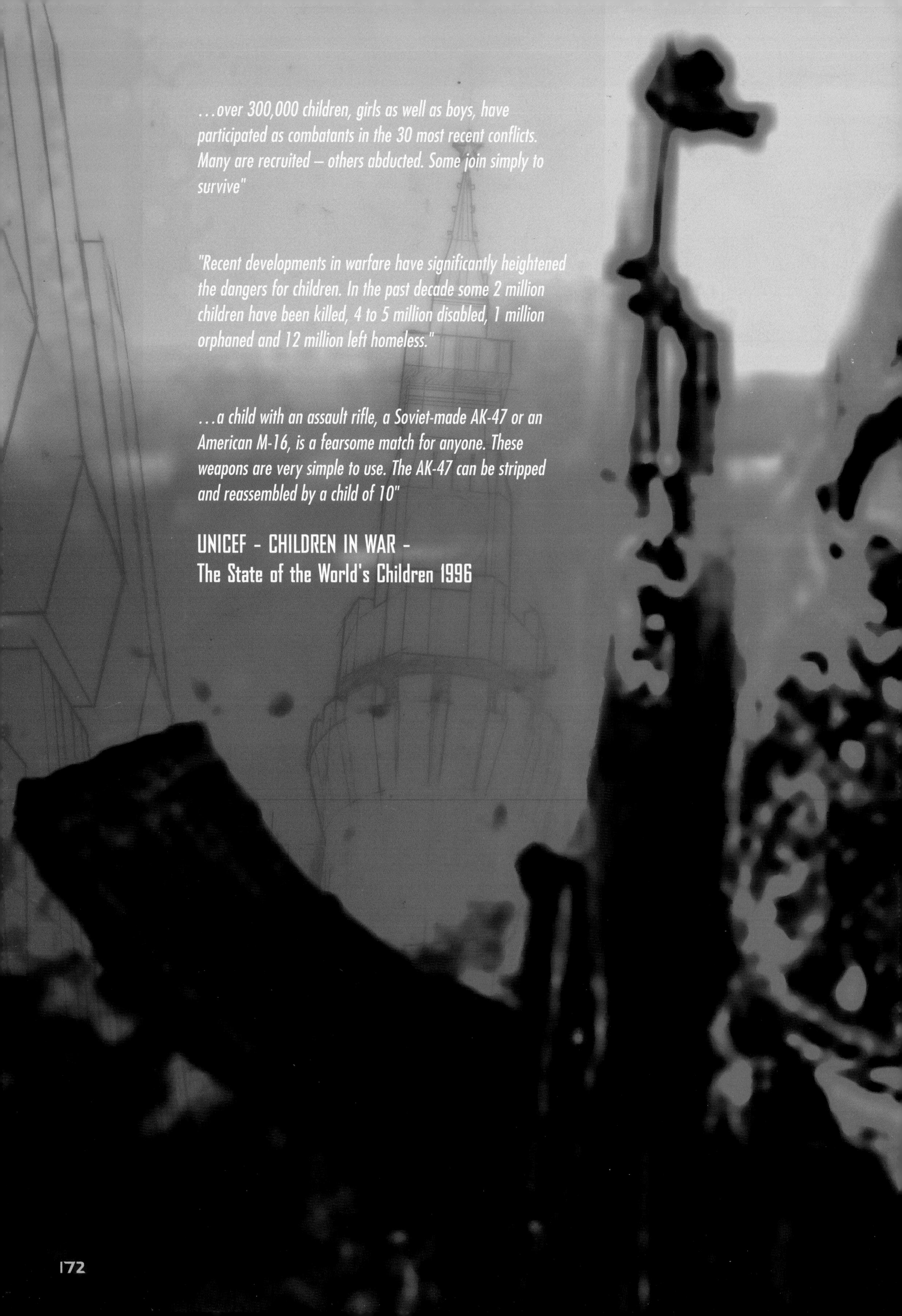

. . .over 300,000 children, girls as well as boys, have participated as combatants in the 30 most recent conflicts. Many are recruited – others abducted. Some join simply to survive"

"Recent developments in warfare have significantly heightened the dangers for children. In the past decade some 2 million children have been killed, 4 to 5 million disabled, 1 million orphaned and 12 million left homeless."

. . .a child with an assault rifle, a Soviet-made AK-47 or an American M-16, is a fearsome match for anyone. These weapons are very simple to use. The AK-47 can be stripped and reassembled by a child of 10"

UNICEF - CHILDREN IN WAR -
The State of the World's Children 1996

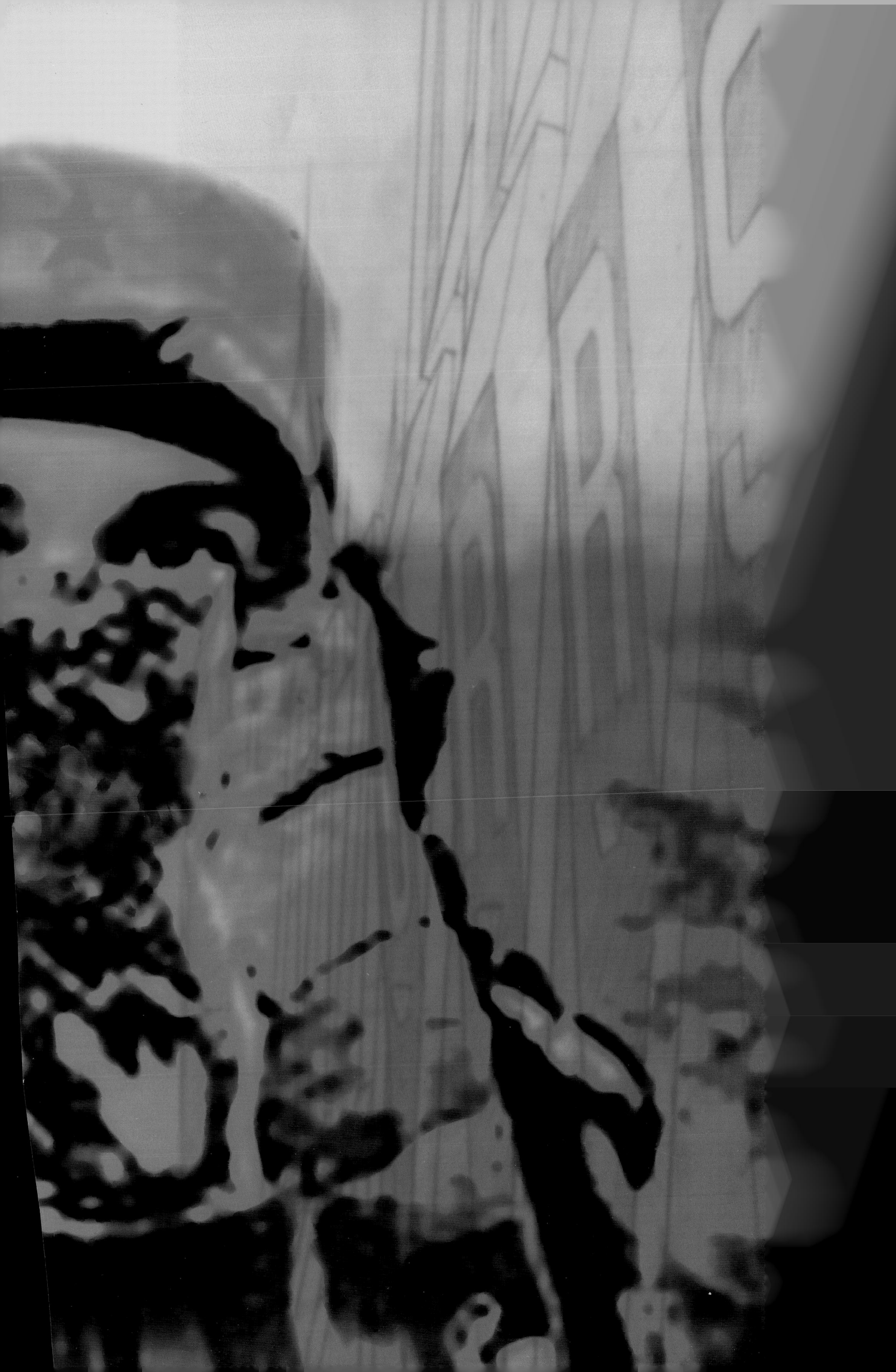

SOURCES CONSULTED

BOOKS

Alexievich, Svetlana, *Zinky Boys; Soviet Voices from a Forgotten War*, Chatto and Windus Ltd., London, c.1992

Davis, Patricia, *201 Russian Verbs*, Barron's Educational Series, Hauppoage, New York, c. 1968

Doyle, Hilary, *Stug III, Assault Gun 1940- 1942*, Osprey Publishing, Oxford, UK, c. 1996

Dunstan, Simon, *Challenger, Main Battle Tank 1982 - 1987*, Osprey Publishing, Oxford, UK, c. 199

Gessen, Masha, *Dead Again; Russian Intellegencia after Communism*, Verso, New York, NY. c.1997

Gogol, Nikolai, *Dead Souls*, Penguin Books, Ltd., New York, NY, c. 1961

Gregory, Paul R., *Soviet Economic Structure and Performance*, Harper Collins Publishers, New York, NY c. 1990

Guggenheim Museum, *The Great Utopia*, The Guggenheim Foundation, New York, NY, c. 1992

Gulland Milner, Robin, *Atlas of Russia and The Soviet Union*, Phaden Press, Ltd., Oxford, England c. 1989

Hutchings, Jane, Russia, *Belarus and the Ukraine*, APA Publications, Verlag, Singapore, c. 1999

Jukes, Geoffrey, *Kursk; The Clash of Armor*, Ballantine Books, New York, NY, c 1969

Katz, Samuel, *Merkava Main Battle Tank*, Osprey Publishing, Oxford, UK, c. 1997

Kennan, George, *Russia Leaves the War*, Princeton University Press, Princeton NJ, c. 1956

King, David, *The Commissar Vanishes*, Metropolitan Books, Henry Holt and Co. , New York, NY c. 1997

Kollontai, Alexandra, *Selected Writings*, WW Norton and C New York, NY c. 1977

Leonidov, Andrei, *Ivan Leonidov*, Rizzoli International Publications, Inc., New York, NY, c. 1988

Moynahan, Brian, *The Russian Century*, Barnes and Noble, Inc. Colville Mews, London c. 1994

Nicolle, David, *Lake Peipus 1242, Battle of The Ice*, R International Books, Great Britain, c. 1996

Pack, Susan, *Film Posters of the Russian Avant-Garde* Benedikt Taschen Berlag GmbH, Hohenzollernring Koln Germany, c. 1995

Platinov, S.F., *The Time of Troubles; A Historical* the Internal Crisis and Social Struggle in Sixtee Seventeenth Century Muscovi, University Press Kansas, Lawrence, Kansas c. 1970

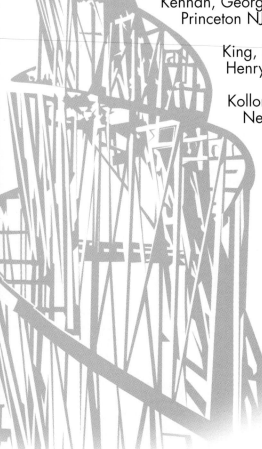

Rabinowitch, Alexander, *The Bolsheviks Come to Power; The Revolution of 1917 in Petrograd,* WW Norton and Co., New York, NY c. 1978

Remnick, David, *Ressurection; The Struggle for a New Russia,* Random House, Inc., New York, NY c. 1997

Rowell, Margarite, *Art of the Avant-Garde in Russia,* Solomon R. Guggenheim Foundation, New York, NY c. 1981

Stanley, Peter, *What Did You do in the War, Daddy,* Oxford University Press, Oxford, NY c. 1983

Steiner, Evgeny, *Stories for Little Comrades,* University of Washington Press, Seattle, Washington. C. 1999

Tucker, Robert, *Stalinism; Essays in Historical Interpretation,* Transaction Publishers, New Brunswick, NJ, c. 1999

Volkogonov, Dmitri, *Lenin ; A New Biography,* The Free Press, New York, NY c. 1994

White, Steven, *The Bolshevik Poster,* Yale University, Boston, Massachusetts, c. 1988

Yergen, Daniel, *Russia 2010,* Vintage Books, New York, NY, c. 1993

Zaloga, Steven, *Inside the Soviet Army Today,* Osprey Publishing, Oxford, UK, c. 1987

Zaloga, Steven, *IS-2 Heavy Tank 1944 -1973,* Osprey Publishing, Oxford, UK, c. 1994

Zaloga, Steven, *KV- 1 & 2 Heavy Tanks, 1941 - 1945,* Osprey Publishing, Oxford, UK, c. 1995

Zaloga, Steven, *The Eastern Front, Armor Camouflage and Markings, 1941- 1945,* Arms and Armor, London, c. 1983

VIDEOS

Liberation, Arnold Schwartzman Film, Simon Weisenthal Center, 1997

Nazi Files, Episodes I and II, Directed and Written by Elizabeth Dobson, 1997

Saving Private Ryan, Directed by Steven Spielberg, Paramount Pictures, 1998

Seven Samurai, Directed by Akira Kurosawa, Toho Studios, 1954

Star Wars, Directed by George Lucas, Twentieth Century Fox, 1977

The Adventures of Buckaroo Banzai, Directed by W. D. Richter, Twentieth Century Fox, 1984

WWII Through Russian Eyes, Historical Achievements Museum, LLC, 1999

MUSIC SUPPORT

Radicals, "Maybe You've Been Brainwashed, Too"

Lola Run, Original Motion Picture Soundtrack

Songs of Russia

the Shell Original Soundtrack

et, "Misconceptions"

175

WHERE WILL SHE TRAVEL NEXT...

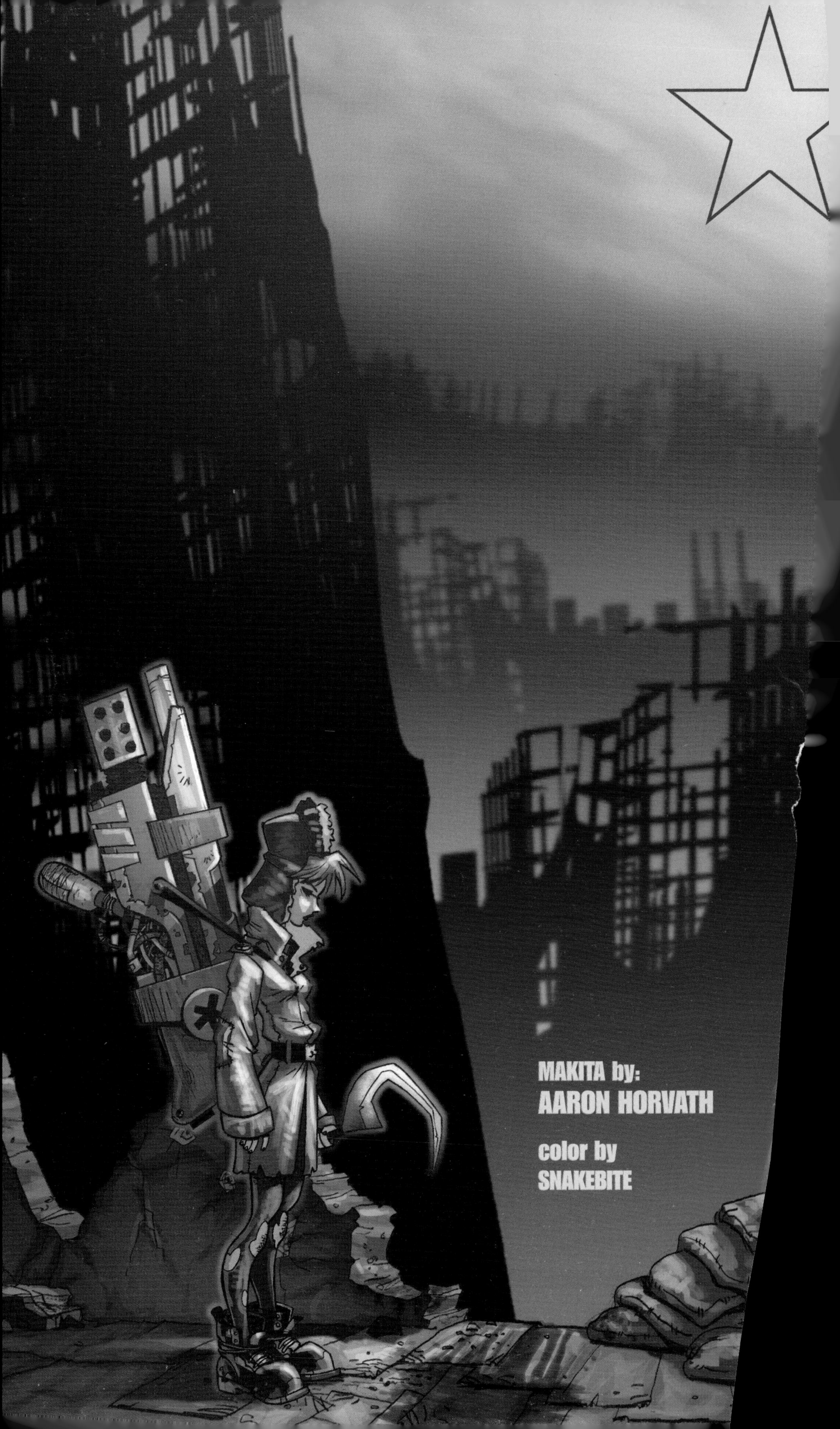
MAKITA by:
AARON HORVATH
color by
SNAKEBITE